Experiences
in a Promised Land

Essays in Pacific Northwest History

Experiences in a Promised Land

Essays in Pacific Northwest History

Edited by G. Thomas Edwards
and Carlos A. Schwantes

Foreword by Robert E. Burke

University of Washington Press

Seattle and London

Library of Congress Cataloging-in-Publication Data

Main entry under title:

Experiences in a promised land.
  Bibliography: p.
  1. Northwest, Pacific—History—Addresses, essays,
lectures. I. Edwards, G. Thomas. II. Schwantes,
Carlos A., 1945–
F851.E97 1986   979.5   85-26470
ISBN 0-295-96328-X
ISBN 0-295-96329-8 (pbk.)

To Our Parents:

Marie and Mac McMullen

and

Frances and Arnaldo Schwantes

Contents

Foreword

Books of readings in U.S. history have proliferated in the last forty years, although recently their number has fallen off. Various economic reasons—declining numbers of students in American history classes, rising costs of printing and publishing, and the rapid spread of copying machines—help to explain this drop-off. We are assured, by publishers and their agents, that "there is always room for a good one," but their words are not uttered with the fervor we heard from their lips fifteen or twenty years ago.

Regional history never has been blessed with useful, teachable books of readings, whether of the document type, or the problems approach, or the collected-essays variety. The Pacific Northwest history field has been especially neglected by anthologists of all sorts, including those who put together books of readings for college history students (and even hope to reach the "general reader," whoever that is).

Now comes a welcome collection of essays written since World War II, most of them from the past decade and several previously unpublished. The editors are college teachers with long experience in the Pacific Northwest, active researchers and writers of their region's history. G. Thomas Edwards, of Whitman College, has specialized in the social and cultural history of the mid and late nineteenth century. Carlos A. Schwantes, now of the University of Idaho, for many years before that at Walla Walla College, has developed the field of American social (especially labor) history of the late nineteenth and early twentieth centuries. Both Edwards and Schwantes have long been collectors, editors, and reviewers as well as writers of Pacific Northwest history material—Edwards has been especially interested in historic photographs and Schwantes in periodical bibliography.

They, like the other college teachers of Pacific Northwest history, soon discovered that their possibilities for assigned readings-in-common were quite limited. They began to tell their colleagues and friends in the field that something ought to be done about it. They found that a great deal of good advice, much of it conflicting, was lying about, ready to be heard (or re-heard). But they persisted, in spite of difficulties of unbelievable variety which, like poetry, they can now consider to be "strong emotion recollected in tranquility."

They have divided their collection chronologically into four distinct periods. Each contains one or two now-classic pieces, old favorite journal articles that they were often told not to leave out, whatever else got dropped. Each section contains two or three pieces that will be less familiar (or quite new) even to experienced college teachers, let alone general readers.

But the editors have not forgotten that these essays are ultimately designed to be read as enhancement for text books and lectures on Pacific Northwest History. They represent, in wide variety, the state of the art of our region's history as written in the past forty years. They provide, so we hope and believe, a stimulating introduction to a big subject that still needs not only exploration but development.

ROBERT E. BURKE

Preface

The editors and other historians believe that there is a need for a compilation of essays on Pacific Northwest history for use in the classroom either as a supplement to a text or as a text itself. Presently there is no general collection of articles covering the history of Oregon and Washington, the two states studied most intensively in Pacific Northwest history classes. The standard textbook of the region, Dorothy Johansen and Charles Gates, *Empire of the Columbia*, is nearly two decades old and does not incorporate the findings of recent scholars. Most of the essays in our compilation appeared after the publication of Professor Johansen's revised edition.

It was not easy to select articles for inclusion. Besides the two major historical journals published in Oregon and Washington, *Oregon Historical Quarterly* and *Pacific Northwest Quarterly*, other scholarly journals occasionally publish materials on these two states. Many excellent articles not included in this collection are mentioned in the suggestions for further reading. Most essays have been reprinted for this volume; six are original. Footnotes are included only for the original essays; all others provide bibliographical notes with readers referred to the original publications for a full set of notes. Abbreviations listed in the citations are keyed to journals listed in the Further Reading section.

We have sought to give balance to this compilation by including selections on political, economic, social, cultural, and minority history. At least half the book is devoted to the twentieth century, an important period slighted by most students of Pacific Northwest history. We have tried to select articles that not only are well written but also will stimulate class discussion. During the selection process we asked colleagues who teach Pacific Northwest history to recommend favorite essays to us, and we tested many of their suggestions in our own classes. We hope that the resulting collection will help students and other readers to gain a better understanding of the dimensions of Pacific Northwest history. Perhaps a few readers might even develop as great an appreciation for our region's heritage as they have for its natural beauty. The editors and authors could not ask for more.

The Pacific Northwest
as Promised Land: An Introduction

A promised land? Can any region of the United States accurately be so described? On the other hand, rare is the region that has not at one time been so promoted. Was the Pacific Northwest a promised land for the region's Indians after the beginning of white settlement? Or for the migratory workers who harvested the region's timber, fruit, and grain? Have the editors, then, suspended or abandoned their critical faculties by the use of the promised land theme? We hope not.

The theme of the Pacific Northwest as promised land is actually quite complex. There are at least three aspects to it: literal, symbolic, and ironic. Only in a limited and highly personal sense do we consider the region a literal promised land. Yet, promised land it was in the realm of myth and symbol created more than a century ago by settlers, promoters, and travelers.

Oregon fever—excitement about the possibilities of the Pacific Northwest—prompted missionaries, promoters, and politicians of antebellum America to lavish praise on the region. Settlers spread the contagion; in fact, hundreds of thousands of people, both residents and visitors, are still apt to rave about the Northwest. Present-day descriptions of its landscape and generally mild winters as well as predictions of a lucrative trade with the "teeming millions" of Asia are reminiscent of the expansive language of the earliest victims of Oregon fever. Examples of the enthusiasm of the pioneer generation are to be found in the words of the promoter Hall J. Kelley, Senator Lewis Linn, and the missionary Jason Lee. Historians have quoted them and others to explain both the American interest in the Oregon country and the westward movement to it. Decade after decade, letters, pamphlets, and newspapers provided numerous examples of regional boosterism, sometimes defined as "puffing" and often induced by the "speculative mania" associated with real estate promotions. Seattle residents in 1871, for example, argued for the supremacy of their raw village over cosmopolitan San Francisco with claims that "the climate is better, the water healthier, Sound deeper, trees taller, rivers longer . . . , clams fatter, fish sweeter, mountains higher, Indians more brave and God-like." In fact, these enthusiasts could voice "a thousand cogent reasons why Seattle should be the garden spot of the earth."

The natural wealth of the Pacific Northwest was frequently described as "boundless," the soil "literally inexhaustible," and the climate "unusually conducive to health." Prospective settlers of the rolling Palouse country of eastern Washington were told in 1899 that "when once the sod is broken there are no weeds for the farmer to fight." Boosters portrayed the Puget Sound as the "Mediterranean of America," an "agricultural Venice," the land of "eternal spring." The Columbia River Gorge was called the "Rhine District of America." No wonder the author Stewart Holbrook said of the booster pamphlets he read as a young Bostonian that they "somehow left the impression that one could have a decent living in Oregon and Washington simply by eating the gorgeous scenery."

The prodigality of nature in the nation's far corner seemed to imply a similar boundlessness of opportunity. Typical was the expression contained in a pamphlet issued by the Oregon Immigration Board in 1888: "All honest, industrious people who desire a location for active work where the chances are largely in favor of their success are invited to come to the 'New Empire.'" The promotional literature, which after the completion of a northern transcontinental railway line in 1883 induced some people unwisely to move to the region in hope of achieving instant success, evoked an angry response from the Pacific Northwest's pioneer labor organizations. Fearful that unemployment and decreased wages would result from an overcrowding of the labor market, organized workers bitterly denounced efforts to promote the region as a promised land. They called immigration boards "undesirable" and warned that the "tons of lying circulars" distributed throughout the East and Europe by real estate promoters and others created a false picture of the opportunities awaiting newcomers.

Such protests were generally futile, for many newcomers were convinced that they had arrived in a veritable Eden. In reality, their crops were bountiful, their health often seemed to improve, the scenery really was magnificent, and a person of average means sometimes did become wealthy. As a region the Pacific Northwest was spared both the ravages of the Civil War and the scars caused by rapid industrialization in the victorious North. And during the twentieth century the cities of the region have remained comparatively free of debilitating forms of urban blight, an accomplishment attributable at least in part to the protective attitudes of enlightened citizens and political leaders, the unusual homogeneity of population, and the abundance of recreation facilities. In recent years, several prominent publications have named Portland, Seattle, and Eugene among the most livable cities in America. Residents are proud to be so recognized but also fear such publicity will spur large-scale immigration to the region.

"It has commonly been remarked," wrote the historian Daniel Boorstin, "that the early New England Puritans could not be disillusioned, for the simple reason that they never suffered from illusions." By contrast, many a newcomer to the Pacific Northwest was transported as much by illusion as by ship, wagon, or train. The more unrealistic the expectation the more likely the newcomer was to be disappointed. Inevitably, there were those for whom the words "promised land" called forth a mixture of sarcasm and contempt.

"For years," a laborer wrote in 1915, "the Golden West has been the Mecca in the dreams of the misguided worker in all parts of the country. If I can only get West has been his only thought." But once he got to the Pacific Coast, the working man frequently discovered that the promised land had already been promised to someone else. As he saw it, he and his fellows supplied the muscle to subdue the "limitless" forests but had little or nothing to show for their efforts; they sawed the timber to build the mansions of the wealthy but lived themselves in shacks. One of their songs talked about digging the mines, building the workshops, and laying endless miles of railway lines, but ended, "Now we stand outcast and starving, 'midst the wonders we have made." The history of the Pacific Northwest is thus filled with paradox, with remarkable achievement punctuated by outbursts of resentment by those whose experience in the region was perhaps best summed up by the headlines of a radical newspaper in the Great Depression: "Oregon, the Promised Land, Becomes Land of Destitution."

Despite such paradoxes the Pacific Northwest retains a promised land image, perhaps more so than any other region of the United States. This is a theme in modern journalism within and beyond the Northwest. *Time,* in a 1977 cover story on the region, judged, "Americans who live in cities or suburbs can look at large parts of the Northwest and glean a true idea of what the nation was like 50 or 100 years ago—a region where small-town accessibility and friendliness come naturally, where people seem to care more about who they are than what they have." The article, with pardonable exaggeration, went on to assert that Pacific Northwesterners were untroubled by typical American worries such as "urban blight, street crime, racial trouble, chronic unemployment."

As if to underscore Holbrook's observation about the region's scenery, *Time* described its farming areas as having a

rare, raw beauty. As winter approaches, the wheatfields in the highlands of the Saddle Mountains and on the Palouse prairie to the east are plowed and furrowed like circles of whipped cream on a pie. A cantilevered bank of clouds passes over a mountainside, and the green landscape turns black and white, resembling a Japanese tapestry. When snow caps the peaks, the Blue Mountains near Walla Walla are indeed blue—electric blue.

Similar in sentiment is Thomas Griffith's 1976 essay in the *Atlantic* on the Pacific Northwest. In addition, Griffith identifies an important factor helping to sustain the popular image of the region: "Newcomers are welcome, so long as they take up the faith in how superior northwest living is, as most do." That faith remains so strong that residents both old and new often turn down better-paying jobs outside the region, and the jobless are reluctant to leave during hard times. In prosperity and adversity, the Pacific Northwest retains a special appeal.

Experiences
in a Promised Land

Essays in Pacific Northwest History

I. Discovery, Exploration, and Settlement

The beaver and the evergreen symbolize the states of Oregon and Washington respectively, but an equally appropriate symbol for both might be a drop of water. In the Pacific Northwest as in few other regions of the United States, water is an abiding, if not always appreciated, presence: fog and rain, glacier and waterfall, irrigation canal and tidal estuary, the Columbia River and the Pacific Ocean—the water droplet symbolizes all of these and more.

West of the Cascade Mountains the endless drizzle of the winter months frequently becomes a source of self-deprecating humor and personal depression, provides a backdrop for the novelist, and adds a somber, brooding spirit to the visual arts. The peculiar pattern of rainfall may well define the region's character for a majority of its residents (see Richard Maxwell Brown's essay). But even in the less populous and more arid country east of the Cascades, where the most common "evergreen" is probably the sagebrush, water is no less important. In the dry sections, people buy rain. Their irrigation networks and multimillion-dollar sprinkler systems deliver the water that grows bounteous crops of wheat, potatoes, and fruit on desert lands. On both sides of the Cascades, water as "white coal" remains a major source of electrical power. And some of the great hydroelectric dams that help illuminate the region also contain locks making commercial navigation possible on the Columbia and Snake rivers as far inland as Lewiston, Idaho, some 400 miles from the sea. At the same time, however, these dams have greatly diminished the once prodigious fish runs upriver.

By far the most important body of water for the Pacific Northwest is the Pacific Ocean. It is today a highway linking the ports of Oregon and Washington with those of Asia, but long before there was a Seattle, Portland, or Coos Bay to utilize its waters for transportation, the Pacific Ocean was the sustainer of life itself for Indians living along its northern shores. No tribes in North America possessed greater material wealth than those that depended upon the abundant wildlife of the North Pacific coast region. Here was a promised land rich in salmon, seal, and sea otter. In later years the Pacific Ocean inextricably linked the region's commercial fishing and timber industries to the outside world. Sea waters drawn aloft by the sun and blown inland as mist and rain made possible the luxuriant evergreen forests that stretched from shoreline to timberline in western Oregon and Washington and the great stands of ponderosa pine east of the Cascades.

Water in various forms also sustains an incredible range of leisure-time activities pursued by Pacific Northwesterners, from scuba diving and rafting to sailing and snow skiing. During certain seasons, residents of the region's largest metropolitan areas can easily spend the morning skiing in mountain snows and the afternoon yachting on Puget Sound or the Columbia River. Such an unusual opportunity contributes to what regional boosters maintain is a superior quality of urban life.

For the Indians of the Northwest coast, the waters that lapped at the edges of their settlements presented a paradox. The same Pacific Ocean that enriched their lives through the gifts of nature also served as an avenue for invasion and European imperialism. In July 1776, the same month that American colonists signed the Declaration of Independence, an expedition set sail from Great Britain on a voyage that would significantly increase European presence in the Pacific Northwest. Captain James Cook's third voyage to the Pacific was primarily motivated by the desire to explore unknown parts of the globe, perhaps even find the fabled Northwest Passage that would give Europeans a short-cut to the Orient. But in the wake of curiosity there usually followed conquest and commerce. These were the three "C's" of empire.

Cook reached the Pacific coast of North America in early 1778, after sailing northeast from New Zealand. From a landfall near Cape Foulweather on the central Oregon coast, the expedition worked its way farther north to the Bering Strait. Cook found no Northwest Passage and missed discovering both the Columbia River and the Strait of Juan de Fuca, but he did visit the splendid anchorage at Nootka Sound on the west coast of Vancouver Island. There his sailors exchanged metal items with the Indians for furs to use as bedding or for repairing their clothes. Leaving the waters of the far North, the expedition sailed south to the Sandwich (Hawaiian) Islands and a fatal encounter with the locals that cost Cook and four crewmen their lives. The British survivors headed for home, stopping at China en route, where they were amazed to discover that the sea otter pelts were worth a fortune. So eager were crewmen to return for more furs that they nearly mutinied. Their officers prevailed, however, and Cook's men sailed home to England to spread news of the fabulous commercial potential of the North Pacific coast.

Cook's third voyage sparked intense interest in exploring and exploiting the North Pacific. In 1792 Captain George Vancouver led an expedition that surveyed the inland sea, which he named for his chief explorer, Lieutenant Peter Puget. But Britain would have to share its prize. Two other European nations, Russia and Spain, had already probed some of the North Pacific's bays and inlets and established a modest presence there before Cook arrived. Russian feelers south from Alaska and, more significantly, Spanish exploration north from Mexico challenged British efforts to dominate the sea otter trade. The vast Pacific was not large enough to contain the imperial ambitions of all three nations, and soon they were joined by Americans seeking new markets to replace those they had lost as a result of their separation from Britain.

Spain and Britain narrowly avoided war at Nootka in 1789–90. Britain held her ground, and Spain progressively lost interest in the Pacific Northwest. Within another decade, however, the Americans who followed in the wake of Robert Gray, discoverer of the Columbia River, had all but driven the British from the maritime fur trade. Perhaps it really mattered little who prevailed, for the trade declined along with the sea otter population and by the early 1800s was overshadowed by fur-trading empires moving west across North America in search of beaver. The maritime fur trade had added greatly to European and American knowledge of the Pacific Northwest. It also constituted the opening chapter in a saga of continuing exploitation of the region for its natural resources. Even in the late twentieth century, a distinguishing feature of the Pacific Northwest economy remains its heavy dependence upon the production of raw materials, primarily wheat and timber.

The principal rivals during the continental phase of the fur trade were residents of the United States and the British Empire, which included not only the English and Scots but also the North American colonials, principally French Canadians living along the Saint Law-rence River. As in the maritime fur trade, curiosity and commerce remained inseparable, one stimulating the other. Although the search for the Northwest Passage ultimately proved fruitless, explorers con-tinued to seek rivers and mountain passes that offered easy overland access to the Pacific Northwest and its furs, especially beaver, with the aim of fusing continental and maritime trade.

Representative of the way that commercial aspirations stimulated geographical curiosity were explorers like Alexander Mackenzie, Si-mon Fraser, and David Thompson, who searched for new routes to the Pacific as employees of the North West Company of Montreal. These three Nor'westers, each of whom gave his name to a major river in the Canadian West, added greatly to the knowledge of remote portions of North America and helped expand the domain of the North West Com-pany from the valley of the Saint Lawrence west to the Columbia. The expedition undertaken by the Americans Meriwether Lewis and Wil-liam Clark further illustrated how curiosity and commerce were linked. At the behest of President Thomas Jefferson, they led a "Corps of Discovery" on a round-trip journey from Saint Louis to the mouth of the Columbia (1804–1806). Publication of articles and the extensive journals of Lewis and Clark encouraged fellow countrymen to seek their fortunes in the beaver kingdom of the far Northwest and, not incidentally, to lay national claim to the land itself.

One of those who perceived the potential riches of the beaver king-dom was John Jacob Astor, a German immigrant to the United States who parlayed his early investments in the fur trade of the Midwest and Rocky Mountains into a real estate fortune in New York City making him the richest American of his generation. In 1811 the employees of his Pacific Fur Company established Fort Astoria at the mouth of the Columbia River, but Astor's poorly led enterprise in the Pacific North-west was cut short by the outbreak of war between the U.S. and Great Britain in 1812 and the subsequent British capture of Fort Astoria. After a treaty was signed in late 1814 with an agreement to restore all captured territory, Americans claimed title to the fort at the mouth of the Columbia. Although Astor lost interest in the fur trade west of the Rockies, the brief flurry of activity by his Pacific Fur Company had helped strengthen America's claim to the Pacific Northwest. During the decade that followed the end of the War of 1812, conflicting terri-torial ambitions were resolved peaceably: the Russians and Spanish surrendered their claims, and the British and American rivals agreed to share the Oregon country for several years.

The joint occupation of the Oregon country—which included all of present-day Oregon, Washington, and Idaho, plus substantial portions of Wyoming, Montana, and British Columbia—worked to the advantage of the fur enterprises of British North America, the North West and Hudson's Bay companies. The Hudson's Bay Company was the older of the two. Some said that its initials stood for "Here Before Christ," although in the Pacific Northwest the North West Company was the pioneer. It had been forced into that role by the other's domination of the lucrative fur trade around Hudson's Bay in central Canada. Nor'westers had to open new beaver country in the Far West or perish. The historic rivalry between the two companies ended in the early 1820s when the Hudson's Bay Company absorbed its rival. Because Americans confined most of their fur trade to the Rockies, the Hudson's Bay Company emerged as the dominant force in the Oregon country (see Keith Murray's essay).

John McLoughlin, the Quebec-born physician who headed the Columbia River District of the Hudson's Bay Company from 1824 to 1845, in effect ruled the Oregon country during most of the years of its joint occupancy. Like many other employees of the Hudson's Bay Company, McLoughlin was first attracted to the frontier in the services of the North West Company and held a variety of posts in both companies before becoming chief factor of the Columbia River District. From his headquarters at Fort Vancouver (in latter-day Washington) and through a series of subordinate forts, he presided over a territory far larger than Great Britain itself. According to McLoughlin's vision, his domain was to be a profitable producer of furs for Europe and of food for local inhabitants. His job was never easy, though, for he had no legal control over Americans who migrated to the Oregon country.

At first, the American inhabitants of the region were scarcely a problem for McLoughlin. Until the early 1840s they numbered at most a handful of missionaries and mountain men in pursuit of furs. But missionaries and promoters proved to be the agents of rapid change. Hall Jackson Kelley, a Boston schoolteacher who had read a version of the Lewis and Clark journals, formed the American Society for Encouraging the Settlement of the Oregon Territory in 1829, which issued countless pamphlets and circulars designed to excite the imaginations of would-be settlers. Nathaniel Wyeth, a New England businessman inspired by Kelley's message, led two overland expeditions to the Columbia. The resourceful but luckless Wyeth hoped to develop Oregon's resources but could not compete against the well-established McLoughlin.

The first American missionaries to the Indians of the Pacific Northwest, the Reverend Jason Lee and his party of Methodists, arrived in the Willamette Valley in 1834, and their reports further encouraged interest in the region's rich agricultural lands. Following Lee by two years were the Whitmans and the Spaldings, sent to the Oregon country by a joint mission board representing the Presbyterian, Congregationalist, and the Dutch Reformed denominations. Roman Catholic missionaries arrived in the late 1830s.

The story of missionary activity is replete with ironies. Protestants preferred to establish mission stations at specific locations, but sustaining a post proved so time consuming that it left little opportunity for extensive religious work with the Indians. The goal, regardless of denomination, was to win Indian souls for Christ, but many missionaries, consciously or not, facilitated white conquest of Indian lands. Ironically, too, McLoughlin generously provided for the missionaries, who subsequently published accounts glorifying the region, which helped attract the settlers who undermined the rule of the Hudson's Bay Company.

Development in the early 1840s of the Oregon Trail, stretching some two thousand miles from Missouri to the Willamette Valley, greatly facilitated pioneer settlement. Families began migrating over the trail in 1841, and despite the rigors of four to six months of travel, their numbers in the region increased with each passing year. In 1845 alone, an estimated 2,500 people traveled overland to Oregon (see Dorothy Johansen's essay).

In time the new people moving to the Pacific Northwest would have overwhelmed the Indians by their sheer numbers, but hastening white conquest of the region was an invisible ally: disease, for which the Indians had no natural immunity. When Jason Lee arrived in 1834 he found Northwest Indians already suffering from the ill effects of white men's diseases. The stream of settlers moving west on the Oregon Trail and stopping at the Whitman Mission in the Walla Walla Valley also brought diseases. Indians living around the mission watched with apprehension and mounting anger as Marcus Whitman, a physician, seemed to save white but not Indian children from the ravages of measles. Unaware of their lack of inborn immunity to such diseases, Indians believed that the missionary doctor was actually poisoning them into extinction. In November 1847 some struck back, killing Whitman, his wife, Narcissa, and twelve others at the mission, but the massacre only enraged whites throughout the Oregon country. Their provisional government sent a militia into the Walla Walla Valley, scattering the Cayuse. Eventually five of these Indians were tried and hanged in Oregon City.

The 1840s recorded some of the most momentous changes in the region's history. During that decade the swelling stream of homeseekers following the overland route to the Oregon country increased the likelihood of territorial and cultural conflict with the Indians. The Whitman massacre marked the beginning of three decades of intermittent but brutal intimidation of one people by another (see the essay by William Robbins). The 1840s also saw important political changes. In 1845, the year that the Hudson's Bay Company patriarch John McLoughlin retired to land he owned in Oregon City, a New York newspaperman coined the phrase "Manifest Destiny" to describe America's expansive new mood. Manifest Destiny was really a catchall label for a number of things, including the nation's desire to acquire new agricultural and mineral lands as well as an outlet on the Pacific to facilitate trade with China. In many respects Manifest Destiny was a fancy new name for the commerce and the conquest that were an integral part of imperialism.

In the Pacific Northwest, Manifest Destiny translated into "Fifty-four-forty or Fight," a slogan that described America's desire to acquire all of the Oregon country north to the Alaska panhandle. In 1846 Great Britain and the United States resolved their territorial claims peaceably, splitting the disputed country at the forty-ninth parallel. The U.S. was fortunate to get as much territory as it did, for in 1845 only a handful of Americans lived north of the Columbia River.

Even as conflicting imperial ambitions briefly pushed the remote Pacific Northwest to the center stage of world affairs, settlers there fashioned a government of their own to deal with pressing local problems such as probating wills, defending their homes, and preserving title to lands. Their creation of a provisional government in 1843 was strictly a grass-roots affair. The homespun government and laws further evolved until in 1848 the federal government, goaded into action by the sensational news of the Whitman massacre, assumed direct responsibility for its lands on the Pacific. The Oregon Territory was created, and Joseph Lane appointed governor. Because the territory was much too large and sparsely settled to be administered effectively from a capital located in the Willamette Valley, Congress in 1853 established Washington as a separate territory. Both were now duly constituted American colonies proceeding at a very different pace toward full acceptance into the sisterhood of states. Oregon became a state in 1859, and Washington in 1889.

One thing did not change: whether as territories or as states, both Oregon and Washington continued to appear to prospective homeseekers as a promised land. For the region's Indians, however, the Pacific Northwest as promised land seemed increasingly like a cruel play on words. After the Whitman massacre shattered any hope of peaceful acommodation with American expansionism, Indians found themselves progressively humbled and displaced from the land of their birth. During the 1850s many tribes in Oregon and Washington were forced onto reservations. A prime mover in quite a literal sense was Isaac Stevens, first territorial governor of Washington and Indian agent, who took upon himself the task of concentrating the tribes of Washington on reservations in order to open more land to white settlement (see the essay by Kent Richards). The process of obtaining land for homeseekers in this manner produced considerable Indian resentment and some bloodshed. Not too many years passed before land-hungry whites crowded onto territory previously set aside for Indians, as happened in the case of the Nez Perce of Oregon's Wallowa country. The resulting conflict in 1877 made Chief Joseph both an Indian hero and a tragic figure, forever reminding Pacific Northwesterners of the dark side of their region's history.

The handful of blacks who early migrated to the Pacific Northwest must also have had doubts whether the region, particularly Oregon, was truly a promised land. Oregon had a Southern and Midwestern heritage. Whites who came from the Old Northwest often brought antiblack prejudices with them. Others had left the South because they hated its slavery and its planter elite, but they also hated blacks. Oregon's constitution, which went so far as to prohibit blacks—slave or free—from settling within the state, was the only constitution of any American state to take so restrictive a stand. Oregon voters approved the ban on blacks by an 8–1 ratio. Asians, too, were victims of the racism so prevalent in the Pacific Northwest. The Chinese came to the region in large numbers to build railroads, but during a time of severe unemployment in the mid-1880s, jobless whites turned on them and attempted to drive them from Oregon and Washington. Anti-Asian prejudice in various forms continued for decades and provided the basis for the wholesale removal of the region's Japanese during World War Two. At no time did an extraordinarily large number of blacks or Asians move to the Pacific Northwest; even today the region is among the most overwhelmingly Caucasian portions of the United States.

Until the 1880s the Pacific Northwest remained one of America's

*most isolated areas, in both a physical and a historical sense. The
American Revolution was only a memory here, one of the political
heirlooms brought by settlers from older parts of the United States.
The Civil War was an epochal event by any standard, but it too had
only an indirect impact on the nation's far corner. Although politicians
in Oregon and Washington furiously debated the war and the issues
that led to it, a young volunteer from the Puget Sound country in
1861 would have required a minimum of six or seven weeks' travel
time to reach the battlefields of northern Virginia. In any case, few
Northwesterners participated directly in the war. Men enlisting in local cavalry or infantry regiments remained in the region, campaigned
against Indians, patrolled the Oregon Trail, and built forts.*

*The Civil War reduced Atlanta, Columbia, and Richmond to smol-
dering ruins years before communities like Tacoma, Spokane, and
Bend were even built. The Pacific Northwest not only escaped the ravages of the war, but it also avoided having to contend firsthand with
the economic, social, or psychological consequences of Lincoln's Eman-
cipation Proclamation or Lee's surrender at Appomattox. This meant,
for example, that the share-cropping system of agriculture that so
blighted portions of the defeated South was absent in the far Northwest. So, too, were many of the war-spawned hatreds that animated
and constricted political debate at the national level for thirty years
after Appomattox.*

*The Pacific Northwest likewise lagged dramatically behind other
states in the race to industrialize. For years it remained untouched by
the rapid industrialization that marred prominent portions of the victorious North. Seemingly the only threat to pure air in the Pacific
Northwest was the frequent summertime haze caused by forest fires.
Oregon in 1880 had a population of 175,000, and Washington had
75,000. Washington's population, in other words, about equaled that
of Massachusetts 160 years earlier; or, more than twice as many people
lived in Washington, D.C., as lived in Washington Territory in 1880.
All of that would change with the coming of the region's first railway
link to the outside world in 1883. The daily spectacle of a train of
densely packed immigrant sleepers and elegantly appointed Pullman
Palace cars rushing across the once trackless wilderness to arrive in
Seattle or Portland on schedule vividly symbolized the Pacific Northwest's sudden integration with the late-nineteenth-century world of
industrialization, urbanization, and standardization. An economic
and social evolution that in the eastern states had required several*

decades to accomplish was telescoped into a few years in Oregon and Washington, creating the impression in the minds of early twentieth-century observers that "in the Northwest everything seems to have happened during the last ten years." The decades of the 1880s and 1890s marked the dawn of the modern era in Pacific Northwest history.

Rainfall and History:
Perspectives on the Pacific Northwest

RICHARD MAXWELL BROWN

The factor of rainfall and climate in Pacific Northwest history is a large one, and I am not attempting to deal with it in its entirety. Rather, I shall focus on the way in which northwesterners have reacted to the pervasive rainfall in terms of ideas, images, attitudes, and emotions.[1] The Northwest regional identity, I submit, is defined primarily not by a personal prototype, but by a condition of climate—namely the rain that falls more or less steadily about half the year.

In a sense, this essay explores the evolution of regional identity.[2] I am using the term *Pacific Northwest* here in a somewhat restricted way, in that I am focusing almost entirely on the part of our region that is west of the Cascades and placing emphasis on the district south of the Columbia River.

My research has dealt less with the conventional secondary literature of historical scholarship, which tends to be silent on my subject,[3] than with three types of primary sources: first, the objective data and patterns of rainfall and climate as revealed in climatological and meteorological writings going back to the nineteenth century; second, the diaries and letters of Northwest inhabitants in which the human, individual response to the impact of rainfall emerges; and third, the imaginative but authentic writings of a group of leading Northwest novelists for whom rainfall is a significant theme. After dealing with the rise of positive and negative images of Northwest rainfall, I shall treat at length the way in which northwesterners toward the end of

This essay is a slightly revised version of the 1979 Beekman lecture in western United States history at the University of Oregon, which was also delivered that year at the Pacific Northwest History Conference in Portland.

the nineteenth century came to terms with the heavy rainfall: by the creation of an *ideology of climate*. Next I shall assess something not addressed by the ideology of climate—that is, the emotive impact of rainfall on northwesterners. Finally, I shall conclude with some speculative observations about the relationship of rainfall and climate to Northwest character in historical perspective.

The late eighteenth-century British explorers of the Pacific Northwest were enchanted by what they saw as they sailed along the present Oregon-Washington coast and into Puget Sound. They likened the sylvan, primitive beauty of the Pacific Northwest to the artfully contrived rusticity of the "elegantly finished" pleasure gardens familiar to Europeans of the time.[4] The garden image did persist into the nineteenth century, but it was deeply eroded by the rise of a negative perspective given widespread currency by the experience of Lewis and Clark, whose description of the lower Columbia region in the winter of 1805–1806 stressed the "repeated fall of rain" that "almost constantly" drenched them.[5]

Others seconded the impression of excessive rainfall given by Lewis and Clark. Dr. John Scouler wrote of "incessant" rains in 1824–26 that he saw as being comparable to equatorial conditions. Some twenty years later, as Americans were streaming into the Willamette Valley John Burkhart wrote back East from Albany, Oregon, of his extreme anguish over the "verry [sic] disagreeable" time of the long "rainy season" from November to March.[6]

By the middle of the nineteenth century, with the American flag flying over present Oregon and Washington, the image of oppressive rainfall was as well established as the homes of pioneers from Puget Sound to the Rogue River. Jokes began to circulate about the persistent precipitation, and by 1863, at least, Californians were referring to the typical Oregonian as a Webfoot.[7] One historian, writing in the 1870s, traced the origin of the Webfoot sobriquet to the rugged frontiersmen who settled on the Long Tom River of Benton and Lane counties. As the story was told,

a young couple from Missouri [took up] a land-claim on the banks of [the Long Tom], and in due course of time a son and heir was born to them. A California "commercial traveler" chancing to stop with the happy parents overnight, made some joking remarks upon the subject, warning them not to let the baby get drowned in the rather unusually extensive mud-puddle by which the premises were disfigured, when the father replied that they had looked out for that, and, uncovering the baby's feet, astonished the [visitor] by showing him that they were *webbed*.[8]

The Webfoot stigma persisted in the early 1870s as the state of Oregon recovered from the internal tensions of the Civil War era and as the region—with Washington Territory nearly two decades away from achieving statehood—settled in for a decade of nationwide depression. But then came a boom time from coast to coast. By the 1880s Oregonians and Washingtonians were caught up in the Northwest's first great developmental fever. Construction of railroad routes linking the region to the east and south lessened the isolation of this far corner of America and made it possible to launch a drive to lure thousands of new settlers from the central United States, especially the Midwest and Great Plains. To forward the development trend, Pacific Northwest immigration bureaus,[9] promotional publications,[10] and the like were established, but boosters of the Northwest had vigorous competition from their California counterparts for migrants from the nation's heartland.[11] Although the Pacific Northwest's image of a garden had not been entirely washed away, the specter of incessant rainfall epitomized in Webfoot lore seriously handicapped efforts to attract settlers.[12]

Yet, the rains of the Pacific Northwest had their defenders as far back as the 1840s. Peter H. Burnett, a famous Oregon pioneer, approved of the western Oregon rainfall, finding it "much less troublesome" than he had "anticipated" and much preferring Oregon's "gentle showers" and mild, "drizzling rains" to the erosion-producing rainstorms of Missouri from which he came.[13] Even more expansive were Overton Johnson and William H. Winter, who published a description of Oregon in 1846. The two men were enthusiastic about the rain, and they concluded their endorsement of Oregon weather by comparing it to that of France, with France, as they asserted, "laying [sic] between precisely the same parallels of latitude" as Oregon and "occupying exactly the same position on the European Continent that Oregon does" on the North American—that is, they said, occupying a westward, ocean-facing location that provided France—as it did Oregon—"a climate which has long since and universally been acknowledged one of the finest on the globe."[14] The ardor of Johnson and Winter in 1846 was mirrored in the local and county histories of Oregon and Washington that began to issue from the presses in the 1880s. One such publication was a history of Benton County, Oregon, which held that the "rainy season" that came with "such remarkable regularity" was actually "the foundation of the agricultural wealth" of the county and the state.[15]

Thus, the Oregon rain had its articulate defenders, but skepticism remained, for spokesmen such as Johnson and Winter were not necessarily unprejudiced, and local histories, such as that of Benton County, were written to promote the future as well as to record the past. The problem was removing the defense of the rainy weather from the realm of subjectivity. What Northwest boosters needed in

order to refute the reputation of excessive rains and lay to rest the
Webfoot bugaboo was the authority of objective science. Related to
the strategy of scientific validation, adopted in the late 1880s and the
1890s, was the tactic of enlarging the scope of the subject from rainfall
to overall climate. This twofold approach depended upon the accu-
mulation of a mass of meteorological records for the state of Oregon—and the Pacific Northwest in general—and also on state-by-
state comparisons. A key factor in the process of modernization in
late nineteenth-century America permitted such endeavor, namely,
the increasing role of government in the collection and distribution
of statistical data of all kinds.[16] In the Pacific Northwest, two governments were involved: the federal government through the army Signal Service, whose weather service was founded in 1870; and the
government of Oregon, whose own weather bureau was established
in 1889. The joint efforts of these weather services did much to negate
the Webfoot image of Oregon, and in this connection we must note a
now obscure but then important figure who played a pivotal role in
this achievement.

Beamer S. Pague, born in 1862 in Carlisle, Pennsylvania, studied at
nearby Dickinson College, and at the age of twenty went into the U.S.
Signal Service, through which he eventually became one of the leading meteorologists in the U.S., a member of the prestigious American
Association for the Advancement of Science, and the president of the
Oregon Academy of Science. After stints of weather observation at
Mount Washington, New Hampshire, Cleveland, and San Francisco,
Pague was transferred to Oregon in 1886, where he took charge of
the second-rank weather station in Roseburg. After two years, he
moved to Portland to head the Signal Service's principal weather station in the Pacific Northwest. There he served as the local forecast
official, but he did not at all restrict himself to predicting the weather.
Rather, he took the lead in a program to collect systematically the
statistics of precipitation and temperature in Oregon on a locality-by-
locality basis. Pague himself had voluntarily begun collecting aggregate data of this kind for Oregon in June 1887, while he was still in
Roseburg. This data he published regularly in the Portland *Journal of
Commerce*. By May 1888, the worth of Pague's reports in the *Journal of
Commerce* was appreciated enough for the state to begin, under his
direction, its own monthly bulletin, the *Oregon State Weather Review
and Agricultural Report*, in an initial printing of 6,000 copies.[17]

Next, Pague engaged in a personal lobbying campaign to push
through the Oregon legislature the act of February 25, 1889, providing for the establishment of the Oregon State Weather Bureau to operate in conjunction with the U.S. Signal Service.[18] In this cooperative
arrangement Pague became the vital link between the two govern-

mental agencies. He served as chief of the Signal Service weather station in Portland and as, in effect, the executive director of the Oregon weather service, in both capacities helping to prove that impressions could be false, that western Oregon was not really as rainy as it seemed.

While B. S. Pague was making an impact in the Pacific Northwest, the Signal Service in Washington, D.C., was contributing to the demolition of the Webfoot stereotype. In this connection there was another key figure of even greater eminence than Pague—General A. W. Greely, head of the Signal Service in the late 1880s. Like Pague, Greely is now forgotten, but a century ago he was widely known for his heroic leadership of a three-year expedition, 1881–84, to the North Pole for weather observation. During the Civil War, Greely had risen from private to major in the U.S. Army. His advance in the army ranks continued, and after the polar expedition he was promoted to major general and made director of the Signal Service.[19] When he took over, the Signal Service had been collecting precipitation and temperature data on a nationwide basis for nearly two decades, and sufficient information then existed for cumulation and quantification in order to identify general patterns and trends. At the same time, the desire for economic development in the boom years of the 1880s—especially in the Great Plains and Far West—bred a demand for the sort of general climatological reports now within the capability of Greely and his subordinates to prepare. The result was the publication of six reports dealing with the climatological features of the western half of the United States. One, an 1888 report entitled *The Climate of Oregon and Washington Territory*,[20] had its genesis in a Senate resolution of July 26, 1888, introduced by Senator John H. Mitchell of Oregon.[21]

Greely's report on *The Climate of Oregon and Washington Territory* proved to be the core document in the scientific campaign to validate the high quality of the Pacific Northwest climate and to diminish the reputation of excessive rain. The report was a substantial pamphlet of thirty-seven pages, heavily illustrated with supporting charts and maps. It conceded that the belt west of the Coast Range crest was indeed the rainiest section of America, with an average annual rainfall of 70 to 107 inches per year, but emphasized that this zone of super rainfall comprised only 6 percent of the geographical expanse of Washington and Oregon. It then focused on the nearly nine-tenths of the land of Oregon and Washington possessing climatic conditions Greely deemed to be ideally suited to agriculture, land in which the "preponderating amount" of rainfall in the winter was followed "by moderate rains at not infrequent intervals" throughout the growing season, thus making for a situation that favored "to a marked extent the growth of most cereals and other important staple crops."[22] The curse of excessive rainfall was denied, and, as of 1888, the farmers of the Great Plains, whose own climate was now entering one of its most severe dry periods in history, had government assurance that optimum weather conditions awaited those who emigrated to the Pacific Northwest, as indeed thousands were to do.

There was an enthusiastic statewide response to this scientific attempt to transfer the perceptions of Oregon weather from the realm of myth to that of reality. On October 1, 1890, the Eugene *Register* commented approvingly that "people who are inquiring about this country" with a view to settling in it "always want definite statistics in regard to climate, and heretofore we have had only general opinions to give. Now we will have reliable records."[23]

The desire for reliable records expressed in the Eugene newspaper was met not only by Greely's report of 1888 but also by the much more voluminous biennial reports of the Oregon State Weather Bureau in 1891, 1893, 1895, and 1897. Of these, the report for 1893 compiled by B. S. Pague, was a landmark in the developing ideology of climate for the Pacific Northwest. A massive publication of 340 pages, it provided exhaustive data on precipitation and temperature in minute daily detail for scores of localities as well as for the whole state. Introducing this archive of data was a concise ten-page gloss on the climate of Oregon written by Pague, and in it the key item was a table that listed comparative annual precipitation and temperature data for thirty-seven American cities from coast to coast. The crucial comparison was between Portland and such cities as New York, Philadelphia, Washington, D.C., New Orleans, Memphis, Chicago, St. Paul, Omaha, and Los Angeles.[24] Supporting Pague's conclusion that the term *Webfoot* was a misnomer, the figures revealed that Portland's rainfall was not at all excessive but about the same as New York's and Philadelphia's—cities not thought of as being especially rainy—and much less than that of New Orleans; further, Portland's clear surplus of rainfall over such Great Plains cities as Omaha—to say nothing of arid Los Angeles—was viewed implicitly as a great advantage.

In regard to average annual temperature, the statistics showed Portland as the happy medium between cold Chicago and New York and hot New Orleans. A list of the annual average number of rainy days helped explain the existence of the Webfoot prototype in the regional and national folklore, for although Portland was really no wetter than New York City or Washington, D.C., it had more rainy days per year—156 compared to only 128 in New York and 127 in Washington. But overall the Northwest's rainfall contributed a great economic benefit to the region, since in the 7 million acres of the

Willamette Valley, crop failures were "unknown due to the fulsome supply of moisture during the year."[25]

With the publication of Greely's report of 1888 and Pague's 1893 report and with both supplemented by monthly reports, the scientific data on Oregon and Pacific Northwest weather were accumulating rapidly. The result, and one that drew also on previous perceptions, was the emergence by the last decade of the nineteenth century of what might be termed the *ideology of climate* of the Pacific Northwest—that is, a system of interrelated ideas which, taken together, represented a full-fledged climatological doctrine strongly favorable to Oregon and Washington west of the Cascades. Remaining with us today for the most part, the Pacific Northwest's ideology of climate as it emerged in the 1890s contained the following half dozen propositions:

1. Although the rain is prolific, it falls gently and does not generally inhibit outdoor work and activity.[26]

2. The total amount of rainfall per year is about average for the U.S. and only seems excessive because it is concentrated in only about one half (or less) of the year.[27]

3. Even when the long fall-to-spring rainy season is taken into account, there are two notable compensating factors: the warm winter weather in comparison to the subfreezing temperatures and blizzards of the central and eastern U.S.; the delightfully dry and sunny but not excessively hot summer weather.[28]

4. The regularity and dependability of Pacific Northwest temperature and precipitation are such that   in stark contrast to other parts of the country—the crops never fail.[29]

5. The climate is unexcelled for the personal health of the individual, who benefits in terms of comfort and longevity.[30]

6. When the climate of the Northwest is compared to climates elsewhere, it is most analogous to those of England, France, and Japan— "all regions inhabited by healthy and progressive peoples"—and is therefore not merely the finest climate in the nation but one of the best in the world.[31]

In summary, then, this ideology of climate plays down the special factor of rainfall (except as an unmitigated benefit) and plays up the more general point that the words "mild and equable" best characterize the Pacific Northwest.

In time, the favorite weather statistic in the Northwest came to be average annual rainfall for New York City. An illustrated broadside published in 1907 by the Eugene Commercial Club asked the question, "What Would Happen to a Eugene Belle if She Stood in a Year's Rainfall?" The belle's smiling answer for Eugene's annual 38 inches was a happy, "Such Joy!"; for New York City's 45 inches it was an exclamation of "Getting Dangerous"; and for the 62 inches of New Orleans it was a prayerful cry of "Help!"[32] Even today a current popular book on the weather of Washington, Oregon, and British Columbia by a Seattle journalist proudly emphasizes that New York City's annual precipitation is two inches greater than that of Seattle.[33] Thus, the old strategy in regional self-defense going back to the 1890s continues to be employed.

Underscoring the ideology of climate for the Pacific Northwest was the completion in 1927 of a 250-page monograph on *The Physical and Economic Geography of Oregon* by Warren DuPre Smith of the University of Oregon. Smith declared that the notion of an "excessively rainy climate" was a "climatic myth"—fostered especially in California. His conclusion was that "Oregon has not only *not* a bad climate but enjoys the climatic optimum" for the entire human race. "Most of the temperate world," he noted, "has a little less than the optimum amount of rainfall. This [rainfall] is the greatest single physical asset of western Oregon and of the Coast Range country."[34]

Why, then, despite the aggressive stance of Smith and others, is the climate still being defended from the aspersions of excessive and intolerable raininess? The answer lies in the realm of individual psychology. It was the Northwest's first notable historian, Frances Fuller Victor, who identified the problem as far back as 1872. In her book, *All over Oregon and Washington*, Victor noted that "during the rainy season those who are already invalids are liable to greater depression of the vital powers by reason of the continuous wet weather. Even a well person, of a peculiarly sensitive temperament," she declared, "may suffer from the same cause."[35] That was the problem—a psychological depression stemming from the long, cloudy, wet, rainy season that afflicted many in the Pacific Northwest and left few entirely untouched. For the evidence of this problem we must turn back from the prosaic statistical data of climate compiled by Greely, Pague, Smith, and others to the testimony of individuals—to the diaries and letters of Oregonians and Washingtonians and to those who have sensitively interpreted Northwest culture in fiction.

In *Honey in the Horn*, his striking novel of western Oregon pioneer life, H. L. Davis wrote that from November "until spring the rain never totally stopped and the light never entirely started." This was the time of the year "that wore people's nerves the hardest," when "old squatters from the creek canyons" picked quarrels with one another and then reverted to the "heart-eating loneliness" of the rainy season.[36]

Nor was the problem by any means restricted to the isolated settlers of back-country western Oregon. At least one sophisticated urbanite, Judge Matthew P. Deady of Portland, felt a spiritual oppression also. Deady's diary, with its lively account of Oregon's Gilded Age, is stippled with insistent comments on the weather, an almost brooding presence in the half year from October to March. The incisive judge's ubiquitous weather entries reveal an individual with great inner strength for whom the pervasive rain was almost too much. There are abundant references to "terrible" rainstorms, "real" winter rains, weeks that were "wet, very wet," days that were "blustery," and daily rains that were "hard" or "very hard" or even "wild." Weather marred the choicest occasions, such as General Grant's 1879 visit to Portland and America's centennial year of 1876, which found Deady complaining that there had not been "one clear day" in March.[37]

Ken Kesey depicts the dispiriting effect of the steady rain of the Oregon coast in his novel *Sometimes a Great Notion;* one of the characters opines fatalistically that the rain is there, that it will not go away, that all winter long the rain "falls on the just and unjust alike"—"falls all day long"—and "you might just as well give up and admit that's the way it's gonna be. . . . Or you'll be mouthin' the barrel of your twelve-gauge the way Evert Peterson at Mapleton did last year."[38]

Other leading writers, however, less grimly describe the regional rainfall, delineating it in terms that are considerably more equable, even comforting. One finds this in Bernard Malamud's fictionalized portrait of Corvallis in the 1950s and in Don Berry's trilogy of western Oregon pioneer life in the 1840s and 1850s.[39] Rain is a predominant theme, also, in the novel *Beyond the Garden Gate,* published in 1946 by Sophus K. Winther. Winther grew up in the Danebo section on the outskirts of Eugene, was an undergraduate at the University of Oregon, and became a professor of English at the University of Washington. The setting of *Beyond the Garden Gate* is modern Eugene, upon which Spencer's Butte looks down like a cloud-wreathed Mount Olympus. Winther's story is one of excruciating emotional pain for his protagonists, but it is the rain that provides an offsetting mood, for the interludes of gentle, nurturing rainfall endow Eugene and the Willamette Valley with gardenlike natural beauty, in studied contrast to the tragic theme of "what it means to be human."[40]

The soothing ambience of rainfall in the fiction of Winther and others is reflected in real life as well. A 1978 poll in the *Oregonian* revealed that twice as many Oregonians welcome the seasonal rains as find them depressing.[41] This, too, is the overall impression conveyed in the literature of personal experience, the letters and diaries of Northwest residents in which, as in Deady's case, rainfall is prominently and continuously mentioned.

Among the leading pioneers of the Puget Sound country were Colonel Isaac N. Ebey and his wife, Rebecca, who settled on Whidbey Island in the early 1850s. Rebecca's diary for the rainy season of 1852–53 shows the importance of the weather, with which each entry begins. For Rebecca the rain is not oppressive but provides a comforting element of stability in a pioneer life beset with uncertainty. Depressed by her husband's repeated but necessary absences and by the news of her mother's death along the Overland Trail, Rebecca did not, however, mind the weather, of which she wrote,

it generally rains of nights. The ground is not muddy and the rain does not make it at all disagreeable; men can continue laboring all day here in the winter, while in the states they are all housed up and can do nothing but keep large fires, and feed their stock; here we have to do no feeding at all. How great is the contrast.[42]

Another pioneer who left a daily record of weather and life in the Northwest was A. R. Burbank, whose diary covered the years 1880 to 1898. Burbank was a typical Pacific Slope frontiersman. Born in Illinois in 1817, he traveled overland to California in 1849. After "a time" at Sutter's Fort and in the California mining country, Burbank returned to Illinois in 1851. With his wife, he came West again for good in 1853, this time to Washington and Oregon. By 1867 the Burbanks had settled down in the old town of Lafayette in Yamhill County, Oregon. Until his death in 1902 Burbank was one of the leading participants in the economic and political life of Lafayette, where he was the proprietor of a store, owned a good farm, and participated actively enough in the Republican party to be on hand at an 1891 Portland reception to honor President Benjamin Harrison.[43]

Rain is a persistent motif in Burbank's eighteen-year-long diary. The pages are peppered with accounts of farming and storekeeping, events in the local Grange Hall, church and Sunday school attendance, Fourth of July ceremonies and picnics, local railroad promotions, and mundane family activities in Lafayette and on periodic trips to Portland. In the record of small-town life, the weather—the rainfall, especially—is a great wheeling theme. Climatic high points move to the fore in the pages of the diary. One was a great windstorm out of the south on February 9, 1882, but the peak event began with a warm but "great and continuous rain" from January 10 to 13, 1881, leading inexorably to the great floods of middle and late January— among the greatest in Pacific Northwest history. The rushing Yamhill River eventually carried away Lafayette's bridge—a structure whose building Burbank had supervised seven years earlier and which he and others tried to save from the rising flood waters—"a great loss to the public and the county," Burbank mourned on February 3, 1881.[44]

But an overwhelming number of Burbank's diary entries about weather and rainfall are entirely routine. Laconic observations of the weather from day to day and week to week characterize Burbank's tireless meteorological record keeping. The regularity of the rainfall in the diary must be viewed against the trauma of the event that came near to prostrating Mr. and Mrs. Burbank in 1880. This was the tragic drowning in August of Eva, their daughter, in the Pacific surf of the Washington coast. Again and again, Burbank recorded the unappeased anguish and sorrow he and his wife felt; he "distributed photographs of [Eva] to lighthouse keepers on the north Pacific Coast, received communications from her via spiritualists in Indiana, and was pleased when Charles Bray," a Portland composer, "wrote a song in her memory" for publication in 1881.[45] In reading the diary for the years following this shattering family tragedy, one senses that the act of recording the weather helped preserve Burbank's sanity. In a very real way he depended on the rain; its powerful regularity, whether light or heavy, enabled him to endure personal disaster.

The theme of regular rainfall and climatic regularity that emerges from the personally recorded experiences of A. R. Burbank and others may be the most important theme of all in assessing the connection between rainfall and history in the Pacific Northwest. In his book, *Times of Feast, Times of Famine*, the great French social historian Emmanuel Le Roy Ladurie focuses on the climatic history of the Franco-Alpine sector of western Europe. Over the nearly thousand years that Le Roy Ladurie surveyed, agricultural abundance and scarcity appear in relation to long-term variations in the climate.[46] Although a full-fledged climatic history of the Pacific Northwest in the manner of Le Roy Ladurie remains to be written, present evidence for the Willamette Valley since 1870 clearly indicates weather of impressive dependability and regularity, interrupted by short-term variations in precipitation and temperature.[47]

American cultural historians and critics have long maintained a tradition of interpretation that links climate and history. Most have avoided climatological determinism in favor of a model of explanation that preserves human freedom of adaptive response to climate. As Warren DuPre Smith stated two generations ago in his consideration of the society and climate of western Oregon, "No progressive people will be content to make their homes permanently where the basic needs of life [or] the necessities of a preferred standard of living are not to be had on fairly favorable terms." Instead, he concluded, "they will reclaim it or leave it."[48] Within the parameters of this explanatory model, there has been considerable stress on climate. Walter Prescott Webb's classic work emphasized the connection between the climatic

extremes of searing drought and numbing cold and extremes of political and personal behavior in the Great Plains.[49]

Also stressing climate has been Kevin Starr in his brilliant study of
California cultural history, *Americans and the California Dream*. Starr
shows Californians affecting a self-styled Mediterranean culture in
response to their sun-drenched weather,[50] and for many observers,
the paradoxical overtones of languor and frenzy summoned up by
the Mediterranean metaphor seem to be an apt characterization of
the schizophrenic social and political life of the Golden State with its
negative aspects of hedonism and zaniness.[51] And in recent years the
popular term *Sun Belt* has conveyed the cultural trend of the southern
U.S. toward zealous economic and political conservatism.[52]

To the mode of regularity in the Northwest climate there is an analogue in Northwest social and political life; the analogue is consensus. In both Northwest climate and Northwest history, the qualities
of irregularity and discontinuity wane in comparison to their oppo-
sites. Thus, regularity and consensus seem to characterize the post-
1840 history of the Pacific Northwest. This is not to say, however, that
significant discontinuity and conflict have been absent. In the early
twentieth century, social and political conflict swept over the Pacific
Northwest in the form of a struggle between capital and labor that
had heavy ideological overtones.[53] That era of conflict faded, but now
another is upon us. This time the controversy involves the relationship of people to the natural environment. Ecologically oriented defenders of nature are locked in political combat with those favoring
greater economic exploitation of natural resources. Similarly, organizations such as the Trojan Decommissioning Alliance in Oregon have
opposed the development of nuclear power favored by the likes of
Dixy Lee Ray, the former governor of Washington.

Despite these examples of conflict, some leading historians who
have viewed the long sweep of Pacific Northwest history emphasize
consensus rather than conflict. Central to this viewpoint is the insight
that from the nineteenth century to the twentieth, Pacific Northwest
society has been distinguished by a cultural consensus whose result
has been moderation in both social and political life. In Oregon history, Gordon B. Dodds sees predominant themes of "moderate conservatism" or "progressive anachronism"[54]—these might characterize the entire region. In their stress on a "tendency toward
moderation and proportion" that is one of the "deepest instincts" of
Portland's citizenry, Terence O'Donnell and Thomas Vaughan[55] strike
a note that is comparable to Roger Sale's conclusion that "from its first
breath" Seattle has been solidly "bourgeois"—a city of "land-
owning, house-building, root-making" inhabitants whose historically
dominant middle class blends without social "demarcation into the

'working' and 'upper' classes."[56] In part because the ethnic and social diversity of the Northwest have been less than in most other sections of the U.S., our region approximates the quintessential American average. The people of the Pacific Northwest, Dorothy O. Johansen once declared, "have pursued an unusually even tenor of existence," our history representing "a recapitulation of the middle way, the historical norm . . . of our national history."[57]

The ideology of climate taught that crops never failed in western Oregon—a claim that was apparently unique to the Pacific Northwest and one that helped lure thousands upon thousands of immigrants from the drought-and-depression-blasted Great Plains. Crops never fail in western Oregon! That would make for great stability in economic, social, political, and individual life. And if calm moderation has indeed been the most distinguishing characteristic of Pacific Northwest history and life, is it not much due to what I have emphasized?: the supreme regularity of the calming, moderating ambience of the Northwest's rainfall. For the protagonist of Sophus Winther's novel, and perhaps for us all, "the misty rain" was soothing and "as welcome on his hot face as balm to a sunburned back."[58]

NOTES

1. Recent general works are Edwin R. Bingham and Glen A. Love, eds., *Northwest Perspectives: Essays on the Culture of the Pacific Northwest* (Seattle, 1979), and William G. Robbins, Robert J. Frank, and Richard E. Ross, eds., *Regionalism and the Pacific Northwest* (Corvallis, 1983).

2. Raymond D. Gastil, "A Symposium: The Pacific Northwest as a Cultural Region," *PNQ*, Vol. 64 (1973), 157; Edwin R. Bingham, "A Convert's Testimonial," *OHQ*, Vol. 75 (1974), 336–38.

3. Geographers who emphasize climate are D. W. Meinig, *The Great Columbia Plain: A Historical Geography, 1805–1910* (Seattle, 1968), and Warren DuPre Smith, "The Physical and Economic Geography of Oregon," *Commonwealth Review of the University of Oregon*, n.s. Vol. 6 (1924), 21–31, 56–89; Vol. 7 (1925), 1–26, 31–61, 135–95; Vol. 8 (1926), 199–253; and Vol. 10 (1928), 158–94.

4. Douglas Cole and Maria Tippett, "Pleasing Diversity and Sublime Desolation: The 18th-Century British Perception of the Northwest Coast," *PNQ*, Vol. 65 (1974), 1–7.

5. Meriwether Lewis, *The Lewis and Clark Expedition: The 1814 Edition, Unabridged*, 3 vols. (Philadelphia, 1961), II, chaps. 20–24; III, chap. 25.

6. *OHQ*, Vol. 6 (1905), 286, for Scouler; *ibid.*, Vol. 53 (1952), 201, for Burkhart. See also Robert Cantwell, *The Hidden Northwest* (Philadelphia, 1972), chap. 1.

7. Mitford M. Mathews, ed., *A Dictionary of Americanisms on Historical Principles* (Chicago, [1951]), s.v. "Webfoot." See also Suzie Jones, *Oregon Folklore* (Eugene, 1977).

8. Frances Fuller Victor, *All over Oregon and Washington* (San Francisco, 1872), 179–80.

9. Arthur J. Brown, "The Promotion of Emigration to Washington, 1854–1909," *PNQ*, Vol. 36 (1945), 7, 11; James B. Hedges, "Promotion of Immigration to the Pacific Northwest by Railroads," *Mississippi Valley Historical Review*, Vol. 15 (1928), 183.

10. Brown, 3–18. Promotion of settlement in the Pacific Northwest was a major thrust of the popular magazine, *West Shore* (published in Portland, 1875–91).

11. Earl Pomeroy, *The Pacific Slope* (Seattle, 1973), chaps. 5–6; Glenn S. Dumke, *The Boom of the Eighties in Southern California* (San Marino, Calif., 1944). On Northwest competition with California for settlers, see, for example, *West Shore*, February 1880, p. 70.

12. See, for example, *West Shore*, May 1888, pp. 237, 263; July 1888, p. 378.

13. "Letters of Peter H. Burnett, 1844," *OHQ*, Vol. 3 (1902), 424–25. See also Peter H. Burnett, *Recollections of an Old Pioneer* (New York, 1880), 139–41.

14. Overton Johnson and William H. Winter, "Route across the Rocky Mountains with a Description of Oregon and California, etc., 1843," *OHQ*, Vol. 7 (1906), 186–87, 191.

15. David D. Fagan, ed., *History of Benton County, Oregon* (Portland, 1885), 309–10.

16. Morton Keller, *Affairs of State: Public Life in Late Nineteenth Century America* (Cambrige, Mass., 1977), 102–10.

17. "B. S. Pague," in H. K. Hines, *An Illustrated History of the State of Oregon* (Chicago, 1893), 561. "Beamer S. Pague," in *History of the Bench and Bar of Oregon* (Portland, 1910), 202.

18. Hines, 561.

19. *DAB Supp. 1*, s.v. "Greely, Adolphus Washington."

20. *Ibid*; A. W. Greely, *The Climate of Oregon and Washington Territory* (Washington, D.C., 1888).

21. Portland *Morning Oregonian*, July 27, 1888.

22. Greely, 5, 7.

23. Eugene *Register*, Oct. 1, 1890. The Oregon State Immigration Board's annual promotional pamphlets for 1889 and 1891 quoted verbatim key passages from Greely's 1888 report. Oregon Immigration Board, *The New Empire: Oregon, Washington, Idaho* (Portland, 1889), 36–37, and *The Pacific Northwest: Its Wealth and Resources* (Portland, 1889), 64–83.

24. *Second Biennial Report of the Oregon Weather Bureau Cooperating with [the] United States Department of Agriculture, Weather Bureau, Central Office, Portland, Or.* (Salem, 1893), xliii–lii.

25. *Ibid.*, xlviii.

26. *West Shore*, April 1885, p. 96; January 1888, p. 56. "The Round Hand of George B. Roberts: The Cowlitz Farm Journal, 1847–51," *OHQ*, Vol. 63 (1962), 124–53. William F. Prosser, *A History of Puget Sound: Its Resources, Its Commerce and Its People*, 2 vols. (New York, 1903), I, 16.

27. *West Shore*, April 1885, pp. 95–96. Hines, 18. Roger Sale, *Seattle: Past to Present* (Seattle, 1976), 3. U.S. Department of Agriculture, Climate and Crop Service, *Climate and Crops: Oregon Section*, Vol 11 (March 1905), 3.

28. Fagan, 309–10. Oregon Immigration Board, *New Empire*, 33–36. *Illustrated History of Lane County, Oregon* (Portland, 1884), 8–9. Dr. Joseph Holt in *West Shore*, October 1888, pp. 584–85.

29. *West Shore*, January 1880, pp. 2–3, 38–40; February 1880; p. 57; April 1885, p. 96; September 13, 1890, p. 80. *Oregonian*, April 17, 1889.

30. Oregon State Board of Immigration, *Oregon as It Is* (Portland, 1885), 7–8. Prosser, I, 16.

31. *West Shore*, April 1885, p. 116; May 1886, p. 160. Prosser, I, iii. U.S. Weather Bureau, *Climate and Crop Service: Oregon*, December 1902, p. 3. Smith, Vol. 7 (1925), 140–41.

32. Eugene Commercial Club, *Who Said Rain?* (Eugene, 1907).

33. Walter Rue, *Weather of the Pacific Coast: Washington, Oregon, British Columbia* (Mercer Island, Wash., [1978]), 64, 66.

34. Quotations: Smith, Vol. 7 (1925), 12–13.

35. Victor, 276–77.

36. H. L. Davis, *Honey in the Horn* (New York, 1935), 194.

37. Malcolm Clark, Jr., ed., *Pharisee among Philistines: The Diary of Judge Matthew P. Deady, 1871–1892* (Portland, [1975]), 11, 37, 67, 100, 171, 200, 212, 288, *et passim*.

38. Ken Kesey, *Sometimes a Great Notion* (New York, 1965), 382.

39. Bernard Malamud, *A New Life* (New York, 1961), 96 *et passim*. Don Berry, *Trask: The Coast of Oregon, 1848* (Sausalito, Calif., 1977), 6 *et passim*; *To Build a Ship* (Sausalito, Calif., 1977), 28, 197–98, 224; *Moontrap* (Sausalito, Calif., 1977). Rainfall and the stormy coastal climate are an integral part of two books by a new Pacific Northwest writer, Ivan Doig: *Winter Brothers* (New York, 1980), a biographical evocation of James G. Swan, and *The Sea Runners* (New York, 1982), a novel.

40. Sophus Keith Winther, *Beyond the Garden Gate* (New York, 1946), 39, 150–51, 157, 289. On Winther (whose late brother, Oscar Osburn Winther, was a leading historian of the Pacific Northwest), see Susan Bowers, "The Immigrant Novelist," *Old Oregon*, Vol. 55 (Spring 1977), 43; *Contemporary Authors* (Detroit, 1962–), Vols. 5–8, 1st revision, s.v. "Winther, Sophus Keith."

41. *Oregonian*, Dec. 3, 1978.

42. Victor J. Farrar, ed., "Diary of Colonel and Mrs. I. N. Ebey," *WHQ*, Vol. 8 (1917), 52.

43. Martin Schmitt, comp., *Catalogue of Manuscripts in the University of Oregon Library* (Eugene, [1971]), entry no. 150.

44. Augustus Ripley Burbank, Diary, 1880–1893 (Special Collections, University of Oregon Library, Eugene), Jan. 10–Feb. 9, 1881; Feb. 12, 1882.

45. Schmitt, entry no. 150.

46. Emmanuel Le Roy Ladurie, *Times of Feast, Times of Famine: A History of Climate since the Year 1000*, trans. Barbara Bray (Garden City, N.Y., 1971).

47. David W. Baker, "The Climate of the Willamette Valley, 1900–1953," M.A. thesis (Oregon State University, 1955); William G. Loy et al., *Atlas of Oregon* (Eugene, 1976), 130–33.

48. Smith, Vol. 7 (1925), 47 (quotation), and 136. Lucien Febvre, *A Geographical Introduction to History*, trans. E. G. Mountford and J. H. Paxton (New York, 1925). Reid A. Bryson and Christine Padoch, "On the Climates of History," and David Hackett Fischer, "Climate and History: Priorities for Research," *Journal of Interdisciplinary History*, Vol. 10 (Spring 1980), 583–84, 821–30.

49. Walter Prescott Webb, *The Great Plains* (Boston, 1931), 17–26, 319–84, 502–506, *et passim*.

50. Kevin Starr, *Americans and the California Dream: 1850–1915* (New York, 1973), chap. 12.

51. For example, Kenneth C. Lamott, *Anti-California: Report from Our First Parafascist State* (Boston, 1971), and Carey McWilliams's earlier, more balanced classic, *Southern California Country: An Island on the Land* (New York, [1946]).

52. Kirkpatrick Sale, *Power Shift: The Rise of the Southern Rim and Its Rise to Challenge the Eastern Establishment* (New York, 1975).

53. Among many works, see Robert L. Tyler, *Rebels of the Woods: The IWW in the Pacific Northwest* (Eugene, 1967); Norman H. Clark, *Mill Town: A Social History of Everett, Washington* (Seattle, 1970); and Carlos A. Schwantes, *Radical Heritage: Labor, Socialism, and Reform in Washington and British Columbia, 1885–1917* (Seattle, 1979).

54. Gordon B. Dodds, *Oregon: A Bicentennial History* (New York, 1977), 185, 229.

55. Terence O'Donnell and Thomas Vaughan, *Portland: A Historical Sketch and Guide* (Portland, [1976]).

56. Sale, xii, 86.

57. Dorothy O. Johansen, "Oregon's Role in American History: An Old Theme Recast," *PNQ*, Vol. 40 (1949), 92. See also, Dodds, 226–28.

58. Winther, 150–51.

The Role of the Hudson's Bay Company in Pacific Northwest History

Keith A. Murray

All thematic approaches to Pacific Northwest history give substantial emphasis to the Great Fur Rush. This phase of the development of the Pacific Coast extended over a period of about eighty years, beginning sometime between the arrivals of Vitus Bering in Alaska (1741) and James Cook at Nootka Sound (1778). The fur trade was tapering off by 1836 and certainly, as far as Washington State was concerned, was at an end in 1845, when Governor George Simpson ordered that the headquarters of the Hudson's Bay Company be transferred from Fort Vancouver to Victoria.

During these two-and-a-half generations, while the sea otter, fur seal, and beaver surrendered their pelts to Frenchmen, Russians, Englishmen, and Americans, hunting, trapping, and trading attracted hundreds of adventurous, reckless young men from the ends of the earth. Some made small fortunes; a few hard-fisted enterprisers made vast fortunes; scores of others found only financial ruin or death. Search for new sources of furs provided a motivation for exploration. Attempts to maintain supply and trading routes compelled some kind of governmental functions. Profits to be made from trading on the tributaries of the Columbia River system or the Strait of Georgia attracted world interest, even though all but the most persistent were distracted by revolutions, wars, and Napoleonic bombast.

Through all of this activity, the outstanding name in the history of the fur trade is that of the "Governor and Company of Adventurers of England trading into Hudson's Bay." The Hudson's Bay Company was not the first to trade in the Northwest. It came after the Russians,

Originally published in *Pacific Northwest Quarterly*, January 1961.

after the Spaniards, after the Astorians, and after the Northwesters. The records of its competitors are now to be found only in the pages of the history books, but the Hudson's Bay Company is still in business. While it no longer plays a significant role in Northwest affairs, its first decades were of such profound importance to the opening of the old Oregon country and British Columbia that it is difficult to tell of its contributions without seeming to indulge in wild exaggeration.

Perhaps a simple statement of its functions and operations may serve both to focus your thinking and to set an outline for my consideration of the role of the Hudson's Bay Company in the development of the Pacific Northwest. First, the company served as government for the vast region north of California and west of the Continental Divide. Second, it obtained much information about the geography and aboriginal inhabitants of the region—modern studies in ethnography, anthropology, or geography would be impossible to complete were the Hudson's Bay Company's records not available. Third, it expected its posts to be as nearly self-sufficient as possible, and it encouraged each responsible trader to develop the natural resources around his trading post or fort to accomplish this end.

American settlers found the Hudson's Bay Company's example and methods invaluable in their own efforts to survive in the western wilderness. While the company was not happy over American immigration into its vast game preserve, the record shows that a fourth function of the Hudson's Bay officials was the protection of lives and property of settlers, and the acceptance, if not the encouragement, of the villages that American missionaries, mountain men, and prospectors built along the waterways of the Northwest.

In the 1670 charter that created the Hudson's Bay Company, the Crown declared the agents and directors of the enterprise to be "the true and absolute lords and proprietors of the same territory." The governing authority of the company was reiterated in 1821 in "A Bill for regulating the Fur Trade and establishing a Criminal and Civil Jurisdiction within certain Parts of *North America.*" The British government expected the company to maintain order, to prevent foreigners from trespassing on British soil, and to keep the Indians quiet. Sir George Simpson, who was appointed governor, became responsible for profits and for peace.

Sir George discharged his assignment magnificently. A competitor, who at first looked upon the appointment with condescension (Sir George was "reputed a gentlemanly man" who would "not create much alarm, nor do I presume him formidable as an Indian trader"), changed his opinion within three years. He grumbled bitterly about the control of the company authorities, and concluded, "In short, the Northwest is now beginning to be ruled with an iron rod."

It is interesting to note that forty years later effective control was still the order of the day. In all the stories told of the wicked deeds of numerous western badmen, there are few told of outlaws living in areas controlled by the Hudson's Bay Company. There were no Dodge Cities, Deadwoods, or Hangtowns on the Fraser. During the 1860s Boone Helm from Montana hopefully sought out the gold camps to earn a few dishonest dollars. He did not find the law as administered by the agents of James Douglas to be conducive to his peculiar talents; therefore, he abandoned the unrewarding river and returned to Virginia City and a hangman's noose applied by a zealous vigilance committee.

The secret of the company's success was simple. It broke the power of the head-hunting northern Yuculta who had terrorized coastal Indians for generations. All leaders who became friendly with the company as a result of this demonstration of power were supported, and attempts were made to placate those who still remained suspicious and unfriendly.

The company guaranteed protection to anyone on his way to trade, while he was inside the walls of the trading posts, and while he was on his return journey from a trading expedition. It punished crimes of theft, violence, or murder against any white man, even its enemies. Otherwise, it left the Indian to his own devices. The company made little or no deliberate effort to impose European customs on him. It played no part in intertribal or intervillage quarrels. It did not interfere with Indian law or justice where it concerned Indians alone. Above all, while company traders did on occasion trick the Indians, the company itself did not cheat them in business dealings, nor did it try to push them off their lands or move them to another part of the continent.

Examples of Hudson's Bay policy toward the Indians are numerous. Doubtless, some readers are familiar with that part of American folklore which tells how Chief Factor John McLoughlin tricked the Indians into presenting themselves in front of the gates of Fort Vancouver for a conference before he made his formal appearance—thus indicating in a prestige-conscious culture that the Hudson's Bay man was more important than they. He did so by the simple expedient of sending a physically huge Scottish bagpiper, complete with tartan and pipes, to play an impromptu concert along the banks of the Columbia; the waiting Indians could not contain their curiosity and gathered around the piper to hear better what wonderful noises he was producing. Suddenly, at the strategic moment and with a fanfare of trumpets, Dr. McLoughlin emerged. The Indians recognized that they had been outmaneuvered, but they respected a man who knew their customs well enough to trick them in this way. In subsequent trading, they were never cheated, and the Indians seem to have felt no resentment over the incident.

Similarly, the company authorities on Vancouver Island taught the Indians there that they could expect justice, but that the white men were not to be trifled with. On one occasion Indians butchered and ate company cattle stolen from the company pasture and defied the whites at Fort Victoria to do anything about it. When Roderick Finlayson, who was in command of the post, ordered the Indians to pay for their meal, the aborigines fired on the fort. By a ruse, Finlayson got the Indians to clear one of their houses nearby, and then he completely demolished it with a charge of grapeshot. Thus, with no loss of life to either party, the Indians were shown the power of the company cannon. They immediately paid for the stolen animals, and trade was resumed without further retaliation or censure. "We parted good friends," Finlayson wrote in his report of the affair.

On another occasion some Whidbey Island Indians were attacked and robbed as they were leaving Victoria. They appealed to the company, and when the trader informed the thieves that Indians trading with the company had the same protection as did the highest officials of the company, the goods were promptly returned. To underline the company attitude, the Whidbey Indians were given an escort of four white men to make certain that there were no other incidents.

All of us are familiar with the story of how Dr. McLoughlin recovered the property of Jedediah Smith, who was attacked by Indians near the Umpqua River. Word went out through the Indian grapevine that the Hudson's Bay Company would protect all white men in its territory, even though they might be rivals of the company. We are equally familiar with the efforts of Peter Skene Ogden to ransom the captive survivors of the Whitman massacre so that it might be known that no white person was to be held at the mercy of the Indians. It should also be noted that it was not the Hudson's Bay Company that carried out the punitive Cayuse War; this was the work of the Oregon settlers.

United States history is replete with cases of carefully planned attempts to change Indian cultural patterns. In general, Hudson's Bay observers simply recorded Indian customs and made no attempt to change them. Men like Alexander Ross, John Work, W. F. Tolmie, James Douglas, and Sir George Simpson, and such guests of the company as Duflot de Mofras, Paul Kane, and David Douglas reported on many aspects of Indian culture: head flattening; shamanism, totemism, and other religious customs; slavery, social organization, and food gathering; customs of birth, puberty, courtship and marriage, pregnancy, medical treatment, death, and burial.

Though company officials did not always approve of the Indian customs they recorded, they left the Indians free to practice their folkways without interference as long as the company ruled New Caledonia (mainland British Columbia). The versatile Paul Kane certainly did not approve of all that he saw—many times he was horrified by the acts of the Indians—but his observations brought no orders prohibiting the Indians from following their old ways. It is difficult to assess properly the debt anthropologists owe to him and those like him for the patient and careful analyses they made of Indian cultural patterns.

Two examples will serve to explain this assertion. In 1839 James Douglas compiled a systematic census of all the men, women, and children, houses, and canoes in the Indian villages along Puget Sound, and since that time every population study made in this region by anthropologists has used this work as a point of reference. A few years later, Dr. W. F. Tolmie of the Puget Sound Agricultural Company made a glossary of the Nisqually language. George Gibbs, the ethnographer and secretary for the Stevens treaty-making team, later incorporated the Tolmie material into his own glossary, and without Tolmie's prior study, the Gibbs work would have had only a fraction of its present value.

The geographical work done by the company was systematic and thorough. Its traders used old Indian trails, and its clerks and map makers recorded the routes thus followed. Modern highways have been built not far from some of these routes. Names like the Cariboo Road, the Hope-Princeton highway, or the Okanogan Trail are used for the old Indian or fur trader trails.

Alexander Ross, the first white man to cross the Cascade Mountains in the present state of Washington, recorded his route from the Methow Valley to the Skagit River; this route subsequently became the first cross-state wagon road, the now abandoned Cascade Pass route. The ubiquitous John Work pushed an expedition from the Columbia to the Fraser west of the Cascades. Other brigades under the leadership of Work and Peter Skene Ogden traveled up the Snake, through Idaho and Utah, across northern California and the Siskiyous to the Willamette Valley, keeping careful records as they went.

Governor Simpson made copious notes of his travels, and it is no coincidence that Isaac Stevens consulted with Hudson's Bay Governor Simpson before he began his own survey of the projected northern route for the Pacific Railway survey. Naturally, the company also used the work of its predecessors: David Thompson of the North-

westers, William Clark's charts and those of the sea captains who
the islands and bays of the North Pacific Coast. The final synthesis,
however, may be credited to the company.

The economic development of the states of Washington, Oregon,
and Idaho and of the province of British Columbia would have
moved forward in any event with the coming of settlement, but the
contribution of the Hudson's Bay Company to this development was
far from negligible.

From the first, Governor Simpson insisted that company operations should include many activities beyond mere fur trading: "Every
pursuit tending to leighten the Expence of the Trade is a branch
thereof," he announced. A trading post might be built beside an important waterway: "The river with a potatoe Garden will abundantly
maintain the Post," Simpson said. McLoughlin carried out Simpson's
instructions faithfully. Among McLoughlin's letters may be found
careful directions to husbandmen regarding approved methods for
planting grain and vegetables, fertilizing crops, increasing milk production, or building dams for irrigation.

The success of such operations is shown by the report of W. A.
Slacum, an agent of the American navy who visited the Hudson's Bay
forts and farms in 1837. He stated that at Fort Vancouver alone there
were 3,000 fenced acres of land under cultivation, and that the previous year's harvest had been 8,000 bushels of wheat, 5,500 bushels
of barley, 6,000 bushels of oats, 9,000 bushels of peas, 14,000 bushels
of potatoes and roots, with pumpkins and other vegetables. He cited
flocks and herds of horses, sheep, goats, and swine; he reported an
orchard with apple, pear, and quince trees all bearing fruit; he noted
two sawmills and two flour mills in operation.

James Douglas, in an official report two years later, acknowledged
only 861 acres under cultivation with yields of only about one-third
as much as Slacum claimed, but this would still have been a substantial farming operation. Add to this the Cowlitz Farms, the farms
around Fort Nisqually, and recall that even the minor posts had some
garden space. Governor Simpson personally supervised the beginning of the potato patch at Fort Colville.

The company actively participated in the cattle business. Ewing
Young's hazardous and difficult drive from California would have
been impossible without the support of McLoughlin, who contributed over $800 to help promote the project. The company complained
in 1860 that during the previous thirty years its white American
neighbors had stolen 6,058 head of cattle and almost the same number of sheep from its lands. If this claim were true, the company obviously was well supplied with animals.

The company did not confine itself solely to farming. Records show that, during the Sacramento gold rush, some Americans going to California by sea stopped in Victoria to buy food and equipment from Hudson's Bay stores. After a brief period of debate over the value of an ounce of gold dust, the traders settled down to conducting retail operations—perhaps the beginnings of the great chain of retail department stores now located in all major Canadian cities.

The company paid little heed to prospecting for its own mines, but when coal was discovered at Nanaimo, it did not hesitate to add this commodity to its growing list of subsidiary activities. The most important mineral strikes in the Northwest—the gold strikes of the Cariboo district—were organized, and for a long time afterward the traders continued to reap a harvest of gold which was faithfully shipped to London. Truly, Simpson's orders that "every pursuit tending to leighten the Expence of the Trade is a branch thereof" took them far afield from the fur trade.

Scientific, cultural, and religious activities were not forgotten by the company. The Royal Horticultural Society sent David Douglas to Fort Vancouver in 1825 to study the vegetation of the Northwest and to search for exotic plants. Douglas and the traders did not work well together, but he noted and named the Douglas fir. (This, as I remember from a college botany course, is not a fir at all, but a false hemlock.) Paul Kane, the artist, has already been referred to. Fort Vancouver had a library of books and newspapers from London. It was small and not much used, but the fact that there was a library at all reflects considerable credit on the management.

If the little school operated for children of the employees can be designated as a public school, it is interesting to note that the first public school music class in what is now the United States met at Fort Vancouver even before Lowell Mason began his considerably better-known work in Boston. To further religious observance, the offices of the company called the Reverend Herbert Beaver of the Anglican Church to the Columbia River to serve his short, unhappy pastorate. It also transported and protected Fathers Blanchet, Demers, De Smet, and others in their work on the Pacific Coast. The Lees, the Whitmans, Parker, and the Spaldings were all entertained at Fort Vancouver.

The Hudson's Bay Company deliberately chose sites for its trading posts and forts that were not likely to be developed into future cities. With the exception of Vancouver (Washington), Victoria, Hope, and Kamloops, not many of its major stations developed into permanent towns. Many posts, like Flathead House, Fort Okanogan, Fort Nez Perce, Fort Hall, Fort Colville, or Fort Umpqua, were completely abandoned; some are buried under many feet of water piled up behind the Columbia power dams. Much the same situation exists in some of the posts in Canada, like Fort Alexandria, which is now marked only by a cairn of rocks and a bronze plate.

The policy of the company was always to keep the number of its employees small. In 1850 there were still only about 600 Europeans, in addition to a fluctuating number of Indian laborers, in all of the posts of New Caledonia, both north and south of the United States–Canada border. This lack of concern for settlement, in truth this hostility to city growth and development, was part of the policy of the directors whose trade with the Indians depended on how successfully they kept out all trespassers, the chief of whom were American land speculators who might have come for various reasons, but all of whom, for only the barest minimum of encouragement, were willing to plat a townsite and sell lots.

The attitude of the company toward settlement, however, does not alter the fact that what American settlement did occur before 1850 was made with the help of the Hudson's Bay officials. When these men made a serious effort to keep out interlopers, they were usually able to do so, as Nathaniel Wyeth, Hall J. Kelley, Jedediah Smith, or Captain Benjamin L. E. de Bonneville could testify.

When the American missionaries Jason Lee, Marcus Whitman, Henry H. Spalding, and others first came, the directors warned Dr. McLoughlin against aiding them. They suspected that "the formation of a Colony of United States citizens on the banks of the Columbia was the main or fundamental part of their plan, which, if successful, might be attended with material injury, not only to the Fur trade, but in a national point of view." In spite of the warning, McLoughlin sold the missionaries clothing, household furnishings, farm equipment, and enough food to last until the following harvest. Other missionaries, encouraged by the treatment of the trailblazers, sailed or walked to Oregon to add to the numbers of settlers in the Willamette, Snake, and Clearwater valleys.

When Ewing Young gave up his life as a wandering mountain man and settled down to farming, he became the forerunner of other American nonmissionary settlers like Joe Meek, Robert ("Doc") Newell, and William Craig, who brought their families (white or red) and settled near the mission stations—sometimes, it might be noted, to the mutual consternation of all concerned. The Hudson's Bay Company grumbled, but contented itself with urging Americans to remain south and east of the Columbia and the Snake.

The company's own negative policy of refusing to grant land titles to prospective British settlers also aided the growth of settlement south of the Columbia. Some of the immigrants to the Northwest from the Red River country joined the Americans where land was available and a man could have absolute possession of what he could clear of timber and hold from claim jumpers or Indians. On the flimsy excuse that the Willamette Valley was more fertile than the Cowlitz Valley, Hudson's Bay employees, who might normally have leased land from the company and held their own claims as tenant farmers, spurned the feudal relationship, quit their jobs, and moved south to join the Americans and other British immigrants who gravitated to the mission stations and the little towns growing around them.

Thus, by protecting the settlers when they first arrived, following a policy of salutary neglect while they grew self-supporting, and failing to recognize the driving force of the hunger of men and women of peasant stock to own their own land, the company saw settlement grow so large that it could no longer control its neighbors, not only south of the Columbia, but north of it as well. It could not prevent the Americans from building stores, mills, and towns anywhere, even in competition with its own older operations, and finally McLoughlin himself gave up, against a background of censure and criticism from his directors, superior officers, and associates, left the service of the company, and himself joined the settlers at the falls of the Willamette.

Curiously, the Americans who wrote the early history of the Northwest were singularly reluctant to give the company credit for the role that it did play in the governing and development of the region. Partly, of course, this was due to the fact that many of those who wrote the accounts had unhappy personal quarrels with the management of the company, or were so deeply suspicious from prior indoctrination that every act of the company was looked upon as part of a sinister conspiracy by an organization of foreigners to destroy honest American citizens going about their daily business on American soil. Naturally, not all of the actions of Hudson's Bay agents were those of selfless men without malice or evil design. Some associated with the company were mean, vindictive, and even cruel. But the wonder is the mass paranoia that seems to have engulfed Americans when they talked or wrote of the company and its operations.

In order to give some balance, and to prevent this paper from becoming a tabulation of only the great deeds and personalities of the company, the comments of these hostile American witnesses might be reviewed briefly.

The Reverend H. H. Spalding insisted until the day of his death that the Whitman massacre was an unrighteous plot of papists and the Hudson's Bay Company to destroy American Protestantism, in spite of the fact that Peter Skene Ogden certainly rescued all of the survivors at the expense of the company, and that Spalding himself was indebted to Father Brouillet for his personal safety, if not for his life. The settlers who framed Oregon's Provisional Government wrote into their organic law a clause specifically prohibiting Dr. McLoughlin and the Hudson's Bay Company from enjoying any holding south of the Columbia, even though some of their deliberations took place in the grain warehouse of the company at Champoeg.

Josiah Spaulding presented a report to Congress, duly printed at public expense, which asserted that depredations by the Hudson's Bay brigades practiced on Northwest Indians were followed by attacks by the maddened red men on weaker parties of Americans who happened along the way later, and thus was the basic cause for the tribulations of Jed Smith, William Bailey, and others. William Slacum's report was strongly slanted against the company, charging, among other things, that McLoughlin's refusal to end Indian slavery was detrimental to the welfare of the Americans in Oregon.

Hall Kelley, in particular, saw only a monstrous evil crouching behind the company's stockades at Vancouver, Nez Perce, Okanogan, and elsewhere. Even when he was imprisoned for debt in Boston, he was convinced that somehow the long arm of the company had reached out from British soil across the continent in an effort to ruin him. On his wild trip alone to California and Oregon, he was incapacitated with fever and probably would have died save for the charity of his enemies; but he found no good in them, only malignant persecution.

Hazard Stevens, the official biographer of his father, Governor Isaac Stevens, claimed without hesitation that the Chehalis treaty council failed because of the opposition of former Hudson's Bay Company employees who believed their liquor monopoly and system of Indian peonage would end if a treaty with the United States government were signed by the natives. He cited as his authority the testimony of a Nisqually Indian. According to the reasoning of American settlers, the Indian wars of the 1850s in Washington and Oregon were in large measure the result of company plotting.

The rampaging forces of Manifest Destiny finally compelled the Hudson's Bay monopoly to retreat north of the forty-ninth parallel. The crowding settlers claimed and occupied land which the British thought to be rightfully theirs. The wagon trains and prospectors used brigade trails to enter regions formerly known only to fur traders. The Indians, decimated by disease introduced by the settlers, were herded onto reservations and systematically badgered, cheated, starved, and shot, until the survivors became sullen, uncooperative hangers-on to the fringes of European culture and were no longer a source of profit. The fur animals became fewer in number, and demand for their pelts in Europe and the eastern United States declined. The United States government determined to resolve potential disputes by purchasing all claims of the Hudson's Bay Company in Washington Territory, allowing the settlers free reign in developing the region.

When tentative negotiations began, the company at first made the fantastic demand of $3.8 million for the few run-down buildings that remained on the trading-post sites, the farms, and property rights on grazing lands. After protracted negotiations that extended through the period of the Civil War, the claims were settled for only a few thousand dollars, and the operations of the company in Washington were over. The triumphant Americans moved in, used timbers from company buildings for their own cabins or for their prospecting operations, converted some of the sites to farms—or even to airports—and allowed others almost to disappear from the memory of man.

Only the prejudices, the legends, and the folklore remain. No living man remembers when the company was a power in the Northwest. The hundreds of thousands of adults who have moved to the state of Washington in the twentieth century, and their children, born in the last few decades, need constantly to be reminded of the past in order to understand the present. An unprejudiced study of the Hudson's Bay Company is essential to this understanding.

BIBLIOGRAPHICAL NOTE

The primary sources for this paper came from such U.S. Public Documents as the multivolumed *Records of the Commissioners for the Final Settlement of the Claims of the Hudson's Bay [Company]* (Washington, D.C., 1865); and Senate Documents "Spalding Document" (41st Cong., 3d Sess., S.D. 37), Slacum *Memorial* (25th Cong., 2d Sess., S.D. 24), and Isaac I. Stevens, *Narrative and Final Report of Explorations for a Pacific Railroad* (36th Cong., 1st Sess.). From the Provincial Archives of British Columbia come records of the Hudson's Bay Company, including the William Fraser Tolmie Diary, the "Journal of John Work," and the private papers of Sir James Douglas.

Contemporary accounts of visitors to the Northwest include: Sir George Simpson, *An Overland Journey Round the World during the Years 1841 and 1842* (London, 1847); Eugene Duflot de Mofras, *Explorations du territoire de l'Oregon, des Californies et de la Mer Vermeille* (Paris, 1844); Paul Kane, *Wanderings of an Artist among the Indians of North America*, ed. Lawrence J. Burpee, in Master-Works of Canadian Authors, Vol. 7 (Toronto, 1925); David Douglas, "Sketch of a Journey to the Northwestern Parts of the Continent of North America during the Years 1824–25–26–27" (*OHQ*, Vols. 5 and 6, 1904–1905); Hall J. Kelley, *History of the Settlement of Oregon* (Springfield, Mass., 1868); and Pierre-Jean De Smet, *Letters and Sketches*, in Reuben Gold Thwaites, ed., *Early Western Travels, 1748–1846*, Vol. 27 (Cleveland, 1906).

There are several secondary sources of differing value. The best include: John A. Hussey, *History of Fort Vancouver and Its Physical Structure* (Portland, Oreg., 1957); John S. Galbraith, *The Hudson's Bay Company as an Imperial Factor, 1821–1869* (Berkeley, 1957);

Clifford M. Drury, *Henry Harmon Spalding* (Caldwell, Idaho, 1936), and *Marcus Whitman, M.D.* (Caldwell, 1937). Also included are Thomas E. Jessett, ed., *Report and Letters, 1836–38, of Herbert Beaver, Chaplain to Hudson's Bay Company* (Portland, Oreg., 1959) and Hazard Stevens, *Life of Isaac Ingalls Stevens* (Boston, 1900).

A Working Hypothesis
for the Study of Migrations

DOROTHY O. JOHANSEN

Although Portland has become, in many other respects, more urbane than it once was, it has a long tradition of being a quiet, early-to-bed town. The story is told that in December 1941, when practice emergency blackouts were ordered at a designated hour, the lively cosmopolites of San Francisco ignored the order, and the lights, though dim in the bars, burned bright on the hills. Seattle's citizens so successfully blacked out that shops were looted, everyone had a riotous time, and, when the lights came on, life went on as usual. In Portland, the citizens turned out their lights and went to bed as they always did.

For their idiosyncracies, Portlanders have no apologies. They are of the opinion that folk who live on the Willamette are "different" from those who live on Puget Sound, on San Francisco Bay, and in Greater Los Angeles. In turn, the residents of each of these areas would protest that they, too, are "different" from each other and from the provincials who live here. Observers have noted that Portland has been dominated by a village mentality that has made its citizens reluctant to face the facts of urban life. They have a tradition of being cautiously liberal in matters political. Oregon was "progressive" and accomplished progressive reforms before there was a Progressive party; there have been few major scandals in either state or city affairs. Portlanders are inclined to be publicly articulate, argumentative, and ambivalent with regard to community problems. As witness to our dilemmas, I mention a half-completed bridge across the Willamette which has been suspended in midair for two years while the

Originally published in *Pacific Historical Review*, February 1967 (© 1967 by the Pacific Coast Branch, American Historical Association).

public debated highway hookups. On the other hand, a citizens' committee tackled the problem of *de facto* segregation in the schools before there was an outright crisis, and apparently its plan has been put successfully to work without public uproar. While schools are supported, the citizenry is notoriously tightfisted, if not penurious, in fiscal matters, and wealth is not ostentatiously displayed. At the turn of the century, when Seattle was booming and building and mortgaging the present for the future, one of the first property managers in this city told me, Portlanders sat on their money and considered any individual who borrowed for capital improvements to be unsound in principle and practice. A large number of Oregonians today are choosy about the industries they want to see move into the state. Their forefathers, a century ago, rejected the offer of an eastern shipbuilding company to remove here if Portland would accord it some special privileges. The answer was that Portland could build its own shipyards if it wanted any.

Oregonians have generally been described as lacking in that "get up and go" which has so remarkably stimulated the development of its sister states. Perhaps California sunshine is so invigorating and the landscape so stimulating that the environment forces its inhabitants to mammoth projects, large thinking, and great ambitions. On the other hand, Oregon's greenery is restful and relaxing, and its tight and fertile little valleys require no great effort to farm. Too, Oregon has not experienced the magnitude of historical events that helped to make California a great state; it did not have *the* gold rush, but a series of small rushes; it had real estate booms, but nothing comparable to those of California; Oregon had no oil boom, no Hollywood. While California's population grows by the thousands per day, many Oregonians resent the hundreds who come in to clutter up its highways and ferret out the natives' favorite fishing spots. California has big industry; throughout most of its history, Oregon had only its timber and farm crops. Recently, it has achieved notice for its almost unique diversification in small and middle-sized highly specialized manufactures. But Oregonians have been modestly prosperous and perhaps immoderately content and, by virtue of their way of life, have considered themselves different from Californians.

In 1873, J. H. Beadle, a prejudiced and acid-tongued correspondent for the Cincinnati *Commercial*, found the "Webfoot *sui generis*":

There is a distinctively Oregonian look about all the natives and old residents which is hard to describe. Certainly they are not an enterprising people. They drifted in here . . . from 1835 to 1855, and some of them at an even earlier period. . . . They left Missouri and Illinois—most of them—because those states were even then "too crowded" for them and they wanted to get away where "they was plenty o' range and plenty o' game" and have a good easy time. . . . They acknowledge their own laziness and talk about it so good humoredly that one is compelled to sympathize with them.

Beadle thought the climate and the ease of farming the fertile soil of the Willamette Valley added something to the Pikers' natural laziness, and he noted that "these old fellows 'hold on to the land like burrs, and die mighty slow.'" From experience with the first families, he was driven to the "painful conclusion that about a hundred first-class funerals would prove a great advantage to Oregon."

There have been several times a hundred first-class funerals since Beadle wrote, but Oregon still receives the bulk of its immigration from the Midwest, and its inhabitants are, in contemporary opinion, still *sui generis*. However, I am told that southern Californians are also *sui generis;* that they have their idiosyncracies, and that these can be explained in part by the presence there of recent settlers from Kansas and Iowa. Since Oregon, too, has large influxes from these states and since there is an increasing interchange of population between California and Oregon, it has been suggested that Oregonians and Californians tend to grow more alike—that the differences which are, in a way, a source of pride to each community will eventually be erased.

However, if a common origin of population is a factor in creating community similarities, then this tendency should have been evident much earlier, for, historically, California has drawn from the same population sources as has Oregon. From 1860 to 1880, New York and Missouri were the top-ranking native states of California immigrants. In the first decade of the twentieth century, 70,000 Illinois born moved into the state, and Illinois became the top-ranking contributor, with New York in second and Missouri in third place. During the 1860–1880 period, Missouri and Illinois were the chief contributors to Oregon; by 1910, Iowa was in first place, with Illinois and Missouri in second and third places. Pushing back to the period of the first American settlement of Oregon and California in the 1840s, we must take into consideration the peculiar pattern of American internal migration, in which the place of nativity becomes less significant for our purposes than the community of origin, the community from which migration took place. In this case also, the Midwest occupied a peculiar role.

Some years ago, the late Jesse Douglas made a study of the original 1850 census schedule for Oregon Territory. He discovered that 74.2 percent of the adults who came to Oregon between 1840 and 1850 were born in the Atlantic states, but 80.8 percent of their children were born in a "child belt" of midwestern states and territories. He was, therefore, of the opinion that the Atlantic coast background was perhaps more important that had been realized, but he concluded that, since it was possible many of those born in the Atlantic states had removed as children with their parents to the Midwest and had lived most of their lives there, that region was the "crucible in which the population of the Pacific Northwest was molded." His general argument is supported by data we have recently processed from the Oregon land claim applications which show that out of 1,300 applicants in Oregon before 1851, married before they arrived here, 66 percent were married in Ohio, Indiana, Illinois, and Missouri. I believe that, if statistics were available for California's population before 1850, the results would be similar.

Dorothy Swain Thomas's pioneer work on migrations was concerned primarily with differences between migrants and nonmigrants, but in framing the larger problem, she isolated three fundamental elements of migration differentials: the types of communities to and from which the migrants move, the distance spanned in the migration, and the time at which the migration occurs. "Specifically," she said, "migrants whose communities of origin differ in certain respects but who have the same or similar community of destination will be expected to differ from each other. The same is true for migrants whose communities of destination differ, but who have the same or similar community of origin."

This is the assumption by which we usually explain differences in communities. However, I believe that historical evidence suggests a different emphasis, and I would reword the statement to this effect: migrants whose communities of origin differ in certain respects but who have the same or similar community of destination will be expected to differ less from each other than those who have the same community of origin but different destinations. In effect, I am suggesting that, in the American experience, the push factors in migration theory are less important than the pull factors; that different communities of destination draw different types of migrants and that in the building of differentiated communities, economic and environmental factors are less important than individual psychological factors. I would suggest that the differentiating features of communities had their origins in the first populations to settle them, and the elements of differentiation were perpetuated by an ongoing process of selective migration.

I emphasize pull factors because it seems to me that they can be weighted, particularly in the case of migrations spanning a distance of some magnitude. During the 1840s, for example, thousands of persons moved into and among the midwestern states and territories. The common pattern of movement was from the state of birth into an adjacent territory; but a secondary pattern of real significance was the movement continuing in lesser numbers to the next territory, and so on. Ohio born moved in great numbers into Indiana, in lesser numbers to Illinois, in still lesser numbers to Missouri and Iowa. Samuel A. Stouffer has found that in contemporary migrations "the number of persons going a given distance is directly proportional to the number of opportunities at that distance and inversely proportional to the number of intervening opportunities." This concept, which Stouffer hoped would provide a "cue for predicting the tendency of different types of population groups to assume certain types of spatial patterns in their mobility," appears historically applicable. Assuming for the moment that it is, I propose that those individuals who rejected the intervening opportunities which the majority of migrants found attractive pushed out toward a distant destination, presumably because it held out opportunities, apparent or actual, which would better satisfy their expectations. Hence, those who chose to move the greatest distance to a common destination had in common some motives and expectations that made them similar, one to another.

The case of William H. Rector illustrates these points. Rector was born in Virginia and, as a child, immigrated with his family to eastern Ohio. He married and moved to western Ohio, then to Elkhart, Indiana. He was a man of some education, a farmer, cabinetmaker, and machinist, and was successful. He invested his savings in an Elkhart store venture just when, in his words, "the great panick seemed to bring out all the meanness that man possessed," and just when his family was seriously afflicted with malaria. Seeking a more healthful location to recoup his fortune, he traveled through Illinois and Iowa, where he found "agua" [ague] everywhere, and thence to Independence, Missouri, where he "liked the appearance of the country and the condition of the people for health and prosperity," and to which he removed.

During the interval of his search, he had read Wilkes's report on the Pacific, which had been sent him by his congressman. "The general caractor of the country all of which was most desirable," he later recalled, "the health of the pine forests and limpid streams took my fancy. . . . I had lost much of my ambitions for welth or society. And often I indulged in visions of a happy retreat from the agua and fevour and from the toils and vexations of a business life." In the spring of 1843, Rector witnessed at Independence the gathering of emigrants for Oregon. "I see there," he wrote, "a number of families of respectable people—the Applegates, Waldo and many others of like good caractor." Two years later, Rector was able to clear up his debts, and, having been reassured that those who had gone out two years before were "doing well and [were] much pleased with the country," Rector in 1845 himself became an Oregon immigrant and was associated closely throughout his life with the Applegates, Waldos, and others of "good caracter" in the new territory.

A further case can be made from the migration of 1846, in which some 2,700 men, women, and children, according to Dale Morgan's estimate, formed two principal wagon trains, one headed for California and the other for Oregon; probably about 200 male adults decided for Oregon; about 250, for California. The alternatives were approximately equal in economic opportunities. If free land were the object, it was rumored that land was to be had in California by Mexican grant or through the revolution reportedly brewing there. The pending treaty with Great Britain would settle the Oregon boundary issue, and it was presumed that Congress would ultimately pass a donation land grant bill for settlers there. The commercial opportunities of both areas were loudly touted; although the emigrants were primarily small farmers with some artisan skills, none was disinterested in commercial possibilities. Oregon had two advantages over California: its farming pattern was familiar to pastoral folk with small herds of animals; and the cattle on California's thousand hills were an unfamiliar economy to people used to prairie land and small valleys. Furthermore, Oregon was to all practical purposes safely American; a local provisional government, framed after the traditional territorial organization, had settled the question of revolutionary independence and was able to maintain order among the settlers. Assuming these migrants were rational folk, they must have considered the alternatives in such terms.

At Independence, according to young Kentuckian Charles Putnam, who with his brother, Nathan, was California bound, "the California fever rages high," and he reassured his family that he and his brother did not go to California to "revolutionize," though he admitted that they would defend their rights if need be. En route the young men's enthusiasm for California wavered. Nathan wrote, "owing to various reports which we have heard about the probility of our procureing land and the supposed unsettled condition in California . . . we think that we will go into Origin . . . and then if not perfectly satisfyed we will go down into California and look at it." And Charles wrote, "It will be in Umqua Valley (Oregon) where most of the Californians will go, if things are not as they anticipated when we left, in fact the *Aristocracy* or respectable portion of the companies will go to this valley if any danger is apprehended when we arrive at Fort Hall." At Fort Hall, the emigrants were met by Jesse Applegate, an Oregon settler of 1843, who offered to guide them to the valley. From the fort, Applegate wrote his brother in Missouri, urging him to come out and reporting that "almost all the respectable portion of the California emigrants are going on the new road to Oregon—and nearly all the respectable emigrants that went last year to California came this Spring to Oregon."

An interesting study could be made to discover what qualities or values were subsumed under the word *respectable,* which in these three cases was used as a criterion for choosing Oregon. I suggest that the word meant recognition of law and order and the United States government, and the Protestant as opposed to the Catholic faith; it represented a Puritan morality with emphasis upon sobriety and thrift, with confidence in the rudiments of education, and with modest ambitions of competence and self-sufficiency. Under this rubric, I think one would not often find the great risk taker, but rather the conservative personality—in the words of Kogan and Wallach, the one who "selectively scans the environment in terms of its success and failure potentials rather than in terms of its other multifarious attributes, and . . . is particularly sensitized to the image that his behavior creates in the eyes of others as well as in the 'inner eye' of his own self-evaluation system." This conception of the conservative personality is especially appropriate to Oregonians, who, while sensitive to public opinion, were in some cases stubbornly adherent to the individualism implicit in a self-evaluation system. Thus, one finds among those considered eminently respectable, the Jeffersonian aristocrat among Jacksonian egalitarians, the Deist among Methodist revivalists. Despite apparent inconsistencies, respectability was equated with Oregon and was one of the criteria by which early Oregonians differentiated themselves from early Californians. It was the theme of an anecdote of the early fifties.

At Pacific Springs, one of the crossroads of the western trail, a pile of gold-bearing quartz marked the road to California; the other road had a sign bearing the words "To Oregon." Those who could read took the trail to Oregon.

Those who chose Oregon had already formulated expectations of a "better" way of life which that particular destination held out for them. Their expectations were derived from what was reported of the territory, and Oregon was, indeed, well reported from 1834 on, giving rise to the "Oregon fever" in 1842. The political situation in the states, with regard to both domestic and foreign policy, had generated an Oregon literature which played up the virtues of the country and its potentials for a chosen people. Oregon was reported as a pastoral Eden, a theme that echoes throughout the history of western settlement. But it is interesting that the very first Americans in the area were aware that rough mountain men, fur traders, and mixed breeds were inappropriate Adams. John Ball, one of the Wyeth party of 1832, remained in Oregon, entranced by the the lush beauty of the valley where he built a habitation, "the walls of which are the cylindrical fir, and the roof thereof cypress and yew." But he found it was a "country of falsehood and low cunning. The whites adopt, in many things, the customs of the natives . . . as it is, and with no prospect of imigrants such as to change the tone of society, I shall soon depart from this coast." The Protestant missionaries, having failed to civilize the natives by Christianizing them, sought to overwhelm their barbarities by the weight of a Protestant population of the "right kind" of people. Petitioning Congress for assertion of American sovereignty over the territory, they rhetorically noted the "vicious" population and asked whether the region was to be settled by the "reckless and unprincipled adventurer . . . the Botany Bay refugee . . . the renegade of civilization from the Rocky Mountains . . . the profligate deserter seaman from Polynesia, and the unprincipled sharpers from Spanish America" or by an orderly people, a colonizing people of moral principles, who would hardly risk their persons and property in a political vacuum.

Hall Jackson Kelley, an Oregon propagandist of unfailing enthusiasm, appealed to "All Persons of Good Character," even a "portion of the virtuous and enterprising but not least faithful population, whom misfortunes have thrown out of employment," to immigrate to Oregon; he invited "pious and well educated young men" to instruct the natives; and "properly educated persons to fill the civil, military and literary roles"—"men possessed of scientific knowledge . . . mathematics and natural philosophy to constitute the corps on engineering, surveying, astronomy, geology and botany" in this western Utopia.

The first large immigration in 1843, according to missionary report, was composed of settlers who appeared "industrious and some of them are religious." They and their followers in 1844 were by their own description "well-to-do farmers or, rather, graziers." John Minto, one of the 1844 arrivals, was an emigrant from England, the son of a labor agitator, and he found his American companions "conspicuous for individuality of character and measure of acquirement."

Town builders were immediately busy advertising their locations. Peter H. Burnett, who later became California's first governor, wrote lengthy and fulsome letters home describing the country, its resources, its advantages. Here, in "this beautiful country," he said, "lazy men have become industrious, as there is no drinking or gambling . . . among the whites; and labor meets with such ready employment and such ample reward, that men have more inducement to labor than elsewhere. This is, as yet, no country for lawyers, and we have the most peaceable and quiet community in the world."

Authors of guidebooks contributed to the body of Oregon lore.

Overton Johnson and William H. Winter noted the advantages of Oregon, but they also warned, "Men are apt to expect too much, to draw their pictures too fair; they look to those wild and distant regions for something surpassing nature, and they are disappointed. The world contains now no Garden of Eden." John Shively spurred on the 1846 migration with just the right mixture of realism and romance: at Fort Vancouver, "It is a pleasant sight, after months of toil through the wilderness to see the ships in the harbor . . . and a general stir of business throughout the vicinity." He warned that the settlement at the falls of the Willamette (Oregon City) was "very expensive living," so he advised, "Be off to the country and take a fresh bag of flour and your family with you, and find a location to suit you—then go to work; a little labor will seed you a fine field of wheat, and this same land that you locate, in a few years will make you rich beyond doubt."

Maria King wrote her family that she had been much opposed to coming to Oregon but, "If I were back there and knew what I know now I should be perfectly willing to come. . . . I write to you as if I expected you to come." Justin Chenoweth, who described himself as a "restless creature," wrote home that "liberty has been the chief object of my life. From this sentiment I was mainly induced to emigrate to this country." He found it met his expectations. Among the first settlers were several from the South who brought with them Negro slaves. Others had left the South because they disapproved of slavery, could not and would not compete in a slave economy, and yet believed slavery was an issue within the rights of individual states to settle. In Oregon they promptly excluded slavery and freed Negroes.

Thus, those first settlers, finding their expectations fulfilled, wrote enthusiastically to their families and friends. It is not unlikely that those to whom they wrote were of their own predilections, shared their own expectations—and people listen to what they want to hear. I believe it was Thoreau who said, "Those who are ready to go are already invited." As a consequence, the next migrations were composed of persons not unlike those who were already in Oregon.

During the decade of the 1850s, California's population increased by about 300,000 persons. The goldfields were a magnet attracting one of the greatest migrations in our history. But in that same interval, while the thousands were flocking to the gold country, some 30,000 moved into Oregon. One cannot help but ask, Why didn't they, too, go to California? The answer seems implicit in what I have said before. Their expectations would not be satisfied in California, or for that matter, in Illinois or Missouri or Texas or Iowa. And, for those whose expectations were not fulfilled in Oregon, another move had to be made—to Washington Territory, which developed its own differences—or to California, or back to Missouri and Illinois. This was one way of removing the conceptual dissonance consequent to a wrong decision. Leon Festinger's theory of conflict, decision, and dissonance is interestingly appropriate here. The conflict between expectations and reality could be solved by removing the cause, as in the case of a Missourian who left Oregon because, as he was supposed to have told a pioneer he met on the trail in 1847, "in Oregon there are no bees, and you can't raise corn, and if you can't raise corn, you can't raise hogs, and if you can't raise hogs, you can't have bacon, so I'm going back to Missouri where I can have cornbread, bacon and honey." But another, and perhaps more common, way of solving conflict, according to Festinger, is to rationalize the choice. Hence, those who made the wrong choice clung stubbornly to it and justified it—in this case, by elaborating the differences which made Oregon preferable to California, despite evidence to the contrary—and in urging others to come and join them, they found content in social reinforcements for their individual situations.

With this brief and sketchy evidence as justification, I come then to what I believe might be a useful operational theory for the study of migrations. Crudely stated, it is to this effect: (1) migrants who choose one destination over an alternative of approximately equal economic advantage have in common a range of value expectations which, insofar as they are realized or rationalized, are factors in the establishment of a differentiated community; and (2) the first settlers determine the character of a community, and by communicating their value satisfactions or dissatisfactions to potential migrants, they, in effect, "select" the migrants who will follow and thereby perpetuate the character of the differentiated community.

If this hypothesis, which relates the processes of migration and community formation, is valid under test, it may in part explain the origin and perpetuation of diversities in our society, which, in so many other respects, has been structured and subjected to seemingly all-pervasive conformities. And, too, it seems to me that, even with such a tentative and highly suppositious guideline as this proposes, our understanding of this peculiar and continuing phenomenon of migration might be enhanced. It might open up the field of our inquiry by asking new questions that are answerable from historical data and for historically valid purposes. This approach may also have the advantage of explaining an event in the framework of an appropriate middle-range generalization of probability with regard to human decisions and human actions without resort to the metaphysics of "forces." In my opinion, this problem provides a felicitous opportunity for interdisciplinary studies, particularly with the behavioral sciences.

History comprises human nature and human action, and human nature is no more a total mystery than history is a mystique. It seems to me that we can find aid and comfort in the provocative work of the behavioral scientists. While their community of origin may be different from that of historians, their ultimate expectations more comprehensive and general, and the means by which they move and the roads they travel different from ours, yet, insofar as historians and behavioral scientists deal with human actions, our destinations are not too much differentiated. To ignore these fellow travelers is by so much to limit our variety of approach, lessen our effectiveness, and reduce our own conceptual experience. We are then somewhat in the same position as the matriarch of a respectable old Portland family who, one evening, sat in the bay window overlooking the city, talking to her granddaughter who had returned to Portland to visit. "You know," said grandmother, "you were not an easy child to bring up." "Well, grandmother," Virginia replied, "it wasn't easy to live with you." "Now, how was that?" "Grandmother, you never distinguished between your principles and prejudices. For example, you felt equally strong about garlic and adultery." "Virginia," answered grandmother, "I don't know how you know about such things, we've never had either of them in the house."

BIBLIOGRAPHICAL NOTE

Sources for this essay include Jesse S. Douglas, "Origins of the Population of Oregon in 1850," *PNQ*, Vol. 41 (1950); "Autobiography of William Henry Rector," *OHQ*, Vol. 29 (1928) and Vol. 30 (1929); Dale Morgan, ed., *Overland in 1846: Diaries and Letters of the California-Oregon Trail* (Georgetown, Calif., 1963); and John H. Beadle, *Western Wilds, and the Men Who Redeem Them* (San Francisco, 1878). See also Dorothy Swain Thomas, *Research Memorandum in Migration Differentials* (New York, 1938); "Intervening Opportunities: A Theory Relating Mobility and Distance," in *Social Research to Test Ideas: Selected Writings of Samuel Stouffer* (New York, 1962); Nathan Kogan and Michael A. Wallach, *Risk-Taking: A Study in Cognition and Personality* (New York, 1964); and Leon Festinger, *Conflict, Decision, and Dissonance* (Stanford, 1964).

Recent studies of overland migration include John D. Unruh, Jr., *The Plains Across: The Overland Emigrants and the Trans-Mississippi West, 1840–60* (Urbana, 1979); and John Mack Faragher, *Women and Men on the Overland Trail* (New Haven, 1979).

The Indian Question in Western Oregon: The Making of a Colonial People

WILLIAM G. ROBBINS

Before the advent of Europeans, the richest people in North America were the Indians of the Northwest Coast. They were among the few hunting and gathering societies in the world which produced wealth beyond that needed for subsistence.—*Uncommon Controversy*[1]

Most of the written history of the Pacific Northwest is mainstream America and as conventional as apple pie and baseball. It begins with the European explorers, followed by the fur traders, the missionaries, the gold seekers, and finally the farmer-settlers who superseded all others. The westering push of these people across the continent is cataloged as progress and success in much of the published literature of the region. For the most part writers have ignored the fact that each of these groups in varying degrees acted as agents of an expanding American empire. This westward movement of the population and the market economy of mid-nineteenth-century America dramatically increased pressure on Indian people and their land base. Eventually, these newcomers, working individually and in concert, either killed off or displaced the native people.

Despite this reality, romance still infuses the traditional story of the Pacific Northwest; writers tell of a region that required only the determination, courage, and hard work of pioneering farmers to be made hospitable and productive. This version of the settling of the Northwest is flawed, however. It does not recognize the dynamics of market capitalism in westward expansion, and it refuses to acknowledge that, from the perspective of the American Indian, the region's history is little more than a chronicle of white covetousness of Indian

land and the consequent effort to exterminate, dispossess, and remove the native population.[2]

The experiences of Indian people in the Pacific Northwest, therefore, differ little from the pattern of Indian-white relations elsewhere
in North America. From the start of European occupation along the
Atlantic seaboard, an overt, but sometimes residual settler prejudice
toward native inhabitants began to crystallize. This combination of
racial and cultural ethnocentrism manifested itself in the earliest histories of the European experience in North America.[3] By the time the
white population had expropriated most of the natives' land east of
the Mississippi River, these attitudes had taken the form of an ideology of conquest. Its justification, however, rested on the simple basis
of power. That power can be attributed to the greater economic capacity of one society and its adverse effect on the other.[4]

Once the superiority of Euro-Americans was established fact, the
conquerors dictated treaties that progressively limited Indian sovereignty and opened Indian lands to white settlement. This process of
subjugation and subsequent removal of Indian people to areas not
desired by white agriculturalists first occurred in Virginia in the
1620s. In this instance, the growing English settlements and the expanding tobacco farms pressed into the homeland of the neighboring
Pamunkey Indians; in self-defense they lashed out at the encroaching
newcomers, only to be driven farther into the interior. Twenty-five
years later under similar circumstances, the Pequot people were
driven from the lush agricultural lands of the Connecticut River
valley.[5]

By the end of the War of 1812, the invading population had effectively reduced most of the native groups east of the Mississippi to a
subject, colonial status. With their inability to resist by force further
incursions into their dwindling lands, Indians turned to the federal
courts and to treaties with the United States government to defend
their right to remain in their ancestral homelands. What followed was
a blatant assertion of imperial authority and a clear indication that
eastern Indians were reckoned a colonial people, to be exploited or
removed at the whim of an arbitrary and powerful central government that spoke for major interests in the emerging political economy. The removal of the Five Civilized Tribes to Indian country west
of the Mississippi River in the 1830s and 1840s cleared the way for
the expansion of cotton agriculture in the South and marked the end
of this process in the East.

But there was more to come, as market-minded Caucasians relentlessly pressed into the trans-Mississippi West in search of furs, mineral wealth, and cheap land. And they came in a flood tide between
the 1830s and 1850s to Texas, the Pacific Northwest, and California.

Everywhere they overran the indigenous population, destroying game animals, fencing in Indian berrying and bulb-gathering grounds, and slaughtering natives. Nowhere were the atrocities more obvious than in the gold rush regions. Theodora Kroeber's *Ishi* is one of several accounts that capture the uninhibited violence and genocide that occurred across northern California during this period.[6]

Similar circumstances prevailed farther north. And in the Pacific Northwest, a protracted period of native resistance intervened before the land was freed for market exploitation. The truth of these struggles has largely been obfuscated and shrouded in the patriotic rhetoric of frontier literature. Robert Faherty accurately describes the pattern that occurred elsewhere in North America: native people were depicted as hostile brutes, "impeding the civilizing process of advancing settlers"; therefore, "the Indian was stereotyped as uncivilized, and mentally, culturally and religiously inferior to the white. Denied equal status as a person, he could be converted, removed, exploited."[7] This scenario was worked out in western Oregon in the second half of the nineteenth century.

During the 1840s and 1850s the Willamette, Umpqua, and Rogue River valleys in western Oregon filled with white immigrants from east of the Rocky Mountains. The native people who had lived in these fertile valleys for centuries were overwhelmed; many were exterminated, and survivors forcibly removed to lands less desirable to non-Indians. To justify their actions, the newcomers refurbished the old argument that they practiced superior methods of cultivation and represented a more advanced civilization.[8] Legal title to land was important to the white invaders—occasionally as a matter of conscience, but more often to legitimize a claim to enhance market value, and to keep other grasping immigrants from interfering. The Oregon City *Spectator*, the first English-language newspaper published west of the Rocky Mountains, urged in 1848 that territorial government be extended to the region and that Congress pass a liberal land law so that white settlers would be secure in their property rights.[9]

The conventional historical arguments concerning the disposal of federal land in the U.S. have centered around two themes: whether the public domain should serve as a resource to enrich the coffers of the U.S. Treasury, or whether its purpose was to provide free land in small allotments to enterprising agriculturalists in the Jeffersonian tradition.[10] The rights of Indian people (who enjoyed "prior occupancy") entered the debate only when incoming white settlers pressured the federal government to extinguish prior title to the land.[11] In many instances treaties were dictated to extinguish Indian title *after* the arrival of large numbers of white settlers. And on occasion, Congress passed land laws that applied to areas where Indian title had not yet been legally voided.

The legal problem for white immigrants who flocked to the Willamette Valley in the 1840s was to gain congressional affirmation of the generous land laws adopted by Oregon's Provisional Government in 1843 and 1844. These laws, modeled on unsuccessful bills introduced in the U.S. Senate by Senator Lewis F. Linn of Missouri in 1841 and 1842, granted a full section of land (640 acres) to each adult white male who recognized the Provisional Government and established himself as a resident in the valley. After the 1846 boundary treaty with England formalized the extension of the American empire to the area south of the forty-ninth parallel, Congress confronted a situation in which white settlers were on the scene prior to the extension of American jurisdiction. In part because of the Provisional Government's overgenerous land allotments, Congress did not establish a formal land disposal program in the Oregon Territorial Act of 1848. The territory's leaders, however, immediately took steps to validate legal title to the land they occupied in the Willamette Valley.[12]

In 1849 the Oregon territorial legislature forwarded a memorial to Congress asking that Indian rights to land in the Willamette Valley be extinguished and the Indians removed from the valley. The memorialists cloaked their request in the paternalist rhetoric that was so typical in frontier-Indian relations: the natives should be relocated because "they were degenerating through contact with whites." Oregon Territory's first governor, Joseph Lane, invoked a similar Jacksonian argument: white residents in the Willamette Valley were destroying the resources of the Indians; thus, "the extinguishment of their title by purchase, and the locating them in a district removed from the settlements is a measure of the most vital importance to them. Indeed, the cause of humanity calls loudly for their removal from causes and influences so fatal to their existence."[13]

A real paradox—Indian people should be removed from their homelands for their own welfare! White paternalists consistently employed the logic that the removal and separation of Indians from white settlements, the destruction of native culture, and the adoption of white agricultural practices were the only viable means to alleviate the Indians' "plight."

So the newcomers continued to press for a resolution to the land situation. The Oregon City *Spectator* reminded its readers that Oregonians were sensitive about the land issue because they had come to the region "under every assurance . . . that they would receive liberal grants of land." Moreover, they had "a right to expect an unconditional grant of their full claims of 640 acres of land each." When

Samuel R. Thurston was elected the territory's first delegate to Congress in 1849, his key mission was to secure passage of the desired land law. He traveled to the East Coast, attempted to gain the support of the editors of major eastern newspapers, and then went on to Washington to lobby Congress.[14]

Thurston and his non-Indian constituents achieved their objective. In September 1850 Congress passed the Oregon Donation Land Law, a virtual facsimile of the bill Thurston wanted. The new law validated legal title to land already occupied by white settlers in the Oregon country (most of it in the Willamette Valley). Congressional supporters viewed the measure as fair reward for white immigrants who had helped the expanding American empire win a very generous boundary concession from England. The donation act was also viewed as an inducement to encourage additional white immigration to Oregon Territory (indeed, before the act expired in 1855, some 25,000 to 30,000 immigrants entered the territory).[15]

But the donation law did not entirely satisfy the constitutional requirement for the transfer of land to non-Indian ownership. The boundary treaty with England in 1846 recognized Indian title to land and specified that "settlers are not to settle on or occupy land in use by the different Indians until such land is ceded to the United States by treaty." In addition, the Oregon Territorial Act of 1848 guaranteed the Indian right to property in the territory "so long as such rights shall remain unextinguished by treaty between the United States and such Indians." The territorial act, in fact, declared null and void "all laws heretofore passed in said territory making grants of land."[16]

America's expansionist policy makers, however, knew the constitutional requirements for the transfer of Indian land. When Congress passed the Donation Land Law, the matter of Indian land title had been resolved by a previous enactment authorizing the negotiation of treaties with the Indians of Oregon "for the Extinguishment of their claims to lands lying west of the Cascade Mountains." Sometimes referred to as the Indian Treaty Act, the measure provided for presidentially appointed commissioners to negotiate treaties, "and if they find it practicable . . . they shall remove all these small tribes east of the Cascade Mountains and leave the whole of the most desirable portion . . . open to white settlers." As territorial delegate, Thurston insisted that Indian removal east of the mountains was the "first pre-requisite step" to settling Oregon's land issue.[17]

Therefore, agents of the U.S. government acted upon Thurston's request and set in motion a policy of forcing treaties upon the Indians throughout the Pacific Northwest. Recently arrived immigrants to the region gave their wholehearted support to the effort to remove native people to lands less desirable to white agriculturalists. White home-seekers favored it for obvious reasons, and eastern humanitarians—self-proclaimed friends of the Indian—supported it because it would also remove Indians from the corrupting influences of white civiliza-tion. The treaty-making spree that took place in the Northwest in the early 1850s was part of a broader oppressive strategy carried on throughout the American West to disappropriate Indian people of their land base. By this time such treaty making was not a diplomatic negotiation between equals but an aggressor offering terms to a sub-ordinate people. The long history of Indian treaties in North America shows clearly a progressive diminution of Indian sovereignty as the invaders moved relentlessly across the continent.[18] Erosion of Indian autonomy was accompanied by expansion of market capitalism, the latter directly influencing the former.

Obviously, treaties explain only legal niceties. And the immigrant rush into western Oregon explains only part of the overall impact of the Donation Land Law. Most of the donation claims were laid out in the fertile valley-bottom lands in the Rogue, Umpqua, and Willa-mette valleys. No large-scale clashes erupted between natives and whites in the Willamette Valley because the resident Calapooya people were few in number and widely scattered. More than 75 per-cent of the Indian population there had been wiped out as a result of a malaria epidemic in the early 1830s. By the 1850s, the Calapooya, not numerous enough to offer physical resistance to the white intrud-ers, found their game being killed off, their rudimentary fences de-stroyed, and in some instances, their houses burned.[19]

The commissioner of Indian affairs, Luke Lea, appointed Anson Dart of Wisconsin to extinguish Indian title to the valuable agricul-tural lands in western Oregon. Lea believed that the white popula-tion was closing up the western frontier, leaving two choices for the Indian: "early civilization or gradual extinction." He urged Dart to rely upon missionaries to use their influence "in restraining [the In-dians'] wild, roving and predatory disposition" and to bring them "to the habits of civilization." These Christian teachers, the commis-sioner believed, would humanize the idolatrous, "wild and ferocious savage." Dart's instructions explicitly stated that he was to provide for the removal of all native people to an area east of the Cascade Range.[20]

Oregon's first superintendent of Indian affairs immediately en-countered problems. The canoe-using forest dwellers of western Or-egon wanted nothing to do with the intemperate land east of the Cascades; and the people east of the mountains, who feared the dis-eases prevalent among the valley Indians, did not want them in their midst. Therefore, Dart disregarded his instructions and made treaties with nineteen groups that provided for small enclaves of reservation land throughout western Oregon. In his annual report for 1851 Dart noted that Willamette Valley Indians were "disease ridden" and that laborers were needed in the valley; therefore, "it was believed to be far better for the country that they should not be removed from the settled portion of Oregon if it were possible to do so."[21]

Dart's troubles, however, had just begun. When the treaties reached Washington, D.C., Commissioner Lea noted their deviation from standard treaty policy established in 1830 (i.e., removal of Indians from proximity to white settlements), but he forwarded them to the Senate without comment. The Senate refused ratification. Dart's decision to allow the Calapooyas to remain in the Willamette Valley ran counter to territorial desires; but for the moment, the valley's first inhabitants held on to a small portion of their dwindling land base.[22]

The immigrant onslaught to the Pacific Northwest continued. The spillover of prospectors in northern California discovered gold in several places in southwestern Oregon, and by the fall of 1851 there were large numbers of miners working the many tributaries of the Rogue. In addition, the Oregon Donation Land Law began attracting settlers to the fertile soils of the Umpqua and Rogue River valleys, and the consequences of white settlement in the Willamette Valley were repeated farther south—Indian dwellings were destroyed, camas fields were fenced, and game became increasingly scarce.[23]

The Rogue Indian bands, undoubtedly aware of the atrocities committed by miners in northern California, reacted immediately to the combined forces of prospectors and settlers flocking into southern Oregon. Stephen Beckham's book, *Requiem for a People: The Rogue Indians and the Frontiersmen*, documents part of the story of white aggressions against the native groups inhabiting the Rogue Valley. This account is a catalog of pillage, murder, search-and-destroy missions, and, for the survivors, removal to an alien land. But there is much more to the story than Beckham reveals.[24]

The concerted effort to expropriate Indian land across North America *always* involved a scurrilous and intense settler hatred of native people. This pervasive racist psychology, coupled with social and economic aspiration, made frontiersmen willing foot soldiers for American westward expansion. The spokesmen and managers for the imperial state forged the diplomacy and shaped the policy that fended off other pretenders to empire in North America. But the active agents of dispossession, believing in the cant of Manifest Destiny and hence marching to the piper's tune, were common soldiers in the regular army, settler-farmers who attached themselves to volunteer forces in the territories, and the innumerable scavengers, ruffians, and soldiers of fortune without a shred of humanity or sense of social justice. All of these elements are evident in the Pacific Northwest in the decade of the 1850s and particularly in Oregon Territory.[25]

Although the activities of settlers during this period were directly responsible for both the destruction and the removal of native peoples, spokesmen for American expansion—men like Senators Thomas Hart Benton and Lewis F. Linn of Missouri—shaped the ideological fabric. Benton, who proposed earlier as editor of the *Missouri Enquirer* that "the Children of Adam" should march west to the Pacific Ocean,[26] later sponsored a land bounty for white settlers who would defend Florida against Indians: "Armed occupation was the true way of settling a conquered country. The children of Israel entered the promised land, with the implements of husbandry in one hand, and the weapons of war in the other."[27] Benton was emphatic about the element of brute force in American expansion: "The blockade, the stockade, the rifle have taken the country and held it."[28] And his senatorial colleague, Lewis Linn (sponsor of early but unsuccessful land bills to encourage the occupation of the Oregon country), was equally forceful about the role of the foot soldier: "These men would fight for their land, and would love it the more because they had to fight for it. . . . They would make a most effective force to grapple with the Indian, knife in hand, and drive him from his fastnesses."[29]

So the stakes were obviously high for these foot soldiers of expansion; if they could kill off some of the Indians and oust the remainder to undesirable locations, a rich land lay beckoning. The Oregon territorial legislature honored these principles (and their promoters) when it created Linn and Benton counties in the 1840s. But the act of settlement was not always an easy one—witness the bitter struggle waged in the Rogue Valley between 1851 and 1856 that brought death and destruction to its first inhabitants. Nowhere else in the Pacific Northwest, with the possible exception of the Puget Sound country, did the white invader act so ruthlessly to subdue the native population. The Rogue people's determined and courageous resistance evoked the racist fury of white settlers and miners. Willamette Valley newspapers were filled with news articles that excoriated the Indians' resistance in the most vicious of frontier rhetoric.

The state of the public's temper and the uninhibited murder of Indians in southern Oregon appalled one government appointee. Joel Palmer, Anson Dart's successor as Oregon's superintendent of Indian affairs, wrote to his superior of the openly admitted war of extermination waged against the Rogue Indians. He attributed most of the trouble between Indians and whites in the valley "to the mistaken policy of permitting the settlement of the country prior to the extinguishment of the Indian title and the designation of proper reservations,"[30] and he adroitly used the conflict in southern Oregon to promote his pet project: a reservation on the Oregon coast.

Because Dart's policy (of allowing native people to remain in tiny enclaves in western Oregon) was discredited, Palmer devised an altered form of Lane and Thurston's removal proposals. The new superintendent claimed that white incursions into Indian lands in the Willamette Valley made the continued existence of the small reservations an impossibility. "The increasing settlements are rapidly diminishing the roots and game on which the Indians of the Valley mainly subsist." Therefore, because "vice and disease, the baleful gifts of civilization, are hurrying them away . . . a home remote from the settlements must be selected for them." Palmer advised seeking out a coastal reservation for all Indians of western Oregon because their habits and language had more in common with each other than with those of the interior.[31]

By 1853 Oregon volunteer forces and a small contingent of U.S. Army troops under the command of Joseph Lane had forced most of the upper Rogue bands from the valley and confined them to a temporary reservation near Table Rock, adjacent to the north side of the Rogue River. While these survivors attempted to subsist on the hilly and rocky reservation, other small bands remained in the hills and mountains, especially in the lower Rogue country. Once again, however, gold discoveries on the lower river, continued incursions into the Table Rock reservation, and repeated murders brought native retaliation. The Rogue people began their last stand late in the summer of 1855.[32]

Superintendent Palmer was outspoken in pointing to the source of trouble. The renewal of fighting in southern Oregon, he insisted, "is wholly to be attributed to the acts of our own people. . . . The future will prove that this war has been forced upon these Indians against their will." Palmer told General John E. Wool, in charge of the army's Pacific Division, that whites in southern Oregon were determined to carry out their effort "in violation of all treaty stipulations and the common usages of civilized nations." Those who precipitated the war he characterized as "reckless vagabonds."[33]

Despite Palmer's recognition of the responsibility for violence in southern Oregon, historians have been unwilling to treat Indian retaliation as a means of resistance and self-defense. A century later, Ray Hoard Glassley, in *Indian Wars of the Pacific Northwest*, wrote of the southern Oregon struggles in terms of Indian massacres, murders, thefts, and robberies. He went so far as to classify the various Indian groups in the Northwest according to intelligence and found the "Rogues and Shastas . . .[the] most primitive in their habits, passions, and morals. With them it was the survival of the fittest by whatever means necessary."[34]

Most recently, in a widely acclaimed book published by a prestigious eastern house, Malcolm Clark, Jr., writes as if in complete ignorance of Superintendent Palmer's assessment. But Clark takes one step beyond Glassley and attempts to distribute blame to lawless elements on both sides:

Faith in the government's good intentions withered, particularly among the natives of southern Oregon. The fragile peace woven together by Dr. Dart and his agents was unequal to fresh strains. Incidents increased—little acts of casual violence involving a few Indians, a few whites. Each side brutalized women and children. Both practiced a chilling savagery.

And, Clark concedes, these "fresh strains" provoked the most upstanding people: "Blood lust among *even decent folk* ran extraordinarily high. Martin Angell, an otherwise excellent citizen, shot down a passing Indian simply for being an Indian."[35] Which is to say, there is still a need for a fundamental reexamination and rewriting of Northwest history. Or, at least, we should take another look at the priorities and the heroes of the past.

So the conquest and plunder in the Rogue Valley escalated toward extermination and dispossession of the native people, and southern Oregon natives found few non-Indian friends in the territory. Indeed, Joel Palmer was the only territorial or federal official who protested the depredations against the Rogue people. Like other progressives on Indian matters, Palmer favored the establishment of reservations to protect Indians from predatory whites: "The peace of society, the security of property, the welfare of the Indian demands it.[36]

One other white person stood with Palmer against popular opinion in Oregon Territory. He was John Beeson, a native of Illinois, and newly arrived in the Rogue Valley in 1853. Some five years after his westward venture, Beeson wrote *A Plea for the Indians: With Facts and Features of the Late War in Oregon*. In it he argued that the Rogue Indian, like his brethren across the continent, "has been constantly the subject of monopoly and wrong, in every shape which the overbearing and all-engrossing spirit of our people could suggest or impose."[37]

His white neighbors in the Rogue Valley, Beeson said, were a people whose "religious and political faith consists in 'Squatter Sovereignty'—the right to do as they choose, regardless of all but selfish interests." There were many men in Oregon, he contended, whose only idea of the Constitution "is that it was made to keep down the

'Niggers.' Of course they understood it to have the same bearing upon Indians, and all others except 'white American citizens.'"[38] Vernon Bellecourt, a former elected official of the American Indian Movement, once characterized the attitude Beeson described as part of white America's "frontier mentality," a state of mind that allows one to make a gift of six-guns to children so that they can shoot "wild Indians."[39]

Like Palmer's, John Beeson's views were not popular in frontier Oregon. The region's newspapers, he claimed, refused to publish his letters defending Palmer because it would be like "throwing a firebrand among dry stubble." At public meetings in the Rogue Valley, Beeson urged the "exterminators" to desist from their genocidal missions; for this he was threatened with bodily harm. Beeson was as certain about the cause of hostilities in southern Oregon as Palmer: "The unpleasant truth stares me in the face, that the guilt and shame of this war rests on others rather than the Indians."[40]

The five years' conflict between the intruding immigrant population and the Rogue River bands reached its tragic finale in the early summer of 1856. The effort to confine the Indian people to a small and sparse reservation near Table Rock failed when the hungry and harassed bands fled into the rugged, mountainous region of the lower Rogue River in the fall of 1855. The Portland *Oregonian* announced that the Indians had "declared a war of extermination. . . . Therefore, we have no other course left, but to go into the contest, and fight until   the Indians are exterminated." While Oregon Territory volunteers and Lane's army contingent fought a series of running skirmishes with the escaping bands, territorial newspapers poured forth unwavering support for the territorial militia in the lower Rogue country: the volunteers "desire to partake of the delightful repast of killing those unaccountable heathens who were brought into existence by a slight mistake, to murder and eat up superior races, destroy their property and put the United States to great expense."[41]

By June 1856 most of the once numerous and vigorous Rogue people had surrendered. Hired by the government, William Tichenor hunted down and shot, and occasionally captured alive, the few who escaped into the mountains. The survivors were loaded aboard steamers at Port Orford, transported to the Willamette and Yamhill rivers, and then marched overland to the newly created (by executive order) Siletz Reservation on the Oregon coast. A people numbering approximately 9,500 individuals at the time of the first white migrations was reduced to fewer than 2,000 by 1856.[42]

The Indian bands in the Umpqua Valley who lived on the periphery of the Rogue Valley conflict were treated in similar fashion. Like the Rogue natives, the Umpquas "signed" a treaty with Joel Palmer early in 1855; despite their reluctance to leave behind their farms and houses, they agreed to cede their lands to the U.S. government and move to a reservation. Palmer also forced a treaty on the Confederated Tribes of the Willamette Valley, which conveyed title to 7.5 million acres to the United States for $200,000. He reported, however, that the Willamette Indians would not agree to leave their homes for a smaller expenditure: "Promises of the government they say are not good, as they have before been deceived."[43]

The colonizing of Northwest Indian people on reservations was largely the accomplishment of Palmer and the Washington territorial governor Isaac Stevens. In western Washington, Stevens negotiated five treaties in 1855 involving some 5,000 Puget Sound Indians; these treaties ceded most of the Puget Sound area and the Olympic Peninsula to the U.S. The basis for the treaty Indian fishery in Washington today, they were signed at Medicine Creek, Point Elliot, Point No Point, Neah Bay, and Quinault River. Between the two of them, Palmer and Stevens negotiated fifteen treaties extinguishing Indian title to millions of acres in the Pacific Northwest.[44] The treaties carried the usual provisions for removal of the Indians from proximity to white settlements, promised payment for the land cession, and provided for annuities once the various groups were confined to reservations.

The western Oregon coastal reservation, surrounded by small forts, provided better security than the lower Rogue River country. One Indian subagent described the mountainous lower Rogue as a region of rocky hills, crags, canyons, and little valleys, "where a few secretive foes might successfully resist and decimate" the white population. Superintendent Palmer concurred that the native habitat of the Rogue bands provided excellent terrain for their defense in warfare. Other whites, according to one source, were "unanimous in sustaining Palmer's decision to move them." Even those bands that had not participated in the southern Oregon conflict were to be confined to the coast reservation for fear that at some future date they might be "liable to take part in warfare."[45]

There are obvious parallels here between the rationale for the Jacksonian removal policy of the 1830s and the strategy to confine the Indian population of western Oregon to a coastal reservation. The Indian Removal Act of 1830 was based on the premise that certain areas west of the Mississippi River would never be suitable for agriculture and, hence, in the thinking of congressional policy makers, were suited to hunters and gatherers. So too, Joel Palmer, in justifying a coastal reservation, cited the area's separation from the Willamette Valley by the Coast Range, its inaccessibility from the sea, and its general lack of agricultural potential. A visiting army officer said much the same in a letter to the secretary of war: "[The] area abounds in game of various kinds, is well watered . . . contains sufficient arable land . . . is heavily timbered and rich in nuts, roots, and other articles of food as these Indians have always been accustomed to,— and has not yet been considered as worth occupying by the whites."[46]

The reservation included the Alsea and Siletz valleys and an area to the north of the Siletz drainage that extended onto the western slope of the Willamette Valley. Since the coast reservation had been decreed by executive order (and not by formal treaty), it proved easier for subsequent chief executives to dismantle the reservation when its resources became valuable for capitalist investment and exploitation. The initial breach in the territorial integrity of the reservation occurred in 1865, when the Alsea Valley was opened to white settlement; subsequent schemes to build railroads through the mountains to the coast, speculation in timberland in the last two decades of the century, and passage of the General Allotment Act in 1887 speeded the erosion of the native land base. In brief, the former Indian lands were integrated into America's expanding market economy. By the time the Siletz reservation was singled out for termination in the 1950s, only a minuscule portion of its once vast acreage remained in Indian ownership. But that is contemporary history.

Ultimately, Joel Palmer, the architect of the Indian removal and reservation policy in western Oregon, fell victim to his own planning. Having antagonized powerful political factions in the territory when he condemned the exterminationists in southern Oregon, he was finally, by an almost unanimous vote of the territorial legislature, removed from office. The petition to the commissioner of Indian affairs referred to certain "foolish and visionary acts and movements" by Palmer, which brought upon the "defenseless [white] inhabitants the combined power and hostility of a horde of ruthless savages." Palmer viewed matters differently, of course. He attributed his unpopularity to the "designation of the Coast Reservation" and to white inhabitants of Benton County (which bordered much of the eastern side of the reservation) who aspired to the valuable farm land across the mountains. Palmer reported that these settlers exhibited "a feeling of hostility toward the Indians, and a disregard for their rights—a feeling that looks to the humane system of annihilating the race."[47]

So the white newcomers in western Oregon and elsewhere in the Pacific Northwest resolved the "Indian problem" to their advantage, at the expense of the original inhabitants. The imperial spokesmen for the United States created the conditions and the ideology for conquest. And the foot soldiers in the immigrant armies that marched to the Northwest in the 1840s and 1850s and overran the native population followed Thomas Jefferson's injunction to "press upon" the Indians much as settlers had on earlier frontiers.[48] Armed with an imposing justification for dispossessing native peoples, the invaders established a record of intrigue, promises broken or delayed, and in the end, extermination and cultural genocide. Enterprising white capitalists (farmers, timber speculators, and town builders) took over most of the Indians' land in the succeeding decades. Market capitalism had arrived.

White contemporaries blamed the struggles that took place on the Indians, specifically, on their barbaric acts and their inability as organized groups to control their members.[49] And for the most part, much of written history has adopted this line of argument. In the Northwest and elsewhere on the American frontier, however, this has been the great lie. In actual fact, neither the federal government nor its territorial managers could control immigration (indeed, they seldom displayed a proclivity to do so). White settlers confidently invaded Indian lands with the knowledge that the government would support such activity. The result of this process was the appropriation of the property and the colonizing of Indian people.

Most of the classic elements that spurred westward migration and frontier capitalist growth are evident in the U.S. expansion to the Pacific between 1840 and 1860: an abundant fur resource; good agricultural land in the river valleys west of the Cascade Range; excellent harbors in the Columbia and Puget Sound waterways, which attracted commercial entrepreneurs; and an economic crisis and depressed agricultural prices in the Mississippi River valley following the panic of 1837. Fur entrepreneurs penetrated the region on an increasing scale beginning in the 1820s; other agents of expansionism followed: missionaries in the 1830s and finally the growing volume of white immigrant settlers in the 1840s. Confident of government support, the newcomers seized Indian land without regard to the legal and sovereign rights of the original inhabitants.

Thus, the 250 years of white expansion across North America and white pressure on the native inhabitants reveal as much about American history as the American Revolution or the Civil War (and maybe more). By the time the United States had extended its imperial control to the Pacific, American Indians were caught in an internal colonialism. The reservation system that emerged in the mid-nineteenth century was a strategic administrative manifestation of that colonial system.

Published literature about the American frontier west (and Pacific Northwest), with a few notable exceptions, still sings loudly in praise of the conquerors, their social values, and their accomplishments. It offers a narrow vision, and a false one: conquest and exploitation of native people are rarely mentioned. This writing fails to address the fundamental relationship between western expansion and the dynamics of capitalist development. If historical scholarship is to inform us about the realities of the westering process, it must move beyond the narrow values of American imperial history.

NOTES

1. *Uncommon Controversy: Fishing Rights of the Muckleshoot, Puyallup, and Nisqually Indians* (Seattle, 1970), 3.
2. For the conventional version of the white occupation of the Pacific Northwest, see Dorothy Johansen, *Empire of the Columbia*, 2d ed. (New York, 1967); Oscar O. Winther, *The Great Northwest* (New York, 1947); David Lavender, *Land of the Giants: The Drive to the Pacific Northwest* (Garden City, N.Y., 1956); and, more recently, Malcolm Clark, Jr., *Eden Seekers: The Settlement of Oregon, 1818–1862* (New York, 1981). The argument presented in this essay is adapted, in part, from William G. Robbins, "Extinguishing Indian Land Title in Western Oregon," *Indian Historian*, Vol. 7 (1974), 10–14, 52, and "The Conquest of the American West: History as Eulogy," *Ibid.*, Vol. 10 (1977), 7–13.
3. See the provocative chapter, "Concerning Violence," in Franz Fanon, *The Wretched of the Earth* (New York, 1968).
4. Francis Jennings, *The Invasion of America: Indians, Colonialism, and the Cant of Conquest* (Raleigh, N.C., 1975). For the influence of European capitalism on hunting and gathering societies, see Walter Rodney, *How Europe Underdeveloped Africa*, rev. ed. (Washington, D.C., 1981), 10–12.
5. For comment on "removal" as an aspect of Euro-American expansion, see Wilcomb Washburn, *The Indian in America* (New York, 1975); Dale Van Every, *Disinherited: The Lost Birthright of the American Indian* (New York, 1966); Francis Paul Prucha, "Andrew Jackson's Indian Policy: A Reassessment," *JAH*, Vol. 56 (1969), 527–39; Reginald Horsman, *The Origins of Indian Removal, 1815–1824* (East Lansing, Mich., 1970); Arthur DeRosier, *The Removal of the Choctaw Indians* (Knoxville, 1970).
6. Theodora Kroeber, *Ishi in Two Worlds: A Biography of the Last Wild Indian in North America* (Berkeley, 1961). Also see Jack Forbes, *The Indians of California and Nevada* (Healdsburg, Calif., 1969); Dee Brown, *Bury My Heart at Wounded Knee* (New York, 1970); Amelia Susman, *The Round Valley Indians of California* (Berkeley, 1976).
7. Robert Faherty, "The American Indian: An Overview," *Current History*, Vol. 67 (1974), 241–44.
8. "Petition of Citizens of Oregon Praying That the Laws of the United States may be Extended over that Territory," in Priscilla Knuth and Charles M. Gates, eds., "Oregon Territory in 1849–1850," *PNQ*, Vol. 40 (1949), 5–7.
9. Oregon City *Spectator*, Dec. 28, 1848. There were occasional early-comers among the whites who argued for the prior rights of Indian land ownership. Samuel Parker, a Protestant missionary who traveled among the Nez Perce in 1833–34, suggested that the question of land ownership rested not with England or the United States, but with the Indians because they "have a priority of claims." See Parker, *Journal of an Exploring Tour beyond the Rocky Mountains* (Ithaca, N.Y., 1838), 260.
10. Roy Robbins, *Our Landed Heritage* (Princeton, 1940), 18–21. Robbins, still consulted as a standard source on U.S. land policy, sometimes writes as if Indian claims to land never existed.

11. Denton R. Bedford, "How to Start an Indian War," *Indian Historian*, Vol. 6 (1973), 11.

12. William Bowen, *The Willamette Valley: Migration and Settlement on the Oregon Frontier* (Seattle, 1978), 69–71; Jerry A. O'Callaghan, *The Disposition of the Public Domain in Oregon* (Washington, D.C., 1960), 21, 34.

13. "Memorial of the Legislature Praying for the Extinguishment of Indian Title," July 10, 1849, in C. F. Coan, "Federal Indian Relations in the Pacific Northwest: The First Stage, 1849–1852," *OHQ*, Vol. 22 (1921), 53; "Governor Lane's First Message to the Legislative Assembly," in Knuth and Gates, 12. For the elaboration of Andrew Jackson's justification for Indian removal see Prucha.

14. *Spectator*, Feb. 22, 1849; Clark, 236–37.

15. Clark, 237; O'Callaghan, 34; Winther, 157. Also see "Petition of Citizens of Oregon," 5–7. Oregon's white population increased 295 percent in the decade of the 1850s; see O'Callaghan, 19.

16. These provisions of the boundary treaty and the territorial act are reprinted in "The Coos, Lower Umpqua and Siuslaw Indian Tribes: An Historical Perspective," unpublished pamphlet distributed by the Coos, Lower Umpqua, Siuslaw Indian Tribes, Inc., Coos Bay, Oregon. Copy in the author's possession.

17. Alvin Josephy, Jr., *The Nez Perce Indians and the Opening of the Northwest* (New Haven, 1965), 286; *Congressional Globe*, 31st Cong., 1st Sess. (1850), 41D; Theodore T. Johnson, *California and Oregon* (Philadelphia, 1850), 266.

18. Allan G. Bogue, Thomas D. Phillips, and James E. Wright, eds., *The West of the American People* (Itasca, Ill., 1970), 81; Steve Talbot, *Roots of Oppression: The American Indian Question* (New York, 1981), 34–35; John C. Ewers, *The Role of the Indian in National Expansion, Part 2: Removing the Indian Barrier* (Washington, D.C., 1939), 105.

19. O'Callaghan, 34; Sherburne F. Cook, "The Epidemics of 1830–1833 in California and Oregon," in *University of California Publications in American Archaeology and Ethnology*, Vol. 43 (1955), 303–26; Wendell H. Oswalt, *This Land Was Theirs: A Study of the North American Indian* (New York, 1973), 567; *Spectator*, Aug. 10, 1848; Lavender, 277.

20. Luke Lea to Anson Dart, July 20, 1850, U.S. Department of Indian Affairs, Records of the Oregon Superintendency of Indian Affairs (microfilm copy, Oregon State University Library), 149.

21. Josephy, 287; Coan, 54; U.S. Department of the Interior, Annual Report to the Commissioner of Indian Affairs, 1851; Records of the Oregon Superintendency of Indian Affairs: Instructions and Reports, 1850–1855.

22. *Congressional Globe*, 33d Cong., 1st Sess. (1855), 744; Lavender, 276–77; Josephy, 287; Clark, 262.

23. Joel Palmer to commissioner of Indian affairs, Oct. 8, 1853, Records of the Oregon Superintendency of Indian Affairs, 239. One person claimed that all the good land in the Rogue Valley was "fenced-up" by 1853; see Wallace Farnham, "Religion as an Influence in Life and Thought: Jackson County, Oregon, 1860–1890," Ph.D. dissertation (University of Oregon, 1955), 25.

24. Stephen Dow Beckham, *Requiem for a People: The Rogue Indians and the Frontiersmen* (Norman, Okla., 1971). Although Beckham is appalled by the senseless brutality committed against Indian people, his account is flawed with repeated references to "thieving," "marauding," and "untamed" natives.

25. Talbot, 101–105.

26. Quoted in Clark, 11.

27. Michael Paul Rogin, *Fathers and Sons: Andrew Jackson and the Subjugation of the American Indian* (New York, 1975), 129.

28. *Ibid.*

29. *Ibid.*

30. Palmer to commissioner of Indian affairs, Oct. 8, 1853.

31. *Ibid.*, June 23, 1853, pp. 86–88.

32. Beckham, 124, 147–51; Coan, 8.

33. *Congressional Globe*, 34th Cong., 1st Sess. (1855), 133.

34. Ray Hoard Glassley, *Indian Wars of the Pacific Northwest* (Portland, 1953), 61.

35. Clark, 263, 265 (italics mine).

36. Coan, 27; U.S. Department of Interior, *Annual Report of the Commissioner of Indian Affairs* (1853), 89.

37. John Beeson, *A Plea for the Indians: With Facts and Features of the Late War in Oregon* (New York, 1858), 10.

38. *Ibid.*, 15, 23.

39. Vernon Bellecourt, address at Oregon State University, Nov. 6, 1973.

40. Beeson, 29, 47–48, 79, 83.

41. Portland *Oregonian*, Nov. 24, 1855; Beckham, 147–67; the quote is from the *Oregon Statesman* (Salem), Mar. 25, 1856.

42. Beckham, 181–89; Alfred Kroeber, "Cultural and Natural Areas of Native North America," *University of California Publications in American Archaeology and Ethnology*, Vol. 38 (1939), 136–37.

43. Coan, 14–16; U.S. Department of Interior, 1856 *Annual Report of the Commissioner of Indian Affairs*, 12; 1855 *Annual Report*, 110.

44. Coan, 14; *Uncommon Controversy*, 19.

45. Timothy Davenport, "Recollections of an Indian Agent, III," *OHQ*, Vol. 8 (1907), 238; Philip H. Sheridan, *Personal Memoirs* (New York, 1888), 91.

46. Coan, 4–5. The army officer is cited in Preston E. Onstad, "The Fort on the Luckiamute. A Resurvey of Fort Hoskins," *OHQ*, Vol. 65 (1964), 175.

47. 34th Cong., 1st Sess. (1856), H.E.D. 53, 133–34; Palmer to commissioner of Indian affairs, Jan. 8, 1856, *Records of the Oregon Superintendency of Indian Affairs*, 4, July 10, 1855, 13.

48. Jefferson's phrase is cited in William Appleman Williams, *The Contours of American History* (Cleveland, 1961), 179.

49. Bedford, 11.

Isaac I. Stevens and Federal Military Power in Washington Territory

KENT D. RICHARDS

Virtually all accounts of Isaac I. Stevens as governor of Washington Territory have uncritically applauded or condemned his conduct. This is particularly true of his role in the formulation of Indian policy, his declaration of martial law, and his relationship with the military. Stevens's actions in each of these areas are interrelated, but this paper will focus primarily upon the relationship between Stevens and the several federal military officers in the Pacific Northwest.

To understand Isaac I. Stevens's position during the Indian wars of the 1850s, it is necessary to be aware of his earlier career, a topic for which, unfortunately, Hazard Stevens's eulogistic biography of pater-familias has been accepted as almost the sole source. This is not the place to consider Isaac Stevens's life prior to 1853, but certain trends and personality traits should be noted. His most obvious trait was a need to prove himself mentally, physically, and morally superior to associates or adversaries in any given situation, and he constantly drove himself to accomplish these ends.

Stevens's physique partially explains his personality. A large head and short stubby legs indicate that he probably suffered from a congenital gland malfunction. His parents doubted that he would live through infancy, and his early years were a struggle for survival. An uneasy relationship with his father provided a second, and not unusual, influence. Isaac resented his father, a stern New England taskmaster, who pushed his son to the limits of his physical and intellectual ability. The death of Isaac's mother in a carriage accident, for

Originally published in *Pacific Northwest Quarterly*, July 1972.

which her husband was responsible, and Isaac's dislike of his step-mother added to a difficult situation. Isaac later complained that he nearly had a mental breakdown as a young man, and there is no doubt that he suffered physically from the hard farm life, for he almost died from sunstroke and sustained a hernia which troubled him throughout his life.

A descendant of New England Puritans who provided more than their share of clergy, prosperous businessmen, and soldiers, Isaac determined not to succumb to his adversities, but to surmount them and prove himself to his father and to the world. He chose a military career because it fitted his desire for an active life and allowed him to escape the farm. The United States Military Academy with its emphasis upon engineering provided a natural outlet for his outstanding mathematical ability. Stevens entered West Point in 1835, earned a creditable scholastic record, and graduated in 1839. For the next fourteen years, he served in the Army Corps of Engineers, constructing coastal forts, fighting during the Mexican War, and working on the Coast Survey. In 1853 he resigned from the army to accept appointment as the first governor of the newly established Washington Territory.

While he was in the army, Stevens became accustomed to holding positions of command, to giving orders, and to expecting obedience from the men under him. He demonstrated great energy combined with a frantic drive for personal achievement and recognition. When working on eastern coastal forts, he insisted that the addition of new duties would not require his release from prior commitments. For example, during one brief period, he no doubt set a record of sorts by simultaneously supervising construction or repair of fortifications at eight different sites from Savannah, Georgia, to Bucksport, Maine. Stevens demanded complete loyalty from his men and in return was generally fair and impartial. It is significant that, with the exception of his year in Mexico, and often even then, he was in an independent command with his superior officers absent at a distance.

Successful in his quest for the governorship of Washington Territory and the leadership of the northern railway survey, Stevens realized that he was leaving military life, but he continued to operate in a fashion which assumed the form of a military command. He asked, for example, that Captain George B. McClellan be appointed as his assistant in charge of the western portion of the survey. General Joseph G. Totten at first refused, pointing out the difficulties that might arise when a military officer received orders from a civilian. Totten admonished Stevens, "With your zeal for command, which is laudable and natural, you should understand how McClellan would feel."

Totten eventually acquiesced, but his prediction was prophetic, for by the end of the year, Stevens experienced troubled relationships with McClellan, as well as with other members of the expedition.

As Governor Stevens began the treaty making which preceded the Indian outbreak of 1855, he left behind a career which had accustomed him to command and to prompt, unquestioning response from his staff. A man who reacted with physical vigor—as long as his health sustained him—to any problem or obstacle, he throve on responsibility and disliked delegating authority in matters he deemed important. In addition, he bristled at personal slights, real or imagined, and he construed differences of opinion on policy as attacks upon his character.

The Indian wars in the Pacific Northwest during the 1850s, like all Indian troubles in the Far West, resulted from long-standing differences between dissimilar cultures. The fact of white settlement perhaps sufficiently explains the outbreaks in 1855. The treaty-making process carried on by Stevens was not his decision, for President Franklin Pierce and Secretary of State William L. Marcy ordered the Washington tribes brought under treaties. However, it must also be recognized that Governor Stevens assumed as his major responsibility the building of an empire of white citizens on the western coast, that he did not carry on treaty negotiations with much tact or diplomacy, that he was unaware of or chose to ignore certain facets of the Indian character and culture, and that he seemed oblivious to the signs of possible hostilities in the months prior to the war.

Margaret Stevens perhaps accurately reflected her husband's opinion of the Indians when she observed in a letter to her mother that "the Indians . . . think so much of the whites that a child can govern them." She believed, as did the governor, that "Mr. Stevens has them right under his thumb—they are afraid as death of him and do just as he tells them."

It is not surprising, then, that Stevens felt safe when he ventured east in the summer of 1855 to conduct the prestigious negotiations with the Blackfoot Indians and their neighbors. He was convinced that he was the only white man who knew how to handle these tribes. George Gibbs, who was with the railroad survey, claimed that the governor was "crazy about this Blackfoot treaty," and he warned that Stevens "ought not desert the immediate interests of his own territory for the mere glorification of making a big talk and swell with the Missouri Indians."

Stevens was near Fort Benton when he learned of the death of the Indian agent Andrew J. Bolon and the general outbreak of hostilities. He immediately decided to brave possible deep snows and hostile tribes to return to Puget Sound by the most direct route. The decision provided grounds for the first disagreement between Stevens and the army, when the governor contended that the military refused to send troops to his rescue and abandoned him to his fate in Indian country.

Stevens made this accusation in February 1856, after General John E. Wool had rejected his counsel. The governor began to build a case against the general, whom he indicted for "utter and signal incapacity" and whose removal from command Stevens demanded. But earlier, when Stevens was at the Coeur d'Alene Mission in November, he had written to the commander at The Dalles to advise him of his plans. At that time Stevens did not seem concerned for his safety, and he did not suggest that he would return through Yakima country. He obviously believed that he and the friendly Nez Perce could cope with any eventuality.

Beneath this first open conflict between the army and Stevens lurked more significant issues than even the safety of the governor— questions of war strategy and an overall policy toward the Indians. Immediately upon hearing of hostilities, Stevens urged vigorous action even though he admitted that, from the vantage point of the Bitterroot Mountains, "it is difficult to get information." This lack of evidence dissuaded him not at all from "earnestly recommending" a winter campaign by the army to break the will of the hostiles and to destroy their provisions and livestock.

Some writers have contended that Stevens's active policy was a consequence of his desire to promote the interests of his constituents, the white settlers. Stevens certainly agreed that the settler had a right to the land. He indicated this in his proclamation issued immediately after the Walla Walla Council, which opened eastern Washington to settlement, and again in a letter to President Pierce, in which he stated that the conflict was simply a question of "whether the Indian or the whites shall occupy the country."

But even if the interests of the settlers had not dictated a vigorous policy, it is doubtful that Governor Stevens would have altered his. He was a man who followed his own instincts, his own sense of right, wrong, and justice. Despite his title, the governor was never a politician at heart. He did not stop to sniff the political wind before making decisions; he was a military man, making military decisions.

More important to Stevens than the desires of the settlers was his conviction that the Indians had betrayed him. He viewed the Indians as children whom he would protect if obedient and to whom he would mete out punishment when they were naughty. In the governor's narrow view of the treaties signed during 1854–55, the Indians' signatures upon a legal document bound them to its conditions, and

the war resulted when certain chiefs treacherously broke this cove-
nant and tribes refused to follow their designated leaders. Convinced
that he was morally and legally right and believing that the broken
treaties reflected badly upon his negotiations, the governor set out to
punish the wayward children.

In contrast, General Wool's initial reaction was to proceed slowly
until he was aware of the extent of hostilities and until the necessary
reinforcements could be moved to the Columbia District. Reports
from officers in the field, particularly that of Major E. D. Townsend,
supported Wool's policy. After examining the troops at Vancouver
and The Dalles, Major Townsend reported that the condition of men,
horses, and equipment would not allow a winter march. But, Townsend noted, even if the troops could go, he would recommend
against the campaign because the well-mounted Yakimas would drive
their cattle and extra horses into the mountains and then keep out of
reach. Further, Townsend added, a campaign would only disperse
the hostiles and perhaps drive them into the vicinity of friendly tribes
who then might be corrupted. And finally, the major observed, there
were neither settlers nor property in eastern Washington for the
troops to remove or save.

With this report in hand, Wool replied to the governor's enthusiastic prompting with the icy comment that the campaign proposed was
an extensive one, and, he reminded Stevens, "You should have recollected that I have neither the resources of a territory nor the treasury of the United States at my command." But, he assured the governor, the army would pursue the war with promptness and vigor
"without *wasting unnecessarily the means and resources at my disposal by
untimely and unproductive expeditions.*" The war would end in a few
months, Wool insisted, if the settlers and volunteers refrained from a
policy of Indian extermination and if the volunteers withdrew from
the field.

General Wool sent troops to Puget Sound and directed Colonel
George Wright to prepare for a swing through Yakima country in the
spring. But Wool insisted throughout the winter that future hostilities
would be more the fault of the whites than of the Indians. There is a
certain irony that, from the beginning of the war, the army represented the voice of compromise and moderation, while the governor,
as the leader of the white settlers, took the position that "*the war shall
be prosecuted until the last hostile Indian is exterminated.*"

Faced with Wool's resistance, which Stevens considered stubborn
and obdurate, the governor called out volunteer forces. He told the
general, "I am . . . too old a soldier . . . to do otherwise than to press
forward with all my energies." Reliance upon volunteers or militia

was a long-standing tradition on the frontier, and Acting Governor Charles Mason had called out two companies while Stevens was still in Blackfoot country.

Suspicion and distrust between regulars and militia was also a long-standing tradition. Lieutenant George Crook expressed the regulars' contempt for militia when he derisively described the mounting of a company of Oregon volunteers. According to Crook, when the volunteers' captain bawled "attentshun the company," his command answered with "go to Hell" and similar epithets. Only after the captain attempted to mount and accidentally hit his chin on the saddle horn, did the company finally move forward. It is unlikely that Crook endeared himself to those within earshot when he remarked that he did not care to ride in the rear of the column, for, in the event of an Indian attack, he would probably be trampled to death. Acting Governor Mason attempted to lessen this mutual suspicion by naming Major Gabriel J. Rains of the army as brigadier general commanding the volunteer companies.

When Governor Stevens began raising his volunteers, he spoke of a spirit of cooperation with the regulars, but he also made it clear that he would be issuing the orders and formulating campaign policy. Ignoring Wool, the governor began urging his policies on the commanders of the regular army in the Northwest, particularly on Colonel Silas Casey commanding at Fort Steilacoom. Blocked in his desire for a winter campaign east of the Cascades, the governor determined early in 1856 to seal off the various mountain passes, isolating the Puget Sound Indians during the winter, and then, as soon as the snow melted, to proceed across the mountains into Yakima country and the Walla Walla Valley.

But the volunteers could not guard the multitude of possible mountain routes, and Stevens attempted to secure the use of Casey's command to supplement the militia. Colonel Casey, however, requested that the governor raise two companies of volunteers and turn them over to the army. Then, Casey claimed, the army could protect the "frontier without the aid of those now in the service of the territory."

Stevens must have recognized the merit in Casey's proposal, for he was plagued with problems within the volunteer organization. Despite his own herculean efforts, the volunteers could not efficiently carry out his ambitious plans. But he rejected Casey's request, predicting a disaster if he called in the volunteers just when they were poised, or so the governor claimed, to strike a decisive blow. More to the point, Stevens declared that, if he did raise additional volunteers, he would certainly not give up control of these units to the regular army. The governor, Stevens insisted, became the final authority in an emergency.

Stevens's argument touched the crux of the dispute. Who was the ultimate authority in the territories in a military situation? The Organic Act for the territory did not define the limits of authority for either governor or commanding general. It seems obvious, however, that if an emergency existed, as Stevens insisted, cooperation between civilians and military was essential, and both the governor and the military were at fault for assuming that either could or should operate without the other.

Colonel Casey, however, was on strong ground in assuming that volunteers would act under regular army officers. This transfer of authority was traditional, and when Charles Mason raised the first volunteer companies, he agreed that Major Rains would exercise command. Stevens ignored tradition, and no doubt further alienated Casey when he made their differences a personal matter. The governor complained that he journeyed twice at great inconvenience to Fort Steilacoom on visits to Casey, whom he styled his inferior, and he claimed that he had waived personal etiquette in his desire to cooperate.

From this point, the two men moved on to a second general area of dispute: policy toward the friendly Indians. Casey assumed that the army would deal with the hostiles, but he readily conceded that Stevens, as superintendent of Indian affairs, was responsible for the friendlies. Relative to the former group, Casey informed the governor in July 1856 that he was sending a command under Captain Erasmus Keyes to check on tribes at the Black River, and he added: "Permit me to remark that I would consider it extremely inexpedient and entirely unnecessary for you to order volunteers to take their [Indian] lives, or to commit any violence on them." The governor heatedly reminded Casey that, as superintendent, he had ordered all Indians out of the area between the east shore of Puget Sound and the Cascades and that any Indians who remained would be subject to punishment. Casey ended this exchange by noting that he would be pleased if Stevens would exercise his responsibility as superintendent and assume control over the one hundred Indians he was feeding at Fort Steilacoom with army rations.

The relationship between the governor and Colonel George Wright followed a similar pattern. Stevens knew Wright and Casey from the Mexican War, and when Wright arrived on the Columbia in January 1856, Stevens exclaimed, "Allow me as an old companion in arms to welcome you to the Territory of Washington." The governor spoke of the "propriety of strong understanding between the regulars and the volunteers" in a united and energetic action.

But Colonel Wright immediately dissuaded Stevens of any notion that he would follow the governor's commands. He took issue with Stevens's argument that the Indians interpreted delay as weakness, and he subsequently denied the volunteer commander Benjamin F. Shaw's request for arms and ammunition. He informed Stevens that the regulars would conduct all summer operations, but added, condescendingly, that the volunteers would do good service if it ever became necessary to call on them.

As Wright attempted to arrange a truce with the Yakimas during the summer of 1856, he found the governor's activities increasingly vexatious. The colonel complained that the Indian agent Michael Simmons attempted to wreck the negotiations by telling the Yakimas that the army would hang any Indian who came into camp. A short time later Wright angrily protested that the governor's negotiations seriously embarrassed the army, confused the Indians, and tended to prolong hostilities.

When the fighting slowed in the fall of 1856, the animosity between the governor and the army did not end. The prime bone of contention involved Indian leaders who had been captured or who had surrendered. Stevens had insisted from the beginning that the instigators of the war would suffer, an assumption based on the governor's premise that a few bad Indians were responsible for the outbreak.

As early as June 1856, Stevens had assumed that he and Colonel Wright were agreed that they would accept only unconditional surrender and would bring murderers to trial. Wright did not commit himself, but after forging a truce, the colonel suggested it would be unwise, if they wished for peace, to punish any Indians. The governor maintained that criminals deserved justice and if the situation were so unsettled that "trials will lead to war, then the sooner the better." Casey entered the debate and supported Wright's position, meeting Stevens's order to turn certain Indians over to him with the suggestion that "the better way would be to consider that we have been at war with the Indians, and, now, we are at peace."

The third army officer in the Northwest with whom Stevens quarreled was Colonel Edward Steptoe. The governor began courting Steptoe's favor in the late summer of 1856, when Stevens decided to hold a second council in the Walla Walla country. He first urged Steptoe to furnish troops at the council to replace volunteers whose enlistments were expiring. Steptoe, then on his way to establish a post in the valley, agreed to accommodate the governor, although he noted that orders prohibited extending aid or encouragement to the volunteers' military operations.

When Steptoe arrived in the vicinity of the council, he resisted the governor's efforts to induce him to enter the volunteer camp, explaining that he needed to prepare winter quarters, and he advised Stevens that, as the Indians seemed unwilling to talk, it would be appropriate to adjourn the council to a more favorable time. But the governor, although admitting the hostility of most of the tribes, insisted that the council would continue, "whatever be the consequences as regards my own personal safety. Such I regard to be my duty to the public, to the Indians, and to my own character."

Soon the Indians attacked the governor and his men. Stevens and the volunteers made their way to Steptoe's camp, joined forces with the army, and together drove off the hostiles. As the combined parties returned to The Dalles, each in bad humor, Steptoe dashed off a hasty note to headquarters, pleading that he had tried to stay out of the trouble between the Indians and Stevens and that he "only took part in it when it was evident that the latter must be destroyed unless rescued. . . . The truth is there would have been no further disturbance whatever in my opinion but for the council; it was premature and inopportune."

Once back in Olympia, Stevens burst out in full fury against the whole military establishment. He complained that it was working against ratification of his treaties, that prohibition of settlement east of the mountains was illegal, and that Wright had perpetrated a surrender to Indian demands "unprecedented in history, and most discreditable to our government . . . a usurpation of my duties, for which he will be held to account. . . . The sole object of the army had been to destroy [my] influence among the Indians and establish the prestige of the army regardless of propriety and honor."

By the end of 1856, Governor Stevens had suffered through a frustrating twelve months, and perhaps the most disconcerting aspect was his association with the United States Army. It seemed to thwart him at every turn, and his relationship with each of the commanders eventually deteriorated into mutual distrust and suspicion. The army and the governor held different basic assumptions about the causes of the war and the correct policy to pursue. Each held a different philosophy of the proper relationship between civilian and military authorities. In this difficult situation, Stevens's attitudes did not improve relationships or help to solve problems. He insisted upon his course of action, refused to compromise with the army, and thus complicated Indian-white relations. In part, at least, Stevens's position during 1855–57 was responsible for the uneasy truce that led to renewed hostilities in 1858.

Although General Wool matched Stevens in his concern for the perquisites of office, Casey, Wright, and Steptoe were reasonable men and inclined to meet the governor halfway in conducting the war, an inclination Stevens did not match. The governor's use of large numbers of volunteers led to huge expenses, and these troops did not prove particularly effective in conducting military operations or negotiations.

Isaac I. Stevens possessed great abilities and many talents, but as governor and superintendent of Indian affairs during the years 1855–57, he was the wrong man in the wrong place at the wrong time. In his relationships with the military, Stevens proved that he did not possess the capacity for cooperation, moderation, and compromise necessary in those trying times.

BIBLIOGRAPHICAL NOTE

Major sources for this paper are the Isaac I. Stevens papers in the manuscripts section of the University of Washington Library; the William W. Miller collection, Beinecke Library, Yale University; National Archives, Record Group 393, United States Army Continental Commands 1821–1920, Department of the Pacific, Letters Received; *Pioneer and Democrat* (Olympia); *Puget Sound Courier* (Steilacoom). The two biographies of Stevens are: Hazard Stevens, *Life of Isaac Ingalls Stevens*, 2 vols. (Boston, 1900) and Kent D. Richards, *Isaac I. Stevens* (Provo, 1979).

Other sources include W. D. Lyman, *History of Walla Walla County* (n.p., 1901); William F. Prosser, *History of the Puget Sound Country* (New York, 1903); William C. Brown, *The Indian Side of the Story* (Spokane, 1961); Murray Morgan, *Puget's Sound* (Seattle, 1979); Norman H. Clark, *Washington* (New York, 1976); Alvin M. Josephy, *The Nez Perce Indians and the Opening of the Northwest* (New Haven, 1965); Martin F. Schmitt, ed., *General George Crook: His Autobiography* (Norman, 1960); James Doty, *Journal of Operations of Governor Isaac Ingalls Stevens of Washington Territory in 1855* (Fairfield, Wash., 1978); Charles M. Gates, ed., *Messages of the Governors of the Territory of Washington to the Legislative Assembly, 1854–1889* (Seattle, 1940).

II. From Frontier
to Urban-Industrial Society

In the fall of 1883 a crowd of notables—including former President Ulysses S. Grant—gathered in remote Gold Creek, Montana, to celebrate the driving of the final spike in the nation's second transcontinental railroad, the Northern Pacific. Henry Villard, financier and president of the road, and the politicians took turns driving home the spike, the same one used when the first tracks were laid near Duluth, Minnesota, fourteen years earlier. If any act symbolized the taming of the frontier, this was it. In the 1840s, when the wagon ruts of the Oregon Trail were fresh, the overland trek from the Midwest to the Willamette Valley required a spirit of adventure and endurance. Now, with the completion of a rail line linking Saint Paul with Portland and the Puget Sound, a person could travel to the Pacific Northwest in luxury and comfort. A journey that once required five months by wagon was reduced to five days.

Before the end of the 1880s, two more transcontinental lines and a rail connection to California linked the Pacific Northwest with the wider world. Never before had the region's natural resources been so accessible to so many people. And never before had any individual or organization in the Pacific Northwest possessed such transforming power as the railroads. They opened remote timberland, hauled lumber to new markets in the Midwest, and created countless new jobs and an occasional family fortune. They spurred agricultural development of the semiarid country east of the Cascades (see the essay by Alexander C. McGregor). They fostered the rapid growth of towns like Tacoma and Seattle and populated the open spaces.

They also excited fear and envy. More than a decade before the north-

*ern transcontinental link was forged, Ben Holladay, a regional trans-
portation magnate, had brought corrupt politics, monopoly, and the
gaudy materialism of the Gilded Age to Oregon. To support his Oregon and California Railroad Company and other interests, Holladay
played a key role in electing a Portlander, John Hipple Mitchell, to the
United States Senate, where, the* Oregonian *later accused, he stood
"for everything that is corrupt, immoral and infamous."*

*Fear of political corruption was only one reason citizens might dis-
like railroads. Towns bypassed or slighted by the companies also resented their power, and none was more bitter than Yakima. The first
train arrived there in 1884, but when citizens refused to pay the price
the Northern Pacific demanded for a station and a switchyard, the
railroad laid out a new town, North Yakima, four miles away. It then
ran its trains through Yakima without stopping. In the end, most citizens moved their houses and business to the new town (subsequently
renamed Yakima), but for years the antirailroad sentiment remained
strong in the Yakima Valley.*

*Also resented were the railroads' vast land holdings, the most tan-
gible symbol of their wealth and power. In order to promote development of the West, the federal government gave railroads millions of
acres of the public domain. The Northern Pacific's grant in Washington
paralleled the right-of-way and formed an enormous checkerboard of
alternating squares of government and railroad land that covered two-
thirds of the territory, stretching from Spokane almost to the Pacific
Ocean. Prior to the coming of the railroad, much of the land had been
unsuitable for farming or ranching. The Northern Pacific sold a large
portion of its holdings for a nominal price to encourage agricultural
development but retained other lands rich in timber and coal. Benefi-
ciaries were naturally grateful to the railroad, but others portrayed the
Northern Pacific's land grant as a black cloud blighting the territory.
Critics charged that railroad power had corrupted legislators and
mocked the democratic process. Such charges formed the basis for several political reform movements that promised to restore the promised
land to the people.*

*Few aspects of life in the Pacific Northwest changed more dramati-
cally during the 1880s and 1890s than the pattern of settlement. Not
only did the railroads make it easy for people to immigrate to the region, but they also actively recruited settlers. Tens of thousands of
pamphlets promoting the Pacific Northwest as a promised land flooded
the East Coast and Europe. By 1883 the Northern Pacific alone had
831 promotional agents in Britain, with another 124 scattered over*

Norway, Sweden, Denmark, Holland, Germany, and Switzerland. In 1888 the Northern Pacific advertised in 3,385 newspapers and distributed 650,000 brochures. Individual communities and real estate speculators added to the effort to attract settlers.

Pamphlets typically portrayed the region's natural resources as "vast and inexhaustible," with one author claiming that it would "scarcely be possible to exaggerate the extent and value of the forests of the Pacific Northwest." Promoters also described the region as a health seeker's paradise, filled with hot springs and mineral baths. Its climate, according to claims, was ideal, sunstroke was practically unknown, and evenings were "cool and conducive to sound slumber."

An often repeated refrain was that success awaited any newcomer who was willing to work hard. A promotional pamphlet issued by the Union Pacific Railroad in 1889 claimed that "nearly all of the people have gone to the Pacific Northwest for the purpose of bettering their condition. Many of them had strong arms and good appetites, but no money in their purse; they had also will and determination to win and have won."

The promotional campaign greatly influenced population movement. During the decade of the 1880s the population of Oregon grew by 80 percent and that of Washington by 380 percent, an astounding rate of increase equaled by few other states or territories in the nineteenth century. Many of the newcomers were women, part of family groups making their way west by rail. Oregon was able to absorb its new residents without much change in customs and traditions that dated back to the pioneer days of the 1840s and 1850s. But newcomers poured into Washington in such great numbers that they altered prevailing patterns of life and gave the territory a somewhat different character from Oregon's. The reverence for the first generation of overland pioneers was far less pronounced in Washington than in Oregon.

There were other differences, too. More foreign immigrants chose Washington, which throughout its history contained a larger percentage of foreign-born residents than did Oregon. In fact, no area received more Swedes and Norwegians in proportion to its already resident population than Washington, which for years ranked third in the United States in Scandinavian population (see Jorgen Dahlie's essay).

Nowhere were the population changes more pronounced than in urban areas. The 1880 census ranked Walla Walla as Washington's most populous community, but then the major railroads passed it by. Seattle sprinted ahead to claim first place, with a population of 42,000 in 1890. During the decade of the 1880s Seattle's population increased by

1,000 percent, Tacoma's by 3,000 percent, and Spokane's by an incredible 6,000 percent. Portland, by contrast, grew by only 164 percent, from 17,557 to 46,385 inhabitants, barely ahead of the upstart metropolis Seattle.

Portland was slow to worry about a Puget Sound rival. Having long enjoyed the trade advantages conferred by two major rivers, the city was confident that it would remain the commercial capital of the Pacific Northwest. The product of slow but steady growth, Portland regarded herself as a model of civility and culture. High society there consciously modeled itself after that in the long-established cities of eastern America.

Portland's civic smugness was reinforced in the mid-1880s by a series of violent outbursts in Tacoma and Seattle, where rapid growth followed by a sudden economic slump led to social instability and anti-Chinese violence by unemployed white workers. Harvey Scott, editor of the Portland Oregonian, *used the troubles to contrast the Puget Sound communities unfavorably with Portland, where the anti-Chinese agitation never amounted to much.*

An especially bitter urban rivalry erupted between Tacoma and Seattle. Tacoma had the advantage of having been chosen the Pacific terminus of the Northern Pacific in the early 1870s, while Seattle was relegated to a branch line. But Seattle conceded nothing and finally won a transcontinental line of its own when James J. Hill chose the city as the western terminus of his Great Northern Railway, completed in 1893.

Like high school rivals yelling at a basketball game, Tacoma and Seattle partisans jeered one another mercilessly. "Seattle, Seattle! Death rattle, Death rattle!" chanted the schoolchildren and businessmen of Tacoma. In 1898 a Seattle partisan gave the rivalry an international twist when, after the battleship Maine *exploded and sank and the United States subsequently declared war on Spain, he scrawled on the men's room wall in the Great Northern station:*

> *Remember the* Maine
> *To Hell with Spain,*
> *And don't forget*
> *To pull the Chain—*
> *Tacoma needs the water!*

So determined was Seattle to become the leading metropolis of the Pacific Northwest that its incessant boosterism earned the label "Seattle Spirit," which was believed by many, particularly the residents of Se-

attle, to be an irresistible force. If Portland was a transplanted New England dowager, Seattle was a rambunctious frontiersman who grew rich through a combination of drive, optimism, wit, and occasional good fortune.

The region's urban promoters and community leaders were typically interested in far more than mere material gain. They believed that cultural institutions, particularly churches and schools, and a sense of order and cleanliness were all desirable and might give a western community a settled air that would dispel the fears any easterner might have about the West's "fancied lack of social advantage." As new as Pacific Northwest settlements were, they fostered philharmonic societies, art associations, libraries, and lyceums (see Karen Blair's essay). Professionals organized into medical and pharmaceutical societies, bar associations, and service clubs. The whole community took pride in the installation of the latest type of streetcar or telephone equipment, the electric lights that appeared first in the mid-1880s, or paved streets—anything that enabled one community to boast of its superiority over its rivals. Social and cultural organizations and technological innovation were all regarded as signs of progress and as evidence of a community's permanence.

The 1880s and 1890s were decades of momentous changes in the Pacific Northwest, a time of abrupt transition from the frontier world of Lewis and Clark, the Whitmans, the Oregon Trail pioneers, and Chief Joseph to the postfrontier world of transcontinental railroads, nationwide markets, commercial agriculture, large-scale industrial enterprise, and professional associations and colleges (see the essay by Lee Nash). Certain statistics suggest the magnitude of the changes: during the 1880s the value of Oregon's industrial production increased by 280 percent, and Washington's by 1,100 percent; the value of Oregon's agricultural production increased by 65 percent, and Washington's by 230 percent. But statistics alone can scarcely convey the meaning of such changes in human terms. For many people the rapid transformation from frontier to postfrontier world was anything but smooth and uneventful, particularly when frontier attitudes and methods were used to solve the problems of the postfrontier world. People who glorified the bravery, foresight, and individualism of Oregon Trail pioneers, for example, were now forced to cope with an unfamiliar world of strikes, social unrest, bureaucracy, and standardization. These two decades, in short, were the first truly modern ones in Pacific Northwest history (see Robert Ficken's essay).

From Sheep Range to Agribusiness: A Case History of Agricultural Transformation on the Columbia Plateau

Alexander C. McGregor

The Columbia Plateau, a mountain-girdled 22,000-square-mile prairie of rolling hills, arid sagebrush flats, and stark "scabland" canyons, has changed in a century from an austere and unpromising region to one of the most productive farming and ranching areas of the American West. The experiences of four Scottish-Canadian brothers—Archie, Peter, John, and Alex McGregor—and their descendants and neighbors exhibit some of the striking changes which transformed this 250-mile-long and 200-mile-wide district of eastern Washington, northeastern Oregon, and northern Idaho from a land of semi-nomadic "tramp" open-range sheep raising to an area dominated by complex capital-intensive agribusiness. Four bench marks in the continuum of change indicate some of the steps of agricultural succession in the remote land: the development of sheep raising from open range to deeded and leased ranchland in the late nineteenth century; the expansion of wheat raising and the elaborate horse- and mule-powered technology of 1910–20; the transition from work animals to fossil fuel–powered machinery during the twenties and the Great Depression; and the striking advances in output and productivity made possible after World War II by the research of agronomists and the chemical industry.

Open-range sheep production was a rapidly growing business in 1882 when twenty-one-year-old Archie McGregor and his twenty-year-old brother, Peter, left their family's farm in the forests of eastern Ontario and came west during the first sustained rush of immigration to the semiarid, treeless lands of the Columbia Plateau. The Mc-

Originally published in *Agricultural History*, January 1980.

Gregor brothers searched for suitable homestead locations. Archie McGregor wrote his father in 1883 and told of going "on foot with my blankets on my back. . . . The longest walk I had without anything to eat was 60 miles. I always felt happy on the way for I could see the country or hunt. So I did and I took up 160 acres of land. . . . Of course I have not the deed yet but I am a Yankee all the same." But this homestead, in the sandy deserts of the Big Bend district, was quickly abandoned. By the winter of 1883–84 the McGregors, like many other young immigrants, decided to become sheepherders "in default of opportunities for more desirable work." The McGregor brothers and many other Scottish, Irish, French, and Canadian herders took only minimal pay, enough to buy overalls, tobacco, and a few supplies, and exchanged their labor for a share in the future increase in the size of the flock. After two years of sheep tending, Archie and Peter separated their nine hundred fifty head from their employer's flocks and purchased an additional fourteen hundred head on credit. The outlook was encouraging, and in 1886 the two men convinced their younger brother John to come west and join the partnership of "McGregor Brothers, sheepmen."

The McGregors and other woolgrowers in the 1880s and 1890s grazed more than a million sheep on rangeland which had once supported huge herds of cattle. The cattleman A. J. Splawn remembered that "cattle were fat the year around. . . . Cattle could be seen in the white sage in the coldest weather absolutely shaking with fat." A pioneer cattleman said of the land, "These hills reach from hell to heaven, with bunchgrass from top to bottom." But a Yakima, Washington, cattleman complained that "cattle-owners are running from a pestilence—sheep." Sheep raisers had several advantages in the competition for the range. Cattle lacked the herd instinct and were left unsupervised and scattered over the rangeland for several months at a time. One herder and his dogs could move as many as three thousand gregarious, docile sheep, trailing them to the best pastures or to protected canyons where they could be sheltered from storms. Cattlemen described the peripatetic sheepmen as "tramps," "hoboes," "coyotes," or "vultures" and claimed that they "just drift around in search of good feeding ground and camp wherever such areas are found, regardless of the interests of anyone else."

The woolgrowers trailed their flocks in a cyclical fashion from sheltered lowland winter ranges to green summer pastures in adjacent mountains. The McGregor brothers, for example, trailed their flocks one hundred fifty miles from scabland winter grazing grounds to summer pastures in the Bitterroot Mountains of Idaho and the Okanogan highlands of northern Washington. Sheepmen encountered sporadic opposition in the forests and bunchgrass ranges. William

McGregor, a visitor at his brothers' camps in the Bitterroots in 1892, wrote his family that

every few miles there are sections . . . left for school purposes so whenever we would strike one of them we would stay a few days. . . . The idea is to get good feed. . . . But these people who live near school sections kick. They want that for their own livestock and they have no more right to it than anybody else. . . . It is pretty nearly all Swedes that settled up here and they are pretty cranky when they see sheep coming into the mountains.

Archie McGregor described the competition for the scabrock winter range in an 1893 letter to his sweetheart: "The French man is camped at Hooper Lake. He herded up to Mr. Town's yesterday and Mr. Town fired him off. Great times in the rocks. Nellie as I read your loving words I feel guilty. I have taken a few chaws of tobacco this spring." The native perennial grasses of these lowland pastures, reduced by decades of heavy cattle raising, were becoming infiltrated with a secondary growth of annual forbs ("weeds") unwittingly introduced from Europe and Asia. Plants of this type, such as "Jim Hill" mustard, made better seasonal sheep feed than the native grasses. But they were only marginally palatable for cattle, and cattlemen complained that their animals "failed to lay on fat as readily as formerly." At a time when beef was a glut on local markets, sheepmen had the further advantage of being able to ship their wool clip by boat around Cape Horn to Boston, an international marketing center for the fiber.

Sheep raisers had to protect their animals from a whole series of dangers: blizzards, cold rainy weather immediately following shearing, poison weeds, scabies, liver flukes, foot rot, "grub in the head," coyotes, bobcats, bears, and the very herd instinct that enabled a solitary herder to move thousands of the animals. If a few sheep became alarmed and started running away from a lightning storm or a predator, the remainder of the band, if not closely watched, would follow the leaders over a cliff or would "pile up" after them in a ravine or against a fallen tree. During lambing, a month-long period which began in early April, herders put in their own sort of eight-hour day— "eight hours before dinner and eight hours after." Ewes would sometimes refuse to suckle a newly born lamb, an obstinance that would lead to the lamb's rapid death unless an alert sheepman intervened. After spending several months with a flock, the naturalist John Muir concluded that "sheep brain must surely be poor stuff." The herder, Muir noted, "is never quite sane for any considerable period of time. Of all nature's voices, 'baa' is about all he hears."

Sheepmen devised various methods for protecting their defenseless animals. Sheep were dipped in a solution of hot water, sulphur, and black leaf (nicotine squeezed from tobacco leaves) to prevent infection from scabies, tiny mites that dug into the skin and caused large patches of wool to fall from the animals. *Ranche and Range,* a Columbia Plateau livestock journal, offered its subscribers advice on how to treat "running of the nose": "Blow tobacco smoke at the sheep's nose through a long clay pipe, and then give a good pinch of fine Scotch snuff blown into the nose as far as possible through a tube of any kind."

The tramp sheep businesses were devastated by collapsing wool and mutton prices during the panic of 1893. The McGregors and other sheepmen told the story of "a fellow [who] sent his wool to Boston. . . . When it arrived it wasn't worth enough to pay the freight. His broker in Boston wired him and told him that he owed $150. . . . The sheepman wired back and said 'I do not have $150. Am sending more wool.'" In the midst of the financial crisis, belated attempts were made to regulate grazing on the unfenced rangeland of the Columbia Plateau. Sheepmen and herders who ignored a ban on sheep grazing in the Cascade Mountains forest reserves were arrested. Other sheepmen were jailed for defying a "quarantine" law designed to keep woolgrowers who used eastern Oregon winter ranges from crossing the Columbia to their accustomed summer pastures. Sheriff's deputies in 1896 delivered summonses to the tents of John, Archie, and Peter McGregor and thirty other "prominent" sheepmen who were grazing their flocks on the land-grant holdings of the North Pacific Railway. Railroad investigators had learned of a "peculiar trespassing law" on the books in Washington designed "to prevent the sheep from trespassing on the unfenced lands of homestead claimants," and they used this statute to obtain an injunction against sheep grazing on 2 million acres of Columbia Plateau rangeland. Some sheepmen evaded the authorities and "sometimes by stealth and in the night have been known to get by certain stations of lookout." Others moved their flocks to Montana and even to an island in the Bering Sea where public domain remained available. The ban on sheep grazing in the Cascades was lifted pending further study, but the Northern Pacific case denied sheepmen access to vast railroad winter ranges and prevented them from reaching an equal area of checkerboard federal lands.

Railroad officials, eager to lease or sell an apparently barren and valueless land, in a sense almost forced prosperity on the sheepmen who decided to remain on the plateau. The Northern Pacific land commissioner William Phipps and western land agent Thomas Cooper began a grazing lease program which would serve as a model for similar leases of railroad lands in other states, a leasing system for federal forest reserves, and a proposed leasing arrangement for all rangeland remaining in the public domain. John McGregor in July 1896 agreed to Northern Pacific Grazing Lease #1—22,359 acres for $200 the first year and $400 thereafter for the duration of the ten-year lease. Many other sheepmen acquired similarly large holdings. But few of the remaining open-range cattlemen were among the seven hundred seventy-seven leaseholders. Most apparently doubted the effectiveness of the railroad plan or expected it to limit sheep grazing while continuing to give them free access to the range. A veteran Columbia Plateau rancher, C. H. Brune, estimated that sheepmen gained control of 90 percent of the bunchgrass range:

The cattlemen, when they had to start buying land, well, by then the sheep-men seemed to outbid 'em or get the land in their possession first. There were sheep ranches from the Cascade Mountains along the Columbia and along the Deschutes River in Oregon, the John Day River, the Snake River, and well, all the rivers in [eastern] Washington.

Northern Pacific land agents urged sheepmen to purchase their leaseholds. The McGregor brothers were told that if they refused to sign purchase agreements the land might be sold to outside buyers. John McGregor in 1897 agreed to buy his leased land within five years for $1.25 per acre and signed long-term contracts for an additional 10,000 acres for 75 cents to $1.25 per acre. When the McGregors and other sheepmen fell behind on lease payments or land contracts, Commissioner Phipps lowered the charges or accepted late payment. A rapid improvement in wool and mutton prices after 1898 improved the outlook for the woolgrowers, and John, Peter, and Archie McGregor convinced their younger brother, Alex, a Chicago druggist, that "he could make dollars in Washington where he had made pennies in Chicago." The McGregor brothers and other sheepmen also benefited from a miscalculation by the Northern Pacific Railway. In their haste to sell apparently valueless land, the railroad had sold or leased vast holdings to sheepmen just as farmers were beginning to move onto bunchgrass pastures. When John McGregor in 1897 agreed to pay a dollar an acre for 5,389 acres on Rattlesnake Flat in the Big Bend, the land appeared suitable only for sheep grazing. Six years later the Washington State Bureau of Statistics claimed that nearby Ritzville had become "the largest initial shipping point of wheat in the United States." Shortly after receiving a deed for the tract in 1902, John McGregor resold the land to farmers for $31,127, almost six times the purchase price. While selling peripheral lands, the McGregors fenced more than 30,000 acres of excellent range, purchased land scrip and used it "to obtain valuable water rights . . . which made it easier to obtain adjoining land for grazing purposes," and encouraged friends, relatives, and sheepherders to claim strategic homesteads or lease state lands on their behalf.

The McGregor brothers in 1905 incorporated their sheep ranch as the McGregor Land and Livestock Company, developed a variety of enterprises, and began purchasing residences and buildings in what would become the company town of Hooper, Washington. Some modifications were made in the sheep business, including "shed lambing," an innovation that required increased labor but enabled woolgrowers to save even orphaned "bummer" lambs. But many of the improvements in the labor-intensive trade were accidental. The *Shepherd's Journal*, a Chicago paper, in 1910 reported that the McGregor sheep foreman Jock Macrae had noticed two sheep suffering from lupine poisoning:

. . . [he] had a bottle of whisky in his pocket and by way of experiment gave the two sheep a small dose of the liquor. Mr. McGregor laughed at the man's action . . . [but] when the band was taken five miles from where the two stricken sheep were left McGregor's attention was called to the bleating of the two sheep . . . running to join the herd, cured. For years the department of agriculture at Washington, D.C. and the Washington State College have been at a loss to know what to do in the matter. To keep herders from drinking the liquor . . . [McGregor suggested] that a small dose of ammonia mixed with the liquor will have the same effect on the poisoned sheep.

The four officers of the new company began searching for ways to make more productive use of their sheep pastures. More than twenty-three thousand acres of their land were in the rugged, shallow-soiled scablands, but an adjacent ten thousand acres were located on the rolling hills of the Palouse country and had soil forty to a hundred feet in depth. Wheat raising had shown great promise on other portions of the bunchgrass prairie: by 1905 Columbia Plateau farmers were raising more than 25 million bushels of wheat annually, and the region had replaced California as the most important wheat-producing area on the Pacific Slope. The McGregors began the second phase of agricultural development in 1905 when they leased some potentially arable land to tenants and hired crews to break several thousand additional acres of Palouse rangeland. Farmhands on the McGregor ranch and elsewhere on the plateau had to become expert teamsters, for horses and mules were required for every aspect of wheat production, from plowing and seeding to harvest. The first teams used in a newly cultivated area were often small, and the implements homemade and crude. But by 1910 multiple hitches of large teams and large, elaborate farm implements had become a striking feature of this agricultural region, to a degree uncommon in most wheat-producing areas. Because labor was more expensive in this Pacific Slope district than elsewhere and farm sizes were large, from the time the land was first broken, the trend was toward limiting human labor by the use of large teams of horses and mules. Whatever the equipment, farmers always had to struggle to get maximum performance out of their work animals. A Walla Walla farmer, Ernest McCaw, "applied the whip to make lazy mules get up and to teach 'em." Another wheat grower, Carl Penner, claimed: "You couldn't beat the meanness out of 'em. It just don't work. But if you'd treat 'em halfway right and try to pet 'em a little bit and curry 'em nice and give 'em plenty to eat, they soon learned who was boss." Even the elaborate "sidehill" combines had to be modified: the skilled drivers who guided the twenty-seven to forty-four work animals nailed buckets to the side of their seats and filled them with rocks to throw at unruly horses and mules. Penner recalled that some farmers tried using air guns to stimulate their teams, "but the humane society got after 'em."

The sheep pastures were first broken with one-bottom two-horse walking plows—aptly known as foot-burners—but these were quickly superseded by two- and three-bottomed plows pulled by six- and eight-horse teams. The seedbed was first prepared with wooden harrows made of thin slices of railroad ties with spikes driven through them. By World War I, manufactured iron harrows were in common use. McGregor tenants in 1905 stood in wagons and hand broadcasted wheat seed. During the next ten years this technique was replaced first by horse-drawn mechanical seeders and then by drills which dug small furrows and dropped the seed. Several varieties of wheat seed were brought to the semiarid land from Australia, California, Arizona, Kansas, and elsewhere. All these wheats had serious limitations, and the pioneer plant breeder W. J. Spillman of Washington State College began crossbreeding different wheats in hopes of soon developing a hybrid exactly suited to the region. Early hybrid strains were not spectacular, but the Palouse country farmer Girard Clark accurately predicted in 1909 that "in the work of cereal improvement there is no limit to the possibilities, hence no stopping place."

Farmers and scientists generally agreed that the lands left fallow had to be cultivated repeatedly to create a "dust mulch" that would preserve a maximum amount of soil moisture. William McGregor recalled that farmers "mulched the soil up fine and harrowed it to death and let it blow awhile." The "dry farming" enthusiast Hardy W. Campbell traveled to the plateau to promote this style of farming and won the support of several Washington State College scientists. The agronomist Byron Hunter in 1907 told of wheat growers who tilled their fallow land six, eight, and ten times in a single year and concluded: "there is much to commend this method." Wind and water erosion, two consequences of this intensive method of cultivation, soon became evident on scattered portions of the plateau. Ernest McCaw recalled that his father "harrowed that whole place fifteen times one year. Made such a fine mulch, packed right down, but when it rained it run off. Too much workin' ruins the soil." But the soils of most areas of the plateau were deep, and despite some gullies and ditches, the cropland in 1919 averaged more than twenty-three bushels per acre—the highest yield of any region in the United States. Major changes in cultivation did not occur until the 1930s, when the federal government began offering subsidies for soil conservation.

Wheat growers battled weeds, insects, and crop disease with indifferent success. Washington State College scientists talked of walking along railroad tracks and pulling out every Russian thistle imported into the region. But, as *The Ranch* noted in 1904, "The whole Russian army . . . if it were here engaged in destroying this thistle, could hardly exterminate it." The Whitman County commissioners in 1909 passed an ordinance requiring farmers "to pull out mustard and other injurious weeds" in an equally futile attempt to eliminate unwanted plants. During April and May 1917 a hundred farmers and scientists fought to keep "coulee crickets" out of wheat lands of the Big Bend. The Washington State Department of Agriculture reported that "six distinct armies of crickets were encountered, moving as persistently in different directions as an army of soldiers. These were all successfully conquered. It is reported that one army made six successive charges against different portions of a four mile defense line." Farmers were troubled every year by smut, a fungus which caused serious reductions in yield and quality of wheat crops. Of even more concern, however, was the explosive quality of the smut dust. A group of wheat growers in 1909 formed the "Anti-Smut Club of the Inland Empire" but made little progress in the battle against the fungus. During the 1914 harvest season in eastern Washington, three hundred separators had fires, causing a loss of grain and machinery of more than $500,000. The agronomist Ira Cardiff found that harvest crews could limit the fire danger by running a ground wire from the threshing cylinder to the frame of the machine. But the fungus remained unchecked. McGregor Land and Livestock in 1920 reported that "the crop all went to smut," and an estimated 70 to 80 percent of the wheat raised in Washington that season was graded "smutty."

Huge crews of local farmhands, high school boys, and traveling laborers handled harvest work during the years of horse- and mule-powered agriculture. On the McGregor ranch as many as 121 men and 320 work animals were required for the work of heading and threshing the grain. Joe Ashlock, writing in 1919 of his experiences as a "green harvest hand," described his first impressions of the work: "A threshing machine, a hot sun that boils the sweat from you in trickling rivulets, seven bathless, shaveless, soapless days with no clean clothing and your blanket roll getting filthier every day." The crews had to remain attentive and careful throughout the long working days that began when the fireman cleaned the steam engine's flues and kindled a fire at 4 A.M. and ended at 8 P.M. or later. The "forker" had the job of jabbing a Jackson Fork, a heavy steel drag dumping device, into the stack of unthreshed grain. The cable used by one of the McGregor ranch outfits broke when a load of wheat was in midair, sending the prongs of the Jackson Fork completely through the body of the forker, Bruce Barr. He miraculously survived the accident and resumed work a week later. A Big Bend farmhand, Arthur Buhl, remembered cleaning a separator clogged with weeds and hitting his leg against a sharp rod in the cylinder:

I jumped on the ground and I felt something in my shoe. It was blood. My leg was cut clear down to the bone. . . . So the fireman says "I got some turpentine." I said "Well, that will hurt, won't it?" He said "No, if you do it right now it won't hurt." And it didn't. Put that turpentine in there and they had a dirty old shirt and he slapped that round there and you know that never did get sore.

Carl Penner recalled working as a sack sewer: "The first three or four days the blood would just run out of your fingers where you grabbed the sacks." Fred Clemens, the brother of one of the McGregor tenants,

well remember[ed] a certain day when I just turning 16 years, was one of the two sack sewers. . . . We threshed that day a few more than 1800 sacks. Their overall weight was about 120 tons. Each sewer sewed about 900 sacks, throwing about 3600 half-hitch "ear" loops, making well over 8000 stitches, and picking up and carrying to the sack pile over 60 tons of wheat. Without doubt that was the hardest physical day's work I ever performed, before or since.

Each outfit had two cooks who worked in mobile "cook shacks" preparing food for a large crew of hungry workers. Lenora Torgeson remembered cooking sixteen hours a day for sixty-four straight days during one harvest season on the McGregor ranch. Header punchers, hoe downs, header box drivers, separator men, flunkies, and several other employees completed each harvest crew.

During the late twenties and early thirties, Columbia Plateau farmers abandoned their elaborate horse- and mule-powered technology and began using fossil fuel as a source of energy for plowing, harrowing, hauling, and harvesting. Signs of the changing circumstances had been evident since World War I. Threshing outfits had begun replacing steam engines with gasoline threshing machines in order to eliminate water and straw haulers from their crews. Combines became increasingly popular after a gasoline engine was substituted for the cumbersome ground-powered "bull wheel" which had provided power to run the sickle bar and threshing mechanism. The gasoline engine helped make horse-drawn combines maneuverable and eliminated some of the problems of switching to a style of harvesting that required only a third of the laborers of a heading and threshing outfit. But these changes did not alter the major flaw of animal-powered agriculture in a semiarid land: the horses and mules could never complete plowing, harrowing, and seeding work on time. William McGregor remembered that "with horses it took so darned long to get the job done that they would end up plowing in July. By that time the ground was hard as a brick and the weeds and volunteer wheat were knee high."

A few farmers had sold their work animals during the boom years of World War I and bought tractors only to find that the available models were heavy, unwieldy, and difficult to operate. Improved tractors were available in 1925, and as the last of the tenant farmers left the McGregor ranch, the corporation began replacing animal power with internal combustion farm machinery. The three Holt "75's" purchased by the McGregors were primitive by later standards. The Holts tilted dangerously on steep hillsides. They were started by placing a crowbar in the flywheel, pulling, and standing aside as the bar flew into the summer fallow. The Adams County farmer Levi Sutton recalled that the 75s offered the operator his choice of two speeds: "slow and damn slow." With all of its limitations, the Holt was an indication that the days of low-investment wheat farming were doomed. When the McGregor brothers had begun commercial wheat raising in 1905, their "wheat ranch" inventory had been valued at $1,559 and included four-horse cultivators, walking plows, sleighs, a grinder, and a fanning mill. Twenty years later the investment had climbed to $102,371. The McGregors had completed the transformation from mules, horses, and headers to gasoline power by 1930. The last separators and steam engines were gone, and four $5,000, sixty-horse-powered tractors, lighter and more versatile than their predecessors, pulled three new combines over the steep hills of wheat. Maurice McGregor noted in 1928 that "the use of tractors is eliminating men." The wheat ranch payroll books showed a 72 percent decline in the labor force during the years 1927–30. The large crews of traveling harvest laborers were gone, and sixteen men, most of them year-round employees, were used as combine operators, truck drivers, and "Cat skinners" (tractor drivers).

Some of the horses and mules were sold at an auction sale. The remaining old work animals were put to use one final time. When the price of wheat fell from a dollar to thirty-three cents in the early thirties, the McGregors bought carloads of hogs from North Dakota, Minnesota, and Montana and fed them carefully regulated diets of wheat, hay, apples from the McGregor orchards, and slaughtered work horses. An Adams County farmer, Ralph Snyder, recalled that "horses were pretty cheap":

Well, a hog needs protein besides wheat. . . . I'd take an old horse and shoot him out there in the corral and open him up. Then those hogs would eat that thing right out from the inside, bones and all. People would buy my sausage and come by and see those hogs eatin' that darned thing and some of 'em got kinda squeamish. But it was fine protein for 'em and cheap as hell. Oh we used to get a little stuff from the packing house at $30–$40 a ton. But I could get a horse for a dollar a ton, with no freight bill to pay.

Columbia Plateau farmers continued to buy tractors even during the worst years of the Great Depression. Clarence Braden, a salesman for Caterpillar Tractor Company, estimated that during the years 1931–37 he accepted ten thousand horses and mules in trade for tractors in the Walla Walla area and adjacent regions. He sold the animals to loggers and buyers from the South. Braden recalled:

With the horses and mules and the hay it was fairly close to an even trade. . . . It didn't cost farmers a lot of money 'cause they had some awfully nice stock in this country. Most of the horses you'd buy . . . for 30, 40, 50 dollars apiece but if you got ahold of some real first class three or four year old mules, you'd go clear to $175 . . . [but] I found lots of 'em you didn't want at all. Take 'em for $5 and kill 'em for meat.

The speed and reduced labor requirements of the tractors were important advantages even during the depression. Even those farmers who were reluctant to change to gasoline power had little choice when the large crews of experienced harvest hands quit making the long journey to the Pacific Northwest interior in the mid-thirties. "You hated to quit the mules," Carl Penner recalled. "They was just some life. You know you get attached to a mule the same as you do people. . . . But you couldn't get anybody to drive the mules. . . . The Caterpillar came along and you bought a Caterpillar."

Columbia Plateau agriculture changed even more rapidly after World War II, a period Wayne Rasmussen describes as the "Second Agricultural Revolution." Chemists, plant breeders, entomologists, and agronomists all contributed to a tremendous increase in productivity. Some of the most dramatic changes came from the introduction of anhydrous ammonia, a concentrated nitrogen source which became available for farm use when ammunition plants built by the federal government were sold to private chemical companies and converted to fertilizer manufacturing. An additional series of commercially produced chemicals was useful for killing weeds, insects, and fungi. Two USDA scientists in 1947 described one of these products, DDT, as being "effective against a wider variety of agricultural pests than any other synthetic insecticide heretofore tested—and, wonderful to relate, its effect lasts, sometimes as long as a year!" DDT represented a significant advance from the earlier insect sprays—such as arsenic, whale oil, and even ice water—and was the first of many insecticides marketed on the plateau. A selective herbicide, 2,4-D, first marketed in 1945, became the first of hundreds of effective weed killers.

Many scientists and farmers were at first skeptical about the usefulness of the new chemical products for wheat production in a semiarid land. "The use of fertilizers for maintaining soil fertility," a 1948 "Progress Report" issued by Washington State College warned farmers, "is not practical for dryland farming. . . . Since moisture is the limiting factor in crop production the yield is naturally affected very little by the application of fertilizer." The veteran researcher Harley Jacquot disagreed, and when his university funds for fertilizer research were discontinued in 1950, he began a career of almost twenty-five years as full-time agronomist for McGregor Land and Livestock. His work on the McGregor ranch brought dramatic results—his first test plots treated with nitrogen produced fifty and sixty bushels per acre from a land where twenty-five bushels was a long-accepted average. Jacquot's later research verified the conclusion that chemical fertilizers could substantially increase wheat yields. His experiments attracted wide attention, and other farmers had favorable results. Fertilizer use in the region would increase sixfold in sixteen years.

The McGregors began their own farm chemical business in 1948 as a sideline for their general merchandise store in Hooper. At first the store clerks Sherman McGregor and Cliff Rollins merely bought bags of fertilizer and sold them to their neighbors. When anhydrous ammonia became available in 1952, they built a derrick on the back of a truck to haul tanks of the product to the field and added makeshift equipment to a plow to inject the chemical into the ground. Unloading the first rail car of ammonia shipped into the town of Colfax, they mishandled the product, and a fog of ammonia vapor forced the evacuation of an adjacent residential area. McGregor and Rollins finished unloading the tank car late at night and shipped the next car of ammonia to a railroad siding in a sparsely settled area four miles outside of town. The transformation of this business illustrates some of the rapid changes that occurred in the nature of wheat farming. The McGregors developed and manufactured ammonia applicators and herbicide sprayers that were big, wide machines—up to 110 feet in width, with masses of steel: complex systems of tanks, valves, and gauges, and huge airplane tires to prevent the equipment from digging up the loose soils. The chemical business gradually expanded to $35 million in annual sales, and by the seventies, sixteen outlets were built in Columbia Plateau towns, and supply depots for applicator parts were established in Alberta, Saskatchewan, and Manitoba.

Use of commercial fertilizers marked the first step in the improvement of wheat yields. Plant breeders worked to develop new strains of wheat that could make efficient use of agricultural chemicals and fought a never-ending battle to develop new disease-resistant varieties of wheat faster than new fungi appeared. The most promising new wheat was Gaines, a variety developed by O. A. Vogel in 1962 from the progeny of his 1949 crossbreeding of a Japanese "semi-dwarf" wheat with Brevor, a Pacific Northwest variety. The agronomist B. R. Bertramson estimated that during the decade from 1964 to 1974 Gaines brought Pacific Northwest farmers a total additional income of $770 million because of its high-yielding capabilities. Yields in the Palouse country climbed from less than thirty bushels in the 1940s to fifty-three bushels during the years 1965–75.

Changes in farm equipment accompanied the new chemicals and wheat varieties. On the McGregor ranch in 1970, seven men, equipped with three self-propelled air-conditioned combines, a "bankout" wagon (a huge diesel-powered machine similar to an earth mover, which moved with ease over the steep hillsides hauling wheat from the combines to trucks waiting at the edge of the field), and three trucks handled harvest operations which fifty years earlier had required more than a hundred men and three hundred work animals.

But the future of wheat raising had become filled with uncertainties. The productivity of Columbia Plateau farms had become dependent on nitrogen produced from Alaskan and Canadian natural gas, phosphate from Florida and Morocco, and hundreds of pesticides manufactured from petroleum. The Swedes, who had presented Paul Müller of Switzerland with the Nobel Prize for his discovery of DDT, later banned the chemical. DDT was one of several agricultural chemicals to be outlawed in the United States. Despite forty years of soil conservation work, the Palouse region alone lost more than 20 million tons of topsoil into its streams every year. "The worst erosion in the United States," a scientist noted in 1973, "is in the Palouse country."

The livestock businesses of the Columbia Plateau likewise underwent a period of rapid transformation. The number of cattle in the region increased rapidly after 1950. Unlike lambs, most of which became sufficiently fat for market on range feed, the cattle had an intermediate stop at feedlots on their way to the slaughterhouse. McGregor Land and Livestock developed a feedlot operation which was expanded to handle 140,000 cattle per year, with 53,000 head in the pens at any one time. The cattle were fed barley, wheat, alfalfa, cull potatoes, and cannery waste plus a whole series of additives including MGA (which stops the estrus cycle in heifers and thus promotes rapid fattening), oxytetracycline (for prevention of scours), and dimethylophysitoxane (a bloat preventive).

Farming, agricultural chemical sales, and cattle feeding all required specialized machines, synthetic fertilizers and additives, and other capital inputs to increase productivity and displace human labor. Only range sheep production resisted these changes and remained labor intensive. Sheep numbers dropped dramatically, both regionally and nationally, after World War II. The McGregors and other sheepmen hired skilled herders from the Basque provinces of Spain when the shortage of domestic laborers willing to live a lonely life with the flocks became acute. But by the early seventies young Basques were able to get better-paying jobs in factories in Spain than on western ranges. Continued difficulties in finding workers and rapidly increasing expenses caused the McGregors to begin shifting to a low-labor range cattle business. After ninety-seven years of sheep raising, McGregor Land and Livestock made plans to sell the last of their ewes in 1979. Even before the corporation had begun phasing out the sheep, the $300,000 of annual wool and lamb sales had become a minor part of a corporate agribusiness with $79 million in annual sales. The area had changed greatly since 1882 when Archie and Peter McGregor first reconnoitered the region with their bedrolls on their backs. The semiarid sheep pastures had been converted into a land of corporate agribusiness. By closely tending to the welfare of their flocks, the sheepmen built the framework for a diverse and highly productive style of agriculture. The veteran sheepman Emile Morod commented on the McGregor agribusiness: "It all come out of them damned sheep."

BIBLIOGRAPHICAL NOTE

The process of agricultural transformation is explored in further detail, in both text and bibliography, in Alexander Campbell McGregor, *Counting Sheep: From Open Range to Agribusiness on the Columbia Plateau* (Seattle, 1982). Major primary sources for this paper include McGregor family and corporate business records, especially Archie McGregor letters (privately held, Glendale, California), McGregor Land and Livestock files (Washington State University), and corporate records still held by the company in Hooper, Colfax, and Spokane; Northern Pacific Railway Archives (Minnesota Historical Society, St. Paul); trespass suits brought by NPRR against stockmen (Federal Archives and Records Center, Seattle); "Archives" file kept and made available by B. R. Bertramson, Department of Agronomy, WSU; business records of Coffin Sheep Company, Yakima; oral interviews conducted by the writer (particularly those with C. H. Brune, Arthur Buhl, Ralph Snyder, and William McGregor); and taped interviews on file at Whitman College (Carl Penner, Ernest McCaw, and Clarence Braden).

Other sources include the Columbia Plateau livestock journal *Ranche and Range* (*The Ranch*), 1894–1906; *Oregon Agriculturist and Rural Northwest*, 1895–99; F. V. Coville, *Forest Growth and Sheep Grazing in the Cascade Mountains of Oregon*, USDA, Division of Forestry, Bull. 15 (Washington, D.C., 1898); S. A. D. Puter, *Looters of the Public Domain* (1908; rpt. New York, 1972); John Muir, *My First Summer in the Sierra* (Boston, 1911); Frank Andrews, *Marketing Grain and Livestock in the Pacific Coast Region*, USDA, Bureau of Statistics, Bull. 89 (Washington, D.C., 1911); Reynold M. Wik, *Steam Power on the American Farm* (Philadelphia, 1953); M. R. Cooper et al., *The Progress of Farm Mechanization*, USDA, Misc. Pub. 630 (Washington, D.C., 1947); Thomas Keith, *The Horse Interlude: A Pictorial History of Horse and Man in the Inland Northwest* (Moscow, Id., 1976); D. W. Meinig, *The Great Columbia Plain: A Historical Geography, 1805–1910* (Seattle, 1968); Washington Agricultural Experiment Station *Bulletin* nos. 89, 118, 294, 310; Byron Hunter, *Farm Practice in the Columbia Basin Uplands*, USDA, Farmers Bull. 294 (Washington, D.C., 1907); and *Agronomy and Men*, WSU Agronomy Dept., yearbooks of 1958–59, 1961–62, 1965–66, 1967–68.

Old World Paths in the New: Scandinavians Find a Familiar Home in Washington

Jorgen Dahlie

In an article entitled "Beyond the Great Divide: Immigration and the Last Frontier," Moses Rischin presents an analysis of the problems faced by historians of Far West immigration. He argues that much of the recent history of the region has been

so stylized and parochialized that it has come to represent the ultimate in American historical discontinuity. . . . The very rapidity and intensity of change in a region so vast with a population so new and so elusive, so mobile and so diverse, so contemptuous of antecedents and yet so hungry for a past, has made it difficult for the historian to find his bearings.

Moreover, the historian has often compounded his difficulty by affecting to see the immigrant in an idealized social order, one singularly free of the tensions and conflicts that usually characterize the world of the immigrant. Rischin goes on to explain the tendency of the historian to write with a "blind spot":

Presumably, in an area distant from the corrupt older America, the troublesome provincialisms of race, region, religion, and nationality that divided and redivided Europe and nearly destroyed the United States could be happily forgotten. . . . Perhaps it would be best to ignore the immediate pasts of immigrants from all the states and all the source countries so that they might all the more readily become Americans and golden westerners.

Rischin's observations provoke a response. It would seem appropriate to take a closer look at immigration from the point of view of

Originally published in *Pacific Northwest Quarterly,* April 1970.

the ethnic community itself. This I propose to do with the Scandinavians in Washington State. Although this view will necessarily be restricted, it may reveal that the Scandinavians who crossed the Great Divide at the turn of the century wanted very much to become "golden westerners."

Even if this observation remains debatable, however, it should be possible to come away with a clearer understanding of how one group of immigrants reacted simultaneously to the desire for American status and to the pull of deep-seated loyalties to an older tradition. If we look at the ethnic community with reference to select factors in immigration—promotion and settlement, occupational choices, assimilation, or acculturation—we can make some assessment of how instrumental the ethnic group was in shaping its own course of action.

A brief résumé of the statistics will underline the central importance of immigration in the history of Washington State. Between 1890 and 1910 the population of the state increased almost fourfold, with well over 1 million inhabitants counted in the thirteenth census. During the decade ending in 1910, the state's growth rate was six times that of the nation as a whole. Even more remarkable was the extremely large proportion of inhabitants of foreign extraction living within the state—more than 500,000 in 1910.

The native-born American in Washington State was likely to find himself working side by side with Germans, Canadians, Irishmen, Russians, or Austrians. His chance of meeting Scandinavians was exceptionally good: nearly 25 percent of all those of foreign extraction— 123,781—were either Danes, Swedes, or Norwegians. As late as 1910, only two of ten Washington residents had been born in the state, so clearly the immigrants, foreign and domestic, had a decisive voice in the rapid developments taking place during this period.

The immigrants from the Scandinavian countries were largely "second-stage" immigrants, having settled first in large numbers in other states, notably Minnesota, Wisconsin, Illinois, and Iowa. The annual reports of the commissioner-general of immigration over the period 1899 to 1910 show only 24,954 incoming Scandinavians who gave Washington as their destination. Yet, in that same period, the state's Scandinavian population increased by almost 100,000, indicating that many must have made subsequent decisions to relocate in the West.

The Washington-bound immigrants definitely preferred certain localities and occupations. In 1910 nine counties—Chehalis, Island, King, Kitsap, Pierce, Skagit, Snohomish, Spokane, and Whatcom— accounted for 75 percent of all the Scandinavians in the state. Of these, Spokane was the only county east of the Cascades to have a substantial number. Evidently, the immigrants favored areas where native-born Americans were in the minority, a condition existing in seven of the nine counties; the exceptions were Skagit and Spokane. Few Scandinavians were to be found in Asotin, Columbia, and Garfield counties, where native-born Americans composed at least 75 percent of the population. The comparative density of Scandinavians in the total population ranged from a low of 10 percent in Spokane County to a high of 25 percent in Kitsap County.

The concentration of this ethnic group in a well-defined area—west of the Cascades and more specifically in the Puget Sound region—was significant because of the economic opportunities and the subsequent occupations taken up by many Scandinavians. Moreover, it raises an interesting speculation for the historian: did these immigrants merely follow the mainstream of migration, as it were, or were they making a deliberate choice brought about by ethnic "pressures" of one kind or another to settle in the region?

In his study of English immigration to the trans-Mississippi West, Oscar Winther has pointed out just how difficult it is to distinguish among the manifold promotional operations that affect immigration. Nevertheless, a good deal of evidence suggests that the Scandinavians in Washington were especially receptive to inducements by their fellow countrymen. Individual Danes, Swedes, and Norwegians, whether in official, semiofficial, or informal capacities, displayed remarkable energy and enterprise in persuading immigrants to follow their lead. One or two examples must suffice to illustrate how successful they were.

O. B. Iverson, a Snohomish County pioneer, is perhaps exceptional. In 1867 Iverson emigrated to Iowa from his native Hardanger, Norway. During the next decade he served on Indian patrols in Montana, worked as a territorial immigration commissioner in the Dakotas, and in 1876 represented Snohomish County in the territorial assembly. Before he moved to Washington Territory, he had returned to Hardanger to recruit a sizable contingent of Norwegian families to settle in South Dakota.

Iverson then directed his activities toward Washington Territory, which he had visited following an exchange of letters with Governor Elisha P. Ferry. His reaction to the Puget Sound area was one later echoed by many Scandinavians, and no doubt it proved to be a potent "selling point" to prospective settlers. "The jagged summits of the Olympics," he wrote, "now appeared clear and cold, sticking out of the dark, green banks of firs on the foothills. I thought of Norway.

This scene was different, but just as beautiful." Iverson reported that many of the original Dakota settlers moved to Snohomish County in direct response to his efforts.

The story of M. E. Poyesen, also a native of Norway, lends additional credence to the belief that ethnic-inspired promotion may have influenced Scandinavians in their migrations. Poyesen found his version of heaven on earth for the Norwegians in the aptly named Paradise Valley in the Palouse region near Moscow, Idaho. He had settled first in Canada and later moved to Goodhue County, Minnesota, where he resided for fifteen years.

Like Iverson, Poyesen had returned to his homeland to help arrange for the immigration of ninety-seven families, most of whom were destined for Minnesota but were subsequently encouraged by Poyesen to seek the advantages of Paradise Valley. Poyesen's efforts and those of a Pastor Andersen of Genesee, Idaho, are indicative of what could be accomplished by individual promoters capitalizing on intimate knowledge of an area and of the immigrants and, in these instances, working outside the main movement.

Not all of the promotional endeavors were as systematic as those of Iverson and Poyesen. In fact, the spontaneous boostings that appeared with mounting frequency in the foreign-language press were perhaps as effective, especially when such unsolicited testimonials contrasted the splendors of Washington with the harsh realities of life previously experienced in the Midwest.

A typical endorsement was that of the Port Townsend immigrant who told the Tacoma *Tidende* readers that his nationwide wandering had convinced him that "of all the states, Washington is that one best suited to the Scandinavians." It had the climate, the scenic attractions, and the economic opportunities—and, in his words, "the delicious fish" available in Puget Sound.

A Vashon Island farmer recounted that many of his neighbors had come from Illinois, Iowa, and the Dakotas in response to firsthand reports of how well the region suited Scandinavians. The reports were justified, he said, because

when a man comes from the East with nothing, and after 10 years work and thrift has himself a fine little fruit farm, cleared and paid for, or else 3 or 4 milk cows and lives well and in peace, that is the evidence of what one can do.

J. K. Stensrue, a Pierce County immigrant, noted that even if the immigrant were well established, as he had been in Minnesota, the Far West offered better opportunities. He claimed that a farmer in Pierce County could net more money in a year on five acres planted in asparagus than could a farmer with 150 acres in Minnesota!

While the promise of economic gain had its fascination for Scandi-navians, it was not the only enticement for these immigrants. Einar Finsand, who periodically described Scandinavian settlements in the Tacoma *Tidende*, reported that the small town of Fir, "scenically situ-ated on the western bank . . . of the Skagit River," was an exemplary place where Swedes and Norwegians lived and worked in a harmo-nious atmosphere. Here the old-country languages were spoken, the Lutheran church was firmly established, and the newly arrived im-migrant could find a miniature version or replica of the homeland which would make the settling-in process relatively painless. That he would prosper was axiomatic—after all, the immigrant would hardly have been unaware of the promise of America—but it was important to begin where he might have reassurance and the security of his own community.

On occasion, an impassioned description of the special appeal of Washington appeared in print. Peter Nicolaisen, who was fifty years old before he left for America, penned his reactions to the two widely separated regions settled by Scandinavians:

North Dakota is not so bad. True, it has its hailstorms and its blizzards, and . . . it *is* possible to get ahead there. . . . But I, who was born and lived to my fiftieth year along the coast of northern Norway, find it wonderful here in Seattle with the saltwater breezes and the evergreens around Puget Sound, where I can watch the waves and the ships coming and going. . . . As a *Nordlaending* (northerner) it does me good to see ocean, mountain, and forest.

Among the many letters in this vein is one by a newcomer to Seattle and Tacoma who wrote about his previous experience in "North Da-kota's treeless and monotonous flats" and was struck by the resem-blance of Puget Sound to Norway's Romsdalfjord.

From the small community of Jordan on the Stillaguamish River, another immigrant noted that "the land around here reminds one a lot of old Mother Norway. Here are hills and dales, mountains and fjords; along the river are trees and flowers in profusion," and he urged other Scandinavians to settle in the community. A Norwegian who must have been one of the first in the Hood Canal area—he arrived in 1869—told the Tacoma *Tidende* editor that after some thirty years he was still overawed by the scenic beauty of Mount Rainier, Mount Baker, and the Olympic Mountains and had never thought of himself as being in a strange new country.

Added to individual claims put forth by enthusiastic immigrants was the strong voice of the ethnic press, which steadfastly endorsed Washington as the choice area for Scandinavians. There is substantial evidence that most of the Washington weeklies—Tacoma *Tidende*, Tacoma *Tribunen, Washington Posten* (Seattle), *Nya Världen* (Bellingham), *Vestra Posten* (Seattle), and *Svenska Nordvästern* (Spokane)—directly influenced Scandinavian immigration. These newspapers pursued vigorous editorial policies, featured success stories of individual Swedes, Danes, and Norwegians, and provided, in their use of the mother tongue, the element which historian Nils Hasselmo has characterized as being most central to the immigrant's whole experience in a new society.

Spokane's Swedish weekly, *Svenska Nordvästern,* might be taken as a model of how the ethnic press served its particular function for the immigrant. Hans Bergman, the editor, took a lively interest in Spokane County and was energetic in drawing its attractions to the attention of Scandinavians. In a special report entitled "A Great Land," he lauded the natural beauty of Spokane and the Coeur d'Alene area and pointed out that it was uniquely suitable for Swedish settlement. He publicized the achievements of Swedes who had "made good" in the American tradition, and his accounts of Enoch Engdahl and Sven Anderson, remarkable by any standard, must have given Spokane's Swedish community pride and inspiration.

Engdahl, who was born in Dalarne, Sweden, in 1874, left home when he was fifteen to join an uncle in Minneapolis. He worked as a carpenter for 85 cents per day to learn cabinetmaking, which was his father's trade. He volunteered for service during the Spanish-American War. In 1902 he settled in Spokane, where he formed a sash and door company and an investment firm, capitalized for $150,000. Following a visit to Sweden in 1906, Engdahl returned to Spokane to manage the apartment complex and hotel business which he had established.

Sven Anderson's career was perhaps more colorful than Engdahl's. Born in Sweden in 1861, he had received a superior education. In 1880 he immigrated to the United States and subsequently spent seven years in the "Wild West" states of Montana, Wyoming, Colorado, Idaho, Washington, and Oregon. He worked as a mule skinner, ox driver, cowboy, mill hand, prospector, mason, and blacksmith. He claimed—perhaps too modestly—that his adventures would rival any of those James Fenimore Cooper wrote about in his stories of the West! He served a term in the Idaho legislature and worked as a cashier for the First Bank of Troy before moving to Spokane. By 1910 he was a senior officer in the Scandinavian-American Bank of Spokane. Hans Bergman implied that similar opportunities were there for any enterprising immigrant. This theme could be found in all the foreign-language newspapers.

As I have indicated, the configuration of Scandinavian settlement, shaped in large part by ethnic promotion, directed the immigrants into specific occupations. This in turn had considerable importance for the Americanization process, which was linked closely to economic progress. It will be useful here to indicate where the majority of Scandinavians worked and what this meant for them in their striving for full acceptance in American society.

Most Scandinavians were engaged in agriculture, the woods industry, and fishing, with perhaps the majority on the farms. Although complete statistics are unavailable, the Dillingham Commission findings (1907) and the exhaustive study by E. P. Hutchinson, *Immigrants and Their Children, 1850–1950,* show that Norwegians especially, and Swedes to a lesser extent, were firmly committed to farming. This was particularly true in Washington and is supported by a number of other semiofficial sources.

The Dillingham Commission also carried out specialized studies of the woods and fishing industries that give a clear picture of Scandinavian preferences. Based on the commission's data gathered in Oregon as well as in Washington, an estimate of 10,000 Scandinavians employed in Washington's woods industry in 1900 appears reasonable. Significantly, many Norwegians and Swedes took mill jobs as a means of accumulating capital to buy farmland. The commission report, which included studies of forty national groups engaged in the woods industry, showed that, of the total number employed, 25 percent were Scandinavians, and they were three times as numerous as the Japanese, who ranked next. Commission investigations of the fishing industry disclosed that Orientals—Japanese and Chinese—dominated the canning industry, but that Scandinavians were by far the largest group in the Fisherman's Protective Union. The Union had a total membership of 6,775 in 1908, and nearly 3,000 were Scandinavians.

While farms, forest, and sea claimed the allegiance of most Scandinavians, another sizable contingent composed of entrepreneurs, professional men, construction workers, artisans, and unskilled laborers sought the larger urban areas. Increasingly after 1910, the immigrant succeeded in making his mark in Seattle, Tacoma, and other cities. But it was as farmers and in the rural environment that the majority of immigrants worked out their destinies and gained full acceptance in society.

It remains to determine how the ethnic community regarded assimilation and to examine this process in the light of Moses Rischin's warning. To ignore the "immediate past" of immigrants might expose the historian to the charge of "presentism," which Rischin fears, and lead to unwarranted assumptions about how easily Scandinavians became Americans. But there is another side to this argument: the experience of the Scandinavians suggests that their "immediate past" *was* the one element which contributed significantly to rapid Americanization. The reason may be, as Timothy Smith has noted, that the immigrant did not see assimilation exclusively as an Anglo-Saxon project.

A key to the Scandinavians' view of themselves is found in their belief that they were not newcomers to American ways, at least not in Washington. One Swedish editor put it this way:

What our countrymen find is that very few came directly to the west coast. The majority have gone through the beginning experience, or if we can use the everyday expression, their "greenhorn period," in the eastern or midwest states. They speak, if not always correctly, the English language quite easily, and read it with ease. In any question of use and customs they are already Americanized.

The same point was made even more emphatically by Ernst Skarstedt, the Swedish author and historian. Writing about his fellow immigrants in 1908, Skarstedt documented the biographies of 372 prominent Swedes in Seattle, Tacoma, and Spokane. Of these, only 51 had come directly to Washington from Sweden; the rest had served their "apprenticeship" in the American way for periods up to twenty years (or more) in other states. By the time they were established in Washington, they had overcome the major obstacles to acceptance by their fellow Americans.

Histories of typical immigrants confirm the fact that many who gained recognition in their communities had adhered to the traditional American virtues: they were hard-working, thrifty, progressive, practical, and optimistic. Men like John Rudene of La Conner, who had been "behind almost every progressive farm movement" in his area, Nels Peter Sorenson, first president of the Whatcom County Dairymen's Association, Nels Jacobson, bank treasurer and president of the Lynden Creamery, and Charles Anderson, township treasurer and a school board director in Whatcom County—these men were the foreign born who adapted easily to American ways, ready to accept responsibilities and to assume leadership when proffered. They saw themselves as Americans first, Scandinavians second. Paradoxically, this is even more apparent in the context of the vigorous debate on language and culture carried on in the ethnic press.

Scandinavians viewed this debate as essentially an internal matter. The issues to be hammered out in a "family argument" were largely unknown and ignored outside the ethnic community. Although many opinions were expressed and disagreement seemed to attend most discussions, it would be misleading to interpret the debate as indicative of conflict and tension brought about by the clash of alien cultures. In the final analysis the immigrants agreed with the dominant note sounded in their own newspapers, and most would have echoed Hans Bergman's response to his own question:

I want . . . to ask my countrymen to consider this advice: be Swedish; is it practical for Swedish-Americans to follow this advice? I say yes, and maintain that to hold fast to all that is good in our national heritage and to throw out that which is poor, is in the best tradition of the Americans themselves. Live for what is right and proper, be American citizens, take an interest in community affairs—and politics.

Bergman's emphasis on *Svenskheten* (Swedishness) carried a strong admonition to retain the native language as long as possible, but his position was not inflexible. In short order the utilitarian view prevailed, and those "with high hopes and ambitions for this great 'golden land' in the west" were advised to learn English as quickly as possible.

Not surprisingly, the ethnic press consistently singled out as models those Scandinavians who had effectively combined the values in their own heritage with the best American virtues. Scandinavians considered themselves as Americans *and* immigrants. They agreed with the Bellingham immigrant who said, "When it comes to reverence for the Stars and Stripes, to loyalty and patriotism, we take a back seat to no one." But they would have little trouble accepting the other view expressed in this description of the "new" American:

We . . . are no vagabonds. We are immigrants. . . . We uprooted our customs and brought them along with us. We are a transplanting with the roots and all; but the roots are not bare. With the roots comes a richness of homeland origin and it is this homeland's rich soil around our roots that has made our transplanting possible.

BIBLIOGRAPHICAL NOTE

The principal primary sources for this paper are the Scandinavian-language newspapers published in Washington State from the 1890s through first decades of this century. These include Tacoma *Tidende*, Tacoma *Tribunen*, *Washington Posten* (Seattle), *Nya Världen* (Bellingham), *Vestra Posten* (Seattle), *Svenska Nordvästern* (Spokane), and *Western Tribun* (Seattle). Other primary documents are Ernst Skarstedt, *Washington och dess Svenska befolkning* (Seattle, 1908); Hans Bergman, ed., *History of Scandinavians in Tacoma and Pierce County* (Tacoma, 1950); *Abstracts of Reports of the Immigration Commission* (Washington, D.C., 1911); and *Thirteenth Census of the United States, 1910: Population*, Vol. 3 (Washington, D.C., 1913).

Other sources include Lottie Roth, ed., *History of Whatcom County* (Seattle, 1926); O. B. Iversen, "From Prairie to Puget Sound," ed. Sverre Arestad, *Norwegian-American Studies and Records*, Vol. 16 (1950), 91–119; Paul W. Gates, "The Campaign of the Illinois Central Railway for Norwegian and Swedish Immigrants," *Norwegian-American Studies and Records*, Vol. 6 (1934), 66–88; Moses Rischin, "Beyond the Great Divide: Immigration and the Last Frontier," *JAH*, Vol. 55 (1968), 42–53; and Charles M. Gates, "A Historical Sketch of the Economic Development of Washington since Statehood," *PNQ*, Vol. 39 (1948), 214–32.

Harvey Scott's "Cure for Drones": An Oregon Alternative to Public Higher Schools

LEE NASH

The report of the United States commissioner of education for 1900 reads rudely to enlightened Oregonians eighty-five years later. Oregon in that year supported a lone quartet of four-year public high schools, widely scattered at Astoria, Baker, Eugene, and Portland. Of the other forty-four states, only Louisiana and North Carolina had fewer free high schools in proportion to population, and both suffered impediments to educational development unknown in the West.

Historians of the American high school have overlooked Oregon's low standing, and none of their varied explanations for the slow growth of those schools elsewhere speaks to Oregon's condition. Less wealthy states, understandably, postponed public secondary education, yet the indexes of affluence offered by the 1900 census place Oregon high. Thirty-three states ranked below Oregon in the percentage of families owning nonmortgaged homes, and sixteen states had a combined per capita agricultural and manufacturing productivity smaller than Oregon's; yet all supported proportionally more high schools. Rural areas were late in founding schools beyond the grades, we are told, but twenty states with a higher percentage of rural population than Oregon had correspondingly more high schools. The presence of many unprivileged blacks had a negative effect upon educational statistics in the South, and yet no less than fourteen southern and border states outstripped Oregon in number of four-year high schools.

Strange it was that this wealthy western state, settled prominently

Originally published in *Pacific Northwest Quarterly*, April 1973.

by public education–oriented New Englanders, should have boycotted so faithfully the great high school movement that swept the nation in the 1880s and 1890s. The fact is that Oregonians generally had come to accept a unique, sophisticated educational philosophy whose most vocal and visible publicist was Harvey W. Scott, editor of the Portland *Oregonian*. This philosophic alternative became enshrined as local educational gospel by 1880 and, through a series of public debates, policy decisions, and a massive, sustained barrage of editorial evangelism, continued supreme over growing heretical opposition for more than twenty years. Finally, the outworn orthodoxy collapsed in an afternoon, like Holmes's One Hoss Shay, its aging evangel exhausted with his anachronistic burden.

The story of this forgotten alternative deserves the telling as a dramatic expression of frontier individualism and as a corrective supplement to the standard histories of free high schools. Many such accounts, old and new, tend to view the movement with 20–20 hindsight through glasses of rose, as though progress were largely unopposed, inevitable, and to be identified with the forces of truth and righteousness and broadened tax bases. As the single most effective holding action against the high school, Harvey Scott's alternative, in fact, was surprisingly successful in educating Oregon youth, featured logic impeccable, and offers liberal educators of today a wholesome, if terrifying, glimpse of the pit whence their forebears were digged.

The roots of Scott's educational thinking thrust deeply into the pioneering experiences of his youth on two frontiers. Born in Illinois in 1838, he studied the McGuffey readers in a log schoolhouse at irregular intervals. Lessons as lasting were learned from hard farm and sawmill work, stern parental discipline, earnest Presbyterian preaching, and the long files of covered wagons that passed the house daily each spring and summer toward yet newer Wests. At fourteen, an age when later generations were entering free high schools, Harvey spent six months guiding oxen over the Oregon Trail, helping to bury his mother and a brother along the way. In Oregon and Washington territories he helped his father clear three farm sites and worked as logger, mill hand, carpenter, and rail splitter. At the age of a high school senior, he fought Indians in the bitter Yakima War of 1855–56, winning a sergeant's chevrons and an honorable discharge in place of a diploma.

As a muscular, six-foot war veteran, Scott finally felt free to leave home and pursue latent educational ambitions. A few months of elementary training were followed by mostly private studies of Latin and Greek, always interspersed with manual labor, and at twenty-one Scott was admitted to the classical course at Pacific University in

Forest Grove. He found at Pacific able, empathetic professors who had been well educated in the East, and a president, Sidney Harper Marsh, who consciously modeled his young Congregational school after "the ideal New England college." The young frontiersman reveled in the new-found bonanza of mind and spirit and never ceased to marvel at how such a school could mediate between culture and barbarism. Of Pacific University he wrote in 1898:

It would seem that in the curious union of interests between the older East and newer West, between the sons of hereditary culture and the sons of the pioneer, the opposite poles of American life had been brought together. Strangely the sympathy has been perfect; and if there is any other place where the spirit of the best New England breeding has been more perfectly fused with and inspired by the spirit of plain American life, we do not know it.

A pioneer's son who experienced this complex cultural alchemy felt grateful.

As an undergraduate, Harvey continued manual labor much of each year, but now his work included teaching summer schools and helping with the instruction at Pacific University's Tualatin Academy. Persevering over all obstacles, he graduated in 1863 at the age of twenty-five, with the first bachelor of arts degree earned in the Pacific Northwest. Little wonder that one of Scott's favorite quotations was a couplet from Dryden's translation of Virgil:

> The father of our race himself decreed
> that culture should be hard.

Two years later the itinerant farmhand and logger was editor of the foremost journal of the Oregon country, the *Oregonian*, and the triumph of self-reliant individualism was complete.

Indeed, the complex of values associated with the term *individualism* suggests the most basic assumptions underlying Scott's educational views. At least by 1880 he was disturbed at the erosion of self-dependence and the growing menace of socialistic doctrines, and he found frequent occasion in editorials and commencement talks to offer correctives. "Men are forgetting their individuality," he said on one occasion, "are losing the sense of their responsibility; are becoming dependent where formerly they were self-reliant and strong. Duty is becoming a word of literary significance merely." The antidote to these noxious tendencies—and the panacea for success—was disciplined hard work. The abilities and opportunities of men "in the mass" were about the same, Scott stressed, and in the end purposeful industry would always distance the "fitful efforts of great talents." "Boys and girls!" ran a favorite bit of rhetoric, "you've got to work; and your school will help mighty little. The less help you have the stronger you'll be—if there's anything in you." Physical as well as mental labor helped to develop individualism, Scott was certain, and rural schoolchildren with their opportunity to do farm work much of the year thus had the advantage over their city contemporaries.

Industry would bring success, to be sure, but the issue, to the editor, was not merely one of material prosperity or adversity. The spiritual implications were much more central, for the discipline of individualism bred character and equipped man's "higher nature" for fruitful labors in the moral realm. "For, if the obscure and intricate existence of man on this planet has any meaning at all," Scott insisted, "he is placed here as in a training school for his character." He deplored the decline of bracing religious influences, despite his regular promotion of liberal theology, and he considered it tragic that the "trifling levity" of modern textbooks had replaced the earnest moralities of McGuffey. He lamented, too, the tendency of a "materialistic age" to overemphasize science. "Great as modern achievement is in this direction," he asserted, "yet without the guidance of moral science it is nothing, or worse."

One of Scott's deepest convictions was that history revealed steady moral progress in Western man and that the most precious legacy passed to each new generation was the accumulated body of moral principles. Concluding an address on the subject, he declared: "And therefore the education of our race, in the highest sense, consists in and requires the bringing of the conduct of man as an individual, and of man in society, into harmony with the moral law of the universe." Every teacher, he said, should urge upon his students this moral key to history and to life.

If the primary goal of education was to inculcate individualism by building character and mental discipline, Scott reasoned, this would best be served by a restricted curriculum intensively pursued. At the elementary level this meant a solid grounding in English studies, the chief of which was history. Taught as he preferred, history included literature and philosophy, as well as politics and war, and went beyond the nation to cover the Western world from ancient times. From the time he became editor, Scott freely advised grade school principals and teachers on curricula, method, discipline, "illustrative apparatus," textbooks, and administration, and he took paternalistic satisfaction in the growth of enrollment and buildings. From 1901 to 1910, he served as chairman of Oregon's first textbook commission, which selected books for the public schools of the state.

Scott's major educational interests and curricular concerns, however, focused upon secondary and higher schools and the careful study of classical languages and literature. As early as 1872, he was reassuring fellow alumni at Pacific University with a talk on "The Benefits of a Classical Education," and his admiring analysis of those benefits continued throughout his career. He qualified his defense of the classics significantly by advocating them only for a limited few of superior ambition and ability who would truly profit by them. From this aristocracy of intellect would come the leaders of thought and action, those responsible for preserving and extending the culture of their generation. Intimacy with Greece and Rome would provide a discipline and a foundation upon which such leaders should erect a superstructure of modern knowledge and expertise.

As a topic perhaps too delicate to share openly with the readers of a widely circulated daily, Scott's view of this limited, undemocratic function of classical education was seldom explicit in his writings. For courses and activities that threatened to filch time from the humanities, Scott had no sympathy. Political economy was a field in which "quackery runs riot," drama drained students' energies and endangered character, athletics were taboo, and oratory produced hollow, artificial speakers.

Closely tied to Scott's preference for a limited, traditional curriculum was his conviction that the ideal educational agencies were the private academy and, especially, the small private college. The large university laid but a sandy foundation for life with its broad, diluted curricula, its impersonal machinery which allowed lazy students to slide through, and its tendency to attract athletes and rich playboys. Isolated from the world's "violent pulsations," the small college provided friendly soil for the quiet nurture of self-reliance and moral principle. The typical student in such schools had little money and needed to work his way, benefiting much thereby, said Scott, since "this necessary conflict with obstacles is the best of all disciplines."

Harried development officers of Oregon's private colleges, still seeking recognition and support sixty years after Scott's death, might well envy the long generation when the Northwest's leading daily was their advocate against all comers. They might, too, do worse than peruse the *Oregonian* file for ingenious editorial defenses of the small college.

We need, must have, must sustain, these local institutions to create an atmosphere of culture at home. This quality never can be imported. It must be home-made. The agencies that produce it are always local. They issue from our academical centers. They are felt throughout the country inversely as the square of the distance, and this is the reason why I cannot think, as some do, that we have too many of these local colleges.

It was as important to have a college close at hand, said the editor, proving the depth of his conviction by the intimacy of his analogy, as it was to have a nearby newspaper.

For years Scott strongly advocated that Oregon young people attend college in Oregon, this in the face of an increasing tendency among some wealthier families to send their heirs to schools in the East. A commencement address at Portland High School in 1891 gave him an excuse to develop the point:

Every person must fix, or "settle," somewhere. He must get into relations with some portion of mankind, at some particular place, and stay there, if he is to accomplish anything and not make a failure of life. So he should know intimately the dispositions and habits, the mental characteristics, the business and other methods and ways of those among whom he is to live and move. . . . Education at home, therefore, is best. It should be aided as far as possible by travel and observation abroad; but it may be said with certainty that no one has ever succeeded well who did not intimately know his own country—that is, the mind of his own country; and this knowledge can only be had by close association with it during the formative period of his own mind.

Besides all this, Oregon students enjoyed a perspective on life and the world denied their fellows in the East. "Mount Hood is remote and alone," said Scott, drawing metaphorically upon the loftiest of local sanctions, "but from Mount Hood how immense the prospect!"

The editor found means more direct even than promotional editorials to act in behalf of Oregon's private schools. For Bishop Scott Academy, which two of his sons attended, he wrote a handsome recommendation that was published for several years in the Episcopalian school's catalog. For Methodist-backed Portland University, he served as trustee president from its founding, in 1891, until 1898, two years before its collapse. He was much interested in the founding of Reed College, and during the last year of his life, 1909–10, he was consulted frequently by trustees of the new school as far-reaching policy decisions were made.

For his alma mater, Pacific University, Scott was the ideal alumnus, and more. As the first graduate and as the controller of the chief publicity organ for the region from which Pacific University found students and support, he personified a college president's fondest dreams. A year after becoming editor, Scott responded to a plug for Willamette University in the Salem *Statesman* with an article extolling the virtues of Pacific, thus introducing a forty-five-year period when the Forest Grove school was unofficially known as the *Oregonian's* favorite college. Regular editorial notices as well as excellent news coverage attested to this status. The inauguration ceremonies of President W. N. Ferrin in October 1903, for example, were given more than ten full columns, including the top news spot, the entire right-hand column on page one.

Scott also wrote promotional material distributed by the college, recruited students, three times served as alumni president, helped prepare a history of the school, and spoke often on campus. He praised the school with warm affection: "Here, an idea has been steadily at work. It has yielded to no discouragement, been ex-hausted by no toil. . . . From a past whose foundations rest in so earnest devotion, what may not be expected of the future?" He served as a Pacific University trustee for the final decade of his life, 1901 to 1910, the last five years as chairman. A working and a giving trustee, he left a great gap in the Pacific University economy at his death. Sadly surveying possible successors to Scott as chairman, President Ferrin confided to his son, "I wish there were someone available more prominent."

The strength and status of Pacific University at the turn of the cen-tury—and, indeed, of all the private colleges and academies of Ore-gon—are attested by contemporary opinion and by an impressive spate of statistics. In 1909 Pacific was the leading private college in the state and second in academic quality only to the University of Oregon among public institutions, according to a Carnegie Founda-tion official who had made a detailed study. This judgment is con-firmed in the report of the United States commissioner of education for 1910, which shows Pacific leading the private colleges of the state in such significant categories as library holdings and endowment.

With seven private colleges in 1900, not including Portland Univer-sity which succumbed that year, Oregon had the third highest num-ber of such schools of all the forty-five states in proportion to popu-lation. (Tennessee and Kansas ranked first and second.) While this may well have been an uneconomic glutting of the educational mar-ket (two of those schools did not ultimately survive), it seems clear that the private colleges played a significant local role. More Oregon public-school teachers holding the life or state diplomas in 1905 were graduates of private colleges in the state than of all six public higher institutions combined.

As for the private academies in the state, they too were numerous and strong in 1900. Oregon ranked fifth in the nation in the number of four-year academies supported in proportion to population, be-hind four New England states which had long specialized in private preparatory schools. School attendance statistics indicate that Ore-gon's academies filled in nicely for high schools. The state was second in the nation in the percentage of ten- to fourteen-year-olds attending school, and fifth in fifteen- to twenty-year-olds attending. That the

Oregon system of education did not neglect public elementary schools was also confirmed by national statistics; Oregon ranked sixth among the states in the smallest percentage of illiteracy among persons over ten years of age. Of course, it is impossible to estimate precisely Harvey Scott's contribution to this vigorous system of public elementary and private higher schools and to the contrasting anemia of Oregon's free high schools and normal schools. The remarkable fact remains that Oregon's educational status quo mirrored faithfully both Scott's likes and his antipathies.

An integral component of Scott's educational ideal, the part that makes his philosophic package unique, was the role he saw for the *Oregonian* in the cultural instruction of adults. From the time he became editor, still firmly muscled from his own struggles for schooling, he expressed concern for Oregon education. Early in his editorial career, he decided that his paper should provide cultural fare for his pioneer readers, who "were not by any means indifferent to the finer impulses," as he once told a friend. That decision and Scott's personal scholarly inclinations and disciplined lifelong study led him regularly for forty years to write instructive editorial articles on history, literature, philosophy, religion, and education. Highly selective anthologies of his cultural writings were published posthumously in no fewer than nine volumes. Such articles appeared alongside standard editorials on political and economic matters, lending the section variety and verve.

Leading American dailies commonly covered cultural subjects during the late nineteenth century, but in weekly columns by experts with by-lines, not on the editorial page. By placing his articles on that page, Scott was able to control directly the *Oregonian*'s cultural curriculum and to be identified with it. Such were the educational possibilities of an era of personal journalism, when a powerful editor could shape his paper into an extension of his mind and personality. And it all seemed to suggest to a frontier clientele that the life of the mind was at least as significant as material gain or public affairs. Indeed, upon occasion Scott would make this point explicit, as in his address before the Oregon Pioneer Association in 1890:

Just now we are having in Oregon a material development such as we never hitherto have known. It is well; we all rejoice in it, and we all try to promote it; and yet we should not become so fully occupied with it as to overlook the greater importance of the other side of life—that is, right development of thought, feeling, character.

In their best expressions, in fact, cultural and economic development were needful complements each of the other. Scott welcomed transcontinental railroads in part because of the cultural stimulus they would bring.

At Scott's death the Oregon Pioneer Association searched for a means of encapsulating his career and found it: "Mainly he was an instructor," said the pioneers; "tens of thousands were his daily students." Scott's editorial page, declared Frederic G. Young of the University of Oregon, "through the thought and discussion it provoked constituted essentially a folk school." Regular readers, said another admirer, received "a liberal education" in any year.

Scott himself referred increasingly to journalism as "that branch of literature to which is entrusted the education of the popular mind," to the newspaper as an "educational agency" or a "department of education," to the editor as a "public teacher." He also compared the *Oregonian* to his beloved "country colleges." Their cantons of culture throughout the region provided vital local support to his efforts to quicken the intellectual life of the region. So powerful and satisfying an alliance could obviously do without certain kinds of lesser educational efforts, especially public high schools and state-supported normals.

The *Oregonian* greeted the 1869 opening of Portland High School—Oregon's first public secondary school—with a happy enthusiasm that gave no hint of contention to come. Scott, in fact, played no part in the national battle for the legality of free high schools, which was fought and won during the next decade in eastern and midwestern states. He was distracted from educational and even editorial concerns by his appointment as collector of customs (a position he held from 1870 to 1876), by intensive political activities, and by a five-year absence from the *Oregonian* desk. Returning to the paper in 1877, he became increasingly aware of the issues, and during the next year he was ready to assume the leadership of the anti–high school forces in his region.

Early in the campaign, before his aims were fully defined, Scott committed a serious tactical blunder. Concerned with crucial political issues during the 1878 autumn session of the state legislature, he evidently neglected to read the many amendments to the Oregon school law before they came up for vote. They passed routinely, and embedded among them was this single sentence under "Duties of Directors":

To maintain at least six months in each school year, in all districts where the number of persons, between four and twenty years is one thousand, as shown by the clerk's yearly report, a high school, wherein shall be taught in addition to the common English branches, such other branches as the directors of such districts may prescribe.

Having failed to comment in season, Scott could only register his regret at the fait accompli. Thus was destroyed an argument he had used just a few weeks earlier, that the high school was "unknown to the law of our state and of most others."

The law, to be sure, was modest enough, and its only immediate effect was to legalize Portland High School, which was the only four-year public secondary school in the state. No other Oregon town could boast the required population, and only four more school districts had qualified by the time the next Oregon high school bill was passed—in 1901. While the act of 1878 was hardly calculated to promote free high schools, to Scott its passage constituted a step backward before his twenty-year mission had gotten well under way.

Typical of Scott's early fulminations on the high school—it could be called his keynote article—is the "Cure for Drones" editorial of April 16, 1879. The piece began with a long case study of a poor Pennsylvania family whose several boys attended high school and became drones in society, unable to find white collar employment and unwilling to do manual labor. It was a typical case, Scott was sure, and it confirmed his conviction that "the only republican idea in public education is to teach people enough to take care of themselves and to keep out of jail."

Since most of mankind was destined for industrial, manual work, the public interest was violated if people were overeducated and made dissatisfied with their lot. Scott declared, in conclusion:

Give every child a good common school English education at public expense, and then stop. There have been two presidents of the United States who received less aid than this in their school education; if any want more, let those who dance pay the fiddler. This is the cure for drones. It is the way, too, to make the public schools a public blessing, instead of allowing them to develop into nurseries of imbecility and idleness.

In later years Scott would refine his concept of state responsibility for education to mean primarily education for citizenship.

The *Oregonian's* periodic editorial thrusts at the high school during 1878 and 1879 kept the issue alive and enabled the editor to test and mobilize his armaments against a favorable opportunity for an all-out offensive. A depressed economy during the 1870s combined with increasing taxes late in the decade to give many citizens itching ears for Scott's preachments. Portland's several private secondary schools, feeling the pressures of subsidized competition, drifted with their constituencies to his camp.

The stage for effective combat seemed set in early February 1880, with the annual school meeting and election a month away. Few could have suspected that Scott's editorial polemic on February 9 was but the opening blast of an intensive crusade that would see thirty-one editorials and nearly twenty thousand words within the next twenty-nine days bombarding the schools from every angle. Early in the crusade the high school emerged as the bête noire that must be destroyed by citizen vote at the open school meeting on March 1. Then the election of a conservative director at the polls on March 8 would complete the business.

Scott marshaled his arguments skillfully, producing fresh recruits to reinforce the old and sending them by waves into battle throughout the month. One must plumb the historical literature of the high school deeply to find points he missed, and some of his arguments seem original. A free ride through high school was "one of the most powerful promoters of communism that could be devised," since it disqualified youth from useful labor and created a class of lazy malcontents. Higher education was scarcely ever beneficial unless earned by one's own exertions.

Emphasis on secondary education, moreover, was corrupting the elementary schools by pressing them to expand curricula under the assumption that all pupils would go on to high school, when, in reality, only 5 percent continued. The secondary curriculum with its foreign languages, higher mathematics, and science was impractical for most and an improper tax expenditure. The high school, in short, was an "aristocratic excrescence," supported by all but attended by few—the children of the wealthy who could afford to keep their sons and daughters in leisure. To let this "class school" live would open the way for the further development of public education, since every argument in favor of the high school applied equally to universities and professional schools. "If we stop at the city high school," he insisted, "we have done too much or too little."

Such charges invited replies. The most effective response came from the widely respected Oregon pioneer educator, the Reverend George H. Atkinson, who became the man of the hour. Using the exact words in one of Scott's summarizing editorials, Atkinson broke down the charges into five counts, laid a sound rationale for investigating and evaluating each, and proposed that Scott's charges be made the basis of a thorough, impartial examination of the public schools. Scott was unenthusiastic about an investigation, since it would delay action on the high school and dissipate the effect of his whirlwind campaign, but he could hardly block it. The school meeting officially commissioned Atkinson's committee, with him as chairman. Taxpayers at the meeting repeated their docile habit of approving the tax requested by the city superintendent of schools and the directors without questioning the figures.

A week later, though Scott's editorial barrage was unabated, in a school election described as "the most exciting ever held in this city" with six times the turnout of the preceding year, the *Oregonian*'s conservative candidate lost by a decisive margin. The next day Scott valiantly professed to be "encouraged" by voter support, but his disappointment must have been keen. It remained only for Atkinson's committee to return a verdict favorable to the school system, and Scott's designs would be thoroughly scotched for that year.

The report read before the adjourned school meeting the following July was a spirited rebuttal of Scott's criticisms, recommending only that tuition be charged for French, German, and Latin courses. The editor might have found short solace in this concession to his conviction that the high school was not the proper institution to instruct in the linguistic skills necessary for college entrance. But the high school, nonetheless, was soundly affirmed as an essential part of public education.

Portland High School was rescued, and never again was Scott to attempt a local campaign on so massive a scale. If he could not turn back the clock, however, he could help to keep it running slow. His continued relations with the high school could be described as a sort of wary truce, for he recurred regularly to his arguments of 1880 and especially to his criticisms of the Portland school "machine." This "artificial, costly, and elaborate system" was created and controlled by "professionals," one of whose ignoble goals was the maintenance and expansion of the high school. They were obsessed, also, with picayune regulations, attendance and promptness statistics, and growing budgets. Scott considered the power, intricacy, and expense of the statewide educational organization to be similarly monstrous, and in 1895 he offered his solution: "The office of state superintendent ought to be abolished. We should not be content merely to hack the limbs; we should first hew the head off."

During the 1890s Scott concentrated his anti–high school efforts on blocking a more liberal high school bill in successive state legislative sessions. Agitation had long been growing for such a bill, and a legislative committee charged with codifying Oregon school laws in 1897 took opportunity to incorporate a section providing for the creation of high schools throughout the state. Learning that the committee report with its impious clause was to come before the 1899 session, Scott sent his most trusted editorial associate, Alfred Holman, to Salem with orders "to do what he could to head off legislation looking toward the extension of public education beyond the elementary grades." Holman's lobbying and Scott's editorial support proved a persuasive team. William Kuykendall, chairman of the education committee in the legislature and leading spokesman for high school legislation, said of the session: "Every move we made in the direction of high school legislation seemed to be blocked."

When the legislature next convened, in January 1901, Kuykendall introduced a revised school code, having sugarcoated its high school clause to provide only for "grades above the eighth grade," hoping thus to forestall the opposition of two years earlier. The bill had experienced no difficulty by January 21, when Harvey Scott strode into the senate chamber and accepted an honorary seat within the bar. Full of foreboding, Kuykendall drew the editor aside for a talk on educational matters. Recalling that conversation twenty-one years later, the former senator said:

He told me that he still held the opinion that the state had no business providing for education beyond the elementary grades. "But," said he, "I am an old man now and I am not going to fight you any longer. Free high schools are coming and I shall cease to oppose them!"

Ready for just such a happy emergency, Kuykendall two days later introduced a comprehensive bill providing fully for the support and organization of district and county high schools. It passed both houses with negligible opposition. That Scott could have postponed such legislation for at least one biennium is certain. It is clear, too, that he had been fighting a delaying action at best and that carrying his crusade against free high schools into the twentieth century would have become more and more painfully anachronistic.

J. H. Ackerman, new state superintendent of schools, had been conducting in public and private an aggressive campaign for high schools. The 30 percent increase in Oregon population between 1890 and 1900 was in large part the result of an influx of progressive easterners accustomed to public high schools. The immigration promised to increase during the next decade, and communities began to see the promotional advantages of a public high school in attracting their share of the newcomers.

Scott could not for long have prevailed against such pressures, and at last he permitted himself to read the unwelcome handwriting of judgment. Before his death in 1910, Scott was to see Oregon pass other laws favorable to public secondary education and establish more than twenty times as many four-year high schools as the state had at the century's turn. No other state approached Oregon's percentage of increase during that decade.

State patriotism and federal land subsidies led Scott generally to favor the University of Oregon in Eugene and Oregon State Agricultural College in Corvallis, though with many others he long advocated their merger. The four church-related academies and colleges that were officially designated state normal schools in the 1880s, however, were an entirely different matter. As they sought and received increasing state appropriations, Scott gave them the lash of his anti–high school arguments and developed new ones just for them. State support for higher education, he stormed, "ought not to be peddled about to every starvling sectarian academy in the land," which would do a bad job of educating teachers anyway. "School-made teachers," said the self-made man, "are often just such practical failures as school-made editors."

With their nonstrategic locations—Ashland, Monmouth, Drain, and Weston—small enrollments, dubious standards, and reputation for political logrolling, the normal schools were vulnerable to Scott's biennial condemnations. In 1905 the normals obtained their appropriations only after waiting a year for a referendum vote, and in 1907 and 1909 opposition had so grown that no support was given. The normal school at Drain closed in 1907. Ashland and Weston shut down with two months left in the 1908–1909 school year; salaries were unpaid; seniors did not graduate. Monmouth hung on until the end of the year and then suspended. Direct responsibility for the death of the normal schools was attributed by their historian and by contemporaries jointly to Jay Boerman, president of the state senate, and to Harvey Scott. During the last year of the editor's life, Oregon had no normal schools.

These negative monuments to Harvey Scott's educational philosophy—four lonely high schools in 1900; four slain normal schools in 1910—have been considered the primary symbols of that philosophy by the few local historians who have studied the matter. One of the most persistent of American cultural convictions has been faith in the public schools—as the partner of democracy, the catalyst in the melting pot, the panacea for all social ills. A man who attacked the accepted natural extensions of this great system was obviously "disputing the passage" with progress. When that man's powers and circumstances were such that he could significantly arrest public educational development in his area, he was certain to be charged with a special species of un-American reactionary villainy.

But understanding is a higher goal than judgment and requires that Scott's educational accomplishments be thrown into the balance. It is true that his powerful ego and superior intellect led him to overgeneralize from his own dramatic success and to expect too much of lesser men in more competitive times. It is true that he insulated himself and his readers from the impressive case for free higher schools in a changing society, a case that was widely prevalent after 1880. But his philosophy was logical, and his program effective; they proved indeed to be a positive cultural achievement, a viable educational option. Scott's militant momentum, his culturally rich *Oregonian*, and a disciplined corps of veteran local supporters brought that option across the frontier of the twentieth century as a vigorous, isolated salient. Past stood in striking juxtaposition to present, and the contrast offered, and still offers, rare opportunity for comparative analysis by students of American culture.

BIBLIOGRAPHICAL NOTE

Primary sources undergirding this paper include regional newspapers, especially the Portland *Oregonian*; Scott family papers, in possession of Harvey W. Scott, Portland, Oregon; Pacific University Archives, Forest Grove, Oregon; seventh annual report of the superintendent of Portland public schools (1880); fourteenth biennial report of the Oregon superintendent of public instruction (1900); laws and legislative journals of the state of Oregon for 1878, 1901, and 1909; reports of the U.S. commissioner of education for 1899–1900 and 1910; Twelfth Census of the U.S. (1900); and *Transactions* of the Oregon Pioneer Association for 1886, 1890, and 1913.

Secondary sources include general and regional histories of American public education, especially Edward A. Krug, *Shaping of the American High School* (New York, 1964); Theodore R. Sizer, *Secondary Schools at the Turn of the Century* (New Haven, 1964); Elmer Ellsworth Brown, *Making of Our Middle Schools* (New York, 1903); Ellwood Patterson Cubberly, *Public Education in the United States* (New York, 1919); Rush Welter, *Popular Education and Democratic Thought in America* (New York, 1962); Henry J. Perkinson, *The Imperfect Panacea: American Faith in Education, 1865–1965* (New York, 1968); and W. Carson Ryan et al., eds., *Secondary Education in the South* (Chapel Hill, 1946); plus several theses and articles in the *Oregon Historical Quarterly*, *History of Education Quarterly*, and *American Quarterly*.

The Seattle Ladies Musical Club, 1890–1930

KAREN J. BLAIR

"Everybody knows America wouldn't have any music if it weren't for women," observed the internationally renowned pianist Harold Bauer in 1924.[1] His remark saluted the phenomenon of women's music clubs, which blossomed in the United States from 1900–1930, and it held a large measure of truth. In thousands of communities during the early twentieth century, women founded and sustained amateur clubs that exhibited an impressive range of musical strengths and achievements.

On the verge of their long-awaited enfranchisement, women developed broad visions of their full participation in society. They dreamed of a world in which their equality would soar beyond the political arena. Many also determined that the richer offerings of civilization, like classical music, would be accessible not just to the wealthy, but to everyone. Women's music clubs became one vehicle for forwarding these aspirations.

Excluded from the male-dominated mainstream of musical performance and composition, women in the late nineteenth century began to form separate music associations of their own. Initially, these groups served to maintain and expand the musical knowledge and skills of women who, though trained in music in their youth, devoted the bulk of their days to running households and rearing families. The clubs soon came to embrace two additional important functions. The first of these was to assist the professional development of women performers and composers. To this end, the all-women's groups established music scholarships for girls, created opportunities for performances of new and old works, sponsored the MacDowell Colony for creative artists, and supported women's orchestras. A second, civic-minded function, which became more prominent after World War I, was to build a nation in which every citizen could enjoy fine music. Working toward that goal, clubwomen brought artists of international reputation to perform in their towns and successfully fostered music education for immigrants in settlement houses and for youth in schools. Less obviously feminist in character, this second function strengthened the public role of women; more subtly, its progressive thrust challenged the elitist priorities of the male musical establishment.

The Ladies Musical Club of Seattle (LMC) is representative of the music clubs that grew and developed in America during the early twentieth century. The organization, which functions to this day, was formed in 1891, when twenty-four women, all musically trained in their youth, met at the home of Mrs. Ellen Bartlett Bacon. Their collaboration was "for the purpose of developing the musical talent of [the] members, and stimulating musical interest in Seattle."[2]

Like most of their counterparts elsewhere in the country, early members of the LMC were middle class and white. Most of the charter members and subsequent participants appear to have been leisured women, married to prominent professionals or businessmen in the community. Among them were the wives of Moses Gottstein, president of Gottstein Furniture Company; John C. Moore, physician; Gustov Schultz, druggist; Mitchell Gilliam, judge; W. D. Chandler, day editor of the Seattle *Times;* William Hickman Moore, city councilman; A. S. Hansen, accountant for the Hansen Baking Company; and Frank Van Tuyl, president of the Black Gold Channel Mining Company. They were women who had forsaken their early musical background, usually in piano or voice, for marriage, child rearing, and participation in Seattle's social, charity, and study clubs. Some, like the German-born pianist Martha Blanka Churchill, were experienced artists, anxious to maintain their facility. The daughter of a professor at the Hamburg Conservatory, Blanka had studied with Franz Liszt and performed internationally. It was while on concert tour in America that she met Frederick A. Churchill, a physician, and retired to make her home with him in Seattle. Rose Morganstern Gottstein had studied voice and sang at weddings in the city's churches. However, her husband, two sons, participation in the Temple de Hirsh, and volunteer work at the Children's Orthopedic Hospital demanded much of her attention, according to her grandniece, Mary McCarthy, in *Memories of a Catholic Girlhood.*

Other members made determined efforts to advance their professional careers, insofar as they were able. Mary Carr Moore blossomed as a composer after arriving in Seattle with her physician-husband in 1901. In 1912, she presented to the public her four-act grand opera,

Narcissa, the story of the early Pacific Northwest missionary Narcissa Whitman. Other working composers in the club included Kate Gilmore Black, wife of an Alaska Fish Company vice-president and organist at Westminster Presbyterian Church. Amy Worth directed the Women's University Club Chorus for twenty-five years and published thirty songs, including one recorded by Lotte Lehman. Daisy Wood Hildreth, whose husband was a salesman at Frederick and Nelson department store, also published her compositions.

Clara Hartle, who had studied voice in Chicago, came to the city when she married in 1904. For four decades, until her death, she instructed students, directed the University Methodist Church choir, and adapted fifteen operas to present in lecture-recital form to audiences all over the state. Cecilia Augsburg developed arts management skills through her LMC music circle. She had studied piano with Emil Liebling in Chicago and then headed the piano department of Kansas State Agricultural College. Having fallen in love with Seattle while performing on a concert tour, she settled in the city as a piano teacher. Her marriage to the druggist Gustov Schultz did not prevent her from becoming a concert manager of the Seattle Symphony Orchestra once she had proven herself as an impresario for the Seattle Musical Art Society.

In any given year, the LMC membership list also contained a handful of names of single women who made music their profession. Most, like Nellie Beach, Fidelia Birgess, Anna Grant Dall, and Leone E. Langdon, supported themselves as music teachers. Nellie Cornish founded a school for all the arts in 1914, known still as the Cornish Institute. She tapped the expertise of Martha Graham, Merce Cunningham, Mark Tobey, John Cage, and the wave of White Russians fleeing their country in 1917 to provide first-rate instruction for her pupils.

Others of the unmarried members were students, like Alice B. Toklas, who took her piano degree at the University of Washington's Conservatory in 1895, before her move to Paris and association with Gertrude Stein. Lillian Miller served as president of the LMC for a few months in 1900, but left for New York as soon as the opportunity arose to study composition with Edward MacDowell, the American composer.

The LMC never lacked for women eager to audition, by invitation only; membership conferred the privilege of paying dues and attending the monthly meetings from October to May. The club's serious attention to music in a community full of fervid women kept its lists full. By 1905, there were 98 active members; by 1916, 150; by 1921, 158; by 1932, 177. The group offered unique benefits to its own musicians, since the primary purpose of the association was performance by the members. If the constraints of the day prohibited a concert career for married women, at least members could maintain their skills by playing or singing for each other at meetings in each other's parlors. They were not only permitted but expected to perform regularly, alone, in duets, trios, string quartets (1922–27), other chamber groups, or in chorus (1913–22). Anticipating cases of stage fright, the early rules stated that "an active member who refuses to perform at the club concerts during six months, will forfeit her membership, unless her refusal has been caused by some reason considered adequate by the Executive Committee."[3]

Club members who were composers, as well as those who were performers, enjoyed regular hearings. Entire meetings devoted to Seattle compositions assured an airing of such works as "I Know Not Why," by Lillian Miller, "Oh Wind from the Golden Gate" for women's chorus by Mary Carr Moore, "Nocturne" and "Mazurka" for piano by Kate Gilmore Black, and songs by Amy Worth. This feature of club life was crucial for the growth of women composers, who in Seattle and elsewhere enjoyed few such opportunities outside the clubs. In this capacity, women's clubs demonstrated their ability to provide a service to women that remained unmet by any other institution in society.

Western classics of the nineteenth century were popular choices for club performers, with Schubert, Beethoven, Wagner, and Tchaikovsky providing the staples. The women did not shy from contemporary music, however, and recent works by English (Elgar), American (Grainger), French (Debussy, Ravel, Saint-Saëns), and Russian composers (Rachmaninov, Borodin), were regularly performed. The newest atonal music, championed by Claire Reis and her League of Composers, was, however, generally ignored by clubwomen, as it was by the musical establishment of the day.

Perhaps surprisingly, LMC members defied general assumptions about European supremacy in music. They broke tradition in their support of American music, performing works by Edward MacDowell, Mrs. H. H. A. Beach, and Louis Gottschalk with regularity. In addition, they pioneered in collecting, analyzing, and listening to native folk music, especially Native American songs and Negro spirituals. This effort brought new respect to an unrecognized American musical heritage. In papers they prepared for their meetings and at conferences, they tapped the scholarship of women anthropologists like Alice Cunningham Fletcher, Frances Densmore, and Nelle Richmond McCurdy Eberhart who were collecting and publishing the music of North American Indians. Likewise, they turned to Natalie Curtis Burlin for lyrics and musical notation of plantation songs.

A notable exception to their commitment to native music was the ban by women's clubs on popular music, especially jazz, even when its elements were wedded to classical forms, as in *Rhapsody in Blue* by George Gershwin. Rejection of popular music served to symbolize opposition to a whole wave of new post–World War I freedoms that clubwomen perceived as shocking. The behavior of young single women, openly smoking, drinking, dancing, and traveling with men in automobiles alarmed many adults. In Seattle, Cecilia Augsberger and other educators damned jazz as a "menace in the community." Clubwomen throughout the nation criticized the sensuous rhythms, dissonances, and incendiary lyrics of popular music for their corrupting influences. Some hoped that the permissiveness of the age might be checked by offering classical music as an antidote. Among Montana clubwomen, for instance, it was said that classics might replace that which was so "inexcusably worthless."[4]

But clubwomen did not espouse classical music solely as a means of subduing popular culture. Long before the advent of the jazz age, they were inspired by the positive idea of bringing the joy and knowledge of music to a wider public. They began by seeking to involve nonmembers in their programs. At first, they simply desired larger audiences for their own performances at club meetings. A member's satisfaction from effort spent on polishing pieces would be greater if she could reach beyond her immediate circle to play for a sizable crowd. Thus, the LMC, like its counterparts all over the country, began to permit "associate members" to attend a special monthly concert—October to May—for a fee, often slightly higher than official dues. Associates tended to be friends and relatives of club members, male as well as female; some associates were music lovers who lacked the talent, training, or courage to perform in public. Numbers of associates at the LMC grew from 217 in 1905, to 266 in 1916, to 360 in 1921, although only a small percentage of the associates actually attended each concert. For these eight occasions, the club required facilities more spacious than homes of participants. Therefore, the LMC rented halls and rooms—at the DAR, Plymouth Church, Unitarian Church, YMCA (1907–13), YWCA (1913–23), Women's University Club (1923–24), Olympic Hotel (the ballroom, 1925–44), Woman's Century Club (1944–60), and Seattle Public Library (1960–present).

Members did not long confine performance of their work to the closed club meetings and special concerts, but soon grew ambitious for wider exposure. They shared their work with other clubwomen in the region, performing, for example, at the Woman's Century Club Arts and Crafts Exposition held in 1906, and bringing their music to the meetings of other societies and conventions as well. An especially gala event for the LMC was the world premiere of *Narcissa*, by Mary Carr Moore, based on a libretto by her mother, Sara Pratt Carr. Moore engaged a tenor and a soprano from the New York Metropolitan Opera and selected seventy local singers for her cast. Among them, naturally, were a great many women from the club, who performed in the chorus and as principals. The first grand opera ever composed and conducted by an American woman, *Narcissa* was produced at the Moore Theater in downtown Seattle in April 1912, winning critical acclaim that brought great satisfaction to members of the LMC.

Anxious to forward the musical growth of its members, the LMC also took seriously its additional goal of bringing good music to the Seattle community. To this end, the women imported the finest talents of the day to the far northwest corner of the nation. One of their major contributions to Seattle's cultural life was the establishment of a concert series that scheduled performances by four renowned recitalists each year. This plan originated in 1901, after the pianist Fannie Bloomfield Zeisler canceled her engagement in Seattle, discouraged by reports of the small turnouts at other classical concerts. A disappointed Rose Gottstein suggested that the club might assure some outstanding performances by guaranteeing the fee of the artist and then recouping the investment through a vigorous ticket sales campaign. Thus Gottstein, acting for the LMC, became Seattle's foremost impresario of classical music events. For nearly forty years, until her death in 1939, she made an annual visit to New York City's concert managers, armed with a purse of at least twenty thousand dollars, and secured four top artists of the concert stage for Seattle engagements. No wonder one local newspaper reporter cheered, "Folks, Meet Mrs. Gottstein: Puts Us on Music Map."[9] This work she did as a labor of love, receiving no payment but an autographed photograph from each performer she introduced. In thanks, the club presented her favorite charity, the Children's Orthopedic Hospital, with a two hundred–dollar donation each year. Upon her death, the group also purchased a hospital bed in her honor, for five thousand dollars. It was a small price in view of the stellar talents she brought to the city.

Thanks to this series, the inhabitants of a remote city could count on regular exposure to the best-known virtuoso performers the world could offer. In the first decade, the club sponsored Fritz Kreisler, Josef Hofmann, and Harold Bauer. Twice, Walter Damrosch conducted the New York Symphony Orchestra with a sixty-member chorus that included vocalists from the Ladies Musical Club. Later, Jascha Heifetz, Sergei Rachmaninov, Pablo Casals, Lotte Lehmann, Yehudi Menuhin, Ignace Paderewski, Artur Rubinstein, Vladimir Horowitz, Rosa Ponselle, Efrem Zimbalist, Mischa Elman, and José Iturbi—a veritable *Who's Who* of international pianists, violinists, and singers—came to serenade the city.

Not surprisingly, the LMC felt a special responsibility to bring women to the stage. During the early years especially, a significant number of the professionals—eighteen of forty-seven—were female. Among the first were the Venezuelan pianist Teresa Carreño, the soprano Lillian Nordica, the contralto Ernestine Schumann-Heink, the singer Geraldine Farrar, and, to rectify past disappointments, Fannie Bloomfield Zeisler.

The prominence of such individual women performers did not mislead women into supposing that their sex had gained a firm footing in the male musical establishment. Male performers, orchestra conductors, critics, and teachers persisted in the view expressed by the writer Anthony M. Ludovici that "woman can at best make only an inferior display, even if she make any display at all."[6] In the orchestral world this attitude was rigid, causing the social critic and feminist Suzanne La Follette, in the 1920s, to rail against "the prejudice of male musicians . . . effective enough to exclude [women] from the personnel of our important orchestras."[7] Sir Thomas Beecham, conductor of the London and Seattle symphonies, summed up the inability of male musicians to take female colleagues seriously.

I do not like, and never will, the association of men and women in orchestras and other instrumental combinations. . . . My spirit is torn all the time between a natural inclination to let myself go and the depressing thought that I must behave like a gentleman. I have been unable to avoid noticing that the presence of a half-dozen good looking women in the orchestra is a distinctly distracting factor. As a member of the orchestra once said to me, "If she is attractive, I can't play with her; if she is not, I won't."[8]

Of similar mind, José Iturbi refused to accept female graduates of the Eastman School of Music in the Rochester Symphony, which he conducted. Only a handful of women, usually harpists, managed to win places in symphony orchestras, until the Cleveland Orchestra admitted a few female musicians in 1923, and San Francisco four violinists and a cellist in 1925.[9] These steps, however, did not constitute a trend, and integration was slight until the 1970s.

Clubwomen sought to counter the exclusion of women from the musical mainstream in several ways. In 1913, the LMC began awarding music scholarships to girls, on the grounds that financial resources tended to be unavailable to them. In 1920, the club initiated an interest-free loan program for promising beginners, and it also aided students at the Cornish School. When women performers, barred from established symphonies, formed their own separate orchestras, women's music clubs everywhere sprang to their support, contributing money, selling tickets, filling concert halls, inviting them to play at their meetings and conventions, and publishing regular reports on their tours and critical triumphs.

The first of these all-women's orchestras, founded in Boston in 1888, was the Fadettes, named for a protagonist in George Sand's novel, *La Petite Fadette*. By 1920, they had performed six thousand enthusiastically received concerts all over North America. Dozens of other orchestras of women playing classical repertoire—in Salt Lake City, Chicago, Philadelphia, Los Angeles, New York, Minneapolis— were founded in the first third of the century and adopted by women's music clubs.[10]

The interest of clubwomen was not confined to women in the performing arts. They saw the importance of supporting women creators as well as performers. Not surprisingly, then, music clubs became financial backers of the MacDowell Colony in Peterborough, New Hampshire, a haven for composers, but also for writers, painters, and sculptors in need of solitude, work space, inexpensive room and board, and prepared meals. The colony was a project undertaken by Marian Nevins MacDowell, a German-trained pianist, upon the death of her husband in 1908. To fund the colony, she embarked upon a forty-nine-year career of regular concert tours to women's clubs and conventions, publicizing her dream of establishing a retreat "where working conditions most favorable to the production of enduring works of imagination shall be provided for creative artists."[11]

Marian MacDowell sought respect, enthusiasm, and money for her colony from the entire spectrum of American clubwomen. In return, she provided over 50 percent of the colony's facilities to creative American women, thereby forging a bond with clubwomen and winning their loyalty and firm support. MacDowell clubs sprang up all over the country. In Seattle, as elsewhere, women's music clubs named Marian MacDowell an honorary member, giving her not only their commendations but also their financial support. Funds from Seattle organizations like the Music Art Society, MacDowell Colony League, and Alpha Chi Omega helped sustain the colony, which still operates today. As long as Marian MacDowell maintained control, the bulk of colony awards went to women. Oddly enough, women working in arts other than music received the lion's share of awards and, later, of recognition. Nevertheless, a significant percentage of colony money continued to come from women's music clubs.

In their support of the MacDowell Colony, as in numerous other projects, music club women made common cause with other American clubwomen. Yet despite their history of encouraging women's abilities and influence, the music clubs had often been at odds with the general movement for women's rights. The turn of the century had seen steady efforts by women to win themselves the vote and find other avenues to political influence; to gain entry into trade unions, schools of higher education, and the professions; and to shape an American future that guaranteed democratic participation by all citizens. Many advocates of these goals discouraged attention to the arts, believing this arena incompatible with the rebuilding of society. Leaders of the politically moderate but powerful General Federation of Women's Clubs, for instance, disdained artistic endeavors, while revering civic reform. "Dante is dead," proclaimed President Sara Platt Decker at the turn of the century,[12] imploring her middle-class, leisured white constituency of half a million members to leave their poetry and pianos in order to lobby Congress for streetlights, public libraries, and child labor laws. Her agenda held no place for women's efforts to reform the cultural life of the nation.

It was the first World War that nurtured the already existing civic strain in the women of music clubs and led eventually to their increasing interest in the democratization of the arts. Patriotic community sings during the war stimulated pride in American songs. In every locale, Liberty Choruses formed in 1918 to lead citizens in public renditions of "Over There," "Swanee River," "A Long, Long Trail," and the national anthem. Huge, enthusiastic audiences filled theaters, halls, and churches; eventually, Chautauqua tents and outdoor sites were needed to accommodate these gatherings. The fervent response to American songs led clubwomen to appreciate the importance of cultivating the indigenous musical heritage and to seize the opportunity to extend the benefits of music to a far broader population than they had heretofore touched.

Although the strong anti-German feelings that swept the wartime nation caused some clubwomen to banish German compositions from their programs for the duration of the fighting, most desisted from such extreme measures. The war, nevertheless, caused them to reevaluate earlier assumptions that the German populace was inherently more receptive than the American listening public, and that German music conservatories must necessarily remain superior to American ones. A Washington State clubwoman wrote in 1917:

Hundreds of thousands of this country's money have been spent yearly by students in music in European cities. . . . We have not the musical atmosphere of older civilizations. It is our privilege to see to it that this atmosphere is created and maintained, in order that American women may be trained under the protection of our own wholesome institutions.

There are indications that we are about ready to replace our old-world culture with something radically our own. Let us make it unnecessary that any of our good American dollars shall be changed into marks in Leipsic [sic] or Berlin.[13]

Indeed, organizations of women provided hearty endorsement for the founding of the great American music conservatories, including the Juilliard, Curtis, and Eastman schools of music. In Seattle, the Cornish School found patronage that permitted expanded programs and the construction of an impressive school building in the wave of patriotic postwar enthusiasm for American musical education.

The drive for enhancing American prestige and power neatly allied itself with clubwomen's hopes for bringing better music to the nation. Members theorized that a common appreciation of classical music could fuse the American populace—people of every age, sex, background, and nationality—into a strong, united, and patriotic body of fine citizens who would create a superior democracy, disdainful of materialism, every bit as cultured and powerful as any nation on the globe. Clubwomen's devotion to this civic mission now overshadowed their emphasis on the musical training and advancement of women.

The clubwomen had an excellent opportunity to apply their civic theories when they found themselves with surplus cash—their profits from the community concerts they sponsored. With no interest in keeping substantial bank accounts, they initiated a spending campaign to elevate good citizenship while building musical taste in America. They chose to invest in groups that had not been reached by American musicians before. Thus, immigrants and children became the recipients of music club programming in the first third of the century.

Realizing that their public recitals were not attended by unassimilated immigrants, women's music societies frequently donated their profits to the burgeoning number of settlement music schools in the cities. If they were to bring good music to all citizens, the women had to encourage music lessons and other means of musical expression in the institutions located within immigrant neighborhoods. Thus, the settlements drew on women's clubs for assistance of endless variety, and the clubs provided money for instruction and supplies, teachers and coordinators, receptive audiences for settlement house performances, and invitations to immigrant musicians to play for club meetings.

The Ladies Musical Club was typical in its effort to insure that the foreign population of Seattle would have access to music. It voted in 1914 to contribute to the new Settlement Music School in Seattle, an appendage of the settlement house in the Russian-Jewish neighborhood. Both settlement house and music school were sponsored by the Seattle branch of the National Council of Jewish Women, a group dominated by women of German-Jewish origins. The school borrowed programs that were effective elsewhere and emphasized the music that clubwomen respected. It provided piano and violin lessons and encouraged ensemble work as well. A boys' glee club, several girls' choruses, and an orchestra were established, and even the performance of operettas grew commonplace. Lessons with able music instructors, Jewish and Gentile, were inexpensive, pupils paying just "enough to make them appreciate the lessons and give them no slightest feeling of being objects of charity."[14] Full scholarships were made available to talented youth who had no financial resources for training.

Settlement house music programs were not limited to children, however. For the general foreign populace, harmonica bands, community sings, choruses for every age group, and celebratory pageants provided music; the programs featured classical and American music as well as native songs from every land. Thus, it was possible to hear mothers sing their folk tunes, kindergartners participate in rhythm bands, groups of boys harmonize sailor songs, young girls perform *Madame Butterfly*, and orchestras and choruses of all ages prepared a varied repertoire for neighborhood audiences on settlement anniversaries and national and religious holidays.

For these newcomers to American shores, clubwomen hoped that music would provide spiritual nourishment and solace in lives sapped by struggle. "If it means a great deal for the rich, who are surrounded by beautiful things[,] to have music in their homes, those who have only poverty have even greater need of it," remarked one settlement music supporter.[15] Clubwomen expected that music would act as a counterbalance to the immigrants' struggles, cultivating qualities contributing to good citizenship. As one of their leaders observed: "It is, of course, a truism that a healthy happy human being makes a better citizen than a morbid unhealthy one; and also that the more normal mental and emotional outlets the individual has, the more chance there is of his remaining healthy and happy and a good citizen."[16]

Some idealists among the clubwomen looked upon music shared by natives and immigrants as a true international language, a vehicle for communication among the diverse groups now settled in America or even, perhaps, around the world. Music, they thought, might contribute to international peace—"Art unifying mankind in the common cult of beauty."[17]

Practically, the women believed that music could instill democratic values in foreigners. Settlement music training could teach newcomers the tunes and lyrics of American patriotic songs. And by encouraging respect for the music of the Old Country, clubwomen could demonstrate open-mindedness. Moreover, the settlement music schools provided access to classical musical knowledge, which in Europe was available only to the aristocracy. How the social workers must have glowed when one little girl declared, "Music is a luxury, but we get it here at Music School Settlement in New York for ten cents."[18]

Music club women believed that exposure to classical music could build good character and loyalty to American values not only in foreigners, but also in their own children. Soon after the war, state and national federations sent representatives into the public schools, promising that new music appreciation and participatory programs could insure everything from good posture to high grades. The women declared that the study of the classics could pull the U.S. through its "grave musical crisis" by checking "degeneracy in our modern public music into rag time" and by luring potential "delinquents" from "the suggestive words of popular songs" and the unacceptable behavior which they believed was sure to follow. So, too, music could enliven the small and sleepy communities from which youth, increasingly, was fleeing. "Make [your town] a lovely place to live in so that nobody cares to leave it," suggested one clubwoman to rural villages afraid of losing their population to the "wicked" cities.[19]

To make good their promises to modify youthful behavior through music education, women's groups quickly developed and then donated appropriate materials to public institutions. They purchased Victrolas and records for the schools and paid to bring symphony orchestras to schools or children to concert halls. In Arlington, Massachusetts, women's clubs deposited a great quantity of sheet music at the public library. The Ladies Musical Club in Seattle distributed bibliographies of music books at the libraries. It urged teachers to make their students aware of the music columns that the newspapers were printing in response to LMC pressure, and the growing number of classical radio programs. On Tuesday nights in 1925, for example, KJR broadcasted the Ladies Musical Club String Quartet on the "Puget Sound Savings and Loan Hour."

One easy way to build children's enthusiasm for the classics was to hold school competitions, which clubwomen sponsored. Musical Memory Contests induced children to memorize compositions by the great composers. Club members persuaded teachers to arrange spelling bee–style competitions, in which children would listen to a piece of music and identify the composition, composer, nationality, and dates, and the musical instruments featured. The LMC also sponsored essay contests on the values of music.

At local, state, and national levels contests were also held to reward young people already devoted to musical study. Beginning in 1915, the National Federation of Music Clubs awarded contest prizes in piano, violin, cello, organ, and voice. Later, the National Association of Colored Women, like multitudes of women's associations, invited students to their conventions, to perform solo, in duets, trios, quartets, and glee clubs, and gave medals and blue ribbons to the winners.[20]

Gradually, efforts to expand schoolchildren's familiarity with music led to after-school music clubs. These soon became institutionalized as regular music courses in the public schools. By the late 1920s, Seattle's music societies lobbied successfully for elective credit for high school students of music and for state accreditation for music teachers. Here was proof of the uniting of cultural and political action.

How acceptable to professional male musicians was women's involvement? Their efforts scarcely constituted a frontal assault on the male-dominated musical establishment of the early part of this century, yet many male critics expressed discomfort at the increased feminization of musical enthusiasts. Failing to appreciate that club members had subordinated their own musical development to champion established musical values among women, children, and immigrants, these men felt threatened by women's presence in the musical world. Walter Damrosch, conductor of the New York Philharmonic Orchestra, complained in his autobiography:

Women's musical clubs began to form in many a village, town, and city, and these clubs became the active and efficient nucleus of the entire musical life of the community, but alas, again principally the feminine community. It is to these women's clubs that the managers turned for fat guarantees for appearances of their artists, it is before audiences of whom 75% are women that these artists desport themselves.[21]

Others, like George Reynolds, expressed their resignation to the phenomenon, and simply assigned cultural concerns to twentieth-century woman as they assigned sports to men:

Most of our Chambers of Commerce, men's organizations, you notice, are strong for good roads and golf links and Sunday baseball, to provide the amenities of life and opportunities for the enjoyment of the leisure with which our society seems almost to be threatened, but it is the women's clubs which mainly advocate those diversions of life which, from the days of primitive man, have enlivened his soul and ennobled his days, the great arts.[22]

Such acceptance of women's growing role in shaping musical taste was the exception. When the Curtis School of Music realized that two-thirds of its students were women when it opened in 1919, it limited acceptances until women represented only a third of the student body by the end of the decade. At Ginn and Company, publishers, the music department head Edbridge W. Newton attempted to bolster male participation in music by hawking its virtues to boys: "To be a good musician requires brains of the highest order. Boys, be not afraid to study music, there is nothing more worthy of the masculine mind."[23] Yet women persisted.

Indeed, the range of opportunities that music associations provided for members and their families was impressive. For the beginner, the loans and scholarships, the instruction and contests, the exposure and support, and even the safe dormitories for music students in strange cities aided the budding performer and composer. For the mature woman artist, who might have been a full-time, widely recognized professional in a world without sexism, the clubs reaffirmed her ability and nurtured its growth through acclaim. They constituted a crucial network for professional women. For example, the teachers shared educational techniques and news of job openings in schools; the ambitious concertizers and composers enjoyed hearings at regional meetings; contests yielded money, exposure, and acclaim.

To tap the enthusiasm of a growing associate membership with no musical skills, the clubs increasingly served to sustain the new auxiliaries and support associations which became the foundations of civic musical institutions. Their focus, away from the individual woman's training in favor of acquainting all segments of society with the classics and indigenous American songs, represented a massive effort unmatched anywhere else in society. Sheer tenacity pushed clubwomen beyond mere lobbying for access to music toward the instituting of contests, concerts, prizes, and classes in school, settlements, and anywhere else the general citizenry might respond.

While members seldom attained praise from the male musical establishment, their efforts made an enormous impact on American musical life. This tireless cultivation of musical taste nurtured the respect Americans developed for and the enthusiasm they applied to the federal music program of the depression years. So too, the clubs' public program shaped the future supporters of the town symphony, the subscribers to the chamber music festivals, and the donors of the music schools throughout the nation.

Without a doubt, club members' motives were many. Their antipathy to popular music, their hopes of homogenizing the taste of youth and immigrants until it conformed to traditional standards, and blind patriotism—all these coexisted with the effort to develop an arena for women's influence in society, to revive the folk music of Indians, blacks, and other neglected groups in the nation, and to share the musical beauty that had heretofore been monopolized by elites. On all counts, their organization was impressive, the variety and ingenuity of their projects were dazzling, and their success was broad. Women's societies, however detached from the musical mainstream, effectively shaped musical taste in the early twentieth century and served as a major force in American music.

NOTES

1. Mildred Adams, "Foster-Mothers of Music," *Woman Citizen* (Jan. 26, 1924), 7.

2. The bulk of the paper's material was secured from the annual yearbooks of the LMC, in the Seattle Historical Society. The origins of the club are noted in C. T. Conover, "Ladies Musical Club's Epochal Cultural Services," Seattle *Times*, July 3, 1959; Mrs. A. E. Boardman, "Early History of the Ladies Musical Club," Golden Anniversary of Artists Concerts, 1900–1950, *Program*, 13; Hazel Gertrude Kinscella, "Seattle and the Pacific Northwest," in Quaintance Eaton, *Musical USA* (New York, 1945), 195–206; and Clarence Bagley, *History of Seattle*, 3 vols. (Chicago, 1916), 1, 615–16.

3. Ladies Musical Club, 1981–92 Constitution, p. 9.

4. "Jazz Is Under the Ban," *Music and Musicians*, Vol. 1 (July 1921), 12; "A Music Club in Every Community, Is Slogan," Miles City (Montana) *Daily Star*, Jan. 15, 1922.

5. Seattle *Star*, Sept. 19, 1924.

6. Anthony Ludovici, *Woman: A Vindication* (New York, 1923), 320.

7. "Opening Doors," *Woman Citizen*, Vol. 6 (Nov. 19, 1921), 187–88.

8. Sir Thomas Beecham, "The Position of Women," in *Vogue's First Reader* (Garden City, 1942), 420.

9. Sophie Drinker, *Music and Women: The Story of Women in Their Relation to Music* (New York, 1948), 239; "Wanted—The Open Door in Music," *Woman Citizen*, Vol. 7 (Feb. 24, 1923), 15.

10. Christine Ammer, *Unsung: A History of Women in American Music* (Westport, Conn., 1980), 105–108.

11. "A Brief History of the MacDowell Colony," MacDowell Colony Archives, Peterborough, N.H.

12. Rheta Childe Dorr, *A Woman of Fifty* (New York, 1924), 119.

13. Ida B. McLagan, "Music," in Washington State Federation of Women's Clubs *Bulletin*, Vol. 2 (November 1917), 40.

14. Nicholas John Cords, "Music in Social Settlement and Community Music Schools, 1893–1939: A Democratic-Esthetic Approach to Music Culture," Ph.D dissertation (University of Minnesota, 1970), 37.

15. *Ibid.*, 287.

16. Clarence A. Grimes, *They Who Speak in Music: The History of the Neighborhood Music School* (New Haven, 1957), 18.

17. Alice Duer Miller, *Barnard College: The First Fifty Years* (New York, 1939), 121; Washington State Federation of Women's Clubs, *Bulletin*, 1925.

18. Christine Rowell, "Where Children Love Music," *St. Nicholas Magazine*, Vol. 47 (February 1920), 352.

19. General Federation of Women's Clubs, *Report of the Colorado Biennial Board for the Twentieth Biennial Convention*, Denver, 1930, 35; Massachusetts Federation of Women's Clubs, *Federation Manual*, 1922–23, 77; Washington State Federation of Women's Clubs, *Bulletin*, Vol. 2 (November 1917), 42–44; Rhode Island Federation of Women's Clubs, 1915–16 Yearbook, 71; Alice Ames Winter, "The Technic of Being a Clubwoman," *Ladies Home Journal*, Vol. 41 (August 1924), 6.

20. *National Notes*, 28 (July 1926), 18.

21. Walter Damrosch, *My Musical Life* (New York, 1926), 323.

22. General Federation of Women's Clubs, 1930 Biennial Report, 363.

23. Massachusetts State Federation of Women's Clubs, 1921–22, *Federation Manual*.

Weyerhaeuser and the Pacific Northwest Timber Industry, 1899–1903

Robert E. Ficken

In January 1900, a group of midwestern investors headed by Frederick Weyerhaeuser purchased 900,000 acres of western Washington timberland from the Northern Pacific Railway and announced formation of the Weyerhaeuser Timber Company. With the signing of the documents, the new company became the second largest private holder of timber in the nation and the dominant force in the forest industry of the Pacific Northwest. The arrival of Weyerhaeuser in the region both symbolized and heightened the revolutionary changes then under way in the timber industry. The company was the foremost participant in the migration of Great Lakes lumbermen to the Northwest following the completion of transcontinental railroad lines to Puget Sound. Its incorporation dramatized the growing concentration of timberland in the hands of large holders, transforming the focus of the industry from sawmills and manufacturing to land and speculation in timber. And its arrival in Washington set off a scramble among the older operators to dispose of their mills and land, if possible to the new giant of the industry.

The Washington lumber industry had changed significantly in the half century prior to 1900. Originally developed by San Francisco merchants to meet the demand for lumber in post–gold rush California, the industry for several decades remained dependent on the cargo trade, dispatching vessels laden with lumber to ports around the Pacific Basin. Timber was plentiful and cheap and, in the early years, often free for the taking. "No one can find fault with them but uncle sam," a visitor to Puget Sound wrote in 1859, "and he is far

Originally published in *Pacific Northwest Quarterly,* October 1979.

distant." Dominated by such firms as the Puget Mill Company, owned by Pope and Talbot of San Francisco, and the Port Blakely Mill Company, the industry underwent its greatest expansion in the closing years of the century. Washington lumber production increased from 160 million feet in 1880 to over a billion feet 10 years later, and by 1905 the state was the largest lumber producer in the nation.

Much of this expansion resulted from the completion of the Northern Pacific and Great Northern railroads, making it possible to ship lumber to the East. In addition, midwestern lumbermen, alarmed over the depletion of timber in the Great Lakes states, began to follow the rails westward in search of new investments and sources of supply. Western Washington, where stumpage was inexpensive, proved especially attractive. In something of a preview of the later Weyerhaeuser deal, Chauncey Griggs and a syndicate of wealthy associates acquired 80,000 acres of timber from the Northern Pacific in 1888. Founding the St. Paul and Tacoma Lumber Company, they built at Tacoma the largest and most efficient sawmill complex in the Northwest.

Other investors, including such important figures as William E. Boeing, Congressman Joseph Fordney of Michigan, and R. D. Merrill, became familiar sights in Puget Sound and Grays Harbor, buying up timber claims from small holders. Agents for John D. Rockefeller, E. H. Harriman, and English syndicates supposedly were at work across the region. "All the choice timber lands are being taken up by capitalists who are able to hold for a higher rate of stumpage," observed Cyrus Walker, manager of the Puget Mill Company and the leading lumberman in Washington. George H. Emerson, the most important operator on Grays Harbor, noted that there were "millions of dollars in the air ready to light on any tracts of timber that can be had at reasonable prices." Timber owners eagerly took advantage of the demand to dispose of their claims. Of an Aberdeen lumberman to whom he was introduced, Merrill wrote, "His first words almost were to ask if we were in the market for timber." The owners of the larger mills and tracts of timber, though not yet desirous of disposing of their own holdings, greeted the boom with approval. Withdrawal of timber from the market, both by speculators waiting an advance in values and by the creation of government forest reserves, would force the adoption of less wasteful logging and manufacturing practices. Restricted access to supplies of timber, Emerson pointed out, would cause lumbermen to "begin to appreciate the value of the property they have inherited, and take proper steps for its preservation and proper harvest." Moreover, timber holdings were rapidly increasing in value. Chauncey Griggs estimated in 1898 that the value of the St.

Paul and Tacoma Lumber Company's timber had doubled over the past decade and would double again in the coming years. Charles S. Holmes, a partner in the Port Blakely Mill Company, expected that stumpage prices would "advance rapidly from now on and well located timber land will be worth a good deal more than it has been in the past."

Frederick Weyerhaeuser kept watch on these developments with a growing interest. Born in Germany in 1834, Weyerhaeuser had started out in the sawmill business on the Mississippi River during the Civil War. In the years following the war, he built, usually by combining his assets with those of other lumbermen, a conglomeration of mill and timber companies that stretched over several states in the Midwest, and he became in the process one of the wealthiest men in America. Searching for new areas of investment, Weyerhaeuser spent much of the 1890s investigating possible timber transactions on the Pacific Coast.

In 1898, Weyerhaeuser and a number of men who later became his associates in the Weyerhaeuser Timber Company organized the Coast Lumber Company. The firm's ostensible purpose was to purchase and market Washington shingles in the Midwest and possibly to acquire a millsite on the coast. Its most ambitious undertaking was an effort in 1900 to "secure under satisfactory contracts not less than ninety per cent . . . of the aggregate output of the exclusive shingle mills of the state of Washington." The attempt to create a shingle trust failed, but other activities of the Coast Lumber Company proved more successful. The company provided a convenient cover for its officers and stockholders visiting the Northwest in search of possible timber purchases. George Emerson wrote to a friend in the fall of 1899 that "the Coast Lbr. Co. representing ten of the heaviest millmen in the East, including Weyerhauser [sic], is on the Coast looking up propositions."

Weyerhaeuser's plans for the Northwest became a leading topic of conversation among timbermen. One trade journal even devoted a monthly column to detailing the latest movements of Weyerhaeuser and his associates. Speculation centered on a rumored deal with the Northern Pacific, the size of which was hard to believe. When Emerson informed him that Weyerhaeuser had secured an option on all the railroad's timberland, an incredulous R. D. Merrill responded that it was "more likely" the arrangement was limited to "the lands in Chehalis [Grays Harbor] County." But by November 1899, the Northern Pacific had removed its timber from the market, and all observers acknowledged that Frederick Weyerhaeuser would soon be the leading lumberman in Washington. "It would seem as though these parties," observed William H. Talbot, the president of Pope and Talbot, "were intent upon capturing a great amount of timber land, and it may be their idea to eventually control the business."

Under conditions of some suspense, a number of major timber companies decided that the time had come to sell out. Among these firms was the Puget Mill Company, the oldest and largest lumber company in Washington. Founded in 1853, the concern operated mills at Port Gamble and Port Ludlow and owned 186,000 acres of timber. Cyrus Walker, manager of the mill company since 1863 and owner of 10 percent of its stock, had become increasingly exasperated with the frustrations of lumbering. "It is a bad business," he grumbled, "where there is no hope of satisfying yourself or any body else." In addition to the chronic problem of overproduction, growing labor militance disgusted the conservative Walker. "I feel sometimes that I have outlived my usefulness," he wrote, "and that it is better to get out of the way, and stop growling at the present improved methods the employees have of running things their own way." The Talbot brothers, Will and Frederick, who had managed the company's affairs from San Francisco since the early 1880s, were also weary of the burdens that the business imposed upon them.

In March 1899, Walker was approached by an intermediary for easterners interested in purchasing the Puget Mill Company. Although unable to ascertain their identities, Walker did learn that they were "capitalists from Minnesota, Wisconsin, and Michigan" who did not at present own property on the Pacific Coast. Furthermore, he wrote, the offer "comes through Judge [Thomas] Burke, who is the Attorney for the Great Northern in Seattle, therefore I presume they are friends of J. J. Hill." And since Frederick Weyerhaeuser and James J. Hill were friends and neighbors, Walker was convinced that "the Warehouser [*sic*] crowd" wanted the property. The prospective purchasers, moreover, were interested in timber. "They do not want to consider any of the other mills here in the proposition," Walker noted, "as [the other mills] have but little timber land, [and] it is timber they want, and not mills." The investors, though, were willing to buy the company's mills, vessels, and other assets in order to acquire the timber.

The prospect of selling to Weyerhaeuser excited the interest of the Puget Mill's owners. Walker responded favorably to the possibility of unloading "this elephant of ours, which is gradually killing off all that have any thing to do with the active management of the concern," and he supported a sale "if any thing like a fair price can be secured for the property." Agreeing with Walker "in every particular as far as selling out is concerned," Will Talbot believed that "it would be best for all concerned if we can dispose of the Company's property." Frederick Talbot acknowledged that it would be "a great blessing for us all" to sell the business. The Talbots and Walker, however, set a high value on their property, contending that even the logged-off land was worth five dollars an acre. Will Talbot feared that "when the intending purchasers learn how much we wish for the timber land . . . they will be scared from considering the subject any longer." In addition, the rapidly increasing value of stumpage raised the possibility that a more profitable sale could be made at a later date. Walker, for one, questioned whether "this is the proper time to sell." Considerations of price and timing prevented the negotiations from proceeding beyond the preliminary stage.

A more vigorous and direct effort to conclude a deal with Weyerhaeuser was undertaken by George Emerson, manager of the North Western Lumber Company of Hoquiam. The mill had been built in 1882 by Captain Asa M. Simpson, one of the pioneer lumbermen on the Pacific Coast, and was the site of the greatest industrial activity on Grays Harbor. The company also operated mills at South Bend and at Knappton on the Columbia River. Simpson, well known for his eccentric behavior, did not get along with Emerson, who often complained of the "degrading abuse" he received from his employer. Emerson also chafed at Simpson's refusal to allow him a voice in making company policy, despite the fact that he was a stockholder. When the Hoquiam mill burned in 1896, the company built a modern facility designed to serve the rail markets opened up by completion of the Northern Pacific to Hoquiam, but Simpson refused to approve Emerson's plans to concentrate on the rail trade.

In frustration, Emerson decided to buy out Simpson. He secured an option on the property but, lacking sufficient funds himself, needed a wealthy partner to carry out the scheme. Through the medium of the Coast Lumber Company, Emerson worked to involve Weyerhaeuser in his plans. "If we could get the Weyerhauser [sic] interest centered here," he wrote, "we think all our holdings would come to the front. I have been therefore very anxious to accomplish that move and sincerely hope I shall be able to get them to consider the purchase of this property without farther [sic] delay." If the rumored deal with the Northern Pacific was successful, Emerson believed, the Weyerhaeuser people would require several sawmills in order to produce enough lumber "to meet their interest and tax account." The North Western mill, with its access to both cargo and rail markets, was ideal for such a purpose.

In November 1899, Frederick Weyerhaeuser and several of his associates visited Washington to examine the Northern Pacific land and other possible investments. The group spent a day with Emerson inspecting the Hoquiam and South Bend mills. "I think I should have talked more fully with Mr. Weyerhauser [sic] than I did," Emerson wrote to the secretary of the Coast Lumber Company after the visitors departed, "but felt he was entirely able to judge the situation and see any point I might make without my pointing it out to him." The response of the visitors was encouraging, and a Weyerhaeuser-Emerson purchase of the company seemed likely. "Mr. Weyerhauser [sic] tells me I shall hear from him as soon as he reaches the East," Emerson informed a friend. The Hoquiam lumberman even began to worry about "being a pebble in so large a pond."

With considerable confidence, Emerson rebuffed the overtures of other parties interested in the property. "I have felt from the first," he remarked, "the Weyerhauser [sic] people were the parties with whom we would eventually deal." But as the weeks passed, Emerson's optimism faded. Meeting with W. I. Ewart of the Coast Lumber Company in mid-December, he learned the bad news. Though "Mr. Weyerhauser [sic] is very strongly inclined toward accepting our proposition," he reported to an associate, other members of the syndicate were opposed, contending that the Northern Pacific purchase was too costly and too immense an undertaking to allow for additional acquisitions. When further efforts failed to convince Weyerhaeuser to take up the option, Emerson resigned himself to a continued business relationship with Simpson.

The Northern Pacific purchase was indeed an immense venture. In the summer of 1899, Frederick Weyerhaeuser had begun serious negotiations with railroad officials, which focused on a million acres of land in western Washington. The purchase price was the main obstacle: Weyerhaeuser offered five dollars an acre; the railroad demanded at least seven. Weyerhaeuser, however, operated on the principle that "the only times he ever lost money on timberlands were the times when he didn't buy," and the Northern Pacific was badly in need of funds. The parties reached a compromise that called for the purchase of 900,000 acres at six dollars an acre. The sale was completed on January 3, 1900, Weyerhaeuser himself providing a third of the purchase price and the remainder coming from the members of his syndicate. "The value of Washington timber land," observed the *Pacific Lumber Trade Journal*, "must be conceded when a capitalist of Mr. Weyerhauser's [sic] calibre prefers a large tract in this state to $6,500,000 in cold cash."

The Weyerhaeuser Timber Company began business in March 1900, operating out of a small office suite in the Northern Pacific Building in Tacoma. George S. Long, sent out from Wisconsin as resident manager, was in some ways a surprising choice for such an important position. A native of Indiana, Long had for many years been sales manager for one of the mills in the Weyerhaeuser syndicate. He had no firsthand knowledge of the Pacific Northwest or of the problems involved in timber management. Readily admitting that he was "absolutely without a particle of experience in the land business," Long set to work acquainting himself with the company's holdings and with the timber industry. "Every time I get out into the woods," he noted, "I learn something that I didn't know before." He proved to be a skilled businessman, not only widely respected as the representative of the largest company in the industry but also esteemed for his expertise and personal integrity.

Long was faced with several immediate and important problems. For one thing, he believed that it was imperative to establish an image of cooperativeness for Weyerhaeuser, to dispel any fear that the company would use its size to the detriment of the public or of other firms.

If you have such a thing as public sentiment . . . to contend with, you want to study that very carefully, and find out who really controls public sentiment; trying to get them friendly towards your interests, and avoid doing things that will irritate the public; in other words, a man has to be a good fellow.

Thus, when Long unwittingly acquired at an auction a section of state timber desired by the Port Blakely Mill Company, he wrote to the manager of that firm that Weyerhaeuser had "no inclination or disposition to interfere with your plans." Long then arranged to sell the timber to Port Blakely at the same price he had paid the state. Close attention to the company's image was from the beginning a characteristic of the Weyerhaeuser operation.

As part of this effort, Weyerhaeuser also sold some of its timber holdings. Many small mills were dependent on the Northern Pacific for timber and feared that their supply would no longer be available. One of Long's first acts was to inform trade journals and newspapers that he would sell timber to mills "which were more or less dependent on the Northern Pacific lands for logs." He did so, Long explained to a member of the syndicate, "for policy, as I thought it much better to have it understood that we are willing to sell, than to have it understood that we would not sell. If we get all the little mill men down on us because we will not sell," Long feared, they might influence county assessors to raise valuations on the company's land. Weyerhaeuser sold its first timber in June 1900 and continued to make small sales, disposing of 19,000 acres by the middle of 1903.

The principal task facing Long, though, was assimilation of the lands acquired from the Northern Pacific. The syndicate had made no detailed examination of the land prior to purchase; it relied on the railroad's figures for the amount of timber acquired in the deal. But the railroad had cruised only a portion of its property, and a fourth of the land sold to Weyerhaeuser had never been examined at all. Within days of his arrival, Long began sending cruisers into the woods in an effort to secure a more accurate idea of the company's holdings.

The results of these preliminary surveys were shocking to Long. "I have tried," he wrote to Weyerhaeuser in late June,

to be not at all prejudiced in this matter, but I cannot get away from the conviction, that on the so-called unexamined lands, we have been imposed upon, and have been equally convinced that there has been given to us a large quantity of isolated, scattering, timberless tracts of land, which it will never pay us to log.

The railroad's figures, Long concluded, "are padded and excessive." Over 200,000 acres had either been logged or burned over or were otherwise without commercially profitable stands of timber. Prolonged discussions between the company and the railroad resulted in agreement for a joint cruise of the unexamined land. Compensation for errors supposedly would be figured into a second Weyerhaeuser purchase of Northern Pacific timber, then in the negotiation stage.

While dealing with the railroad, Long initiated a vigorous timber purchase program that focused on the even sections within the boundaries of the Northern Pacific grant. His policy, Long wrote to Weyerhaeuser, was "to clean up the individual small ownership as much as possible." This required a great deal of expense and time. "The buying up of these lands adjacent to our holdings," Long noted, "is somewhat of a tedious process, as we have innumerable people to deal with; in most instances buying single claims of 160 acres from homesteaders, or people who have quarter sections they have taken up for timber claims." By the end of 1900, he had purchased 1.5 billion feet of timber from private holders. Weyerhaeuser holdings in Washington, including a second purchase of 261,000 acres from the Northern Pacific, amounted to 1.3 million acres by mid-1903. These acquisitions filled in the checkerboard squares missing from the original purchase and assured efficient timber management.

Concentrating on its timber holdings, Weyerhaeuser did not immediately enter the manufacturing end of the business, though the company had expected to rapidly commence lumber production in Washington. "We bought this timber not to look at but to cut," a member of the syndicate told reporters in February 1900. Other lumbermen welcomed this news, believing that the giant firm would be a stabilizing factor in the industry. "The more property and plants which they control," observed Frederick Talbot, "the better it will be, . . . for us and the balance of the people in the same line of business, and as they are not cheap people by any means we do not think that they will be strong competitors, that is, at a cut rate." Long, however, soon concluded that weak markets meant that the manufacture of lumber would produce little or no profit. To begin lumber milling "at the present time," he informed Frederick Weyerhaeuser, "would probably demoralize business, and do more harm than good."

When it became evident that Weyerhaeuser would not immediately begin lumber production, concern over the company's plans became widespread. Newspapermen and lumbermen clamored for information. "This whole country seems to expect that we will build mills at once," Long complained in January 1902. "The newspapers have been building some more mills for us," he noted on another occasion, observing that "while these edifices are hardly air-castles, they are at the same time newspaper mills." In statements and interviews, Long repeatedly stressed that Weyerhaeuser would not manufacture lum ber until market conditions allowed. "You have to say something to these newspaper fellows," he wrote to Frederick Weyerhaeuser; he added that he was studying "the art of saying nothing that can be misconstrued, and [trying] to leave the impression that we are ready, willing and anxious to build mills, and apt to build them at any time."

Weyerhaeuser's hesitancy to add sawmills to its holdings was not for want of opportunity. The extensive Puget Mill facilities were available, and the owners of that company continued to discuss a sale with persons they assumed to be Weyerhaeuser representatives. However, Seattle attorney Maurice McMicken, acting for a syndicate of Michigan lumbermen, presented a more detailed and direct proposal for the purchase of the company. Discussions ended when Pope and Talbot suggested a price of $6 million for the mills, timber, and other assets, a figure McMicken believed ruled out any possibility of a deal. "He considers the price named for the timber land so high," Cyrus Walker informed Will Talbot, "that in his judgement, it will be useless to present any such figures to his people." Walker and the Talbot brothers consoled themselves with the knowledge that their timber would continue to appreciate in value. But disposal of their property remained a major goal, and Walker hoped that "some day, the Puget Mill Company may be lucky enough to unload their holdings here, on to some Lumber Syndicate, from the Middle West."

Pope and Talbot continued to look for an opening that would allow a linkage with Weyerhaeuser. In early 1902, the company made elaborate arrangements for an "accidental" meeting between Walker and Frederick Weyerhaeuser. "There may be no material advantage from such a meeting," A. W. Jackson, a Pope and Talbot official, pointed out, "still there might be material benefits aris[ing] from such a meeting." The two lumbermen might establish a personal rapport that would lead to a cooperative effort to monopolize the Washington timber industry. Will Talbot, for one, desired the "eventual coming together of the large timber owners, thereby creating a Timber Trust which can control the mkts & prices of the world." Despite the preparations, Walker and Weyerhaeuser did not meet, and Pope and Talbot continued to operate as an independent concern.

Owners of other mills and timber properties, however, had more success. In April 1900, George Emerson secured financial backing for his effort to buy out A. M. Simpson; his new partner was C. H. Jones, a wealthy Michigan lumberman and important stockholder in the St. Paul and Tacoma Lumber Company. Jones and Emerson spent 10 days in San Francisco working out the details of an arrangement whereby they would purchase the Hoquiam mill and its 22,000 acres of timber for $550,000, most of this sum to be in deferred payments. Simpson would retain ownership of the South Bend and Knappton mills. But no sooner had Emerson and Jones returned to Washington than news arrived that Simpson had changed his mind and refused to sign the contract. The sale, Simpson now insisted, would have to be on a cash basis.

While Emerson despaired, Jones turned to Weyerhaeuser as a possible third participant in a cash purchase of the property. "I let him do most of the talking," Long reported of his first meeting with Jones. Long favored Weyerhaeuser participation, pointing out that it would be a good idea to "get acquainted with the details of the manufacturing end of the business." But given the eccentricities of Captain Simpson, there seemed to be no hurry to rush into the purchase. "That property will be down there ready for us whenever we want it," Long believed. Discussions between Jones and various members of the Weyerhaeuser syndicate continued on into 1901.

In April 1901, though, Simpson suddenly agreed to sell the property to Emerson and Jones under the terms of the original agreement. Long decided that this outcome was all for the best, as "we would [not] have made any money to speak of if we had bought the . . . plant." Besides, a connection with Emerson was probably not in Weyerhaeuser's interest. Emerson was nice enough, Long conceded, but he was "getting a little old, and [was] not as enthusiastic as would be required to put life into a plant." Still, Long was annoyed at being left out of the deal and at not even being informed of it in advance.

Weyerhaeuser gave less consideration to other possible purchases. By the end of 1899, the operators of the Port Blakely Mill Company had decided to sell their holdings, including one of the largest sawmills in the world and over 60,000 acres of timber. Weyerhaeuser was the first prospect approached by Charles S. Holmes and John and James Campbell. "If these people would be willing to sell out their holdings for about one-half of their present asking price," Long wrote to Frederick Weyerhaeuser in late 1900, ". . . we might then feel inclined to make further investigations." But Holmes and the Campbells were not willing to reduce the price and in February 1903 sold the company to two Michigan investors, David E. Skinner and John W. Eddy.

The operators of another major concern, the Grays Harbor Commercial Company, also approached Weyerhaeuser with an offer to sell. Long was "quite in favor of buying the Grays Harbor Commercial Co's plant, if we can get it at the right figure." But Weyerhaeuser was not prepared to pay the price demanded by the mill's owners, and serious negotiations never got under way. The timber company had a chance to pick up a remnant of A. M. Simpson's Washington properties when Harry Heermans, a Grays Harbor real estate speculator, obtained an option on the South Bend sawmill. Heermans, reported Long, "naturally came to us with it." Long and R. L. McCormick, the timber company's secretary and a member of the Weyerhaeuser syndicate, examined the property and found that it lacked adequate railroad facilities and that the mill's timberlands were badly scattered.

In January 1902, Weyerhaeuser finally became a lumber manufacturer by acquiring the Bell-Nelson Lumber Company of Everett. Originally, the mill was to have been purchased by the Coast Lumber Company, but during the negotiations the latter firm was supplanted by the Weyerhaeuser Timber Company. The mill was small and inefficient and owned only a small quantity of timber. "I am afraid some of you will not like the saw mill," Long informed the members of the syndicate, "for it is not a first-class one by any means, and [it is] one which will either have to be re-built before a great while or else run . . . in a way that may not be entirely satisfactory." But the mill provided an opportunity for experience in the lumber business, as well as the company's first direct involvement in logging Washington timber. Although it was rebuilt in 1903, the mill continued to be a relatively minor factor in the lumber trade, and for a decade it was the only Weyerhaeuser manufacturing venture. Aside from the relationship between rising stumpage values and log prices, the direct impact of Weyerhaeuser on lumbering remained one of potential.

The original purchase from the Northern Pacific and the subsequent acquisitions from the railroad and other holders dramatized the concentration of Washington timber in the hands of large operators. "It will not be long before the timber in small tracts, will be used up," Cyrus Walker pointed out in March 1901. Heightened by the Weyerhaeuser purchases, speculative mania produced an abrupt increase in the value of stumpage. By mid-1901, Weyerhaeuser itself was forced to cut back on purchases because of the high prices demanded by timber owners. "There is no question about the sharp advance in the price of stumpage being on account of the large purchases of timber land, made in this country," Walker observed. The boom continued until the panic of 1907, and Long reported at the end of 1906 that the company's "stumpage has increased 50% in value during the past twelve months." Even after the panic, according to the Bureau of Corporations, "this great [Weyerhaeuser] holding exerts a continuous stiffening effect upon the market."

Concentration of ownership raised the possibility that the large holders might achieve control over the manufacturers of lumber. Already small mill owners were having difficulty acquiring supplies of timber. Frederick Talbot welcomed the Weyerhaeuser purchases, for "the fewer hands the timber gets into the better position we will all be in to dictate terms re prices of timber lands etc." Cyrus Walker believed that the time was not far distant when "the large holders will have it in their power to controll [sic] the price of stumpage." Long too was confident that control of stumpage was the only course that could result in stable lumber prices. The big firms, he argued, should "continue the policy of adding to their holdings, . . . and thus bring about at an earlier date the time when they can control the market conditions." The arrival of Weyerhaeuser signaled the beginning of the era when control of timber, not ownership of sawmills, was the key to success in the Northwest forest industry.

Recognizing the new order, other lumbermen deferred to the leadership of Weyerhaeuser, and the company responded in a fashion new to the Northwest. In September 1902, a series of large forest fires devastated western Washington and Oregon, burning over 2 billion feet of timber. Smoke darkened the Pacific Northwest and drifted as far south as San Francisco where, wrote Will Talbot, "mixing with the fog [it] makes a very dreary day for all of us." The old-fashioned lumber companies, accustomed to cheap timber, had never paid much attention to the forest fire problem, despite frequent heavy destruction in the summer months. But Weyerhaeuser and other recent arrivals had invested millions of dollars in timber, and fire represented the most serious threat to their investments. Twenty thousand acres of Weyerhaeuser timber had been killed in Clarke County alone, and Long was determined to secure governmental assistance to protect the company and the industry from the danger of further losses.

The attention devoted to politics by lumbermen had been as sporadic as that centered on the fire danger. They had been more concerned with preventing actions detrimental to their interests than with positive accomplishment, and when political action was required, they traditionally preferred to rely on what George Emerson called "Metallic argument." In the aftermath of the great fires of 1902, however, Long decided to "strike while the subject is warm." He organized a committee of lumbermen to formulate a fire protection program and subsidized a publicity campaign in trade journals and newspapers.

When the state legislature convened in Olympia in January 1903, Long hired a confidential lobbyist to press legislators to approve the lumbermen's program. "No one will know that he is looking after our interests," Long noted of the lobbyist. The result was legislation establishing a state fire warden, deputy fire wardens in the counties, and a system of burning permits. An additional act in 1905 created a state forest commission. With Long's backing, similar legislation was approved in Oregon in 1905. These laws were an important step in the direction of conservation of natural resources, and the lobbying efforts were an early demonstration of the new type of sophisticated leadership brought to the timber industry by Weyerhaeuser.

The arrival of Weyerhaeuser in the Pacific Northwest transformed the region's timber industry. Declining in importance, the old San Francisco–based companies sold out to midwestern investors or went out of business altogether, especially if they lacked sizable timber holdings. Of the old firms, only Pope and Talbot continued to be a major force in the industry. Henceforth, those companies that had failed to take advantage of the once cheap prices of timber to acquire extensive holdings were doomed to extinction, while the rapidly increasing value of timber caused lumbermen to search for efficient methods of production and for means of utilizing species of wood previously left to rot in the forest. As new issues of conservation and taxation, overproduction and shifting markets came to the fore, Weyerhaeuser expanded its leadership role in the Northwest. Soon, other lumbermen would take no collective action unless the giant timber company agreed to participate, and the firm became the single most important unifying factor in a notoriously chaotic industry.

BIBLIOGRAPHICAL NOTE

Research for this paper concentrated on the records of lumber companies and the papers of individuals associated with the industry. The records of the Weyerhaeuser Timber Company, consulted at the company's archives in Tacoma, are an indispensable source for the firm's activities. The University of Washington Libraries hold sizable and important collections of manuscripts. The Ames Collection includes the records of Pope & Talbot and the letterbooks of Cyrus Walker. The George Emerson Letterbooks are crucial to an understanding of the situation on Grays Harbor. The records of the Port Blakely Mill Company and of the Merrill & Ring interests were also of considerable value in the preparation of the paper.

As for secondary sources, Thomas R. Cox, *Mills and Markets: A History of the Pacific Coast Lumber Industry to 1900* (Seattle, 1974), is invaluable for its coverage of trends in the industry at the end of the nineteenth century. Based on extensive research in company records, Ralph W. Hidy, Frank Ernest Hill, and Allan Nevins, *Timber and Men: The Weyerhaeuser Story* (New York, 1963) is the standard history of the firm. A similar work is Edwin T. Coman, Jr., and Helen M. Gibbs, *Time, Tide and Timber: A Century of Pope & Talbot* (Stanford, 1949). Robert E. Ficken, "The Port Blakely Mill Company, 1888–1903," *Journal of Forest History*, Vol. 21 (1977), covers the turn-of-the-century activities of that important concern.

III. Reform and Repression

The events of July 17, 1897, were like the sunburst that follows a violent storm. In a single day, or so it seemed, the gloom and pessimism caused by four years of economic depression and social turmoil disappeared. It all happened when the Alaskan steamer Portland nosed into Seattle's Elliott Bay and brought news of an incredible gold discovery in the Yukon. Passengers holding up sacks stuffed tight with thousands of dollars' worth of the yellow metal disarmed even the most stubborn skeptics.

Within days, parlors and pool halls from Puget Sound to Massachusetts Bay buzzed with talk of finding fortunes in Canada's fabulous Klondike. Merely thinking about the precious metal revived hopes and dreams battered by years of monetary crises, widespread unemployment, and popular unrest. Pacific Northwest merchants, eager to capitalize on the Klondike trade by mining the miners' pocketbooks, intensified their long-standing commercial and urban rivalries. Similarly, astute land speculators, industrialists, financiers, railroad barons, and others realized that the economic revival made the vast natural resources in Oregon and Washington every bit as attractive as those in the remote Klondike.

The trains that brought thousands of Klondikers to the Pacific Northwest occasionally carried dreamers of another sort as well, people seeking not gold or glory but a chance to build a brave new world in the wilds of Washington. Their utopias bearing such quaint names as Home, Equality, and Freeland arose on Puget Sound's isolated bays and tidal flats, and although these settlements differed on such matters as distribution of wealth and free love, each embodied its founder's vision of a better life under anarchism or socialism. Their hope was to transform Washington into a model commonwealth, a workable alternative to the larger industrial society that seemed with each passing year to suffer more social tension and economic dislocation. These social pioneers could not imagine that they would fail.

For world savers in the 1890s, the compass of opportunity pointed unmistakably to a promised land in the nation's northwest corner. Why? For one reason, the severe depression of the decade caused a number of Americans to consider alternatives to the prevailing economic system. And no part of the country had a more pronounced tradition of receptivity to the new ideas and patterns of behavior than the Far West. A Chicago newspaper observed in 1886 that for "some reason that is not easy to explain the West Coast has always had a strange attraction for people of a romantic and unpractical turn of mind." Long before the 1890s, eastern reformers had believed that the Far West offered them "the most opportunities and the fewest obstacles to overcome." The political and social traditions and institutions that discouraged innovation by keeping people loyal to inherited beliefs and ways of doing things were weaker there. After all, migration to the Far West was an act that required the courage to break old family and community ties and forge new ones.

Innovation took many forms. Everything from new systems of medicine to new systems of government interested reformers in the Pacific Northwest (see the essay by G. Thomas Edwards). As early as the 1870s, agrarian protests occurred in Oregon against banks and transportation monopolies. During the 1880s reformers won for Washington women the right to vote (although the territorial supreme court took it away) and for Oregon workers the first legalized Labor Day holiday in the United States. During the anti-Asian agitation that swept the region during that same decade, reformers promulgated an innovative political program that served as the ideological foundation for two decades of protest politics (see the essay by Carlos Schwantes).

By the concluding decade of the nineteenth century, the Pacific Northwest was well on its way to developing a tradition of receptivity to innovation; it also retained an almost pristine natural environment that appealed to reformers. In their eyes the region possessed an unspoiled quality at a time when major industrial centers in the East and in Europe seem prematurely old and used up. At a time when blast furnaces colored Pittsburgh skies a sooty amber, and dirt, disease, and unpleasant industrial odors blighted working-class neighborhoods in cities such as Cincinnati and Chicago, the undeveloped Pacific North-

west still offered an outlet for a nation's pioneering urge, especially when that urge expressed itself as social experimentation and reform politics. A government clerk who abandoned his job in Washington, D.C., for a chance to create a model commonwealth on Puget Sound spoke for many who shared his dream when he declared that "a pioneer project would have a better chance for success in a pioneer environment."

No less a figure than John R. Rogers, Washington's governor from 1897 to 1901, encouraged the visionaries who made the pilgrimage to the nation's far corner. He himself was living proof of the unusual opportunities that awaited them there: a journalist and pamphleteer whose head was filled to overflowing with ideas for refashioning society, Rogers moved from Kansas to Washington in 1890 and scarcely six years later was elected governor on a reform ticket. He actually joined one of Puget Sound's utopian colonies in order to participate in its insurance program, thus becoming probably the first American governor ever to "belong" to a communitarian experiment while in office. Washington, a reformer noted in 1899 after surveying the string of innovative proposals that kept surfacing there, was home to "more 'isms' and 'osophies' than any other state in America."

Oregon, which was settled earlier and under somewhat different circumstances than Washington, had the reputation of being the more conservative of the two states. In fact, however, developments in Oregon during the 1890s frequently paralleled those in Washington, much to the dismay of the region's conservatives. And although Oregon had no real counterpart to the communitarianism on Puget Sound, the Populist revolt that swept John R. Rogers and other reformers into office in Washington had a major and lasting impact on Oregon politics and government as well.

As a third-party alternative to Republicans and Democrats, the People's or Populist party was in the long run no more successful in the Pacific Northwest than elsewhere. But as a protest movement it provided an agenda for a subsequent group of reform-minded Republicans and Democrats, who in the early twentieth century successfully turned many an innovative proposal into law. Perhaps the Populist party's most lasting contribution was to make issues and individual candidates more important to Pacific Northwest voters than party labels.

No one was more responsible for establishing the electoral machinery that restricted the power of party organizations than William S.

U'Ren. Although he never advanced any higher in politics than the lower house of the Oregon legislature, his influence was so great that American history texts occasionally identified him erroneously as the state's governor. U'Ren was more than a regional reformer. His proposals to take power out of the hands of political bosses and give it to "the people" inspired emulation in many parts of the United States and Canada. The "Oregon System" became a synonym for U'Ren's machinery of the direct primary, initiative, referendum, and recall; and Oregon voters remain the nation's most frequent users of the initiative (see Robert Woodward's essay). Because the system de-emphasized party politics, it is no accident that maverick and independent-minded politicians have flourished in the Pacific Northwest.

The tolerant climate of opinion that encouraged U'Ren to promote the Oregon System and the Puget Sound utopians to build their model commonwealths also provided a congenial home for a variety of people best described as romantic rebels (see Edwin Bingham's essay). Notable individualists like John Reed and Charles Erskine Scott Wood were romantic rebels, and so, too, were members of the Industrial Workers of the World, the Wobblies. As much a part of the region's folklore as its history, Wobblies attracted popular attention during the years 1905–19 by their unorthodox protests against poor working conditions in the forests and fields.

The Industrial Workers of the World particularly attracted the migratory workers so numerous and so important in the Pacific Northwest. Migratory workers supplied the muscle needed by the region's basic industries. They felled the trees and milled its timber, dug its precious metals, and harvested its wheat and other crops. Numbering among them such men as the future Supreme Court justice William O. Douglas, the migratory workers frequently traveled from job to job precariously perched on the undercarriage of a fast-moving passenger train, suspended only inches above sudden death, and blasted by the cinders, sand, and dirt of eastern Washington and Oregon. Douglas remembered one migrant whose worldly possessions consisted of a battered suitcase, a pair of high-heeled shoes for a girl friend in Seattle, and a single extra shirt. Wobblies attracted attention to the exploitation of migratory labor by singing bitter songs of protest and by staging street-corner rallies that often developed into clashes with municipal authorities determined to stop them. These protests were called free speech fights. In 1916 one of the free speech fights resulted in a bloody confrontation known as the Everett massacre (see Norman Clark's essay).

Could it be that a common thread linked the region's romantic rebels, utopian visionaries, political reformers, and hardheaded capitalists? If so, that thread was called opportunity. The Pacific Northwest at the turn of the century was another name for opportunity. It beckoned to capitalists large and small to seek their fortunes in the mining regions of north Idaho, the British Columbia Kootenays, and the Yukon. It fired the hopes of a variety of visionaries and cranks. It provided a congenial home for the individual who had a dream to pursue.

With the entry of the United States into the First World War, the generally tolerant climate of opinion changed. People would still pursue their dreams, but the range of popularly accepted behavior contracted dramatically (see the essay by Paul Holbo). The draft, enacted in 1917, symbolized as nothing else the changes overtaking the region. Loggers, metal miners, and clerks from the Pacific Northwest were sent to fight in the trenches alongside pipefitters from Brooklyn and Boston. With the stroke of a pen, desk-bound bureaucrats in Washington, D.C., significantly changed the lives of every citizen. Nationwide crusades urged Americans to buy savings bonds and to conserve fuel, wheat, and meat. The war, in short, placed a premium on centralization and conformity.

During the war, reform was easily equated with disloyalty. As a Walla Walla commercial journal phrased it, the Pacific Northwest had long been known for its "freak candidates with freak political ideas and platforms." In a country at peace, the journal explained, "a few political mountebanks may make little difference, but when our country is at war it must have sound, orderly, stable, able government." The magazine believed that it would do no harm if the region's numerous "disturbers, detractors, and wind bags" were "put on ice" until the war ended. No group in the Pacific Northwest learned more about the repressive power of the wartime state than did the Wobblies. Their nonconformity, their opposition to the war, and their power in the lumber industry made them special targets in the government's drive for conformity. Raids on Wobbly halls netted scores of prisoners.

To the Pacific Northwest, World War I meant a combination of regimentation, optimism, sorrow, and prosperity. Before 1916 the economy had been in a slump. The war made jobs plentiful. Women entered the work force as never before, although in most cases their employment was only temporary. Many wartime jobs were in shipbuilding, which became a major industry on Puget Sound. The growing demand for food and timber raised the prices of those two basic resources and greatly benefited the Pacific Northwest economy. Spruce, a light, strong wood, was especially needed for aircraft construction, but in 1917 Wobblies curtailed its production through a series of strikes and slowdowns to protest miserable working conditions. Their actions forced the federal government to intervene in the name of military necessity. To get the spruce, Uncle Sam brought military discipline to the timber industry and helped correct many of the conditions that had long irritated Wobblies.

During the war one of the commonest acronymns to appear in the newspapers was "HCL." Everyone knew that HCL stood for the "high cost of living." The cost of food, housing, and other necessities rose so rapidly that it became a chief topic of conversation. Workers worried about wages that failed to keep pace with rising prices, but as long as the war continued, many grievances went unspoken in the name of patriotism. But when the fighting ended in late 1918, a time of reckoning was at hand. Conflict in the postwar era threatened to tear apart the region's social fabric.

Dr. Ada M. Weed: Northwest Reformer

G. Thomas Edwards

When the doctors Gideon A. and Ada M. Weed settled in Salem, Oregon, in 1858, they brought to this frontier capital the latest in eastern hydropathic medicine and a reforming spirit. They had attended Dr. Russell T. Trall's Hygeio-Therapeutic College in New York City, where the faculty not only provided medical education but also urged students to campaign for societal reform. Thus, Ada's work for woman's rights owed much to Dr. Lydia Folger Fowler, teacher of clinical midwifery and lecturer on woman's rights.

A few months after the Weeds opened an office, Ada began lecturing Oregonians about the need to improve the condition of frontier women. She was probably the first female to deliver a series of lectures on behalf of her sex in Oregon. Informed listeners, many of whom had never heard a woman lecture, realized that the speaker advanced ideas similar to those espoused by eastern women in the controversial woman's rights movement and that she and her husband as practitioners of hydropathy—popularly known as the "water-cure"—championed an alternative medical system that prompted quarrels wherever it was practiced. While advocates of other controversial movements and fads, like temperance, spiritualism, and phrenology, enjoyed success in antebellum Oregon, it proved impossible either for the Weeds to continue their hydropathic practice or for Ada to carry on her efforts on behalf of her sex. Her lectures on woman's rights had no significant impact: there was no major attempt to improve the condition of Oregon women until Abigail Scott Duniway's organized efforts of the 1870s.

Originally published in *Oregon Historical Quarterly*, March 1977.

During the 1850s—the early years of the national woman's rights movement—dedicated women, assisted by some male allies, sought to improve educational and employment opportunities and to attain a variety of legal rights. Susan B. Anthony and a few others also advocated equal suffrage. To win these reforms women held both national and state woman's rights conventions, wrote public letters, and made lecture tours. These female lecturers were a novelty; while many men and women in the audience sympathized with the speaker, scoffers came in hopes of hearing a heated exchange.

The actions of these women reformers in the 1850s, like those of participants in the current women's liberation movement, led to a national controversy over the role of women in American society. Ministers and editors tended to ridicule women advocating additional opportunities for their sex. The editor James Gordon Bennett, for example, argued:

They want to fill all other posts which men are ambitious to occupy, to be lawyers, doctors, captains of vessels and generals in the field. How funny it would sound in the newspapers that Lucy Stone, pleading a cause, took suddenly ill . . . and perhaps gave birth to a fine bouncing boy in court! . . . or that Dr. Harriot K. Hunt while attending to a gentleman for a fit of gout . . . found it necessary to send for a doctor, there and then, and to be delivered of a man or woman child, perhaps twins. A similar event might happen on the floor of Congress, in a storm at sea or in the raging tempest of battle, and then what is to become of the woman legislator?

While woman's rights leaders of the 1850s complained about such rhetoric, they won an unknown number of female and male allies and even savored some victories, including laws granting women property rights in Massachusetts and Ohio. Many female leaders, while championing their sex, also supported abolition, temperance, and education. They engaged in a short-lived dress reform but ceased advocating the bloomer costume because it detracted from their cause. Several female leaders besides Miss Anthony became disgusted with conventional physicians and discovered both the therapeutic value of hydropathy and the sympathy expressed by its practitioners for dress reform and for women seeking status.

While Ada shared goals—including changes in education, professional opportunities, marriage, and dress—with leaders of the women's rights movement, she gave no indication that she had participated in the movement. Instead, Dr. Weed's enthusiasm for the struggle against male domination resulted from her study of unorthodox medicine. Fully aware that as a hydropath and as an advocate of woman's rights she would meet indifference and ridicule, Ada, one of the first professional women in Oregon, instructed women that they should emulate their eastern sisters who sought to improve their lives. From the summer of 1858 into the spring of 1860, she lectured pioneer women about their problems, engaged in a revealing newspaper exchange with the region's most powerful editor, Asahel Bush, championed health reform, and favored temperance.

Born of Southern parents in Illinois, Adaline Melinda Willis (1837–1910) moved from her home in Marion, Iowa, to New York City, where she enrolled in the 1856 summer term of Dr. Russell T. Trall's Hygeio-Therapeutic College, an institution whose admission requirements were "a common school education, the possession of common sense," and fees, including a $50 summer tuition. Two graduates of the school, Drs. George E. and Frances A. Kimball, might have influenced Ada's decision to study hydropathy under Trall. The Kimballs came to Iowa in 1855, practiced hydropathy (she specialized in the treatment of female diseases) in Iowa City, and he—aided by a skeleton, manikin, and illustrations—was a zealous itinerant lecturer for health reform.

An early, energetic, and influential proponent of hydropathy, Trall in the 1840s played a major role in establishing this medical system in the United States; in the 1850s he trained men and women—most of whom came, Trall boasted, "from the ranks of the working class"— as hydropathic physicians in New York City. The professor hoped his graduates would "go among the people and teach them, and their drug-doctors too, a better way of life than the horrible plan of swallowing poisons." During a time when it was difficult for women to gain admission into medical schools, about a third of Trall's graduates were females. Rejecting the limitations society placed on women, the reformer defended training them for a variety of reasons. "The indecent behavior, boorish manner, and debauched habits which are so rampant, if not unavoidable, where young men are long associated together without the refining influences of women, are unknown in the Hygeio-Therapeutic School." More important, Trall argued, since "three-quarters or more of all the doctors' bills of our contry [*sic*] come from prescriptions to women and children, there seems to be a natural demand for more female professors of the healing art than of males," and "the most successful practitioners in the diseases peculiar to [females] in all ages have been women." Trall predicted:

Our hydropathic school is . . . bound to take the lead in bringing females into the ranks of the medical profession. And our female graduates are destined to be the reformers also. They will become teachers as well as doctors. They will do among their sex a work incomparably more important than the mere curing of disease; they will instruct the mothers, the wives, and the daughters of our land how to preserve health; and mothers, through them, will learn how to rear all their children so as to establish them in correct physiological habits; and thus the greater portion of the $50,000,000 now paid annually to our forty thousand male physicians, with the snug little item of a few millions annually expended at five or six thousand drug-shops, will be saved for other and better uses.

When Ada studied at the medical school, its prospectus listed nine teachers and announced: "Increased facilities will be provided for practical anatomy and dissections and all the departments of an educational course will be more thorough and complete than ever before."

Very likely Dr. Lydia Folger Fowler, who taught clinical midwifery at the college, influenced Ada. Fowler, the second woman to receive a medical degree in the United States and the first woman professor in an American medical college, had lectured at various places to women on hygiene and physiology, participated in woman's rights conventions, and promoted the temperance movement. The noted female reformer's recollections of lectures, especially a tour of Wisconsin in 1853, as well as personal encouragement, might have been major factors in Ada's unusual decision to take hydropathy and the woman's rights cause to a distant frontier.

Ada attended lectures, debated, declaimed, and read essays during the required two terms; thus in April 1857 she—the youngest member of her class—received an "irregular diploma" because the school had not yet received a charter.

A few months later she married her classmate Gideon Allen Weed (1833–1905) in the school's lecture hall before professors and students. An observer concluded that the newlyweds "have now united hands, hearts, fortunes, and diplomas in the place and among the associations where they had so faithfully studied the laws of life, and so attentively prepared themselves for future usefulness and duty, and, we hope and trust, abundant happiness."

Unlike some graduates who returned to the college and studied for a "regular diploma," the Weeds decided not to delay their battle for frontier reform. Early in 1858 the young doctors sailed to San Francisco. Mrs. Weed later explained: "We came, not as many do, in search of a fortune, intending to store it in a strong purse, and then go back to our old home again; but we came, expecting to make it a home, and to live and labor for perhaps our whole lives in the young, the rich, and the lovely state of California." She was vague about their next move: "Circumstances merely personal influenced us to continue our journey" to Oregon Territory in late February.

Oregon seemed promising. In 1857 Trall listed it among the newer states and territories sympathetic to his medical system. Further-more, there was no hydropathic physician in the territory, Oregon bookstores advertised hydropathic publications, and items in the *Water-Cure Journal* showed that devotees of hydropathy lived in the Willamette Valley. A few Oregonians had furnished testimonials for hydropathy in the journal; some residents, including more than forty from Oregon City, subscribed to it.

After renting an office in the City Book Store in Salem—then the second largest city in Oregon with about 1,500 inhabitants—the Weeds' first requirement was to establish a hydropathic practice that would furnish a living and funds for a water cure establishment. Such a building would contain bathing facilities, a gymnasium, and rooms for boarding patients. On July 30, 1858, the couple advertised:

G. A. & Ada M. Weed, Physicians, offer their professional services to the citizens of Salem and vicinity. They will practice the Hygeio-Medical (better known as the Hydropathic) system; believing all drugs to be not only unnec-essary in the successful treatment of diseases but injurious to the constitution of the patient, and relying upon Hygenic appliances. Special attention will be given to obstetrics, and those diseases peculiar to women and children by Mrs. Weed.

The Weeds, for a variety of reasons, soon became controversial and engaged in many disputes, especially with professional men. Out of necessity pioneer women "doctored" their families and neighbors; however, Ada was suspect because she held a medical degree (she was the first female in Oregon with one) and, unlike other females, she advertised. Moreover, she and her husband were so-called irreg-ular practitioners. In Oregon as elsewhere in America, there was bit-ter disagreement over the merits of various medical systems, includ-ing allopathy (regular physicians prescribing drugs), homeopathy (irregular physicians advocating "very minute doses of medicine"), and hydropathy (irregular practitioners advocating the therapeutic value of water, vegetable diets, Graham crackers, fresh air, light clothing, and proper rest). The newcomers were also suspect because they advocated change. The Weeds not only wanted to cure physical ailments but also to remedy societal ills. They informed friends that they labored in "the field of human reformation."

One of Ada's first lectures favored woman's rights and attracted Asahel Bush; his response was the first and best-publicized attack on either of the reform-minded Weeds. Bush was territorial printer, edi-tor of the *Oregon Statesman*, a leader of a group of Democrats known as the Salem Clique, and a practitioner of the so-called Oregon style of journalism—"a species of storm-and-stress composition, strong chiefly in invective." Bush devoted most of his energies to political vituperation but occasionally denounced reformers, including advocates of temperance—"corrupt demagogues and narrow brained fanatics"—abolition, and woman's rights. In the fall of 1858 he was embroiled in a major political fight with Oregon's congressional delegate Joseph Lane, but the combative editor found time to engage a different kind of opponent—a female urging improved conditions for her sex. During the 1850s Bush was the target of many personal and political epithets and slurs, including "Ass-A-Hell," and "the father of lies." Today he would be aptly described as a "male chauvinist pig."

Soon after hearing the reformer's speech, Bush published his critique under the title of "Woman's Sphere":

On Wednesday evening last, Mrs. Dr. Ada M. Weed delivered a lecture in the "Christian Church," in this place to a very large and respectable audience, upon the subject of "Woman: her Education and Development." Mrs. Weed has a good voice, and a rather pleasing countenance; and she read her lecture with a generally correct intonation, and in a tolerable manner. She was listened to with very respectful attention; and her occasional happy hits were greeted with rounds of good humored applause.

Some of the statements made and arguments advanced by Mrs. W. were correct enough, and many of her suggestions might be profitably acted upon by the fairer portion of her audience, but the whole lecture was leavened with the "Woman's Rights" and other modern "reform" humbugs. We cheerfully acquiesce in the opinion that woman should have better opportunities for physical and intellectual education than are generally afforded her; we would be glad to see new avenues of industry opened up to these unfortunate females who are compelled to toil for a livelihood, in our large cities, and elsewhere; but we opine that in the selection of occupations for females, some reference should be had to the fitness of things. We concede to woman certain rights, but among these we do not place the right to lay aside her womanly modesty, and, forgetting her true mission in the world and her obligations to society, to dispute with the sterner sex the palm of mental and physical vigor and endurance.

The true sphere of woman is in the domestic circle. There the true woman finds abundant scope for the exercise of the highest and best faculties with which God has endowed her; there she is the chief ornament and attraction, and there she excites the holiest and purest emotions of which the heart of man is capable. Those women who, from misfortune, are compelled to seek employment in other directions, invariably call forth our pity and sympathy; but when a woman voluntarily leaves the domestic walks of life, and embarks in those pursuits which properly belong to the ruder sex, our pity gives way to quite a different emotion.

Mrs. Weed argues that woman should practise medicine and law; that they should become surveyors, navigators, etc. To our mind, the stern warrior Achilles, dressed in woman's garb, and spinning flax with the maidens, was not more out of his proper sphere than would be a woman engaged in either of the above mentioned avocations. We are aware that several women have recently adopted the profession of medicine, and we have Mrs. Weed's authority, that a female is successfully practising law in Philadelphia. But these are women who have unsexed themselves, and who consider themselves highly aggrieved in that they were not formed in masculine mold. It is clear that the duties pertaining to those professions, are entirely incompatible with the relations of marriage and maternity. Imagine, for instance Madame the Doctress, making her usual morning round of visits, with a pair of pill-bags upon one arm, and a squalling babe of six months on the other; or Madame the lawyer, in an "interesting situation," arguing a case of *crim. con.* before a judge who divided her attention alternately between the suit in progress, and the suckling of a pair of twins. Our readers may pursue the *reductio ad absurdum* at their leisure. With the proposition of Mrs. Weed, that there are some of the offices of a physician more proper to be performed by females, we are not disposed to quarrel.

There is a disposition to go to extremes upon this question of woman's rights. Many are disposed to deny to women the rights which clearly ought to belong to them; while others, with even less show of reason, claim for them rights and privileges which are utterly at variance with female character and with all our pre conceived notions of womanly modesty and purity. The truth lies between the two extremes. Give to woman proper advantages of education; open up to her those avenues of industry, or of distinction, if you will, which are suitable for her; but above all, let her cultivate those charms and graces which adorn and beautify female character, and which alone can render woman attractive in the eyes of the other sex. Fit her for the proper enjoyment of home comfort and happiness, and she will cease to aspire to the forum or the quarter deck.

Relishing his attack on Mrs. Weed in particular and women in general, Bush delivered other slaps. Perhaps he had not written them but had been waiting the proper time to print them.

Ah, how much meaning is comprised in that simple expression, *the old fashioned mother.* It carries our thoughts back to those women whose home influence was pure and elevating; who taught their daughters how to be blessings to society, by their goodness, their diligence, and their useful knowledge. We think of the lofty heroism, the brave endurance, the thousand virtues they inculcated, and sigh at the contrast between the past and the present. How few modern mothers understand or perform their duty in training their children. A smattering of this, that and the other, is considered quite sufficient education, and to show off to advantage is made the great business of life. No wonder there are so many desolate firesides, so many unhappy wives—so many drinking, gambling husbands.

Naturally, Ada, who anticipated personal ridicule in the press, could not absorb an editor's attack without offering a rebuttal. On November 30, 1858, Bush published it and his demeaning reply:

Mr. Editor—In looking over the editorial columns of *The Statesman* of Nov. 9th, I find, under the above heading, a notice of the lecture delivered at the Christian Church on the evening of the 3d. I am not surprised to see it mentioned and commented upon in your paper. Your report of the meeting is plain, simple, and without exaggeration, but in the report of the lecture, I am pained to see, you have selected the points of minor importance upon which to found your principal remarks.

You say, "some of the statements made and arguments advanced were correct enough—but the whole lecture was leavened with the 'woman's rights' and other modern 'reform' humbugs." The lecture contained not a word on woman's rights, farther than her right to an education, her right to a broader field of labor, and to receive a just remuneration therefor. The words were not made use of but once, and then, in a quotation from an eminent divine. As to "other modern reform humbugs," I do not know to what you refer, unless it be the discontinuance of the use of tobacco and the brandy-bottle; these perhaps you term "reform humbugs."

Again you say, "we cheerfully acquiesce in the opinion that woman should have better opportunities for physical and intellectual education," etc. To enforce these particular points was the main aim of the lecture. "But we opine," say you, "that in the selection of occupations for females, some reference should be had to the fitness of things." Now, you say, "Mrs. W. argues that women should practise medicine and law; that they should become surveyors, navigators," etc. As to medicine and law, I did say that particular parts of these professions were better adapted to females; but in speaking of surveying and navigation, I had reference, as you say, to the "fitness of things," I said, "surveying and navigation appear to me to belong as strictly to woman's circle of action, as do midwifery and ribbon-selling to man's." You say I argue that women should become surveyors and navigators.—Every attentive listener that heard the lecture, certainly knows this was not the fact. It was used, simply to show the want of fitness in men's occupations. This point you have grossly misrepresented.

Your illustration of Achilles dressed in woman's garb and spinning flax with the maidens, embodies the idea I wished to make appear. Man is constantly making similar innovations upon that which he chooses himself to term "woman's sphere."

In your *"reductio ad absurdum,"* you seem to have drawn upon your imagination very extensively. "Madam the doctress making her round of morning calls, with babe and pill-bags." I would say, leave the pill-bags at home; and the babe might certainly be left with as much propriety on such occasions, as when its mother makes her round of fashionable visits. And your case of "a judge, who divided her attention alternately between the suit in progress, and the suckling of a pair of twins" her condition, extreme as you would have it appear, is certainly far superior in every respect of that of thousands of females of the present day, who, from want of employment, either sit by the pavement, with babes at their bosoms, asking for alms, or nightly walk the streets, bartering their virtue for that which honest industry would not bring.

You say, further: "With the proposition of Mrs. W., that there are some of the offices of a physician more proper to be performed by females, we are not disposed to quarrel;" but in a previous paragraph you say, in speaking of women who perform these offices: "But these are women who have unsexed themselves," etc. Now, according to your own idea, it is necessary for a part of womankind to unsex themselves, in order to perform those duties which you think are most proper for them.

"We concede to woman certain rights." Will you please explain how you became possessed of her rights? Her rights are God-given. "But among these rights we do not place the right to lay aside her womanly modesty." Woman's sphere has been defined as being "wherever good may be done;" and I have yet to learn that in filling this sphere, she will have, in any degree, to lay aside her womanly modesty.

You would "give her proper advantages of education," etc., but *above all*, you would have "her cultivate those charms and graces which alone can render her attractive in the eyes of the opposite sex." Develope woman properly both physically and mentally, and you *will* render her attractive, without making that the especial aim of her education.

Instead of the lecture being designed to induce woman to desert the domestic circle, as you would make it appear, its main object was to enforce the necessity of a good physical and mental development, and an enlarged circle of thought and action, which (whatever else they may prepare her for) *will* fit her to fill, and to fill *well*, her highest and holiest of all offices—those of the wife and the mother.

Bush retorted:

We give place to the above communication from Mrs. Ada M. Weed, in reply to our notice of her lecture, delivered some three weeks ago in the "Christian" church in this place. It is not our intention to hold a controversy with Mrs. Weed, although we have no doubt that is precisely what the lady most desires; as a public discussion would give her the notoriety to which women of her class chiefly aspire. However, as she alleges that we have misrepresented her in our notice of her lecture, our respect for the sex to which Mrs. W. claims to belong demands that we should give her the benefit of a hearing in our columns. We have therefore taken some pains to correct the errors in orthography, syntax and punctuation, which abounded in the manuscript of our fair correspondent, so as to make it presentable to our readers. This Mrs. W. may attribute to our gallantry; as our rule in cases where correspondents attack us, or attempt to criticise our articles, is to publish their effusions *verbatim et literatim*.

Mrs. W. charges us with misrepresenting her, in stating that her lecture was "leavened with the 'Woman's Rights' and other modern 'reform' humbugs." We were an attentive listener to the lecture, and we repeat, that with the exception of an occasional fling at the male sex, (for which she seemed to entertain a most profound contempt,—we hope not drawn from her own experience,) her lecture was mainly devoted to the threadbare story of woman's rights and wrongs, interspersed with an occasional eulogy upon the style of dress known as the "Bloomer." The lady's intimation in regard to "the use of tobacco and the brandy bottle," is entirely uncalled for and gratuitous. We apprehend we use as little of either of those articles as she does; and possibly less, for, with more generosity than she manifests, we might suppose she has carried her endeavors to become a male, to the extent of adopting tobacco chewing and whisky drinking. And the only reference to either of these articles which we remember in the course of her lecture, was when she was venting her wrath upon some ungallant individual (probably Amory Holbrook in one of his relapses) who stood upon a corner of the public street, "with a bottle of brandy in one hand and a plug of tobacco in the other," and had the ill-manners to laugh at her appearance as she strode along, attired in the costume (minus the wooden shoes) in which Chinese mandarins are represented in the picture-books.

Mrs. W. says we "grossly misrepresented" her, in stating that she argues that women should become surveyors and navigators. She certainly did use some language; probably, however, she was only quoting from some "eminent divine." If she disclaims the doctrine, of course we shall not insist.

Mrs. W. quotes our remark, that "with the proposition of Mrs. W. that there are some of the offices of a physician more proper to be performed by females we are not disposed to quarrel," and assumes from it that we admit the truth of the proposition. This is assuming too much. We made no such direct admission, but merely declined discussion of the question. Therefore the point which Mrs. W. makes on our claimed admission will not stand.

We have had neither time nor inclination to notice further this production of Mrs. Weed; and we must here close our columns against a continuance of this controversy. Should Mrs. W. desire to prolong it, (as she doubtless will,) she will probably find editors in the Territory who will be willing to devote a portion of their otherwise useless space to her behoof; and who will perhaps be glad of an opportunity to display their gallantry towards an "unprotected female." And should she at any time be disposed to be severe in her strictures upon us, we shall console ourselves with the reflection that we are not under her hands for *medical* treatment.

Because Bush closed his columns, it is impossible to ascertain the community's response to the exchange. One Salem resident complained that Bush eschewed argument and "resorted to ridicule and burlesque." Influenced by Ada's reforming spirit, Abigail Scott Duniway, who became Oregon's leading suffragist, might have had Bush in mind when she accused in April 1859: "It has long been a proverb concerning Oregonians that men cannot argue without resorting to ridicule or circumvention." Probably the controversy between the Salem editor and the physician sparked the extended debate over woman's rights that appeared in the *Oregon Argus*. Its editor, William L. Adams, was a political foe of Bush but shared Bush's sentiments about the bloomer costume. Adams complained: "We never can make 'trowsers' look natural on a woman. Pantalets do well enough for girls, but on a lady 'shin curtains' do look horrible."

Bush's brusque treatment failed to silence Ada. At the same time that he ridiculed her, she gave a series of addresses in Salem but restricted them to female listeners. In the autumns of 1858 and 1859 the Weeds also made two lecture circuits in the Willamette Valley. As they started their first tour the Weeds described medical conditions in Oregon.

There are a good many radical hydropaths here who eschew tea, coffee, meat, drugs, etc. and the people generally seem to be in a transition state. They are opposed to the allopathic system of drugging, and, although not exactly prepared to indorse the "Cold Water-Cure" are leaning toward our system, which unfortunately is misrepresented by this term. They have seen the evils of the drug system, and are looking about for something better. Nearly all with whom I converse have facts enough at their command, many of them obtained by bitter experiences, to satisfy themselves, and which ought to satisfy everyone, of the fatal working of the theory of drug medication. The people here, as elsewhere, are in advance of their physicians, scores of them knowing more about this treatment of disease, and the laws of health, than they do.

The doctors are nearly all of the "Old School." Since we have been in the Territory we have treated a number of desperate cases successfully, but have lost none; but we have been charged with losing patients that we never had, and who were already dead when we arrived in the Territory! But finding they could not dislodge, nor even intimidate us in this way, the doctors have lately taken another tack; they now say that they believe in the use of water in the treatment of disease, and claim it as part of their system; only a little while ago they could say nothing bad enough against it. Now they recognize it as an important auxiliary in their practice. A wonderful conversion, truly! but I suspect the almighty dollar to be the principal cause.

There are several of these new converts who live not much more than a stone's throw from where I am writing. One of them who, last winter, publicly denounced Water-Cure as a "perfect humbug," told me, the other day, that he used water extensively in his practice. He said that he supposed he was the strangest man I ever saw, for sometimes he used cold water almost entirely, and at other times the most active and powerful drugs, and that it was just as a notion took him!

The cause of Hydropathy has suffered more from such drug-doctors who apply water according to their theory of disease, than from all other causes combined; for the people being generally unable to discriminate between different theories, imagine one to be just as good as another; and if water fails to cure, no matter how absurdly applied, the system gets the blame. We have found many warm friends here who are willing to help us in any way they can. We have a good deal of encouragement to locate permanently in this place. Invalids are very numerous, and consumptions and female diseases are alarmingly prevalent.

The Weeds expounded their reform message and practiced medicine in settlements scattered between The Dalles and Eugene City.

The hydropaths remained several days in towns, where both talked in churches or courtrooms. Between platform appearances each was available for medical consultation. In free lectures or those with a fifty-cent admission charge, Gideon championed hydropathy; his wife—praised by one listener as "an intelligent, enterprising, and reformatory lady"—spoke on other topics, including "Marriage, Domestic Happiness, and Social Discord," "Woman, Her Education and Development," "Causes and Cure of Consumption," or on subjects restricted to female listeners.

Ada's lecture on "Marriage, Domestic Happiness, and Social Discord" has not survived, but undoubtedly she, like eastern women advocating rights for their sex, deplored the condition of married women. Although Dr. Weed recited the wrongs husbands inflicted on wives, it is doubtful that she was as critical as Elizabeth Cady Stanton, who argued that marriage reform deserved primacy. Taking her own marriage as a model, Ada probably urged men to be more considerate and to ponder the results of male domination. Reason and tolerance, she believed, would lead to domestic tranquility.

Lectures on consumption were always appropriate, for Trall warned: "Consumption of the lungs is the most general evidence and the most fatal result of the artificial and enervating habits of civilized society"; moreover, "Females, from their more sedentary indoor, and relaxing habits, are rather more liable to this malady than males." Trall censured allopaths for their "senseless and murderous practice" on patients weakened by the disease. "The ordinary treatement," Trall concluded, "may be resolved substantially, into opium, bleeding antimony, blisters, and expectorants. Each article and each process, I affirm is individually injurious, and all are collectively pernicious."

What Ada said at meetings limited to her own sex is unknown, but she obviously relied on the hydropathic system espoused in Trall's lectures and his writings as they related to women. Like other eastern hydropaths, she underscored the fact that women were more frequently under physicians' treatment than men. Lack of exercise, seclusion, tight garments, improper diet, and drug medicine all contributed, the reformer argued, to the alarming condition of women's health. Ada insisted that any female suffering from any disease must immediately reject medicine and embrace hydropathy. She damned patent medicines advertised in Oregon newspapers and stocked by local druggists.

To avoid illness Ada enthusiastically recited Trall's rules of universal health: "plain unmixed food, free breathing, correct bodily positions, and various exercises." Abigail Scott Duniway shared Ada's concern about the well-being of frontier women and furnished readers similar advice: the "secret of . . . good health is proper clothing, bathing, exercise and food, and *no* strong medicine."

In lectures open only to women, Ada conveyed information about birth control and sex; such talks were probably the basis for accusations of obscenity. According to the historian Andrew Sinclair, "Every woman's physician repeated endless cases of women begging him for methods to stop having children. Most of the methods peddled by the doctors were worse than useless." Ada's advice on birth control is unknown; Trall refused to publish his system. In 1857 he boasted:

We are in possession of the knowledge of a physiological law, by the application of which, any female may prevent conception at will, without injury or inconvenience, and without in any way interfering with the conjugal relations. The process is as simple, almost, as the act of willing; but for obvious reasons, we can not publish it. Indigent and sickly married females, who do not desire, and should not have children (and these alone) may apply to us privately and confidentially.

Ada must have reiterated Trall's judgments on sexual intercourse. He permitted "a monthly or semi-monthly indulgence, a habit in accordance with rules of temperance, chastity, and reason" and warned: "Excessive sexual indulgence in the marriage bed not only destroys the health, temper, and disposition of the wife, rendering her gloomy, peevish, hysterical, and querulous, but often destroys the happiness of the family circle entirely." She probably said something to the effect that "a married couple should no more allow a child to be conceived when either of them is in a state of fatigue from a hard day's work, or in any condition of bodily exhaustion, or mental disturbance, or agitation, grief, despondency, anxiety, passion, or fretfulness, than they would allow themselves to commit murder." Certainly Dr. Weed discussed pregnancy and confinement, accusing regular practitioners of prescribing drug-poisons that threatened the health of the mother and baby.

The lecturer must have warned about masturbation or referred her audience to Trall's *Home Treatment for Sexual Abuses.* In this pamphlet the author insisted that many people, especially boys, masturbated and that this distressing habit could be terminated if parents cautioned their children: they would hardly ever engage in "habitual self-pollution . . . if he or she knew at the outset that the practice was directly destroying the bodily stamina, vitiating the moral tone, and enfeebling the intellect."

Perhaps Ada recommended Trall's *New Hydropathic Cook Book* that rested on the premise that human beings would never have "peace within . . . until a thorough and radical reform is effected in the eating habits of the civilized world." Insisting that "vegetarianism is the true theory of diet," the New York physician lamented "that most cookbooks contained recipes blending seasonings, spices and greases. . . . No wonder the patrons and admirers of such cookbooks are full of dyspepsia, and constipation, and hemorrhoids, and biliousness of every degree, and nervousness of every kind!"

Since Ada and her husband took subscriptions for such items as the *Water-Cure Journal*, the *Hydropathic Encyclopedia, Uterine Diseases and Displacements*, and *Home Treatment for Sexual Abuses*, it is safe to assume that she advised her listeners to consult these publications.

As a result of her lectures, Ada's name was associated with woman's rights. Many Oregon ladies considered her a fanatic, rejected her call for additional opportunities for females, and refused to attend her meetings. Thus Ada asked Adams that, when he published her notice announcing a free and restricted lecture on a subject "in which all females are interested," he stress that she would not speak on woman's rights.

In May 1859 Gideon Weed summarized the results of their first lecture tour:

> We have lectured in all the principal towns, and met with much better success in our enterprise than we anticipated, not only in a pecuniary point of view, but in arousing the people to think on the subject of Health Reform.
>
> Our lectures have generally been well attended, and not unfrequently we have had crowded houses. Mrs. Weed's lecture on The Education and Development of Woman, in particular, has been very well attended and has excited considerable discussion, both favorable and unfavorable, through the Press, and otherwise. But notwithstanding the bitter and mean opposition we have met with in many cases, we are gaining friends from every part of the State; and what is more cheering still, they belong to the intelligent class. . . .
>
> In one town in which we lectured, the dupes of drugs and rum tried to put us down. They circulated a story that we were "Free Lovers," and that Mrs. Weed's lectures "were too obscene for any decent person to listen to." . . . Mrs. Weed has had quite a number of obstetrical cases, and has a good prospect for as much as she will want to do in that line.

Ada also wrote to Dr. Trall and recalled:

> We traveled much of the time, visited the principal towns and villages, and lectured upon hygiene and hydropathy in all parts with a good degree of success. . . . On our second tour it was very encouraging to meet a person here and there who had put into practice our teachings; to find a young man who had been induced by our admonition to free himself from the use of tobacco; to hear a mother say she had ceased to feed her little ones on pork and grease, tea and coffee; and to find the wholesome Graham loaf on the table, where bakers' bread or soda-biscuit had ever been before. Yes, this was

encouraging. This was pay. It was a very great stimulus to the flagging energies. It was the "oil of gladness" on our hearts, and Heaven knows health-reformers on the Pacific need it.

But the Weeds neglected to tell Trall about their financial difficulties; in fact, Ada later misled her teacher, "We had a good practice . . . and [as] many patients as we could accommodate in our house." The couple had won converts to their medical system, attracted patients, and covered the costs of their first lecture tour; however, they failed to prosper. Because of Oregon's depressed economy, patients could not pay. After failing to find a better location in the Willamette Valley in the spring of 1859, the hydropaths, who had acquired a partner to help finance the outfitting of a house in Salem, took in some patients, and advertised: "Patients at a distance visited on reasonable terms. They may be consulted personally or by letter, free."

In the summer the Weeds, believing that they could afford a hydropathic establishment, again searched for a site in the Willamette Valley.

Gideon complained to an admirer late in 1859 that a money shortage made it impossible to open a water cure establishment and lamented: "We have a thousand enemies who are ready to take advantage of our difficulties and to circulate stories that we are 'starving out'—that 'we cannot pay our rent' that 'we are running in debt' etc., etc. You can not imagine with what a fiendish chuckle of satisfaction our enemies here and everywhere hail such an event." The doctor disclosed that "the proceeds of our lecturing this fall did not pay our expenses. Our free lectures were generally well attended; but our pay lectures were not." One reason for the financial failure of the tour may have been that Oregon newspapermen gave little space to the Weeds.

Unable to find a promising situation in the Willamette Valley, the doctors returned to California in April of 1860. For several months they campaigned for health reform in central California. Both of the Weeds portrayed their tour. California, Gideon concluded, "contains more active, wide-awake men—more enterprise—more perserverance—more politicians—more office seekers—more scamps—more vice—more bad whiskey, and more men that drink it, than any other country in the world."

In the spring of 1861 the Weeds opened a Hygeio-Medical Institute in Sacramento; this was the type of establishment they had hoped to outfit in some Oregon town. But the Weeds were not settled; in the fall of 1861 they followed the silver rush to Nevada's Washoe mining district, residing at Washoe City. In 1868 they returned to California. Two years later the Weeds left Vallejo and cast their fortune with Seattle, where they employed different tactics and had greater success improving society than they had in Salem. Gideon—by acquiring 18 weeks of allopathic training in 1869–70 at Chicago's Rush Medical College to increase both his knowledge and his status—placed a brief card in a Seattle newspaper announcing that he was a physician and surgeon. Thus he avoided a repetition of the controversy that had followed his hydropathic advertisement in the *Oregon Statesman*.

A lucrative medical practice and shrewd investments in real estate furnished a good living and a financial basis for reform activities. Gideon's major contribution was to the improvement of medical conditions. According to a contemporary, "The need of medical attention and proper care for the many who are annually injured in the logging camps and saw mills around the Sound" induced Weed to found the Seattle Hospital in 1874. A few years later the doctor provided free medical service to the indigent sick at Providence Hospital. He helped organize the Territorial Medical Society and the King County Medical Society and played a major role in securing passage of a law creating the state medical board. From 1879 to 1888 he was a regent of the University of Washington and urged the territorial legislature to fund a medical school. Weed actively supported the Republican and then the Prohibitionist party. Although badly defeated in seeking election to the city council in 1875—Ada blamed his failure on the saloon vote—Gideon was elected on a nonpartisan ticket as mayor in 1876 and was the first mayor to be reelected. "During his term," writes a biographer, "he instituted many reforms in the management of municipal matters and earned the approval of citizens irrespective of party lines." To check the anti-Chinese rioters of 1886, the physician and his son served as privates in the Home Guard.

Ada also acquired a local reputation. She did not practice medicine in Seattle—she, like her husband, did not advertise their hydropathic medical degrees—or follow the lecture circuit. As a member of Seattle society, Mrs. Weed lived a busy life: she hosted a variety of entertainments in a mansion they built in 1876; raised two children, Benjamin and Mabel; assisted her husband in his reform activities; served as a director of the Library Association; promoted Plymouth Congregational Church; represented her church at regional meetings, where Ada was twice elected secretary of Woman's Board of Missions; supported charities; and labored for temperance, serving as president of the Seattle branch of the Woman's Christian Temperance Union (WCTU).

Clearly the Weeds' efforts to improve their community through orthodox methods earned them social respectability in Seattle that was in marked contrast to the confrontation in Salem that resulted from their crusading zeal. A lengthy article in the Seattle *Pacific Tribune* of

October 25, 1877, described their twentieth wedding anniversary, for which leading citizens gave the couple valuable china pieces that were "testimonials of the esteem in which they are held by the community of which they are a part."

In 1883 Ada departed from genteel reform and ran against three men for the position of Seattle school director. Although the Seattle *Post-Intelligencer* believed that she was as competent as the other candidates, she received only 1 of the 154 votes cast—which included 12 by women.

Mrs. Weed allied with temperance workers and shunned the Washington Territory suffragists who waged a long struggle from 1871 until their victory in 1883. Although she had not worked for the law of 1883 that enfranchised her sex, sometime thereafter she recognized its importance: women voted for prohibition. In January 1887 she wrote a public letter favoring equal suffrage, insisting that the visit of temperance leader Frances E. Willard in 1883 was a major reason why the legislature granted the vote to women. "Her ringing arguments in favor of Woman Suffrage, coming from her high Christian standpoint, were effective shots in the stronghold of Christian conservatism." The region's most vocal suffragist, Abigail Scott Duniway— who railed at those combining the suffrage and prohibition movements—called Ada a "negative suffragist" and argued that Susan B. Anthony and local leaders, including herself and her newspaper, the *New Northwest,* deserved more credit for the victory in 1883 than Miss Willard. Despite disagreement over the WCTU, Weed, a recent champion of equal suffrage, and Duniway, a long-time suffragist, generally agreed on the impact of woman's suffrage. Ada commended women because they voted for honest candidates and prohibition and because they were conscientious jurors. She stressed the importance of suffrage:

It comes in the great mental uplift given to the mothers of our people. It plants her feet on the lofty uplands where she is compelled to look beyond herself, and those things pertaining to herself, and the everyday circumstance of existence; and she comes to place the immediate at its true value, as seen in relation to the great aims and ends of life. Responsibility is a great educator. Life comes to have more meaning; it is enriched; individual womanhood is dignified; to home is added fresh honors; a new halo encircles the head of its goddess, and upon man in all coming generations falls the benediction.

A few weeks later Ada joined other writers disagreeing with Seattle's leading newspaper, the *Post-Intelligencer,* for its editorial opposition to woman suffrage. Ada, in what she called "a suffrage fight with the *Post-Intelligencer,*" delivered the sharpest rebuke, charging that the newspaper had "allied itself with the narrow, the base, the untrue," and added:

There is one, and only one interest, business, cause or class of people that today and yesterday and during its existence, is, and was, and will be a unit against the woman's vote. That is the liquor traffic. This prolific source of crime, the corrupter of the ballot, this organized defier of law, this hotbed of riot and treason, this monster that fattens on and gloats over the depravity and weakness of our people and laughs and sneers at the wretchedness, the want, the woe and the ruin it leaves behind; this devil-fish, that with its millions of money, its myriads of conscienceless men; its compact organization and its extended control of the press threatens the very life of this Nation; this is the one united power, this is the unbroken phalanx against woman suffrage. And the *Post-Intelligencer* by espousing the restriction of the suffrage proclaims itself the ally of this most damnable iniquity.

Mrs. Weed assumed that the newspaper spoke for the Republican party and predicted the party's demise if it rejected equal suffrage— "Starved to death in the house of its friends, who refused to pour the nourishing food of living issues into its blood."

Responding to Ada's attack, an editorial in the *Post-Intelligencer* generalized that a majority of American men and women opposed woman suffrage. But Duniway set aside her disagreements with Ada and praised her "ringing letter of protest" against a newspaper that had sided "with the elements of bigotry and licentiousness."

Soon after Ada's denunciation of the newspaper, the Supreme Court of Washington Territory invalidated the legislation that had enfranchised women. This peculiar decision immediately prompted controversy. The *Post-Intelligencer,* the only Seattle newspaper hostile to woman's suffrage, allowed angry opponents to use its columns. One of the editor's responses to these attacks on himself and the judges was a familiar ploy: he shifted attention to the question of woman's role in society. The editor's piece, entitled "The Perfect Woman," reasoned: "If history teaches us anything, it teaches that in the field of thought and intellect woman can accomplish anything that can be accomplished by men. It teaches, then, the absolute equality of men and women." But the writer quickly qualified his lofty sentiments:

Nature . . . leaves to man the work for which he is especially fitted, while woman assumes that which is her own. . . . The ideal American woman, then, is the woman who best performs the work for which she is fitted; the woman whose first interest is her home, and who, after that, devotes her time to the church and to the amelioration of the condition of her brother men and sister women.

Such a description of woman's role in society must have prompted Ada to recall her conflict with Bush nearly 30 years earlier, and so must the editor's ruling in mid-February that suffragists could no longer publish letters in his paper.

Meanwhile, Weed was among Seattle leaders mobilizing men and women exasperated by the court ruling. As president of the local branch of the WCTU, she helped members pass indignant resolutions and a vote of appreciation to a sympathetic newspaper in the "War on Women." Ada attended a general meeting called to oppose the court decision, served on the executive committee, and argued in fervid if mixed metaphor: "Revolutions never go backward, and notwithstanding we have a decision of the Supreme Court against us, we should not give up the ship." But she found it necessary to abandon the meeting. Unwilling to cooperate with women hostile to temperance, she resigned her position on the executive committee.

Chastened by this unhappy experience, Ada was more careful in choosing allies in the continuing fight against the court decision. She joined twenty-six other ladies—two ladies known to be unsympathetic with prohibition were excluded—in calling a protest meeting for February 21, 1887, at Frye's Opera House. Unlike the earlier gathering, this group avoided taking sides on liquor; in fact, women did not address the protesters. It seemed in better taste, possibly safer, and politically wiser to have a man preside and to invite prominent men as speakers.

The degree of Mrs. Weed's subsequent participation in the futile struggle for suffrage is unknown. Organized protest waned in 1888. Such an extreme statement as that of the *Post-Intelligencer*—"As a rule modest and good women have not voted—at least not the second time—while vicious women and women of the coarser class have been vulgarly conspicuous at the polls"—aroused much less reaction than the newspaper's more moderate criticism of woman suffrage in 1887. Ada and Gideon, disenchanted with the Republican party, championed the King County Prohibitionist party in 1888 (Gideon unsuccessfully ran under the party's banner for county commissioner) because it condemned alcoholic beverages and endorsed woman suffrage.

Although defeated in her last attempt to reform society, Ada received praise for her accomplishments. A sympathetic biographer, for example, summarized: Mrs. Weed "has always been foremost in religious, philanthropic and moral reform work. She is a lady of culture and possesses literary taste and ability of a high order. Her influence upon the social life of our city has been pronounced and in every way beneficial."

In 1890 the Weeds began their move in steps to Berkeley, where

Gideon practiced medicine and the children attended the University of California. Ada maintained her social conscience to the end of her life, offering financial assistance for victims of the San Francisco earthquake and worrying about dishonest public leaders. In her old age she nursed her paralytic husband, suffered from a variety of ailments, and sought medical advice from her nephew, Dr. Park Weed Willis, a Seattle physician who had assumed Gideon's practice. Remembering her hydropathic training, she drank large amounts of water and might have felt a small victory for hydropathy when her nephew, an allopath trained at the University of Pennsylvania, approved her self-treatment: "Water I think is often very good treatment without any additional medicine."

Ada died of cancer in 1910, but she lived long enough to see the start of her daughter's career dedicated to improving the condition of the less fortunate. Mabel carried on her parents' reform spirit by serving as secretary of the Charity Organization Society of Berkeley, general secretary of the San Francisco Community Chest, and assistant director of the State Department of Social Welfare. Through these positions Mabel assisted twentieth-century California women, some of whom—according to her official reports—faced difficulties similar to those that Ada had complained about sixty years earlier.

BIBLIOGRAPHICAL NOTE

This paper is based on primary materials, including *Oregon Statesman* (Salem), *Oregon Argus* (Oregon City), *New Northwest* (Portland), *Post-Intelligencer* (Seattle), *Water Cure Journal* (New York), and various publications by Russell T. Trall, including *Hydropathic Encyclopedia* (New York, 1852), *Home Treatment for Sexual Abuses* (New York, 1854), *The New Hydropathic Cook-book* (New York, 1857), and *Water-Cure for the Millions* (New York, 1860).

Other sources include the Henry Cummins Collection and the Park Weed Willis Collection, University of Oregon Library, Eugene; Harry B. Weiss and Howard R. Kemble, *The Great American Water Cure Craze* (Trenton, 1967); George S. Turnbull, *History of Oregon Newspapers* (Portland, 1939); Eleanor Flexner, *Century of Struggle* (Cambridge, Mass., 1959); Edward T. James, ed., *Notable American Women, 1607–1950,* 3 vols. (Cambridge, Mass., 1971); and Ida Husted Harper, *The Life and Work of Susan B. Anthony,* 3 vols. (Indianapolis, 1898).

Unemployment, Disinheritance, and the Origins of Labor Militancy in the Pacific Northwest, 1885–86

CARLOS A. SCHWANTES

Confrontation and violence loom large in the histories of the North Pacific industrial frontier. Seattle's general strike, bloodlettings in Everett and Centralia, and shoot-outs in the silver camps of northern Idaho constitute a major part of the region's folklore. And these are only the best-known examples in a lengthy list of protracted strikes, lockouts, dynamite blasts, and broken heads and bodies. Any time resolute lumberjacks, sawyers, and coal and metal miners confronted equally determined employers, they risked violence. Because both entrepreneurs and workers on the North Pacific industrial frontier asserted the right of the individual to control his own destiny, struggles over such bread-and-butter issues as wages and hours frequently escalated into bitter contests to determine how much power workers would retain over their lives. Some might argue that the region's industrial conflict was rooted in the class consciousness of its workers, particularly those living in isolated lumber and mining communities. But there is an alternative, non-Marxian explanation for labor's militance. It is the ideology of disinheritance, first popularized in the Pacific Northwest during the unrest of the mid-1800s. This ideology not only explains the broad appeal of several protest movements, such as the Populist revolt that united farmers and workers in the 1890s, but also suggests why so many professed radicals eventually moved into the region's political and economic mainstream.

The events of one episode in particular—the anti-Chinese crusade that erupted during the hard times of the mid-1880s—initiated and legitimated the militant stance that became a hallmark of organized

Originally published in *Western Historical Quarterly*, October 1982.

workers in much of the Pacific Northwest. This crusade is significant because it resulted in the region's first major outburst of industrial violence and its first widespread, sustained interest in radical social and economic commentary. Apart from the obvious desire to rid the area of competing Chinese labor, the crusade of unemployed Caucasians and their allies generated and popularized a series of explanations for hard times. In a larger sense, protesters sought to comprehend the sudden economic and demographic changes that severely strained the region's social fabric during the 1880s. Partisans impelled as much by circumstances as by conscious effort proceeded to promulgate ideas that accounted for jobless white workers' abrupt decline in status to outcasts in a promised land and to offer a remedial program. In the process, they popularized a crude ideology of disinheritance that was the chief legacy of the crusade, an ideology that has contributed to a notable strain of militance in the Pacific Northwest.

Though contemporaries did not speak of an ideology of disinheritance as such, they often voiced an unmistakable fear that monopoly unfairly threatened the political egalitarianism and economic opportunity that they believed to be the birthright of settlers in America's undeveloped West. They worried, too, that the growing power of big business undermined the dignity and worth of individual producers—farmers and industrial workers alike. The Seattle *Daily Press* in the mid-1880s, for example, warned that "probably no other part of the country presents greater opportunities for the growth of corporate monopolies than this territory. Nowhere is it more the duty of the people to see to it that the grasp of these corporations is not confirmed, and to see to it that the people themselves and not the corporations are the governing power." The region's newspapers also published crudely drawn maps depicting the Northern Pacific Railroad's land grant as an enormous black cloud blighting two-thirds of Washington Territory. It made little difference that the land grant was actually a gigantic checkerboard minutely divided into alternate sections of railroad and government land. The real issue for many people was that the railroads and other forms of massed capital had already, or would soon, usurp the individual opportunity that settlers presumed to be their inheritance. The ideology of disinheritance criticized the growing political and economic power of the region's new land and mineral barons and challenged their influence by proposing a variety of remedial, sometimes even revolutionary, steps.

During the course of the anti-Chinese crusade, agitators seized numerous opportunities to expand the vague and poorly articulated protest against unemployment initially used to foment the trouble into a more encompassing ideology of disinheritance. Their new ideology enjoyed widespread appeal because they not only cloaked it with the mantle of a popular movement against the Chinese but also promoted it in terms of ideas already well established in the value system of the people. Included were the tenets of New Testament Christianity, the promise of the American Revolution, and the democracy of Abraham Lincoln. "Labor," anti-Chinese orators fondly quoted Lincoln as saying in his first annual message to Congress, "is prior to and independent of capital. Capital is only the fruit of labor, and could not have existed if labor had not first existed. Labor is the superior of capital, and deserves much of the higher consideration." As interpreted by Lincoln and most of the anti-Chinese agitators, labor encompassed the producing classes in general, not just industrial workers or a proletariat. In the context of the anti-Chinese crusade, remarks such as Lincoln's served easily to goad unemployed Caucasians into illegal acts of protest against capital's supposed pawns as they sought to restore the lost destiny of America's working citizens.

The anti-Chinese agitation began as a popular response to the depression that swept menacingly across the North Pacific industrial frontier in 1884. The economic downturn was really nationwide, but it dealt Oregon and Washington an especially severe blow. Completion of the region's first railway links to the East in mid-decade and the collapse of the building booms in Seattle and Tacoma released thousands of workers to compete for jobs that hard times made scarce. Many of those seeking work were Chinese immigrants imported during the two decades just past to build the Pacific railroads.

In the struggle for jobs, Caucasian workers reluctantly conceded that the Chinese were formidable competitors—"industrious to a fault, apt, skillful, obedient," able to live on wages "upon which a white man would starve, and in a condition utterly repellent to him. Without families to support, except in rare cases, their advantage over the American laborer [is] enormous." "Heathen John," added another observer, "is, of course, quite as willing to work on Sunday as on any other day." Caucasian workers and their middle-class allies especially feared that the region's new industrial monopolies would import a potentially unlimited supply of Chinese labor, thereby permanently reducing whites on the Pacific Coast to "inferiors in power and numbers."

Whites who saw themselves battling Chinese for jobs drew inspiration from the cultural prejudice and anti-Chinese racism prevailing on the West Coast. The Seattle *Daily Call*, for example, a paper popular with the unemployed, variously labeled the Chinese "treacherous, almond-eyed sons of Confucius," "chattering, round-mouthed lepers," and "yellow heathen." Complaining about the "mysterious language" and "vicious and demoralizing" habits of Chinese, whites loudly warned that the only way to compete with a "Chinaman is to adopt pagan ideas and pagan modes of life." Caucasian coal miners in the camps east of Seattle and Tacoma lustily sang:

> We rather live amongst the fleas
> Than be with you—the old Chinese. . . .

"The Chinese must go!" was an utterance heard frequently in Pacific Northwest communities in September and October 1885. Residents became obsessed with expulsion. Daily they grew more excited—or anxious. It was "War! War! War!" screamed an advertisement for Seattle's great IXL clothing store, which catered to a mass market. "The Chinese must go! The IXL says so."

The person who did the most to give the expulsion crusade direction was Daniel Cronin, a thirty-eight-year-old carpenter who came from California to Puget Sound in the summer of 1885. A man of mystery, he proved a skillful orator and persuasive genius. As organizer for the Knights of Labor in Washington Territory, Cronin exploited the discontent caused by hard times and seemingly overnight transformed a faltering, intimidated band of workers into a militant and idealistic brotherhood widely believed to number several thousand. Only nominally linked to the national organization of Knights, the territory's first large-scale labor organization bore Cronin's highly personal stamp.

Cronin used the growing power of the Knights to grasp the leadership of the anti-Chinese crusade. To a September meeting of Seattle's milling and disorganized Sinophobes, he boasted that he had a plan to rid Puget Sound of Chinese within a few weeks. "I was in Eureka, California, when the edict went forth that the Chinese must go," and he proposed to inform listeners how Eureka had successfully expelled its Chinese the previous February. He ominously warned that if Seattle's Chinese were not removed, "there will be riot and bloodshed this winter." Cronin and a group of associates who had worked themselves into the leadership of the region's Knights of Labor rapidly perfected plans for Chinese expulsion. They maneuvered Sinophobes into calling a territorial anti-Chinese congress, which met in Seattle in late September 1885 and decreed that all Chinese must leave Washington no later than November 1. Once local coordinating committees formed, Cronin, for reasons that remain unknown, temporarily stepped aside and let others handle the details of expulsion.

Among the prominent community leaders involved in the movement was a German immigrant shopkeeper and member of the Knights of Labor, R. Jacob Weisbach, mayor of Tacoma. The journalist Emma Adams, who happened to be touring Puget Sound during the uproar, interviewed Weisbach and asked him how he planned to get rid of the 700 Chinese who accounted for approximately one-tenth of Tacoma's population. The mayor replied, "I can not now state exactly. They have been informed that they *must* leave. The time allowed them for preparation has expired. They are aware of that. If any of them choose to tarry and take the consequences, we can not help it." Adams wondered if many of Tacoma's citizens opposed the movement "against cheap labor." "Not many," answered Weisbach, as he proceeded to explain the broader implications of the struggle. "We have here two classes. One lives on the products of its own labor. The other subsists on the fruits of other people's toil. The latter class laments the loss of the Chinese."

Weisbach's sweeping division of society into producers and drones language more akin to that used by the Knights of Labor and later the Populists than by Marx—exemplified one of the most ambiguous aspects of the evolving ideology of disinheritance. Some listeners might interpret such rhetoric as a call for class warfare to eliminate the capitalists, while others, believing that it implicitly rec ognized the American dream of economic plenty and social advancement for all honest toilers, heard it as a challenge to reform the economic system by eliminating its worst abuses.

The *Oregonian* editor Harvey Scott had no doubts about where Weisbach stood. To Scott, Weisbach was a "German Communist," but like most other observers he probably remained unaware of the secret ties linking Weisbach, Cronin, and other revolutionary Knights who plotted the anti-Chinese crusade. In various ways all were associated with the International Workingmen's Association of San Francisco. Describing itself as a "secret, mysterious, world-wide" organization that was "quietly honeycombing society," the IWA claimed to be a branch of the Marxist First International. Actually, the IWA to which Cronin and his associates belonged was a product of the feverish imagination of a young San Francisco attorney, Burnette G. Haskell. "Perpetually playing games," Haskell was, in the words of the historian Alexander Saxton, "a kind of Tom Sawyer never grown up; yet the games he played were at the shadow line of nightmare." His radical faith was a strange and confused blend of anarchism and socialism. He organized several secret groups under the names "Invisible Republic" and "the Illuminati" before boldly appropriating the title of Karl Marx's defunct First International.

Unfortunately, the clandestine nature of the IWA makes it impossible to assess accurately the full extent of its influence, to know precisely which turns and twists of the anti-Chinese crusade resulted from prior planning and which grew out of popular sentiment. It is possible—even probable—that Cronin left Eureka, the most important center of IWA influence outside San Francisco, fully intending to organize unemployed Pacific Northwest workers for the IWA. One point is clear, however; with its members or sympathizers leading both the local Knights of Labor and the anti-Chinese movement, the IWA operated like a wheel within a wheel, intending to use the popular issue of Chinese expulsion to foment fundamental economic change. Racism and radicalism thereby joined hands.

In the frequent torchlight parades in Tacoma, Seattle, and elsewhere, white workingmen displayed banners reading "Discharge Your Chinese" and "Down with the Mongolian Slave," but some banners also boldly proclaimed "Elevate the Masses." Despite occasional talk of class warfare by self-educated political theorists like Weisbach and Cronin, most participants in the movement apparently did not intend to overthrow capitalism but wanted, rather, to curtail the power of those who abused the system by degrading white laborers. In any case, an ideology of disinheritance soon evolved from the level of crude anti-Chinese epithets and ambiguous references to class warfare to a set of political demands embodied in the platforms of regional protest parties and candidates.

The evolution of the ideology of disinheritance was largely a process of education, of making people see things in a new way, of recasting vague resentments into a set of specific demands. The twentieth-century tendency to equate education solely with formal schooling obscures the way that public lyceums and study clubs once functioned as agencies of adult education. "The Knights of Labor," observed the Seattle *Daily Call*, "is the best organization ever inaugurated to unite and educate the industrial people. Each assembly is a school where true political economy is discussed." Thus, even if the majority of jobless participated in the Sinophobic crusade solely to remove their Chinese competitors—real or imagined—they could not avoid insinuations about the relationship between unemployment and political and economic power. In street-corner forums and Knights of Labor lyceums, agitators energized listeners by the sneer they attached to such words as *Chinaman* and *Northern Pacific* railroad. The two hateful terms grew intertwined in the minds of many of Washington's unemployed. The issue was power. The Northern Pacific, it was widely believed, had the power, and "the people" did not. The railroad not only owned an immense amount of land in Washington but also allegedly corrupted legislators, controlled newspapers, and attempted to stifle public protest. The railroad was believed to exploit Chinese labor in an undisguised effort to undercut prevailing wage rates and displace white workers.

Ironically perhaps, agitators endeavoring to generate popular resentment for the power of the new industrial monopolies had an unlikely and unwitting set of allies: land speculators and urban boosters. Most were more or less honest, but some had sold their souls for a fistful of dollars. All tended to exaggerate the virtues of Oregon and Washington in the promotional literature they issued by the ton. In the mid-1880s one agency alone—Oregon's state board of immigration—distributed more than 400,000 copies of pamphlets such as *Oregon as It Is: Solid Facts and Actual Results*. Among the "solid facts" was a guarantee of success to any laborer willing to work. The speculators and boosters were dream makers. Thousands of immigrants who believed along with Thoreau that "eastward I go only by force but westward I go free" set out for the great Northwest, transported as much by myth as by rail or sailing ship. The coming of hard times in 1884 that brought wageworkers reduced incomes and unemployment also snuffed out their dreams of a good life in a promising new land. Hard times mocked promoters' guarantees of success and bred hard feelings in many of the newcomers. Bitter and discontented, the jobless easily believed that their inheritance had been snatched unjustly from them.

Instead of resigning themselves to poverty as they might have done, the unemployed grew militant. The agitators who educated them to see corporate power and the capitalist system in a new light first suggested what they could do about the immediate problem of unemployment. The most popular solution—Chinese removal—was to deny monopolies the pawns they used to drive down wages and reduce proud men with a rich heritage to begging for jobs and food to sustain their families. People who believed that monopolies used their power over legislators to thwart the democratic process—to prevent the passage or enforcement of laws designed to encourage Chinese to leave the Pacific Northwest—were not above adopting extralegal methods.

In her interview with Jacob Weisbach, Emma Adams asked whether acts of violence would be committed against the Chinese:

"None whatever," responded the Tacoma mayor. "The probable course will be a strict system of boycotting, which will certainly result in their departure."

"You are confident that the order of the Knights of Labor will succeed in expelling these men from the city?"

"It will. Undoubtedly it will."

Despite Weisbach's rejection of violence, agitators used claims of Caucasian disinheritance to justify actions that transgressed the thin line between order and violence. Because so many Chinese were supposedly smuggled into Oregon and Washington after passage of the

Chinese Exclusion Act of 1882, the Seattle *Daily Call* charged that their ways "are so dark and furtive that their tricks cannot be detected and unearthed. They come here like an army of rats to gnaw—of grasshoppers to consume." Warning that "self-preservation is the first law of nature," the paper pointedly reminded workers that the Chinese were in the United Sates in defiance of the law and thus had "forfeited the protection of our laws." Thus, participants in the anti-Chinese movement were taught to regard their victims as subhumans who could claim no legal rights. That notion animated Puget Sound's Sinophobes and encouraged them to take a militant stance that risked violence.

In early September 1885, a short time prior to the calling of Washington's territorial anti-Chinese congress and less than a week after Knights of Labor miners in Rock Springs, Wyoming, wantonly attacked Chinese miners and killed twenty-eight and wounded fifteen, violence erupted on Puget Sound. A small group of whites and Indians murdered three Chinese hop pickers in the Squak Valley east of Seattle. Four days later, on September 11, at the Newcastle mines of the Oregon Improvement Company, one of the largest and most powerful coal operators in the territory, a dozen masked men ignited the quarters where thirty-seven Chinese workers slept. The Chinese escaped the blaze but lost their belongings. Finally, on the morning of November 3 the screech of a steam whistle signaled the last phase of Tacoma's efforts to expel its Chinese. While the mayor and sheriff stood by as spectators, members of the Committee of Fifteen (a coordinating body), the Committee of Nine (a semisecret group probably allied with the International Workingmen's Association), and several hundred others invaded the Chinese quarters. The methods they used to rout the remaining Chinese bore no resemblance to a boycott.

Because detailed accounts of the Tacoma and Seattle expulsions have already been published, it is necessary only to summarize these two incidents and add a brief description of agitation in Portland before analyzing how confrontation and violence fostered further interest in the ideology of disinheritance and led to its incorporation into the platforms of the region's several new labor-oriented parties and candidates. The crowd of whites that visited Tacoma's Chinese quarters ordered inhabitants to "pack up at once." Most complied; some begged for more time. In the afternoon about 200 Chinese, accompanied by several wagons of luggage and an escort of whites, journeyed out of Tacoma to a small Northern Pacific station nine miles away. A cold rain fell steadily as the strange procession passed into open country. The Chinese women rode on the wagons; some of the men stumbled through their tears. After an overnight stay in the

Northern Pacific station, during which two Chinese died of exposure, the remainder were forced aboard a train for Portland. Meanwhile, fires of suspicious origin reduced Tacoma's Chinese quarters to smoking debris. Everyone suspected arson. Police promptly arrested one tarrying Chinese but soon set him free for lack of evidence.

The expulsion was a classic case of frontier vigilantism. And as was typical of such episodes, it enjoyed the active support of many prominent community leaders, including Mayor Weisbach, the probate judge James Wickersham, two councilmen, and the editor of one of the city's influential daily newspapers. Their involvement is no doubt the major reason the expulsion proceeded so smoothly.

News of the event traveled to Seattle and Washington, D.C., at telegraph speed. While Seattle's Sinophobes excitedly discussed the virtues of the "Tacoma Method," as the expulsion was euphemistically labeled, President Grover Cleveland acted. He ordered troops from Fort Vancouver to Puget Sound, believing the area to be in a state of insurrection. "What insurrection?" asked perpetrators as they returned peaceably to their homes. And they wondered what soldiers would do when they reached Tacoma:

> "How will they manage to put down a people who are not in rebellion?"
> "Let them come," said the calm minded. "We shall be glad to see them. It will give the boys a change."

The soldiers soon appeared, a portion encamped in Tacoma, and 350 proceeded to Seattle to prevent any expulsion attempt there. A grand jury that was hastily convened in Vancouver indicted twenty-seven Tacoma citizens, charging them with conspiracy and insurrection in violation of the 1871 Ku Klux Klan Act. The same act was also used to jail Cronin and sixteen other prominent members of Seattle's anti-Chinese movement. The action prevented trouble but also made martyrs of those arrested.

Alleged conspirators were indicted several times during the course of the anti-Chinese crusade, but no jury ever found any of them guilty. After a lengthy trial in Seattle in January 1886, for example, jurymen took less than ten minutes to find Cronin and his codefendants innocent. At about the same time, the upper house of the territorial legislature narrowly defeated several popularly demanded anti-Chinese bills. Angered by what they regarded as legislative arrogance and emboldened by the outcome of the conspiracy trial and the removal of federal troops from Puget Sound, Seattle's Sinophobes sprang into action. As in Tacoma, a coordinating committee and a crowd of sympathizers assembled at the sound of a prearranged signal, and on the morning of February 7 they swept noisily through the city's Chinese quarters. They pounded on doors, broke windows, and warned the Chinese to prepare immediately for the afternoon departure of the *Queen of the Pacific*.

Unlike the Tacoma expulsion, the one in Seattle resulted in bloodshed when whites divided into two opposing groups. The King County sheriff John H. McGraw worked with the city's upper class, or Opera House party, to oppose any extralegal action. The Knights' expulsion efforts faltered in the face of opponents determined to uphold the law. Last-minute legal action instituted by a Chinese merchant to halt the removal caused the Chinese to remain at the dock overnight. A skeleton guard of Knights maintained a vigilant watch, while deputies protected sleeping Chinese in a nearby warehouse. The *Queen* sailed the next day with 197 Chinese aboard, about as many as the steamship could safely hold. That afternoon a crowd of workers clashed with citizen deputies, or Home Guards, who attempted to escort the remaining Chinese from the dock back to their homes to await another ship. Curses led to hand-to-hand fighting and then to gunfire. Five people were wounded in the melee, one workman fatally. Shocked and sobered, the anti-Chinese crowd retreated and milled around while leaders desperately worked to prevent further bloodshed. The Territorial governor Watson C. Squire declared martial law and suspended the writ of habeas corpus. Once again President Cleveland dispatched federal troops.

As soldiers patrolled the strangely subdued streets of Seattle, the focus of the anti-Chinese movement shifted south to Portland, where lived more Chinese than in all of Washington Territory. Some of Portland's white workers had begun in early September 1885 to take the same organizational steps that culminated in violence and martial law on Puget Sound. The seasoned agitator Cronin offered guidance to the nascent movement. When he arrived in Portland in late January 1886, Knights of Labor and members of the Anticoolie clubs gave him a tumultuous welcome. Hailed as a hero and martyr of the "late Ku Klux farce in Seattle," Cronin participated in a grand procession that had all the trappings of a coronation or an affair of state.

Joining Cronin was another agitator, Burnette Haskell, self-proclaimed head of the IWA on the Pacific Coast. At Cronin's urging, radicals in the Portland assemblies of the Knights of Labor had invited Haskell to lead the expulsion crusade. He arrived on February 9, the day after martial law had been declared in Seattle. If he had any plans to visit the Puget Sound region, he wisely abandoned them. Together with Cronin and visiting Knights from Salem and Tacoma, Haskell staged an anti-Chinese congress in Portland on the eve of Washington's birthday. The meeting passed resolutions calling for impeachment of Governor Squire of Washington Territory, removal of Portland's Chinese within thirty days, and a boycott of the Portland *Oregonian*, the only prominent paper in the Pacific Northwest to defend the Chinese. Haskell, Cronin, and Nathan Baker, a leader of the local Anticoolie association, also launched a new journal, the *Oregon Alarm*, which had as its motto, "The Tools Belong to the Toilers; the Products to the Producers."

The Chinese fled or were driven out from some of the surrounding communities, but in Portland itself the racist campaign sputtered and eventually stalled in the face of determined opposition. The radical Knights of Labor who believed Haskell's presence would somehow guarantee Chinese removal were disappointed. Haskell quietly sailed back to San Francisco after spending less than two weeks in the Pacific Northwest, and a Portland grand jury charged Cronin with conspiring to deprive the Chinese of their rights. Portland was clearly not another Tacoma or Seattle, a fact that imperious Scott of the *Oregonian* alluded to with pride and relief.

Scott attempted to analyze the successes and failures of the agitators. The Tacoma expulsion, he said, was successful only because Tacoma was still "raw and immature." Having been founded only recently as the western terminus of the Northern Pacific Railroad, Tacoma retained many characteristics of a company town. Consequently, claimed Scott, "much of its population, so hastily gathered, is of the unstable class. Innovation is their motto, conservatism they detest." Furthermore, "the better class of inhabitants are new to each other and to their situation, and scarcely know how to meet new emergencies." The Seattle agitation, the *Oregonian* editor similarly argued, "could take place only in a frontier community, governed like a mining camp, under a very primitive civilization." Census figures support Scott's implication that Tacoma and Seattle, unlike Portland, contained a majority of newcomers. During the decade of the 1880s, Seattle's population increased by over 1,000 percent, and Tacoma's population by an even more astounding 3,000 percent. Among the newcomers were those who had journeyed west expecting to claim the promised land, but hard times dashed their unrealistic aspirations and expectations and made them susceptible to the notion that they must fight to regain their inheritance. In other words, as the labor historian Herbert Gutman has noted, "Aspirations and expectations interpret experience and thereby help shape behavior."

In terms of its immediate goal, the crusade to expel the Chinese from the Pacific Northwest achieved only partial success. Apart from Tacoma and a few small towns—mostly Cascade-area coal camps— the effort faltered. In Seattle whites battled whites in a brief but bloody confrontation, and in Portland, Cronin's attempt to generate enthusiasm for Chinese removal backfired. Indeed, the whole affair split the city's labor movement, discredited the Knights of Labor, and led General Master Workman Terence V. Powderly to recall Cronin's commission as an organizer. Thereafter, Cronin dropped from sight and apparently joined a small utopian commune on the Oregon coast.

In another sense, however, the crusade of the disinherited was notably successful: it called widespread attention to the grievances of workers. Because the 1886 violence in Seattle occurred almost simultaneously with bread riots in London and industrial violence in the Pittsburgh area, alarmed conservatives linked events on Puget Sound with an international revolutionary conspiracy. Chicago's Haymarket riot followed by a sensationalist grand jury report on the Seattle outburst seemingly confirmed their worst fears. Thus for many non-working-class residents of a hitherto geographically isolated region, confrontation and violence on Puget Sound represented a frightening introduction into the mainstream of the nation's social and economic controversies. It startled people who had previously been uninterested in, or unaware of, the Pacific Northwest's growing number of wageworkers and their struggle with unemployment. In many quarters the outburst earned organized labor a new measure of respect.

The worldwide unrest prompted the moderate Tacoma *Daily Ledger* to speculate that "there must be some monstrous evil at the foundation of our political and economic structure to render it as weak and toppling as it is." Suggesting just how deep the notion of disinheritance had penetrated community consciousness, the *Ledger* argued that the unrest was caused by the "unjust and inequitable distribution of the products of labor whereby thousands live from hand to mouth in filthy, disease and crime engendering hovels, while the lucky few waste the substance of the land in vain displays and luxurious living." The paper called for a modification of the present system to effect "a more just distribution" of the products of labor without removing proper incentives to sobriety and industry. The signs of the times so disturbed E. V. Smalley, editor of the booster publication *Northwest Magazine,* that he publicly urged ministers to consider laying aside their "out-grown theology to grapple with the real troubles of humanity which concern the ways of living decently and happily in this world and not how to get to Heaven." Society, said Smalley, could no longer afford to ignore the workers' cry that the "fruit of their labor is not equitably distributed." Such social and economic critiques appearing in two publications generally regarded as spokesmen for Northern Pacific interests helped further legitimate the ideology of disinheritance.

As a result of labor's new prominence, it wielded increased political influence in several important urban centers in Oregon and Washington. Many who had opposed labor's extralegal action against the Chinese nonetheless favored their removal. Thus, in all communities where anti-Chinese passions ran high, astute politicians knew what course to follow when the Knights steered their crusade into the political arena. Sylvester Pennoyer of Portland, a cultured, Harvard-educated lawyer, was one of those who clearly recognized an opportunity. Though he had little in common with the likes of Cronin, he was a popular figure with workingmen. Largely because of his outspoken anti-Chinese stand, Pennoyer captured the Democratic party's gubernatorial nomination. His campaign speeches brought cheering workers to their feet and popularized the ideology of disinheritance when he warned that "to-day the great producing and laboring classes of our state are being ground down between the upper and nether millstones of corporate power and cheap servile labor" and that if Chinese immigration continued "it will only be a few years until the Willamette valley will be the home only of rich capitalists and Chinese serfs."

Pennoyer led the Democratic party to victory in Oregon's June 1886 election, and as governor he did not forget the workers who had voted for him. In his inaugural address he urged legislators to abolish the state's immigration board so despised by organized labor. Said Pennoyer, "If the early pioneers of forty or fifty years ago could find Oregon without a trail through the forests or over deserts, immigrants that desire to come here now can undoubtedly find their way." The governor also convinced legislators to make Oregon the first state officially to recognize Labor Day as a holiday.

Left-wing Knights, buoyed by the success of their protest parties in Seattle and Tacoma municipal elections in mid-1886, launched a territorial People's party later that year. As Washington's congressional delegate they nominated William Newell of Olympia, a former territorial governor, who eagerly accepted. They also drew up a platform that began with the words, "The People's Party announces this truth: That when bad men and drones combine, the industrials must associate or they will fall an unpitied sacrifice in a contemptible struggle." Among the platform's twenty-six planks were calls for legislation to exclude all Chinese from the United States "except the authenticated agents of the government of that country," increasing the money supply, a graduated income tax, abolition of convict labor, factory and mine inspection, direct election of U.S. senators, elimination of free railway passes and discriminatory rates, a mechanic's lien law, and the suppression of the use of "intoxicating liquors." One plank idealistically proclaimed that "we believe that equal duties and equal responsibilities should receive equal remuneration regardless of race, color, creed or sex, and we will oppose all efforts to disenfranchise the women of Washington Territory," but another denounced the Chinese as a "standing menace to our laboring classes and a disgrace to a civilized nation." Their multifaceted platform represented a significant milestone in the perfection and promotion of the ideology of disinheritance. It survived the defeat and demise of the People's party movement of the 1880s and the Republican resurgence that accompanied the return of prosperity a few months after the Seattle riot. In 1891 the document served as a model for the first platform adopted by a far more successful protest party—Washington's Populist party of the 1890s. Many of the founding fathers of the state's Populist party, incidentally, were Knights formerly active in the anti-Chinese crusade. Also converted to populism in the 1890s was Oregon's Governor Pennoyer.

Participation in the anti-Chinese movement taught Pacific Northwest labor contradictory lessons. The skilled workers—who supported the newly formed American Federation of Labor (1886), put down roots in the community, enrolled their children in public schools, and planted roses around their bungalows—generally cast aside the idealism of the Knights and rejected even the radical elements of the ideology of disinheritance. Members of this moderate-to-conservative group, according to the Knight-turned-AFL-organizer C. O. Young, "began to learn what the organization of labor really meant. We ceased to some extent at least to live in the land of dreams and faced realities. We began to struggle for economic necessities, the reduction of hours, increase of wages, and other conditions of employment." Young's view may have been colored by his experience in jail as a participant in Seattle's anti-Chinese crusade, but he probably spoke for many of those members of the working class who learned that their skills enabled them to enjoy a modest portion of the world's goods—to claim, in other words, an acceptable inheritance.

The ascendant craft unionists like Young scornfully derided the Knights for their "impractical visionary philosophies" and expelled them from the communitywide labor councils that Knights had helped to found. But as the Knights declined in the late 1880s, AFL affiliates proved philosophically and organizationally unprepared to unionize the unskilled and semiskilled workers formerly attracted to the Knights. Thus, the Pacific Northwest's numerous migratory lumberjacks, hard-rock miners, coal miners, and harvest hands remained outside the mainstream of organized labor for several decades. At the same time, the old dreams of coming west to claim the promised land and with it a secure position in American society continued to exert a powerful attraction. As late as 1915 a member of the Industrial

Workers of the World complained that for years "the Golden West has been the Mecca in the dreams of the misguided worker in all parts of the country. If I can only get West has been his only thought." Thus, for reasons not unlike those that motivated people to participate in the anti-Chinese crusade of the 1880s, successive members of the region's sometimes downtrodden, but always expectant, producing classes gravitated into economic and political organizations that transmitted and updated versions of the ideology of disinheritance— the Alliance and populist movements and later parties, the Socialist party, the Western Federation of Miners, and the Industrial Workers of the World. All such organizations provided members a sense of social solidarity, enriched individual lives through a feeling of participation in epochal world events, and encouraged them to fight for their inheritance.

As for the Pacific Northwest's anti-Chinese crusade of the 1880s, it was without question a deplorable episode of racism—sordid, ugly, and thoroughly paradoxical. If it convinced one group of workers that the Knights were on the wrong track, it taught another lesson to those who continued to see themselves as outcasts and downtrodden in a promised land: confrontation got results. Even the bloody setback in Seattle attracted attention to their grievances and helped win a measure of popular support for political expressions of the ideology of disinheritance. The virtue of militance was a lesson that organizations animated by the ideology of disinheritance would not soon forget. Paradoxically, too, the ideology that encouraged their militance and protests also accounts for the ease with which all but the diehard radicals abandoned the cause after gaining what they regarded as their legitimate, if modest, inheritance.

BIBLIOGRAPHICAL NOTE

    Among the newspapers consulted for this essay were the *Daily Press* and *Post-Intelligencer* of Seattle; the *Daily Ledger* of Tacoma; and the *Daily Oregonian* of Portland, all for the period 1885–86. Presenting labor's side of the controversy were the *Daily Call* (1885–86) and *Daily Voice of the People* (1886) of Seattle, and the *Puget Sound Weekly Cooperator* (1886) of Port Angeles.
    Scholarly studies focusing on the expulsions include Jules Alexander Karlin, "The Anti-Chinese Outbreak in Tacoma, 1885," *PHR*, Vol. 23 (1954), 271–83, and "The Anti-Chinese Outbreaks in Seattle, 1885, 1886," *PNQ*, Vol. 39 (1948), 103–30; Murray Morgan, *Puget's Sound: A Narrative of Early Tacoma and the Southern Sound* (Seattle, 1979), 218–52; James A. Halseth and Bruce A. Glasrud, "Anti-Chinese Movements in Washington, 1885–1886: A Reconsideration," in James A. Halseth and Bruce A. Galsrud, eds., *The Northwest Mosaic: Minority Conflicts in Pacific Northwest History* (Boulder, Colo.,

1977), 116–39; and Robert E. Wynne, "Reaction to the Chinese in the Pacific Northwest and British Columbia, 1850–1910," Ph.D. dissertation (University of Washington, 1964).

The story of the Knights of Labor in the Pacific Northwest is detailed in Carlos A. Schwantes, *Radical Heritage: Labor, Socialism, and Reform in Washington and British Columbia, 1885–1917* (Seattle, 1979), 22–29.

William S. U'Ren:
A Progressive Era Personality

ROBERT C. WOODWARD

A frail, sickly young lawyer arrived in Tin Cup, Colorado, early in 1888 to become editor of an obscure newspaper. His emaciated body was at times convulsed with a wracking cough as he went about his duties in the small mining town. He was finally forced to seek medical care. The doctor told him that he had tuberculosis and that he could not live more than a few months. The only advice the doctor gave was that he should live in a milder climate. Within a few weeks, William Simon U'Ren, twenty-nine years of age, was on his way to Honolulu to die.

During his brief sojourn in Tin Cup, U'Ren read Henry George's *Progress and Poverty,* and immediately he became a rabid disciple of George. "I went just as crazy over the single tax idea as any one else ever did," he said. "I knew I wanted single tax, and that was about all I did know." *Progress and Poverty* answered many questions that plagued the young lawyer; and here he found what he believed to be the solution to the problems of poverty in a land of plenty.

For generations the U'Rens had been blacksmiths and preachers. They had been French Huguenots, Dutch Dissenters, and for three centuries English Dissenters. Early in the nineteenth century, U'Ren's parents came to the United States as followers of John Wesley. From the time of his birth in 1859, at Lancaster, Wisconsin, Will U'Ren lived in an atmosphere of mysticism and devotion to God. The religion of the U'Rens did not always conform to the orthodoxy of the Methodists, and eventually they drifted from the fellowship of the church. Frances U'Ren, nevertheless, read the Bible to her children and im-

Originally published in *Idaho Yesterdays,* summer 1960.

parted to them a genuine faith in God. U'Ren later said, "I was especially fond of the Old Testament leaders, Moses and the rest; I suppose it's because they were never satisfied with things as they were, they were always kicking."

In 1876, U'Ren left home to work in the mines of Colorado. Two years later, at the age of nineteen, he attended a business college in Denver and read law in the office of France and Rogers. He was admitted to the bar in 1881.

After working for a year in the Hawaiian Islands, U'Ren decided that he would rather die in the United States than continue to live in the middle of the Pacific. He returned in 1889 to San Francisco, where he transferred to a ship destined for Portland, Oregon. But before he left California, a stranger handed him a pamphlet on the initiative. For the first time, he saw a means to the reforms he read about in *Progress and Poverty.*

E. W. Bingham, secretary of the Oregon Australian Ballot League, became acquainted with U'Ren; soon he began teaching U'Ren practical politics. In regard to reform organizations, Bingham told his young student: "Never be president. Never be conspicuous. Get a president and a committee; and let them go to the front. The worker must work behind them out of sight. Be secretary."

U'Ren had become a spiritualist medium, and he held séances in the homes of Seth and Alfred Lewelling, near Milwaukie, Oregon. In addition to holding séances, the Lewellings also held Farmers' Alliance meetings in their home, and many farmers from the Milwaukie community came to discuss their problems. At one of the meetings, Alfred Lewelling gave U'Ren a paper-covered book entitled *Direct Legislation by Citizenship, through the Initiative and Referendum*, written by James W. Sullivan. "I read the book through before I slept that night," U'Ren recalled later. "I forgot for the time, all about Henry George and the single tax. . . . The one important thing was to restore the law-making power where it belongs—into the hands of the people. . . . Once give us that," he concluded, "we could get anything we wanted[,] single tax, anything."

U'Ren presented a resolution at one of the meetings requesting the state executive committee to invite the state grange, the Portland Chamber of Commerce, the Oregon Knights of Labor, and the Portland Federated Trades to form a joint committee to educate the people about direct legislation. With the exception of Portland's chamber of commerce, each of the organizations sent a representative to form the Joint Committee on Direct Legislation. They proposed to call for a constitutional convention to add the initiative and referen-

dum to the constitution. Within a year, the Populist party was organized, and U'Ren became secretary of the state committee.

The "hold-up session" of the state legislature in 1897 was possible
because the Populists held a balance of power over the legislature
and U'Ren, who was a member of the lower house, controlled the
Populist votes. The Populists were able to take advantage of an intra-
party squabble among the Republicans over the appointment of a
United States senator and prevented the organization of the lower
house. By holding up the legislature, U'Ren was able to dramatize
the importance of direct legislation.

U'Ren's propaganda efforts through the Joint Committee on Direct
Legislation had successfully educated the people about the initiative
and referendum. In an article written for the *Direct Legislation Record,*
he estimated that two years previously not more than one in a thousand in Oregon knew about the initiative and referendum. Now
three-fourths of the people favored direct legislation reform.

During the spring of 1898 the National Direct Legislation League
recognized U'Ren's importance to the movement by electing him to
the National Executive Committee. He had become known to the national movement through publicity he had been given in the *Direct
Legislation Record* concerning his part in the hold-up session. He had
previously discussed the session as being an "example of the failure
of representative government" and suggested that no hold-up would
have been possible if the people could have voted on the acts of the
legislature.

In the fall of 1898 a meeting was held to organize the Nonpartisan
Direct Legislation League of Oregon; U'Ren took his usual position
as secretary. A seventeen-man committee was elected, representing
all parties and many factions of parties in the state. Anybody could
join who was willing to work and who would not make reform a
party issue. They planned to circulate literature, write letters to editors, and make speeches until a constitutional amendment was
passed.

Two successive state legislatures reluctantly passed the initiative
and referendum amendments, and in 1902 a state plebiscite made the
amendments final by a vote of 62,024 to 5,668. In 1903 U'Ren organized the Direct Primary Nomination League and became its secretary. The following year the legislature passed a direct primary law.

The original draft of the direct primary law was written by U'Ren.
He based some of his ideas on work done in Minnesota and Maryland, but gave special attention to the Stevens bill in Wisconsin,
which Governor Robert La Follette was promoting. The object of the

bill was to make party conventions and caucuses unnecessary in nominating all state officers and to make direct election of United States senators constitutionally possible. The writing of a direct legislation bill required considerable skill in law making in order to circumvent the federal constitutional requirement that state legislatures elect senators. U'Ren asked Judge Thomas A. McBride, who later would serve on the state supreme court, to help write the final draft to insure that the amendment would be constitutional.

The ingenious feature of the amendment that facilitated direct election was called Statement Number One. The statement was a voluntary pledge made by a candidate for the state legislature, committing himself to vote for the person chosen by the voters in the general election. Since candidates did not have to take the pledge and could not be legally bound to it if they did take it, the constitution remained unviolated. But the politically wise knew they would have to take the pledge to win.

By mid-October 1905, U'Ren had started to organize the People's Power League to be responsible for several initiative measures the following June. Jonathan Bourne, Jr., was eager to participate in the new movement and at the same time prepare himself to run for the Senate. He asked U'Ren to "jot down a skeleton of the main points you would cover in an open letter addressed to each voter of the State, giving me the benefit of your views as to what the leading questions are today and your convictions on same." U'Ren responded by taking charge of Bourne's campaign.

Professor James D. Barnett called U'Ren's People's Power League "by far the most important organized influence in direct legislation." In 1906 U'Ren filed five reform initiative measures in the name of the league. These included a law prohibiting free passes on railroads and four proposed amendments to the constitution. The People's Power League measures were passed by the people in the June election. Two years later, in 1908, the Republicans won generally throughout the state with the notable exception of Governor Chamberlain, who was chosen over a Republican for the U.S. Senate. Four "U'Ren measures" sponsored by the People's Power League passed, including a corrupt practice law. And if the newly elected members of the state legislature who were pledged to Statement Number One kept faith with the voters, a Democrat would be elected to the United States Senate by the Republican legislature. The *Oregonian* sadly commented, "The Republican Party of Oregon behaves as if it had made up its mind to do nothing rational anymore."

In the following January, Chamberlain was elected to the Senate on the first ballot. Some who voted for Chamberlain did so under protest but felt obligated to abide by the pledge. The *Oregonian* foresaw a dreary future for the Republican party regulars and considered the election "as much a triumph for Bourne and U'Ren as for Chamberlain."

Although the single-tax movement had preceded the progressive era and continued after the period nominally ended, Georgeism reached the zenith of popular appeal simultaneously with the progressive era. Single taxers fought independently for the initiative, referendum, direct election of senators, and tax reforms under their own banner; thus in a measure, the single-tax movement became a part of the progressive movement. But single taxers were bound by a dogma to oppose tariffs, imperialism, and government-controlled land conservation, whereas many progressives felt that some degree of tariff protection was necessary, that imperialism brought progress to backward peoples, and that conservation of natural resources was more important than the people's using the land. Neither were the single taxers noticeably of the mugwump type, who represented an elite leadership of the past, interested in good government for its own sake, and the victims of economic and social upheaval created by an *arriviste* class. On the contrary, single taxers were either from families of little reputation and fortune, represented by Henry George, Joseph Dana Miller, Daniel Kiefer, and U'Ren; or from families of wealth, political power, and prestige, such as Joseph Fels, Charles Ingersoll, Tom Johnson, and Leo Tolstoy, whose fame and wealth were unaffected by the single tax.

The single taxers turned indifferently from arguments about whether industrial trusts should be "busted" or regulated. The twin scourges of poverty and corruption could be cured not by treating the symptoms, they reasoned, but by restoring man to his birthright, the land. A belief in land ownership, plus a faith in the people's ability to govern themselves, was a type of Jeffersonian philosophy held by the single taxers. Momentarily, the progressive movement held largely to the same Jeffersonian ideal, until Theodore Roosevelt's New Nationalism, inspired by the anti-Jeffersonian Herbert Croly, helped to return the Republicans to their traditional conservatism. Except for a few Republican insurgents, Jeffersonianism was nominally restored to the Democratic party. Henry George's faith in land and democracy had stemmed not from political traditions, but rather from a reaction to conditions he had observed. In like manner, single taxers of the progressive era did not predicate reform upon affiliation with a particular party but sought to work within the party of their choice or birth. When parties tended to become reactionary, the single taxers denounced the tendency but did not renounce their party affiliation. Although the progressive movement succeeded in achieving reform legislation and the single-tax movement failed completely, the progressive era created a favorable climate in which the single-tax movement flourished.

William U'Ren, not unlike other single taxers, was an avowed progressive; he worked with the progressives and they accepted him. U'Ren was not much different from the typical California progressive, who, according to George Mowry, was about forty; was born in the Middle West; had a north-European name; was an attorney, journalist, or businessman; had a New England religion; and was a Republican. U'Ren did not fit the California mold, however, by being "well-fixed," a pro-McKinley Republican, and "violently opposed to the nineteenth-century agrarian radicalism of William Jennings Bryan and the Populists." Being anti-Populist and anti-Bryan was characteristic not only of California progressives, but also of most progressives. It should be remembered that U'Ren joined the Populists to secure direct legislation primarily and not the whole Omaha platform.

In October 1909, U'Ren was elected vice-president of the Short Ballot Association. He shared the office with the novelist Winston Churchill and served under Woodrow Wilson, the association's first president. A year and one month later, while attending the first annual Single Tax Conference in New York City, U'Ren paid Wilson a visit. Wilson had just successfully completed his campaign for governor of New Jersey and had returned to Princeton.

If the short ballot was to be the subject of discussion, it was soon forgotten when U'Ren found Wilson interested in how the initiative, referendum, and direct primary worked in Oregon. For years Wilson had confidently told his students that direct legislation could not work. In a volume published some years before, he wrote about the use of the initiative in Switzerland and found that "it [the initiative] has not promised either progress or enlightenment, leading rather to doubtful experiments and to reactionary displays of prejudice than to really useful legislation." As for the referendum in Switzerland, "It has dulled the sense of responsibility among legislators without in fact quickening the people to the exercise of any real control in affairs."

Wilson, the unbeliever and critic, became the student as U'Ren retold the story of "people's power" in Oregon. He recounted how the people had fought to get the initiative and referendum and then broke the Republican machine with the direct primary law and Statement Number One, which made possible the election of Bourne and Chamberlain to the United States Senate. U'Ren's reputation for persuasiveness, logic, and debate was not diminished as a result of his visit with the eminent scholar of government and history. The governor-elect conceded that Oregon's example added validity to U'Ren's arguments, but he concluded that the initiative and referendum would have to be restricted "tools for an emergency."

Wilson's victory over the New Jersey machine is a tale often told, but U'Ren's visit during the crucial and formative moments of Wilson's preparation to enter the governor's office could well have given Wilson moral encouragement for the battle he faced. On the day preceding his inauguration, Wilson held a meeting at the Martinique Hotel in New York with the leading members of the New Jersey legislature and several newspaper editors. He insisted that he expected nothing less than the whole progressive platform from the legislature. Although his program did not include the initiative and referendum, he talked about how they had worked in Oregon and how U'Ren had convinced him of their practical possibilities.

In his inaugural address, Wilson expressed faith in people's ability to govern themselves if they were properly enlightened, which he considered his responsibility. The message concluded with words that echoed across the United States and were heard with delight by some in Oregon, as he said that the laws of Oregon "seem to me . . . to point the direction which we must also take before we have completed our regeneration of a government which has suffered so seriously and so long . . . from private management and organized selfishness."

In May 1911, Wilson began a trek into the West that eventually took him to Oregon. The farther west he went toward Oregon, the more he praised the initiative and referendum.

In Portland Wilson greeted reporters with the comment: "In the East I am counted intensely progressive. In Oregon I am not so sure. But I am a great admirer of the Oregon system." However, in answer to a question, Wilson expressed his opposition to the recall of judges. "You hire a man to tell you what is the law. He does tell you and the information doesn't sit well on your stomach. Should you then discharge the man? Better make the law right."

Wilson spoke during the evening to a Democratic gathering at the commercial club. After praising the Oregon System for having destroyed "the machine," he spoke warmly of U'Ren. He had read that Oregon had two legislatures, one at the capitol and "one under W. S. U'Ren's hat." He concluded it was better to have one under U'Ren's hat where it could be found and held responsible than the one at the capitol, which could not be found. Wilson did not mean, however, that direct legislation should replace the legislature. "I do not think the legislature should be considered a necessary evil," he declared.

After Wilson's visit, U'Ren's Republicanism was substantially shaken. U'Ren wondered whether Wilson was the only man that the progressives could support in 1912. If so, he would want to be in a position to lead the Oregon Progressives into the Wilson camp. Although he was a staunch supporter of Robert La Follette, whom he considered the strongest and most desirable Republican, he feared that no progressive could prevent a regular convention from nominating Taft. He reveled in the prospect of both parties nominating progressives, but added that the party that nominated a tory would be beaten. As for himself, he told Senator Bourne, "the party collar does not bind me any closer than it does you, and if necessary to strengthen the People's Power I shall vote and talk for a Democrat." But, he added, "The Democratic Party cannot be as progressive as the . . . Republicans until the negro question is settled."

Herbert Croly, reading a paper at the American Political Science Association meeting in Buffalo in December 1911 attacked the Oregon System. U'Ren, who was a member of the association and attended the meeting, presented some "remarks" in refutation. Croly first attacked direct legislation in general by saying it would have "a period of efflorescence, like Know Nothingism, Grangeism, and Populism, and then gradually . . . sink into utter and deserved oblivion." While admitting that state legislatures were not truly representative and often were corrupt, he insisted that reforms could be made by strong leadership held responsible to the people in both the legislative and executive branches of government. He implied that direct legislation made Oregon's legislature a "rump" in which no "self-respecting man or useful public servant" would want to be a member. Furthermore, the initiative and referendum accomplished no reform that could not have been accomplished equally well by some other means.

In response to Croly's views, U'Ren asked if it would not be better to be a member of Oregon's legislature than a member of a legislature tainted with bribery, such as New York's or Illinois's. In Oregon the legislator would not be bribed to vote for a senator or offered railroad passes, since the state had the initiative and referendum. U'Ren did not believe that there had ever been representative government in the United States. Representatives were often elected by pluralities, and third parties were seldom elected to Congress. He did not advocate the initiative and referendum as "the principal and ordinary method of making laws," but "it seems to be the best means available." He agreed with Croly that other means might be better, but the "fact is that no such results were obtained in any American state by other methods until the way had been staked out by use of the initiative."

Through the People's Power League, U'Ren promoted several

amendments in addition to the all-important single tax in 1912 and did what he could to help the cause of La Follette. The amount of work involved in so many activities forced him to refuse the additional task of managing La Follette's campaign in Oregon. U'Ren's faithfulness to La Follette persisted until Roosevelt received the nomination from the Progressive party, and he then supported Roosevelt in the election.

Just before the primary election in 1912, La Follette spoke in Portland and Salem in support of Bourne. In spite of the efforts of his progressive friends to nominate him, Bourne lost to Ben Selling by a substantial vote. It was generally conceded that Bourne's refusal to campaign in Oregon cost him the nomination. Some, however, held that Bourne's relationship with U'Ren had hurt him politically. Indeed, early in the campaign George Brownell broached the delicate subject to Bourne by suggesting that any connection with the single tax would hurt the senator's chances. As for U'Ren, Brownell wrote, "There are thousands of people in this state who are getting tired of his method and his measures."

Two features of the People's Power League measures that U'Ren was especially interested in were to abolish the state senate and to give the governor complete control over introducing appropriations bills. The election returns of 1912 spelled defeat for U'Ren on three fronts. The People's Power League measures, the single tax, and Bourne all went down in defeat. As in the presidential election, the independent progressives and the Republicans split a segment of votes, giving a plurality to the Democratic senatorial candidate.

The day after the election, U'Ren announced that he was a candidate for governor in 1914. His platform included the single tax, abolishment of the senate, minimum wage scale, short ballot, more people's power, and proportional representation. He believed that his candidacy for governor would give impetus to his legislative program. In 1913, the question remained whether he would run as a Republican. Although he insisted he was a Republican, the *Oregonian* wanted to know what kind. U'Ren answered by declaring that he had always been a Republican except from 1892 to 1898, when he was a Populist. Furthermore, he had voted for all major Republican candidates since 1898 with the exception of Taft and Selling in 1912. He estimated that he had spent more than $13,000 of his own money in advocating good Republican legislation including the recall, corrupt practice law, Statement Number One, and the initiative and referendum.

As the campaign in 1914 got under way, U'Ren added two more planks to his platform. Prohibition was one; the second was to build roads and pay for them from an inheritance tax on estates of fifty thousand dollars or more. Any person unemployed would be offered a job, which would solve the problems of poor roads and unemployment. The *Oregonian* considered the amendment "U'Renic," "socialistic," and "the last word in communism."

When the votes were counted, U'Ren was a poor third. Yet, a tribute to the badly defeated reformer was the fact that an overwhelmingly Republican state chose to reelect a very popular Democratic senator, George Chamberlain, thereby demonstrating the influence of people's power.

To some, the victory over U'Renism was an occasion for rejoicing. But to him who had again tasted the bitter dregs of defeat, the occasion was an opportunity to survey glorious past victories—the initiative, referendum, direct primary, Statement Number One, and recall—and to say of the future:

> "Again to the battle, Achaeans,
> Our hearts bid the tyrant defiance!"

BIBLIOGRAPHICAL NOTE

Primary and contemporary sources include the Bourne (Jonathan, Jr.) Papers 1895–1915, Oregon Collection, University of Oregon, Eugene; Oregon City *Courier*, 1905–15; Oregon City *Enterprise*, 1906; *Oregon Journal* (Portland), 1911, 1927; Portland *Oregonian*, 1902–14; *Direct Legislation Record*, Newark, New Jersey, 1897, 1898; *Direct Primary Nomination League Pamphlet*, 1904; Herbert Croly, "State Political Reorganization," and William S. U'Ren, "Remarks on Mr. Herbert Croly's paper on 'State Political Reorganization,'" *Proceedings of the American Political Science Association*, Vol. 8 (1912) 122–39; Burton J. Hendrick, "The Initiative and Referendum, and How Oregon Got Them," *McClure's Magazine*, Vol. 37 (July 1911), 235–48; Lute Pease, "The Initiative and Referendum: Oregon's 'Big Stick,'" *Pacific Monthly*, Vol. 17 (May 1907), 563–75; Lincoln Steffens, "U'Ren, The Law Giver: The Legislative Blacksmith of Oregon and the Tools He Has Fashioned for Democracy," *American Magazine*, Vol. 65 (March 1908), 527–40; William S. U'Ren, "How Oregon Secured Pure Elections," *La Follette's Weekly Magazine*, Vol. 3 (Jan. 28, 1911); William S. U'Ren, "The Initiative and Referendum in Oregon," *Arena*, Vol. 29 (March 1903), 270–75.

Other published sources include James Duff Barnett, *The Operation of the Initiative, Referendum, and Recall in Oregon* (New York, 1915); Charles Albro Barker, *Henry George* (New York, 1955); Richard Hofstadter, *The Age of Reform* (New York, 1955); Eric F. Goldman, *Rendezvous with Destiny* (New York, 1953); James Kerney, *The Political Education of Woodrow Wilson* (New York, 1926); Fred E. Haynes, *Third Party Movements since the Civil War* (Iowa City, 1916); Lewis Filler, *Crusaders for American Liberalism* (New York, 1912); Norman Hapgood, *The Changing Years* (New York, 1930); Belle C. LaFollette and Fola LaFollette, *Robert M. LaFollette*, 2 vols. (New York, 1953); George E. Mowry *The California Progressives* (Berkeley, 1951); Woodrow Wilson, *The State* (Boston, New York, Chicago, 1898); Arthur S. Link, *Wilson: The Road to The White House* (Princeton, 1947); Ray

Stannard Baker, *Woodrow Wilson: Life and Letters* (London, 1932). Unpublished sources include Paul Thomas Culbertson "A History of the Initiative and Referendum in Oregon," Ph.D. dissertation (University of Oregon, 1941); Russell Gordon Hendricks, "The Effects of the Direct Primary upon Senatorial Elections in Oregon, 1900–1909," M.A. thesis (University of Oregon, 1951).

Oregon's Romantic Rebels: John Reed and Charles Erskine Scott Wood

Edwin R. Bingham

The lives of John Reed and Charles Erskine Scott Wood were curiously like their names. The one, short and explosive, ended abruptly before it was well under way; the other, long and sustained, threatened not to end at all. Although contemporaries for a time, Wood and Reed were of separate generations. When John Reed was born, in 1887, C. E. S. Wood was thirty-four, an age Reed never attained. When Reed died in 1920, at thirty-two, Wood had just entered a new, and in some respects the richest, phase of his ninety-one-year career.

For a substantial period, each man was closely identified with Oregon. Reed lived in Portland for the first half of his life, and Wood spent nearly forty years there. Jack Reed was the sometime companion of Wood's younger sons and was influenced by their father, although probably not profoundly. Both men left the Pacific Northwest permanently, and Reed repudiated Portland; yet the region left its mark on them both, and Wood, at least, reciprocated. Both men thought of themselves first of all as poets, although each achieved his greatest distinction through prose. Wood cannot match Reed in national and international reputation, but some of the writing of each has had currency abroad through German, Russian, and Danish translations. Both men were rebels, and, where they are known, they still stir controversy and arouse conjecture.

Charles Erskine Scott Wood, born in Erie, Pennsylvania, early in the tense decade of the 1850s, was a schoolboy during the Civil War, and his early memories were of that era, reinforced by stories his father told of duty as a navy surgeon with the Atlantic blockading

Originally published in *Pacific Northwest Quarterly,* July 1959.

squadron. After the war the family moved to Rosewood Glen, a farm on the outskirts of Baltimore. Wood remembered the years on the Maryland farm as an idyllic period for the most part. The house was an old colonial brick, rising from a shallow slope crowned by great oaks. A swift stream flowed through the property, threading the nearby stands of hickory, maple, and red gum. In the autumn the trees were hung with purple clusters of fox grapes; and spring brought trailing arbutus, spangling the ground with pink stars, and laurel, wild honeysuckle, and azaleas sweetened the woods. At Rosewood Glen, Erskine learned to swing the scythe, to hunt coon and possum, to pick eggs; and here his speech took on the suggestion of a drawl that it never lost. His formal education was as a day scholar in a small private school adjoining his father's property.

Wood also remembered and resented the taut household his father ran, wherein naval discipline was imposed upon Erskine and his five brothers. The military rigor of the Wood ménage was eased by the fact that the boys had access to their father's extensive library. Indeed, the elder Wood was himself the author of several competent and colorful accounts of his experiences in the Caribbean and China seas, and Erskine, his second son, gave evidence early of a literary bent. All in all, C. E. S. Wood grew up in a conservative, upper-middle-class environment, where duty, courtesy, order, and propriety were considered cardinal virtues.

John Reed's boyhood was spent in the quiet backwaters of Portland. The war of his youth, the one with Spain, did not amount to much. Like Wood, he came from a secure and privileged home. His maternal grandmother, Charlotte Green, widow of a pioneer in Portland industry, entertained grandly in her West Hill mansion, where on summer evenings guests danced on the lawn, casting grotesque shadows in the flaring light of natural gas piped to jets in the tops of Douglas firs. Reed's reluctance to conform stemmed in part, perhaps, from the example set by this spirited lady who went her own way.

John Reed's father was not so conspicuously successful as were the Greens, but John and his younger brother, Harry, lacked for little in a material way and enjoyed the sense of ease and place that belongs to the well off and the well born. Jack Reed, too, had a private school education, first in the Portland Academy and then at Morristown, New Jersey, in preparation for Harvard. His interest in writing developed early, and in his mid-teens Reed was publishing verse in the *Morristonian* and the *Pacific Monthly*. In this first stage of his writing career, Jack Reed had some contact with C. E. S. Wood, but if the older man contributed to the boy's drift into radicalism, Reed failed to mention it in his autobiographical sketch entitled "Almost Thirty."

The experiences of the two men with higher education were

sharply different. Wood's father, William Maxwell Wood, used his influence to procure from President Grant an appointment-at-large to the United States Military Academy for Erskine. Any ambition Wood might have had to be a professional soldier he lost at West Point, where his academic performance was generally undistinguished and his military record bordered on disgrace. In his own words it was

work, work, work, from reveille to taps. Sunday had a brief relaxation period but was really a study day. Saturday afternoon was a holiday for the orderly and well-behaved but I walked about every Saturday afternoon with a rifle on my shoulder . . . for punishment.

More than once Erskine accumulated demerits just short of the number that would bring dismissal, and it is not surprising that in four years he never held a cadet rank.

Despite the demands of the academy regimen, Erskine found time to read the novels of William Gilmore Simms, Bulwer-Lytton, and Scott, as well as parts of Spenser, Chaucer, and Shakespeare, and to carry on a romance (with the girl he later married) so intense as to cause her guardian to forbid the sweethearts to correspond. Doubtless such beyond-the-border-of-duty activities contributed to Wood's indifferent showing at the academy. Nevertheless, in the tightly prescribed curriculum heavily weighted on the side of mathematics, engineering, and the physical sciences, there was little to inspire interest or effort on the part of a young man with creative inclinations, and although Wood stood well in ethics and law, only in military drawing did he excel.

Generally, however, for C. E. Scott Wood, as he was invariably listed on military rolls, the cadet years were unnaturally formal, gallingly restrictive, and depressingly drab—a time to be resented and endured, and little more. Years later in New York, Wood wrote in his journal: "I never pass West Point without thinking of my cadet days. . . . I *hate* the memory of it even now."

Erskine's poor record in discipline, his harsh criticism of the West Point system, his threats to resign and offer his services to the Mexican or the Egyptian army or to go to Florida and grow oranges or, most persistently, to embark on a writing career worried his mother and brought long, measured, elegantly phrased letters of censure and advice from his father. In a typical letter written in Wood's fourth year, the father spelled out his son's shortcomings:

It is this unreasonable desire to escape from the present to an unknown and uncertain future, which has been from the beginning . . . one of the causes of your demerits. Again, I am pained to see the disrespectful manner in which you refer to your Commander in Chief, the President. You may not think of it, but such expressions are a violation of your oath, and if your language corresponds to your writing, upon a report, you would be justly disciplined. . . . My earnest and final advice to you is to abandon all feverish and restless desire after change . . . and address yourself with honest and unceasing vigilance to the labor, the claims and obligations of the present around you—and of the place and position to which you are called.

His father's counsel prevailed, for when the class of 1874 was graduated, reduced from an entering strength of sixty-seven to forty-four, the rebellious Erskine stood academically almost precisely in the middle.

In clear contrast to Wood's four-year confinement in what seemed to him an educational straitjacket stands John Reed's experience thirty-six years later at Harvard in an academic atmosphere that Reed labeled approvingly as anarchistic. Allowed to select freely from a rich curriculum, Reed avoided the physical and social sciences, specializing heavily in writing and literature with a smattering of philosophy and the fine arts, in a course of study perhaps more narrow in this direction than was the West Point curriculum in the other. The difference, of course, was that Reed could choose.

At Harvard, John Reed continued to write—poetry, stories, plays, editorials, jokes, lyrics—whatever came to mind and hand. He showed facility and promise rather than genius, but writing was important to him, for it gave him the same assurance in the intellectual sphere that his unquestioned skill in swimming and water polo gave him in the physical sphere, and it helped him to social status as well.

By far the most profound personal influence on John Reed at Harvard was exerted by Charles Townshend Copeland, who was convinced of Reed's promise and gave him unstintingly of all that a dedicated teacher can impart to an eager disciple—criticism, encouragement, technique, inspiration, friendship. John Reed's deep gratitude to "Copey" was gracefully expressed in the dedication to *Insurgent Mexico*, the book that made Reed nationally known.

Three thousand miles west of the Charles on the Willamette was another man who had an interest in John Reed's writing career. In 1910 C. E. S. Wood wrote the Harvard senior a rambling, friendly letter about poetry, urging that Reed avoid the easy road of imitation and strive to achieve a new poetry that

must not be a moral essay nor an economic tract but it positively must have the pulsing thought of the modern man. If it be full of the surge of the ocean and the wet south wind of an ever-recurring Spring it must also be full of the surge of human life-blood and wet with the tears of humanity. . . . I am looking for the young poet who will . . . breathe the thought of his time and the gospel of the masses of men—in a form eternal.

A large order, and one that Reed failed to fulfill.

With the outstanding exception of his intellectual debt to Charles Copeland, Reed was critical, almost contemptuous, of the university's academic aspects. For him the heart of Harvard lay outside the formal curriculum, and he classified himself as an activity man rather than an athlete or scholar. As an outlander, Reed hungered for the social acceptance he had easily won in prep school. To gain it he spread his energies in a sweeping arc. He was editor of the *Lampoon*, captain of the water polo team, frenetic song leader, president of the Cosmopolitan Club, vice-president of the Dramatic Club, elected to Hasty Pudding to write the lyrics for its annual musical comedy, leading spirit in the Western Club, member of Oracle, Round Table, and Symposium. Unquestionably he made his influence felt, but socially he never reached Harvard's top tier.

In the light of the rebel he later became, John Reed's position at Harvard was equivocal. Although in sympathy with its aims, he did not join the Socialist Club led by Walter Lippman; and in the democratic revolt of the Yard (the outsiders) against the Street (the insiders), Reed, although he lived on the Street, remained aloof until his senior year when he joined the aristocrats just in time to share in their defeat in the contest for class honors. At Harvard, John Reed was torn by a genuine ambivalence; a rebellious impulse against snobbery and injustice was countered by a strong urge toward the rewards that went with social distinction.

When Jack Reed left the university, he carried away a resentment against the Harvard patriciate that later hardened into hatred. He carried away, too, a firm conviction that he wanted to write but without knowing just how to begin. Following Copey's advice, Reed set out for Europe in the summer of 1910 in search of something to write about.

A Harvard man might pause for a time on the edge of a career; a West Point graduate had orders. Second Lieutenant C. E. Scott Wood was assigned to frontier duty with the 21st Infantry, reporting in 1875 to Fort Bidwell in the northeast corner of California about 14 miles from the Oregon border. On the march from there to Fort Vancouver, his permanent post in the Pacific Northwest, Wood had his first contact with the Harney Desert, which he was later to evoke so powerfully in his poetry.

On the frontier Erskine got some of the adventure his restless and romantic temperament craved. He escorted a member of the United States Coast Survey on an early exploration of Alaska, returning in time to serve as aide to General Oliver O. Howard in the difficult and frustrating pursuit of the Nez Perces in their flight toward Canada and freedom that ended at Bear Paw Mountain, Montana Territory, 30 miles south of the international border. Lieutenant Wood's eloquent summary of Chief Joseph's sentiments when he surrendered can be found in most textbooks of United States history. Detached service in Washington, D.C., permitted the young Indian fighter, now a first lieutenant, to return to the national capital to marry his sweetheart of cadet days, Nanny Moale Smith, in November 1878.

Lieutenant Wood's far western experience gave him a taste at first hand of the power of the state in using its military arm to crush the rebellion of a desperate and dignified people whose major crime was simply that they were in the way. Further, his frontier service provided him with literary material. *Century Magazine* published pieces by Wood on his probing of Alaska and on Chief Joseph.

With the Pacific Northwest secure, General Howard was transferred from Fort Vancouver to West Point to head the United States Military Academy, and Wood returned with him to the scene of his unhappy cadet days, this time as adjutant. Not only was West Point duty dull, but Wood had had enough of a career not of his own choosing, and he was eyeing the law as a way out of the army. Under justification of improving his military efficiency, he was granted leave of absence to enroll in Columbia for courses in political science and law.

Shortly after Columbia granted Wood a bachelor of laws degree, in 1883, he resigned his commission and joined his wife and two children in Portland. There he began his career as attorney, a career he maintained for thirty-four years. His rise in the legal profession was not spectacular, but it was sound. In 1887 when George H. Williams, attorney general under Grant, joined Wood as a partner, the firm took on considerable prestige. By the turn of the century, Wood's family had grown to five children, his law practice was large, he represented an international banking firm as land agent for a vast wagon road grant, and he was a member of Portland's exclusive Arlington Club. Moreover, as a specialist in maritime and corporation law, he had become legal adviser and friend to some of the wealthiest and most influential people in the city, and he and his gracious wife moved on terms of easy intimacy with the Charles Ladds, the Henry Corbetts, the W. B. Ayers, and other members of Portland's social elite.

But there was another side to the Portland lawyer and man of distinction, a bohemian and rebellious side. "Colonel" Wood had not lost his creative impulse. He continued to write and sketch and paint wherever and whenever he was able. His journals are full of sonnets, ballads, ideas for stories, character sketches, snatches of dialogue, vignettes, philosophical and nature essays. Much of the work was facile or fragmentary. A good deal was personal, written to his wife to mark an anniversary or to his children and friends to remember a birthday. Despite his writing for the *Century*, Wood seems not to have been in a fever to publish.

Apparently Wood wrote and painted largely spontaneously and because this brought him satisfaction in a way that the practice of law did not. Much of his writing gives the impression of great vitality and considerable talent with but little discipline or direction. In costume and appearance Colonel Wood suggested the poet or artist rather than the professional man. When he dressed for the evening, he affected spotless, ruffled shirts of silk, which set off to full advantage the heavy, handsome beard he had worn since his army days. With his mass of curly hair, his wide-spaced, heavy-lidded eyes, a soft broad-brimmed stetson, and a dramatic black military cape to turn the Oregon weather, he made an elegant and romantic figure.

Inseparable from C. E. S. Wood's literary and artistic development was a gradual growth into radicalism. From the outset he had rebelled against authority, but these were abortive revolts. As he came into maturity and found himself secure in his surroundings, he began to release his resentment through his writing and to seek some theory or ideal through which he might express his belief in freedom and his contempt for any institution, code, or influence that inhibited the unfolding of the individual or suppressed the free exchange of ideas. Reading in Thoreau, Herbert Spencer, Henry George, Proudhon, and Kropotkin helped him to arrive at what he called philosophical or enlightened anarchism.

Other factors in his experience propelled him in the same direction. He disapproved of federal policy toward the Indians, and he was an outspoken anti-imperialist. He decried what he termed the feudal system of land tenure whereby property was distributed and held by virtue of the deed in fee simple. He was drawn to the cause of the underdog, and the unequal struggle against things as they are intrigued him.

In his associations with conservative colleagues and businessmen of wealth and power, he found them in the main uncomplex, narrow, ordinary. He preferred Bill Haywood to Harvey Scott. He found the steerage passengers of a coastal steamer more genuine, more alive, more colorful, than his first-class traveling companions. He could be counted on to bail Portland's radical labor agitator Tom Burns out of jail. When Emma Goldman was scheduled to appear in Portland on her more or less regular tours to the Pacific Coast, it was C. E. S. Wood who paved the way, arranging for halls in which "Red Emma" could be heard, lending the drawing power of his name to swell the crowds, and giving her legal counsel and defense when she was arrested. Restrictions on free speech aroused him to anger and scorn of a society that feared the airing of ideas such as single tax, birth control, free love, and anarchism.

Meanwhile, Colonel Wood had been provided with an outlet for his creative writing as well as a vehicle for his views. When the *Pacific Monthly*, a promotional and literary magazine, was launched in Portland in 1898, Wood was asked to become a contributor, and for more than a decade he obliged in a profusion made possible by manuscript reserves that had been accumulating for years. To disguise the degree of the monthly's dependence on him, Wood frequently wrote under such exotic pseudonyms as Felix Benguiat or Francis du Bosque, providing poetry, short stories, book reviews, and art criticism. "Impressions," a monthly feature, appeared under his own name, and here he expressed his unorthodox ideas with vigor and candor. Between 1898 and 1911, when it merged with *Sunset*, the *Pacific Monthly*, with a peak circulation of over 100,000, was the primary vehicle of cultural expression in the Pacific Northwest, and Wood was its most versatile contributor and the only one to appear throughout the life of the magazine.

Colonel Wood was quite aware that the voluntary organization of society advocated by anarchists was not likely to be achieved, at least not for generations; but he used the anarchist position as a kind of touchstone against which to measure issues that confronted society, and this helps to explain his consistent support of liberal causes. Thus, although he was not a dominant figure in state or national politics, Wood entered the arena from time to time: he joined William S. U'Ren in the forging of direct legislation; he helped manage the Democrat Harry Lane's successful senatorial campaign in 1912; hoping to stay out of the war, he took the public platform in support of Wilson in 1916. To an uncompromising anarchist like Emma Goldman, this was opportunism, and she said so. Wood merely replied serenely, "I will take any wagon going my way."

Although Wood loved the natural beauty of the Pacific Northwest, he felt the cultural isolation that life in this far corner imposed. He could find no one equipped or inclined to share the creative and rebellious aspects of his life. Mrs. Wood's energies were absorbed by the family and by the limited but intense activities of their social set. She did not reproach her husband for his preoccupation with poetry and painting or for his radical views, but she was not sympathetic, and of course she could not join him. Wood maintained a secret office in the chamber of commerce building to facilitate his creative work, where, perhaps, it pleased him to turn out pointed social criticism from a stronghold of the status quo, just as later, all through the prohibition period, he delighted in fermenting wine from the grapes in his Los Gatos, California, vineyards. Salvaging hours at night and on weekends from his busy life, Wood withdrew to this office retreat to write or sketch or paint.

Early in 1911, C. E. S. Wood met a young woman, thirty years his junior, who exerted a marked influence on his writing and who ultimately changed his life. Sara Bard Field, wife of a Baptist minister, had come to Portland with her husband from Cleveland, where she had played a small role in the reform administration of Mayor Tom Johnson. She and Colonel Wood met at a dinner given by Clarence Darrow. "This girl," Darrow told Wood, "is an ardent Socialist. She has seen poverty at first hand in a poor parish in Cleveland." "Socialist?" Wood repeated seriously, but with friendly humor in his eyes. "That's all right for the immediate but she'll become an Anarchist in time. Socialism is just a halfway station toward that goal."

Similar interests in poetry and social reform quickly cemented a friendship between the two, and one day Erskine asked Sara to look through his writing that had piled up in a chest in a corner of his private office. She found the chest full of manuscripts, some prose, more verse, many fragments. She turned over one after another with mounting disappointment. There were too many trifles, too much occasional verse, too many threadbare themes unrelieved by original treatment, too much imitative style, and all of it evidence that Wood was wasting a portion of his power in riotous writing. Then, near the bottom, she uncovered a yellow-sheeted, paper-covered notebook containing free-verse sketches of the desert, which made the search worthwhile.

From the time of his military service on the desert's edge, Wood had returned again and again to this "lean and stricken land." To him the desert meant youth and freedom and peace. For him there was no fragrance to match the spicy scent of sagebrush after a rain. The desert's blinding light, its jutting rimrock, its crags and pillars of basalt or obsidian—bare monuments in a barren waste—its wide-arching skies were beautiful to his eyes, intoxicating beyond green mountain or restless sea. With Sara's help, expanded and chiseled as much as Erskine's free-moving hand would allow, these sketches and verse fragments became *Poet in the Desert*, in Wood's mind his major achievement.

The poem opens with a prologue describing the signs of the desert and comparing it romantically to a beautiful and imperious woman, infinite in the variety of her moods. Then the image of truth is evoked, and through a long series of poetic passages, some of them resembling psalms, some dialogues, some sermons, the poet seeks to weigh the world man has made out of bondage against the world nature makes in freedom.

The performance is uneven. There are passages of serene beauty simply and cleanly wrought. There is passionate denunciation of war with morbidly realistic descriptions of the destruction it brings. There are melodramatic vignettes of sweatshop and mine, and an ostentatious paean to bastardy. There is a gentle hymn to nature, rich in imagery and restrained in statement. The fifty-second segment, which brings the poem to a close, is a sharp cry for revolution. One reviewer described the work as a series of alternate "rhapsodies and recriminations." To another it was "a terrifying cosmic outcry against things as they are." William Allen White wrote: "In another day when democracy has served its place . . . some man delving in volumes of forgotten lore will find these songs . . . and will cry, 'Here is yesterday singing for today.'"

Poet in the Desert appeared first in 1915 and then went into three subsequent editions in English. The various versions reveal the continuous struggle within Wood between poet and propagandist. In a cheap 1918 edition, the special pleading was muted at Sara's insistence, and Wood worked for smoother articulation of the poem's parts. Bearing out her judgment, there is general consensus that Wood is most effective in the descriptive passages free from radical sentiment.

In the same year that *Poet in the Desert* appeared, C. E. S. Wood wrote a brief dialogue poking fun at Anthony Comstock, that "roundsman of the Lord," and his efforts to suppress Margaret Sanger's birth control movement. He sent the piece to the *Masses,* and the editors Max Eastman and Floyd Dell asked for more. Erskine struck off a number of dialogues, one after the other, and when the *Masses* was suppressed in October 1917, many of these satirical conversations, most of them unpublished, were returned to the author. Ten years later they were collected and brought out by Vanguard Press under the title *Heavenly Discourse.*

Little is sacred in these conversations in heaven among such personages as God (Wood in thin disguise), Jesus, Rabelais, Voltaire, Saint Peter, Teddy Roosevelt, Mark Twain, and Bob Ingersoll. The satirist had a good time with his subjects. There was Teddy Roosevelt storming heaven like a Cuban hill and threatening to marshal the angels in military order; Rabelais constantly lamenting having to leave his gullet on earth; and Anthony Comstock crying in high heaven for just one fig leaf. Frederic C. Howe, then commissioner of immigration, considered the dialogues one of the best things the *Masses* had printed. On the other hand, in the words of Vida D. Scudder, professor of literature at Wellesley, "the smart and cheap vulgarity of that thing was too much for me."

In one sense, of course, *Heavenly Discourse* is definitely dated, but some of the tendencies it attacked—war and censorship and discrimination—still threaten. Whether because this is true or because of its wit and humor, *Heavenly Discourse* has had a surprisingly tenacious hold on part of the public, having gone through more than twenty-five printings. Nothing else Wood wrote remotely approached it in popularity, and until recently the book was available in a Penguin paperback edition.

C. E. S. Wood spent more than a third of a century in the Pacific Northwest. During these years when his physical and mental powers were at full strength, he saw the region develop from frontier to settled community. Living in one of the hubs of the area and traveling from it in all directions, Colonel Wood could claim a hand in the transition. As a successful attorney, he maintained a varied practice and cared for a large family. Although his poetry and stories and editorials reached but a relative handful, through *Heavenly Discourse* his satire ultimately commanded a healthy following. His work with U'Ren, his fight for free speech, and his support of Lane and Wilson permitted him a measure of influence on the level of political action despite views that were considered quixotic, if not downright dangerous. As a self-proclaimed anarchist, he tried mightily to ruffle Portland placidity.

The question arises: Why did generally conservative Portlanders suffer such a man to live and work and thunder in their midst? Wood was tolerated, perhaps, in part, because his views were regarded as too chimerical to pose a genuine threat to society. More important probably, Wood was a compelling and polished personality, as much at ease in a banker's drawing room or at a full-dress dinner as he was on Bill Hanley's ranch or at a mass meeting protesting social injustice. Prominent Oregonians who detested and decried his radical doctrines liked his company, admired his style, and respected his judgment.

In the winter of 1910–11, the same winter that C. E. S. Wood and Sara Bard Field met, John Reed returned from Europe to learn that family finances were such that he would have to earn his own living. Certain that Portland was no place for a writer to make his start, Reed left for New York, where Lincoln Steffens, his father's friend, promised that the boy should have his chance. Jack Reed took a suite of rooms, with three other Harvard graduates, at 42 Washington Square and, thanks to Steffens, a job with *American Magazine*. He then set out to make himself a writer.

For some months after graduation, in fact all through his European tour, the undergraduate years at Harvard had loomed as the most significant experience in Jack Reed's life. Now, in New York, Harvard was quickly reduced to size, as Reed's postgraduate education began. He virtually devoured the city, wandering wide-eyed and restless from side to side and end to end, probing corners, learning the brilliant, sophisticated facets of New York life as well as its somber, wretched, sinister ones. His writing and conversation were full of the city expressed in extravagantly romantic terms. New York ratified his imagination and then transcended it. Much of his enchantment was poured into the ears of the tolerant and sympathetic Steffens who, after the death of his first wife, had come to live on Washington Square. Finally, Steffens, in order to reserve part of his nights for sleeping, urged Jack to "write it down."

This was 1911, and Greenwich Village was on the edge of its first great period of intellectual upheaval. Emma Goldman's *Mother Earth* office was a gathering place for anarchists and assorted rebels. Alfred Stieglitz was operating an unconventional American center for post-impressionist artists where the password was "experimental." Mabel Dodge was back from Italy, busy mixing people, ideas, and good food and drink in a salon where only bankers and "bourgeois pigs" were barred. Into this eruptive milieu, a tangle of unruly hair topping his moon-round Boy Scout face, burst John Reed.

While rejoicing in the rebellious and uninhibited side of the Village, Reed also yearned after conventional writing success. The Harvard ambivalence was with him yet, and he longed to see his name in the slick magazines along with the names of Julian Street, Owen Johnson, and Robert Chambers. For three years Reed courted the national magazines with moderate success, publishing in *Century, Smart Set, Saturday Evening Post,* and *American,* but he did not feel that these sketches and stories and poetry genuinely said what he wanted to say.

Reed was taken into the Dutch Treat Club, a weekly luncheon gathering of successful New York writers, illustrators, and editors, and he was flattered that he was selected to write the lyrics for their annual supper show at Delmonico's in 1912. With Bill Daly as composer, Reed produced a deceptively gentle satire called *Everymagazine, an Immorality Play.* In facile, clever verse Reed lampooned the popular monthlies. Representing the family magazine, a club member, swathed in bombazine and wearing sawdust curls, knitted primly as he sang:

> I'm a literary virgin—
> All the warmness of a salmon.

All the passion of a sturgeon.
I'm aristocratic, very.

I'm a live obituary
Of the giants literary
   Who have given up the ghost.
In illuminating snatches
   Since the spring of Sixty-one
I've been publishing dispatches
   From the battle of Bull Run.

Of refinement I'm a symbol
   On your literary table;
All of culture in a thimble
   By the new Atlantic cable.
And though Congress does not heed me,
And the public does not read me,
I'm convinced the people need me
   From the Hudson to the Coast.
O when Trollope kicked the bucket
   And when Dickens was no more
I had half a mind to chuck it
   Till I found the Civil War.
Aristocratic rather,
   Exclusiveness my boast
In fact I am the Father
   The Son, and Holy Ghost.

In eight lines Reed nailed the *Cosmopolitan* to the wall:

Every month I'm full of spice
And naughty Robert Chambers makes it nice.
Some lingerie, a glimpse of stocking.
Lips unlocking, nothing shocking.
And Gibson hints at hidden beauty,
Lovers' booty, tutti frutti.
Read me once and I'll bet I can
Refresh the tired business man.

At the time none of the show was taken as serious satire, but there were enough barbs lying in the lyrics to cause uneasiness among a number of the Dutch Treaters. Something about the whole production was just a shade improper and unfair. One member, some years later, put into a pungent phrase the feeling of the more conventional segment of the club: "The trouble with Jack Reed was that he wasn't housebroken."

The defiance that lay beneath the surface in the Dutch Treat show broke out sharply when John Reed deserted "Everymagazine" for the *Masses*. This was a revolutionary magazine, revolutionary not merely in the disciplined Marxian pattern (although that was part of it), but in the broad, indiscriminate sense of striking out against complacency, convention, and compromise. Its contributors were a strange assortment—Gelett Burgess, Amy Lowell, Lincoln Steffens, Sherwood Anderson, Charles Edward Russell, William Rose Benét, John Sloan, Art Young, Floyd Dell, Louis Untermeyer, Carl Sandburg, Max Eastman—but they were united in rebellion and agreed with Floyd Dell that the *Masses* stood for "fun, truth, beauty, realism, freedom, peace, feminism, and revolution." The January 1913 *Masses* carried a story by Reed that had repeatedly been rejected by the national magazines because its theme was deemed unfit for family reading. Two months later Reed was listed as a contributing editor, and with Max Eastman he drafted a spirited statement of purpose, emphasizing the magazine's defiance.

Meanwhile, John Reed's social education proceeded apace. Lincoln Steffens introduced him to radicals of all sorts—single taxers, socialists, anarchists, labor leaders, atheists, and feminists. At Mabel Dodge's he heard Bill Haywood describe the class struggle as exemplified in the Paterson silk workers' strike and was so impressed that he went to see what was going on, was arrested, and spent four days in jail with Carlo Tresca, Bill Haywood, and the strikers. Out of this experience came the idea for the pageant staged by Reed and others under the auspices of the Industrial Workers of the World in Madison Square Garden, which massed the workers and their wives before a huge New York audience. Reed was becoming increasingly implicated in the radical movement, and although he left after the pageant's one-night stand to spend a romantic interlude with Mabel Dodge in Italy, he had taken a stride along the path that ended under stone beside the Kremlin wall.

Back in New York in October 1913, as managing editor of the *Masses*, Reed found himself drawn in two directions: pulled by the possessiveness of Mabel Dodge, on one hand, and moved toward Marxism and the class struggle, on the other. Moreover, he had not yet found his "lay" or "line," as Lincoln Steffens pointed out. The dilemma was shortly resolved when *Metropolitan Magazine* hired Reed, on Steffens's recommendation, to cover Francisco Villa's exploits against the federalists in northern Mexico.

Characteristically, Reed lost himself in the local struggle. He met the Mexican leader and became an ardent Villa partisan. He was ignorant of Mexican history and only superficially aware of the issues, but he loved the simple, lusty peons and quoted approvingly one compañero's definition of freedom as "the right to do what I want to." Reed rode, slept, ate, and fought with the ragged troops, risking his life and learning that he could tolerate being under fire. As he ran headlong across a chaparral-studded plain, a federalist in hot pursuit, he kept repeating to himself: "Well, this is certainly an experience. I'm going to have something to write about." This was not the expression of a reporter exultant over a prospective scoop, but rather the delight of an artist and poet living through an experience that was providing him with something to say.

That John Reed had truly found his "line" was apparent in the enthusiastic reception of the dispatches he sent back to the *Metropolitan* and the New York *World*, and which formed the substance of his book *Insurgent Mexico*. Reed's undisputed ability to use his eyes and to record in rich, relevant detail and with a kind of impassioned precision all that they took in made of *Insurgent Mexico*, despite its lack of perspective and unity, a memorable book. For the moment, John Reed was the most popular correspondent in the country.

Between his Mexican adventures and the outbreak of war in Europe, Reed had one notable assignment. He was sent to Ludlow, Colorado, to investigate the violence in the coal mines. His report on the Ludlow strike was much less impressionistic than were his stories from Mexico, but there was little question where his sympathies lay, and the experience recalled him forcibly to the clash between the classes.

In Europe in 1914, the *Metropolitan* reporter could not identify himself with the struggle as he had in Mexico. To Reed this was strictly a war for profits; furthermore, it was dull, mechanistic, impersonal. News of one ill-advised and irresponsible attempt made by Reed and a companion to get the feel of the fighting by firing from the German trenches in the general direction of the French lines leaked and followed Reed the rest of his life. His work was a disappointment to the editors of *Metropolitan* as well as to himself. He returned to the United States with the laconic but emphatic message, "This is not our War." A month later John Reed and an artist from the *Masses* were back in Europe covering the eastern sectors and proceeding recklessly into Russia without proper passes. After a series of arrests and narrow escapes from imprisonment, expulsion, even execution, they were at last permitted to leave by way of Rumania. This trip was more exciting than the first, but Reed's conviction that it was a capitalist's war remained firm.

Once again in the United States, John Reed went home to Portland, where he met Louise Bryant Trullinger. They fell in love, and shortly Louise Bryant left her husband to join Jack Reed in New York, where he was busy with the *Masses*, writing up interviews for the *Metropolitan*, and, in the summer, helping to organize the Provincetown Players.

Reed's energies, however, were mainly enlisted in fighting the nation's drift toward involvement in the war. When pacifists and liberals and radicals of various shades and descriptions reversed their positions after Wilson's war message, Reed remained adamant against what he continued to call a trader's war. Disillusioned with the patriotism of the European socialists and discouraged by the docility of the American worker, John Reed, by this time a Marxist, left for Russia in August 1917 to report for the *Masses* and the Socialist *Call* the progress of the revolution then in the provisional government stage under Kerensky.

In Petrograd Reed sought to follow the mercurial scene with the same avidity that had characterized his observation of the Mexican insurrection, but this time with an intellectual as well as an emotional commitment. Reed roamed the streets and haunted the meeting halls, searching out the substance as well as the color of events. He got as close to the revolution as possible, shuttling from one faction to another to see how things were going and ripping posters from walls to help document the story that was taking shape in his notes and in his mind. By November 13 the Bolsheviks controlled Petrograd, the revolution was spreading through Russia, and Reed hailed the Red victory as the beginning of "a kingdom more bright than any heaven had to offer, and for which it was a glory to die."

After six months in revolutionary Russia, John Reed came home in the spring of 1918, having promised to carry the story of the struggle to the American proletariat. Reed's last sixteen months in the United States were troubled and strenuous. Along with other editors of the *Masses*, he faced charges of conspiracy to obstruct recruiting and enlistment, and when he spoke in eastern and midwestern cities in support of the revolution, he picked up other criminal indictments. Although he resigned from the staff of the *Liberator*, which had succeeded the repressed *Masses*, because he would not share editorial responsibility for a magazine which existed upon the sufferance of Postmaster General Burleson, he continued to contribute to the magazine as well as to the Socialist *Call*. The national journals that had once welcomed his work were, of course, closed to him. At the time of Reed's resignation from the *Liberator*, C. E. S. Wood wrote to him approving his action and offering financial aid.

With the armistice, left-wing radicals tried to organize bolshevism in the United States, and Reed was in the vanguard of the movement. The Socialist party splintered, and the left wing split into two factions, the Communist party and the Communist Labor party, each claiming to be revolutionary. Reed was a leader in the latter. His program called for the immediate training of the working class for the seizure of power. It was to gain recognition in Moscow for the Communist Labor party that Reed sailed for Russia late in September 1919.

Meanwhile, in March, his *Ten Days That Shook the World* had appeared, selling 9,000 copies in the first three months. This was the best writing of Reed's career. It had cohesion and a controlled vigor that *Insurgent Mexico* lacked. Although frankly pro-Bolshevik and sometimes in error, it was a full and faithful account of what Jack Reed had seen, backed up by substantial documentation. No other firsthand account of the Bolshevik rise to power is in its class.

In Russia Reed lived in a working-class quarter; he talked with Lenin from time to time, wrote about the revolutionary situation in America for the official Communist organ, and wandered about tirelessly, ranging as far as the Volga. When the executive committee of the Communist International produced a plan to secure the fusion of the two American Communist parties, it was time for Reed to return to the United States. He made two abortive attempts to do so, on the second try spending three months in a Finnish prison awaiting release through either the United States State Department or Moscow. The Russians acted first, exchanging two captive Finnish professors for Reed.

As a member of the executive committee planning for the second congress of the Communist International, Reed moved into full participation in the construction of the new social order. In the excitement of the congress's closing day, Reed, another American, and an Australian delegate, at Reed's signal, hoisted Lenin on their shoulders to receive the tribute of the people in the proper American grandstand manner. As the uncomprehending crowd gaped, Lenin kicked vigorously until the three set him down. There was still a streak of playfulness left in Jack Reed, and it had betrayed him into a breach of revolutionary decorum.

At the end of August 1920, Reed was sent to a congress of Oriental nations at Baku. When he returned to Moscow, his wife, Louise Bryant, was there to greet him, having made her way from the United States. They spent a handful of days together in happy reunion, and then John Reed, his health already shattered by scurvy, fatigue, and strain, was stricken with typhus. By Sunday, October 17, 1920, three days before his thirty-third birthday, John Reed was dead.

When Reed was fighting indictments, writing up the Bolshevik revolution, and working to organize a properly activist American Communist party, C. E. S. Wood was immersed in final negotiations for the sale of the wagon road land grant running from Albany on the Willamette across the Cascades to Ontario on the Snake. It was

Wood's million-dollar commission from this transaction that freed him from his law practice and permitted him in 1919 to break with his family, after providing for them financially through a series of trust instruments that are among the most lucid and thoughtful and moving things he ever wrote. He left Portland for northern California, where he spent the quarter century that remained to him in writing and sharing a rich and intellectually fruitful companionship with Sara Bard Field.

Most of the California years were spent on a Los Gatos hill in an unusual home of stone and steel and glass built under the colonel's supervision. A steep and narrow road twisted down from the house to the highway below, where two huge stone felines—one awake, the other dozing—guarded the entrance and gave the estate its name, "The Cats." Above the currents of reaction that characterized the 1920s, C. E. S. Wood continued to criticize society, and because he and Sara Bard Field were people of sympathy and warmth, The Cats was a kind of clearinghouse for causes and a place of appeal for victims of various forms of injustice and discrimination. On one occasion Wood, at seventy-eight, came through a heavy California storm to galvanize a Tom Mooney protest meeting from listlessness into shouting enthusiasm. Both poets spent hours of their time in writing letters on behalf of such lesser-known figures as Ella Young, an Irish poet who sought to avoid deportation; or Max Hayek, translator of Whitman and Tagore and of Wood's *Poet in the Desert* into German, who needed sponsors if he was to escape the anti-Jewish terror of the Nazis; and there were many more. Erskine and Sara, despite the possibilities of withdrawal at The Cats, were very much of this world.

Even in swiftly summarizing these California years, it is impossible to treat Wood apart from his companion, Sara. It is true that the creative work of the two progressed independently, but in a deep sense there was constant collaboration and consultation between them. Out of devotion to one another and from the beauty and grace of their surroundings they shaped a way of life that was as impressive as anything they wrote.

The last years of Wood's life were marred by illness. In 1937 he sustained a coronary thrombosis from which he made remarkable recovery, considering that he was eighty-four, but failing eyesight and ebbing vitality prevented his completing a number of projects. Charles Erskine Scott Wood died January 20, 1944, just one month short of his ninety-second birthday. His body was cremated and his ashes strewn through the live oak grove at The Cats, as he wished.

The quality of C. E. S. Wood's revolt is difficult to define. It is not surprising that a man who, until his late sixties, felt repressed by one kind of authority or another—father, the army, the legal profession, middle-class convention—should rebel in the direction of anarchism, a theory that provides the utmost leeway for the individual. However, he was not the same kind of rebel in 1918 or in 1935 that he was in the first decade of the century. In the early period his anarchism was clearly egoistic. It sprang largely from having to subdue artistic, romantic, and literary urges in the face of more demanding responsibilities imposed by family and law practice, both of them growing. There is a strident, vainglorious note in this passage from Wood's 1905 journal:

I rebel against the suppression of the individual, the lack of freedom and the falsity—the hypocrisy of the smooth successful life. . . . I am sick of worthy men who force others to their own ideas of worthiness. . . . Let each be free and the worthiest will come to the top. . . . I would have more hope from a society where men gambled freely if they wanted to, than from a society made to be good by force of law and by the thunders of the pulpit. . . . I have more hope that the uplift of the physical and mental man will be resumed when society permits free love than I have from a society which forces the passing glance of young nature to be one dead, eternal gaze. . . . I deify Rebellion. I glory in being a rebel—and a fanatic. These are only other names for mind—progress—earnestness.

Albert Camus describes a type of romantic rebel that he calls the "Dandy." Camus's Dandy delights in shocking people with extreme pronouncements. In Baudelaire's phrase, he achieves coherence in the ambition to live and die before a mirror, and he finds his mirror in the eyes of others. He can exist only through defiance. If he neither commits suicide nor goes mad, he sets out to amass wealth and become a success. There is a suggestion of the Dandy in the Wood of 1905—handsome, a bit vain, dramatically dressed, vociferous in his anarchism, and demanding for himself in Portland something of the freedom that John Reed, Floyd Dell, Mabel Dodge, and others were soon seeking and finding in Greenwich Village.

By 1918 Wood's anarchism is much broader, less self-centered, more humanitarian, less shrill. In Poet in the Desert, condemnation of the state and authority is explicit and hard hitting, but Wood does not renounce law; rather, he proclaims the impersonal law of nature as supreme. If man can only learn to understand and to submit to nature, then she will evolve his soul as she has his body. In this poem Wood is often closer to transcendentalism than to anarchism.

In the late 1920s and through most of the thirties, Colonel Wood turned to direct attack on some of what were to him currently remediable abuses of authority—prohibition, censorship, the Ku Klux Klan, the concentration of corporate power, judicial review. He watched the Russian revolution and the Soviet experiment with interest and approval as a heartening attempt at realizing much of what he had been advocating for more than twenty years. But he was suspicious of the Stalinist purges, and in a letter to the *Daily Worker* he penned a sharp remonstrance to American party-line Communists for being unable or unwilling to think independently of Moscow.

Young radicals who began with admiration for the colonel often became disillusioned, writing him off as a wily old hypocrite, living in comfort and mouthing rebellion. Reed may have been among these. In time, however, some came to believe that Wood was a shrewd and reasonable man with a keen knowledge of what was possible in human affairs, a man whose compromises were more a result of this worldly understanding than of ambivalence, weakness, or hypocrisy. Long life, broad employment of diverse talents, flexibility in point of view—these help explain why C. E. S. Wood cannot be confined to a label or captured in a phrase.

The road that John Reed took to radical rebellion, although circuitous, is reasonably well marked. There were first the Harvard years, when Reed discovered the conflict within him that he strove the rest of his life to resolve. Then came the heady experience of Greenwich Village, balanced by exposure to the poverty and depravity of New York's East Side pointing to the gulf between the privileged and the poor, with Lincoln Steffens standing by all the while as guide and father-confessor. There was the dramatization of the class struggle at Paterson and Ludlow; the romance of four months with the simple, beautiful Mexicans in their struggle for liberty and land; and finally, the workers, soldiers, and peasants of Russia showing timid American workers the way to a proletarian heaven.

Perhaps the quality that best explains why John Reed construed his experiences as he did is his proclivity for total, if temporary, commitment. He was forever throwing himself into some project or toward some person and in the process sacrificing perspective and balance for deep involvement in the immediate. Thus he sank himself in the cause of the Paterson strikers and worked to the point of exhaustion in planning a pageant that, however, impressive, could be staged but one night and shrank rather than swelled the strikers' fund. Reed fled from that scene into the arms of Mabel Dodge and an interlude of unalloyed bohemianism. He carried identification with Villa's mestizos to the point of jeopardizing his life in a cause which he accepted but scarcely understood.

The sympathetic interpretation is that, after fighting through various stages of indecision, Reed finally found himself in Marxism and the Bolshevik revolution. Fortunately perhaps, for this school of thought, Reed died in the early stages of the Soviet experiment. Even so, there is some testimony, albeit of questionable reliability, that dis-illusionment had set in before typhus struck him down. Still, it is more likely that after October 1917 the revolution was almost Reed's entire life. He spoke for it, wrote for it, hurt his mother and lost friends for it, wasted in prison and finally died for it. Marxists ac-cepted this as a fitting climax to a life of persistent, if deviant, growth toward truth. On the other hand, Lincoln Steffens lamented the loss of a free and laughing spirit.

One of Reed's biographers implies without undue regret that a great poetic talent, perhaps genius, was lost in the making of a rev-olutionary. Reed himself once remarked to Max Eastman, "This class struggle plays hell with your poetry." Is it not possible, however, to argue that Reed may have embraced communism because he feared to face his failure as a poet? In a conversation with Sherwood Ander-son, Reed confessed to doubts about his ability to write poetry, and certainly there is little in his published verse to suggest anything be-yond competence.

Malcolm Cowley believed that Reed became a revolutionist for fun-damentally literary reasons. Reed, he felt, could write superlatively on only one subject—"on men revolting against the institutions that prevented them from leading *human* lives." Reed discovered this first in Mexico and then again in Petrograd; and each time the romantic poet and journalist was transformed into a writer who had something close to genius. If Cowley's insight is valid and had John Reed lived to mature with the revolution, Boris Pasternak might have had an American-born counterpart.

There is not apt to be agreement on the meaning or the perma-nence of John Reed's rebellion. As George Kennan insists, after point-ing out Reed's manifest weaknesses, "John Reed's was *one* American way of reacting to the Revolution. It deserves to be neither forgotten nor ridiculed."

Amid the festivities and ceremonies of this centennial year, when platoons of prominent and proper Oregonians are being called from quiet, honored graves and required to pass in historical review, it is perhaps also appropriate to have surveyed these two from out of the state's past who refused to stay in step, each counting a cadence pe-culiarly his own.

Bibliographical Note

Aside from John Reed's own works and his autobiographical essay "Almost Thirty," reprinted in the *New Republic*, Vol. 131 (Nov. 22, 1954), this article leans heavily on *John Reed: The Making of a Revolutionary* (New York, 1936), a persuasive biography by Granville Hicks with the assistance of John Stuart. A more recent life of Reed, published a number of years after this essay, is Robert A. Rosenstone, *Romantic Revolutionary: A Biography of John Reed* (New York, 1975). The entry in the *Dictionary of American Biography* is by Ernest Sutherland Bates.

There is no full-scale biography of Charles Erskine Scott Wood. The best and most convenient treatment is Sara Bard Field's introduction to *Collected Poems of Charles Erskine Scott Wood* (New York, 1949). C. E. S. Wood's son, Erskine, has written a life of his father published in a privately printed limited edition in 1978. The entry in the *Dictionary of American Biography* is by Thurman Wilkins. The largest body of Wood papers is in the Henry E. Huntington Library, San Marino, California. This collection was the gift of Sara Bard Field and has been used in the preparation of this paper with the kind permission of the donor. Other important Wood materials are housed in the Oregon Historical Society Library, Portland, and in the Hubert Howe Bancroft Library, Berkeley, California.

Everett, 1916, and After

NORMAN CLARK

Everett, Washington, lies on a wedge of high ground between Port Gardner Bay and the Snohomish River. The mountains to the east are covered with timber and loaded with minerals; the salt water to the west opens to avenues of world commerce. Jim Hill unlocked these potentials when he brought the Great Northern Railroad down the mountains to the bay, and he, more than anyone else, determined who would make the great fortunes from the natural resources of the region. His favors fell upon Frederick Weyerhaeuser, the timber king, David Clough, former governor of Minnesota, and a loosely extended family of their friends and relatives.

In 1890 the mouth of the Snohomish River was a green expanse of wilderness. By 1900 Hill, with his friends and agents, owned a city of 30,000. By 1910 boosters of Everett called it the City of Smoke-stacks, which indeed it was. Forty mills circled the high ground, darkening the sky with smoke and cinders as they turned out lumber and shingles twenty-four hours a day. Within a decade, a small group of capitalists had industrialized a frontier, and the history of their town is a dramatic case study of the economic, social, and political tensions which came west with the railroads to the shores of Puget Sound.

During these few years, Hill and his friends had created an industrial barony with many of the classic symptoms of industrial unrest: there was absentee ownership, and the iron law of wages seemed to many workers to be an immutable law of life. The impact of primitive capitalism was mollified, however, by a vigorous middle class of mer-

Originally published in *Pacific Northwest Quarterly*, April 1966.

chants, saloonkeepers, and professional men whose welfare depended upon the loggers and the millworkers and whose aspirations were not always those of the master class. After 1900 political and social conflict was constant, always personal, and usually acrimonious. The conflict had alternately sharpened and then blurred the lines of class interest, but it had never shaken the certainty of many wage earners that they were in fact industrial serfs.

It was this certainty, reinforced by the actions of the millowners, which perhaps more than anything else led to what has been called the Everett massacre of 1916, or Everett's "Bloody Sunday." In 1916 the shingle weavers' union demanded the restoration of a wage scale which they had lost the year before. In most areas of the state, mill operators raised wages rather than lose the promising wartime prosperity in an inevitable strike. But not in Everett. Millowners there announced that the real issue was not wages but a man's right to conduct his own affairs, that industrial peace would be impossible until the owners could "run their business without interference from the union." The picket lines went out on a symbolic date, May 1.

Through the summer months, professional strikebreakers came, and smoke again poured from the smokestacks. The pickets shuffled around the mills, their spirits soured by the apparent futility of their sacrifice. Lumber was leaving the harbor again. By August the picket lines had thinned out in hopelessness, leaving the daily vigil to the few who were most dedicated or most bitter. On August 19 an insult from the picket lines ignited the strikebreakers, and, urged on by a millowner, they attacked a small group of pickets and beat them without mercy. That evening when the whistles blew, the union men came out with reinforcements to meet the strikebreakers and to return the violence. Everett policemen, who had done nothing during the morning conflict, came to rescue the strikebreakers during the second encounter. Thereafter the strikebreakers marched with armed guards and with the obvious blessing of the Everett police. To union men the choice then seemed to be that of desperation or despair. Then the Wobs came—the Industrial Workers of the World, the "bummery" as they proudly called themselves, the legions of unwashed, uncouth, and irreverent wage slaves from the logging camps and the mills who had organized the most egalitarian and most radical industrial union in the country. IWW members in Seattle and Chicago had watched events in Everett with an eager interest, impressed by the sheer beauty of historical determinism. They saw a perfect case study in the abuses of capitalism. By August they had decided that conditions in Everett offered a perfect opportunity to dramatize the nature of the class struggle.

The Wobblies did not come as strangers. The socialists had been strong in Everett unions since 1912, and the differences between socialists and the IWW in the Pacific Northwest were seldom emotional ones. In 1913 Big Bill Haywood had spoken to a large group in the city, where the IWW idiom had already become a part of the standard vocabulary. In 1916, the Wobblies came up from Seattle to Everett to strengthen the picket lines, to revive sinking spirits with their songs, to flood the city with their rhetoric—in defiance of an ordinance against street meetings—and to give the bosses a taste of the terror implicit in civil disobedience and passive resistance. At first by the dozen and then by the score, they came to put Everett on the map of social revolution.

Middle-class citizens of Everett shuddered. They knew that the soldiers of discontent had descended upon Spokane in 1909 to protest by passive resistance an ordinance against street meetings, and that their "free speech fight" there had filled the jails with Wobblies until the police were helpless. Spokane spent a quarter of a million dollars jailing Wobblies. For months the city lived in fear. The Wobbly victory for free speech was for the citizens of Spokane a victory of anarchy and chaos over social order. To polite society in Everett, the songs of discontent threatened to bring a long night of lawlessness.

When the Wobs came, the Commercial Club of Everett, then completely dominated by the millowners, called an emergency meeting. Fred Baker, the president, was furious with the mayor and the chief of police, whose excuse was that the city treasury could not support the number of extra policemen necessary to clear the streets of Wobblies. Then Baker asked the county sheriff, Donald McRae, if the sheriff's office could help. McRae assured the club members that, with their help, he could protect Everett from an invasion of big-city radicals. He would call for five hundred volunteers, deputize them, and circle the city with armed guards.

McRae found about two hundred men, mostly from the ranks of mill management and white collar workers, though a few must have been professional scab guards. He saw that each had a gun, a badge, and a club, and he led the drills in the meeting rooms of the Commercial Club.

To his friends, McRae was a man of heroic proportions, tall and strong with a will of steel, a man with guts enough to save a city. To his enemies, he was a tool of privilege, a powerful, drunken sadist who cracked skulls at night and then "blubbered" in remorse the next morning. During September and October, his vigilantes took Wobblies off the trains and trolleys, beat them with clubs and guns, then shoved them down the tracks toward Seattle. He broke up meetings, beat men on the street, hauled them to jail to beat them again, then sent them off with a warning that the next time would be worse. But for each Wobbly deported, two could break through the blockade the following day.

On October 30, forty Wobblies came to Everett from Seattle by boat to engage in a free speech demonstration, each prepared to be mashed and mangled in his role as a martyr for freedom. McRae and his men took them from the boat, beat them, jailed them, then at night took them all to a quiet piece of forest called Beverly Park. Here they stripped the invaders, whipped them, and as the rain began to fall, nearly killed them in a gauntlet of blows from rifles and clubs.

The next morning, a chilling fog of fact and rumor gripped the city. A group of citizens visited Beverly Park, where, even after a night of rain, they could find the bloody ground. The Reverend E. E. Flint of the First Congregational Church was there, and the following Sunday he preached against lawlessness and violence, fully aware that some in his congregation would take his words personally. Knowing that many people were now near hysteria in their fear of Wobbly retribution, he called for a full review of recent events before all the citizens of Everett. He scheduled a public meeting for Sunday afternoon, November 5.

Even before the sermon, IWW leaders in Seattle had sent out a call for two thousand volunteers to bring a massive free speech fight to Everett. McRae, they reasoned, could not wade in blood forever. After Flint's call for a public meeting, the Wobblies also chose that date. In Everett a free speech committee, risking McRae's clubs, circulated thousands of handbills urging that everyone come out on Sunday to "help maintain your and our constitutional right." In Seattle maybe five hundred responded to the call for volunteers. Down from the logging camps, up from the railroad jungles, up from the Skid Road, they came to the IWW hall. They swaggered with memories of Spokane and talk of brotherhood, wage slavery, social revolution, and the obligations of all workingmen to stand up for the rights of fellow workers in Everett. Some were cocky with confidence—it would be a great day. These were men who all their lives had flirted with danger—one knew a shingle weaver by the fingers missing from both hands. Sunday would be part picnic, part holy war. Others, who had felt McRae's wrath, were fiercely determined not to suffer Everett's clubs again.

On Saturday night in Everett, the manager of the Employers' Association of Washington told members of the Commercial Club that Everett was known across the land as a "city of red-blooded Americans who had shown that they would not be bullied." The only way to combat force, he said, was with force. McRae showed the group the black cat card—a Wobbly symbol of sabotage—that he had received in the mail, and he discussed plans for Sunday. Before the meeting ended, three hundred men signed cards for the Open Shop League of Everett.

It was probably this number that responded to the call for assembly the next day. Throughout that Sunday morning, William Butler, the banker, and John McChesney, Jim Hill's agent, sat at their telephones. And as their paid spies reported, they could follow every move in the Seattle IWW hall, and they even heard the singing as the men moved away from the hall and toward the docks. When Butler and Mc-Chesney knew that about 250 Wobblies were aboard the passenger vessel *Verona*, they ordered a blast from the mill whistles in Everett. Then, in the manner of staff generals, they retired to a private club-room while the deputies marched.

The deputies filed down the hill to Port Gardner Bay—clerks, mill-owners, foremen, thugs—armed with shotguns, rifles, pistols. Some of them were already awash with the courage of whiskey and had forgotten whatever discipline McRae may have planned. An enter-prising salesman circulated among the marchers, doing a brisk busi-ness in accident insurance. A crowd of several thousand gathered along the railroad track on the ground above the dock. At Pier 1, the deputies milled around for a while, then many of them concealed themselves in the warehouse and on the several tugboats that formed a rough semicircle around the dock where the *Verona* would tie up.

As the vessel came into the bay, those who were high on the hill could hear the singing from Wobblies on the *Verona*. McRae waited. When the Wobblies secured their lines, he stepped toward the gang-plank with two deputies. There was a sharp exchange of words be-tween the men on the dock and those on the boat. Someone fired a shot, and then a barrage of firing began.

The men on the deck of the *Verona* were crowding tightly toward the gangplank when they caught the murderous crossfire. In con-sternation and terror, they rushed toward the other side of the boat. The shift of their weight almost capsized it. Men fell to the deck, and some slid overboard. The fire from both sides was relentless. There was shooting from the *Verona*, too, for at least a few of the Wobblies had armed themselves in their determination not to be clubbed again.

McRae fell, shot in the leg, and others fell behind him, probably victims of the sloppy crossfire which the deputies themselves had patterned. As deputies ran from the warehouse, they were hit by bullets from fellow deputies stationed in the tugboats. Others knelt behind bags of potatoes on the dock and fired into the mob on the *Verona* or at those who had fallen into the water.

Inside the *Verona*, a Wobbly forced the engineer to reverse the en-gines. The pull broke the tie-up lines, and the boat churned into the bay again, still under heavy fire. On the deck, four were dead, one was dying, and thirty-one were wounded, many seriously. On the dock, one deputy was dead, another was dying, and twenty others were wounded. The number of Wobblies who fell from the boat and were killed in the water, their bodies swept under the sea, can never be fixed with certainty. But one man on the dock, an excellent marksman who fired with some precision, later claimed that he alone had accounted for at least eleven.

This is a tragic chapter in the history of the city and the IWW, written with a hard and grim bitterness. Even today this bitterness restricts the historian. For example, a popular point of departure in analyzing the event is the question, Who fired the first shot? And here the historical method yields only slight satisfaction. If one insists, like Thucydides, upon the firsthand accounts of participants, he can, if he works at it, stack such accounts into impressive piles of mutually contradictory evidence. The accounts of some informants— gathered yesterday or forty-nine years ago—conceal the truth; others distort it. But it may have been that no one really planned to fire first, and to many men on the boat or on the dock, it may have seemed at the moment that the first fire came from the enemy.

The deductive approach is, if anything, more hazardous. One can ask why the Wobblies would have fired first. In view of their purpose, which was to push McRae to the grotesque extreme of his determined course and to prove to the world how rotten the Everett barons were, they had nothing to gain by shooting McRae. This thought gives credence to the stories that McRae signaled for fire by raising his hand, and to the story that the widow of a slain deputy later whispered that her husband would not have died if the sheriff had not chosen to kill Wobblies. But underlying this thought is the assumption that each of the Wobblies acted soberly and rationally and would have done nothing inconsistent with the best interests of the group. One would then have to believe that in the excitement, fear, and passion of the moment of confrontation, each individual aboard the *Verona* found the inner strength to discipline any explosive drives toward boozy martyrdom or blind venegeance. Quite clearly, the history of the Wobbly movement cannot support such a premise.

And surely this is not the most significant question, for it has to do only with who should receive the blame. It in no way illuminates the cause of the event or clarifies the social antagonism and turmoil which made the event possible. It is better to ask, first of all, why in Everett in 1916 there was no spirit of compromise which might have helped both sides avoid killing each other.

In the attitudes and the actions of men with power in Everett in 1916, there is little to suggest that compromise was possible. To John McChesney, to the Cloughs, and their friends Roland Hartley and Joe

Irving—all owners of large mills—the industrial frontier was a wilderness in which only the fittest survived. A man's fitness for survival was measured by his physical prowess, his ruthlessness, his self-confidence, his unbending determination. Herbert Clough once grabbed a planer's knife and almost killed a man who had been drunkenly insubordinate to him in his own mill. John McChesney used his considerable intellectual talents to solidify his economic control over the entire community. By finesse, by trickery, by bluffing, he outmaneuvered the reformers, thus sustaining the vast power Jim Hill had given to him. He did not compromise. Roland Hartley, the pugnacious and earthy manager of several mills, boasted that he could do any job he had ever created and do it better than any man he had ever hired. He never euphemized his contempt for any man who had never earned money with sweat and muscle. Joe Irving, who employed twelve hundred men and had begged the Wobblies— for the welfare of Everett's children—to leave the city, even in his old age spoke freely of the Wobblies he had crippled, bloodied, and beaten nearly to death.

All of these men believed that their enterprises were the solid extensions of their own characters, and they would allow no one to dictate to them in any way. Their open shop fanaticism was an integral part of their value system. They would never recognize a union—they would fight and club and shoot, or close down forever. To retreat from this position would have been for them to expose a soggy lack of principle, a streak of moral and spiritual decay.

Against this background of values, one can begin to understand their frustrations. For four years McChesney had been losing his battle with reformers who favored municipal ownership. They took his water company away from him, and they were after his docks and his electric company. William Butler and David Clough had lost some of their power to elect city officials and to determine tax policy; the people had voted in a reform mayor and a single tax. Hartley, who as mayor had acted as if he ruled a principality, gave up the office in 1912 to a minister—a soft-mannered, white-handed, Populist-socialist preacher who wanted to spend money but who had never met a payroll. Irving, who regarded his workers paternally but sternly, had once threatened to close his mills if his workers listened to speeches by Wobblies. He suffered to see his mills closed by the workers themselves in 1915 and 1916.

All of these men felt that the beauty and the security of their feudal power were challenged by softheaded, gutless "I Won't Workers" who had no respect for property and even sneered at Christianity. The millowners could easily see themselves as the only strong defenders of red-blooded virtue and the American way of life—the way of life that had made them masters. In 1916 they thought they could destroy the union forever. In a world at war, they were confident that war prosperity would mean great wealth, and with great wealth they could regain their lost power. Then the Wobblies came. The millowners determined to crush them in a conflict that would measure strength and integrity on an industrial frontier.

The union men and their Wobbly supporters were no less adamant. Fifteen years of bleeding humiliation were proof enough that they could not reason with the master class. Fifteen years of failure had driven out the moderates and left the radicals to say yes or no. There was also the iron law: mills in other areas had granted the wage increase; if the union had failed in Everett, the competitive advantage of the Everett operators would force wages everywhere inexorably downward. With their own snarling fanaticism, the union men saw a sacred obligation to the great brotherhood of the working class, an obligation to strike hard and to accept nothing less than total victory. If it cost blood, then let it cost blood: the conflict would measure their strength and integrity on an industrial frontier.

From these extreme positions, the massacre seems inevitable, a showdown of strength implicit in the view of the world shared by the protagonists. Or one can see it as a failure of intelligence, the kind of social intelligence which helps men retreat, gracefully or not, when they know that bitterness can linger on to rot away the victories which they might for a moment cherish. There were victories in 1916: the millowners killed some Wobblies, and the Wobblies won their martyrs. But in a few short years the IWW lost its power, and for many years now the Clough mansion in Everett has been an apartment house, and the Hartley mansion a rest home, both unnoticed by the casual visitor. Nobody won for long.

The fanaticism of 1916 is a depressing contradiction to our view of a period which we study because it does illustrate social intelligence. The decade before the war was a period of progressive reform, a period of general humanitarian concern when Americans found many sensible cures for many of the social bruises and lacerations left in the wake of 19th-century industrialization. The second question about Everett, 1916, then, is this: Where were the progressives, the men of conscience, moderation, and intelligence? What happened to them on November 5?

Everett, like most communities in the West, had gone through a progressive upheaval: a new city charter and a single tax in 1912, a successful campaign for municipal ownership of the city's water system that same year, the recall of corrupt politicians in 1914, by which time the city had already voted for woman suffrage, for chasing out the prostitutes, and for closing down the saloons. The Commercial

Club itself was something of a progressive achievement. Organized in 1912, it was at least a forum where millowners, merchants, professional men, ministers, and labor leaders came together to consider the city's future. It had structured a responsible ventilation of opposing attitudes and harsh feelings. But in 1916 the structure disintegrated when the moderates in the club abstained from voting on an open shop resolution. Maybe they failed their community because William Butler held their mortgages, but more likely it was because of a paralyzing ambivalence: their customers were wage earners, but they distrusted the radicalism of the union—its unsubtle, loud-mouthed pronouncements against private property, Christianity, and individualism. Many club members resigned rather than make a choice, and their resignation left the millowners in control.

The Reverend Mr. Flint was a member of the club who had at times given his pulpit to labor leaders for lay sermons on child labor, wages, hours, and working conditions. In 1909 the editor of the Everett *Daily Herald* wrote that "Everett occupies a foremost place in the growing good will between organized labor and the churches. . . . Our most influential ministers do not hesitate to speak . . . upon the great questions that affect the welfare of laboring men." Flint worked in this tradition. But he left the Commercial Club when the deputies began to drill there, when it seemed clear to him that a man of conscience could no longer oppose the club from within. In church and in public parks, he spoke against fanaticism—but not in the club or in the IWW hall or on the dock. He spoke in vain.

Another significant figure in the Commercial Club was A. A. Brodeck, the owner of Everett's largest dry goods store and a community leader since 1903. In a sense, the progressive upheaval began when Brodeck organized the small businessmen, professionals, and wage earners against McChesney's politicians and attacked McChesney's monopoly of land, public utilities, and banking. Though the word came down the Great Northern line that Jim Hill would frown on Everett if the people there did not vote for McChesney's man, the people did not, and Brodeck won. Later it was he who took labor's cause to Jim Hill and persuaded Hill to employ white workers rather than Orientals.

Brodeck's career in reform ended, however, in 1910, when the great issue was voting out the saloons. Representing the businessmen who depended upon the saloons to lure the loggers into Everett, Brodeck worked with Clough, McChesney, and Hartley to frustrate the reformers. These same men alibied for him in 1913 when the state indicted and tried him for adultery. In 1914, when Brodeck was mayor, his office became notorious for corruption and graft, and then not even his powerful friends could save him from recall and ruin. In 1916 his prestige was gone, and he could speak for no one.

The most pathetic failure was Donald McRae, who, in a remarkable way, had also been a progressive. He was elected sheriff on the Progressive ticket in 1912, and his public life was a striking study in contrasting loyalties. He had been an official of the shingle weavers' union, an engagingly personable and fair-minded man described by the union newspaper in 1913 as "an employee of the people who has always realized the obligations of his office." In 1914 an Everett newspaper carried a story about a confessed murderer described as a maniacal "halfbreed" who was captured and jailed by McRae. When this man left the county jail for the state penitentiary, he said that the sheriff was "the most humane officer I have ever had dealings with. He treated me like a man." What happened to McRae? How could he have become the drunken sadist—as his enemies insisted—who blubbered over his violence?

The evidence concerning McRae is about as shaky as that concerning the first shot. Informants differ, but those who hated him—and a few who did not—have said that McRae had been broken by campaign expenses and by a style of life he could not afford as sheriff, that he had been befriended by David Clough, who helped him through an election and entertained him at a private club. Toward 1916, they say, McRae developed a nervous aversion to radicalism. He began to drink heavily and decided that he had found no personal satisfaction in either politics or law enforcement. He wanted a good job, and David Clough had promised him one. Thus, when Clough needed a hero in 1916, McRae was his man.

Because of these failures, there were victories, but there was no real peace. A few days after the shooting, McRae said that the treatment his deputies received from the thousands of citizens who watched from the hill above the dock hurt more than the battle itself. An editorial condemned "the despicable cheers of the crowd that could rejoice when wounded men and the dead were carried away from the wharf." There were reports of still "half a thousand" men under arms determined to crush the IWW, but at least that many more were ready to express their rage against the deputies.

In this atmosphere, union leaders called off the strike following a plea from ministers that further violence must be avoided. But after a few weeks, when it was clear that the millowners would concede nothing at all, the leaders called the strike on again. Picket lines dragged on through the winter months of 1917, and the currents of tension were constantly recharged by a sequence of ugly episodes. For example, the Socialist paper in Everett printed an unsigned letter which, according to the editor, had been received at the IWW hall in Seattle. It represented, he wrote, the "True Commercial Club Spirit." It read in part:

You know you are a God-damned liar and a son-of-a—— when you wired the president saying the Everett men fired first. . . . I wish they had a machine gun and killed all of you sons of —— and threw your bodies in the bay. . . . I hope the president drives all you I.W.W.'s out of the country, as you are nothing but a bunch of murderers, trouble makers and loafers.

In every issue of this paper, for months on end, there was a column headed "We Never Forget," in which Commercial Club members were mentioned by name. The *Labor Journal* of Everett published the names of merchants who opposed the Commercial Club, listing about a hundred grocers, tailors, barbers, and shopkeepers, all of whom were suffering in 1917 because the men from the camps were staying clear of Everett.

In February the IWW opened a new hall in Everett. It was quickly raided by a group of deputies led by a mill executive who had arranged for the police to be in another part of the city when the raid occurred. The deputies emptied the hall of literature and papers, burned it all in the middle of the street, then placed a small American flag on the pile of ashes.

During these months, the churches of Everett apparently moved in full retreat away from any sort of social action. In the minutes of the Snohomish Valley Ministerial Association after November 5, 1916, there is no suggestion that the city of Everett had seen violence or bitterness. In the records of the Reverend Mr. Flint's First Congregational Church, there is the same void.

This silence, however, brought no relief. The trial of a Wobbly indicted for the murder of the deputy sheriff who died following Bloody Sunday was in the headlines for months. The jury found the Wobbly not guilty, and the state dropped its case against the others who might have fired from the decks of the *Verona*. The state never pressed charges against any of the deputies, however, and in refusing to do so, it handed the IWW a moral victory in which it has ever since gloried. The preface to *The Everett Massacre*, published by the IWW in 1917, reads:

It is with regret that we view the untimely passing of the seven or more Fellow Workers who were foully murdered on that fateful day, but if the working class of the world can view beyond their mangled forms the hideous brutality that was the cause of their deaths, they will not have died in vain.

This book is published with the hope that the tragedy at Everett may serve to set before the working class so clear a view of capitalism in all its ruthless greed that another such affair will be impossible.

But it could happen again—and did, at Centralia in 1919, when one Wobbly was lynched and others were beaten, brought to trial, and then convicted. After the hysteria of 1919–20, the Wobblies were through. Branded as traitors because they had opposed the war, their leaders went to prison, and their power dissipated. Their threats became empty, their songs died away, and no one would tremble again at the slogan "A poor day's work for a poor day's pay."

The Wobblies did not return to Everett after the war. In the years following, only the undercurrents of bitterness suggested that preachers had ever sympathized with wage slaves or that tattered and unshaved radicals had ever challenged the city's masters. The Reverend Mr. Flint was gone. Businessmen avoided the Commercial Club. Donald McRae found himself a farm north of the city, but he became—according to those who knew him—a haunted man, afraid of the shadows, afraid of the light. Unidentified snipers shot his animals and put bullets through his house at night. His wife killed herself, and the former hero was a shattered and sullen wreck when Roland Hartley, the millowner, became governor of the state in 1925 and found McRae a job in the state capital.

It was a significant sign of the times that Hartley did become governor. Not universally admired at home, he nevertheless won the governorship with his rabid anti-union speeches and his promises that he could manage the state in the same tight-fisted way he had managed an Everett lumber company. Later, during the depression, he choked on these words, because he never understood the differences between government and primitive capitalism, never accepted a world in which strong men must submit to law, never comprehended a society that wanted the law to protect those who are least able to survive in an industrial wilderness.

He was not a great governor. There is no statue of him—or of anyone else—in Everett. The city has never made an honest attempt to commemorate, or even to come to terms with, any reality of its recent past. In Everett today one can learn more about George Vancouver, the explorer who went ashore at Port Gardner Bay in 1792, than about Roland Hartley, David Clough, E. E. Flint, or the IWW. Though there still are some who remember the events of 1916, one can live a lifetime in Everett and never hear anything about Bloody Sunday.

Recently this silence so impressed one resident that he set for himself the task of breaking it, of learning the details and telling the story. For a decade Edwin Parker, a retired engineer, interviewed the old men who could remember, read the old newspapers, and searched for books or records that might clarify the distortions of the IWW accounts. He found that old men remember only what they want to remember, that newspapers do not always tell the truth, that records disappear when the word goes around that someone is prying into a past that old men have forgotten.

But Parker was persistent. He continued to pry; he wrote down his discoveries and his frustrations and eventually completed a manuscript of more than two hundred pages. But it was never published, because he could not give it the objectivity, the unity, or the coherence of authoritative history—there were too many contradictions, too many half-remembered impressions. He returned, then, to the heart of his evidence, the reminiscences of the old men, and convinced himself that there was a great story here which he could perhaps stitch into the fabric of fiction. In a few years he had a novel, which he called simply *Timber* and published privately in 1963. Though the book has some strengths and many weaknesses, it does bring 1916 into emotional focus. And while Parker makes no assumptions of proletarian nobility, his emphasis is clearly upon the mistreatment of Wobblies and the outrages of vigilantes. In his narrative, there is no doubt about who fired the first shot. The book was the talk of the town for a while, especially among those who could see the images— and even the names—of friends or relatives in its pages. It was reviewed politely, if not deeply, in the local paper.

For a moment, it seemed as if the past might be examined critically and openly. Some community leaders who regarded Parker's work as of at least local significance scheduled an oral review and discussion of *Timber* for an evening meeting at the Everett Country Club. They invited Parker to attend. But several days later, they canceled the meeting without any convincing explanation.

Parker smiles when he tells of this. He is sure he knows who and why. He understands, though he must regret that his work serves only as the grist for neighborhood gossip rather than as a lens through which the failures of the past might be seen in fine detail. He feels today, perhaps more poignantly than ever, what he felt when he wrote the introduction to his unpublished history. "I have been left alone," he said, "in my search for what it is that makes decent men willing to kill one another."

Bibliographical Note

Primary sources for this paper are the "Everett Interviews" recorded by Edwin S. Parker and filed in the Everett Public Library; the author's interviews with David Hartley, Everett, 1963, and Herbert Clough, La Jolla, Calif., 1966; the papers of Governor Ernest Lister, Washington State Archives, Olympia; the Everett newspapers, 1900–18—Everett *Herald, Labor Journal,* Everett *Tribune, Northwest Worker, Commonwealth, Cooperative News,* Everett *News;* and Ernest P. Marsh, "Everett's Industrial Warfare," published in the 1916 *Proceedings of the Washington State Federation of Labor.*

Other sources include William Whitfield, *History of Snohomish County,* 2 vols. (Chicago, 1926); Edwin S. Parker, "They Cleaned up the Woods," unpublished manuscript; Albert F. Gunns, "Roland Hartley and the Politics of Washington State," M.A. thesis (University of Washington, 1963); Robert L. Tyler, "I.W.W. in the Pacific Northwest: Rebels of the Woods," *OHQ,* Vol. 60 (1954), 3–44, and "The Everett Free Speech Fight," *PHR,* Vol. 23 (1954), 19–30; David C. Botting, Jr., "Bloody Sunday," *PNQ,* Vol. 49 (1958), 162–72; Walker C. Smith, *The Everett Massacre: A History of the Class Struggle in the Lumber Industry* (Chicago, 1917); and Harvey O'Connor, *Revolution in Seattle: A Memoir* (New York, 1964).

Senator Harry Lane: Independent Democrat in Peace and War

PAUL S. HOLBO

The progressive era and the First World War, prominent features of national history in the twentieth century, left their marks on the Pacific Northwest. These events were particularly important in the life of Harry Lane, a colorful Oregon Democrat whose political career reached its zenith with his election to the United States Senate in the progressives' banner year, 1912, and ended five years later—as some progressives and some later historians claim the progressive movement itself did—with the entry of the United States into the Great War.

Progressivism meant, and still means, different things to different people. Harry Lane's brand of progressivism was highly individualistic—an early manifestation, perhaps, of a pattern of individualism that Oregonians have boasted is characteristic of their state's politics, presumably as evidenced by such public figures as Senator Wayne Morse and Governor Thomas McCall. There are, to be sure, similarities between Lane and later politicians, especially Morse, but there are differences as well; and it would be too much to assert that the earlier senator influenced the more recent one, or that Oregonians are more independent politically than many other Americans. What can be said is that Lane was a progressive Democrat, independent, cantankerous, outspoken, suspicious, and inclined to battle against what he considered "the interests." As a result of his behavior, his career ended in virulent controversy.

Almost from the outset of his senatorial career, Lane differed with the policies of his party and its eloquent leader, President Woodrow Wilson. Denouncing Wall Street or the railroads during political campaigns in Oregon was one thing; opposing the determined, moralistic

Wilson was quite another matter. The odds against Lane seemed to drive him on. Convinced that Wilson's foreign policies not only were mistaken but also served selfish financial interests, he became relentless in his opposition to involvement in the European war.

All that he accomplished was to stir the wrath of the president and the public at large. Wilson, who believed that the president, like the British prime minister, could demand party loyalty, brooked no differences of viewpoint. Americans generally were far less tolerant of dissent then than they were, for instance, during the Vietnam War. As the United States moved toward war in early 1917, a surge of doctrinaire interventionist opinion and patriotic feeling in the nation's capital and in Lane's home state swept over the stunned and uncomprehending senator like a gigantic wave striking the Oregon coast. As fate would have it, Lane's life ended before the furor subsided.

It is easy to understand why Harry Lane adopted a stubborn and individualistic political course. His stance was not something new or peculiar to him but was rather an inheritance from one of his forebears, a pioneer of Oregon politics.

Some of Lane's earliest memories concerned his grandfather, a man whose life had been exciting enough to impress almost any boy. Joseph Lane had been a general in the Mexican War, Oregon's first territorial governor, a delegate to Congress, and Oregon's first U.S. senator. He was the most prominent man in the state and, it was said, he would "fight at the drop of a hat," especially for an underdog. This attitude no doubt influenced his grandson.

As a youngster, however, Harry, who was born in 1855, was more interested in his grandfather's career as an Indian fighter. General Lane had defeated the Rogue Indians at the Battle of Table Rock, and they were removed to an area near the Lanes' Corvallis home. "They taught me to make bows and arrows, and I wanted to wear a feather in my hair," Harry later reminisced. "My youth was the most utterly dreary period of my life. I wanted to be an Indian. . . . Instead, I was a clerk in a backwoods store. Clerking—clerking was tame business. We dealt in molasses, kerosene, and codfish, but my soul was far away."[1]

The political excitement that perpetually surrounded his grandfather periodically shattered the boy's reveries. In 1860, Carolina-born General Lane, intensely proslavery and sympathetic with the Southern states, ran for vice-president of the United States on the secessionist Democratic ticket with John C. Breckinridge of Kentucky. Senator Lane's views were extremely controversial in unionist Oregon, and his popularity dipped except in communities settled by Southerners. When "Old Joe" appeared at The Dalles in 1861 to speak at a Democratic rally, supporters of President Abraham Lincoln suspended an effigy bearing the inscription "Joe Lane, the Traitor" near his quarters.[2] We will hang "the old traitor" from a gibbet, "if he gives occasion," the Portland *Oregonian* warned. "His toad-eaters may yet see it done."[3]

As Harry Lane grew older, his father "pestered" him to study law or medicine. "The professions were teetering up and down in my mind," he recalled years later, "when the attorney for the accused in a murder case hired a witness and established an alibi for his client. . . . Personally, I charged the outrage to the whole legal profession, from Blackstone and John Marshall down. So, I studied medicine."[4] Medical school at Willamette University, in the state capital city of Salem, went well enough, but Harry could not escape his family connections or avoid controversy. A trustee of the university accused him of using profanity. Summoned before the board, Harry denied the charge. The trustee called the young man a liar. Trouble-making student friends convinced Joe Lane's grandson that he must redeem the honor of his name. Harry angrily called on the trustee, and both parties adjourned outside. The trustee slapped Lane; Harry replied with an uppercut. Both men rolled off the board sidewalk into a mud puddle, Harry on top.[5]

Surprisingly, Lane graduated, in the class of 1876, at the age of twenty. "I . . . looked so young and was so young," he said, "that nobody would hire me and nobody did hire me during the next five years."[6] So he read medicine, worked with a prominent surgeon in San Francisco, and eventually settled down to practice. Dr. Harry Lane was a charter member of the Portland Medical Society.

In 1887 the Democratic governor, Sylvester Pennoyer, appointed the deserving grandson of Joe Lane superintendent of the state insane asylum. The young superintendent promptly tore down the institution's walls and probed into everything else. Harry found coarse feed in a barrel of corn meal and learned that contractors who had political connections supplied the asylum with poor food and shoddy clothing.

Dr. Lane complained loudly, canceled contracts, and changed personnel. His refusal to purchase some wagons from a local Democratic chairman led to one fight. When he replaced a Pennoyer Democrat with a Republican, the governor asked for his resignation. "You can go to hell," Lane replied spiritedly. "I will not resign and you can't make me."[7] Governor Pennoyer agreed emphatically with the contractors that Dr. Lane should not be reappointed for another term. Lane's final report recommended establishment of a board of charities and corrections for the protection of the inmates—and the superintendent. He explained: "The management of an insane asylum is not the easiest task. . . . With a daily average of 639 persons living under one roof, 574 of whom are insane . . . it is not possible to always have everything gentle and serene . . . still, as a rule, it has gone along very well."[8]

Leaving the state Democratic organization seething, Harry departed for Europe to see the sights and to study. He felt that "too many kings and high churchmen" were buried in Westminster Abbey to suit his idea of the "proper balance," but Temple Court greatly impressed him. Alas, he wrote to friends, all England was bound up with an internal problem:

You can't get into a water closet after breakfast without paying a penny, if there is not a man on watch to get your penny, they have an automatic lock on the door . . . into which you have to drop your penny, turn the knob four times to the left and sing "God save the queen." . . . It is offering a premium upon constipation and accounts for the wealthiest modern dealer in England having made his fortune out of a pill.[9]

Back in Portland in 1892, Lane attempted once more to settle down in medical practice. "I am beginning to get business and will do more and more right along," he informed a friend.[10] Lane served as president of the City and County Medical Society, then was chosen president of the Oregon State Medical Society. In 1903 he was appointed to the first Oregon State Board of Health.

In office again, Harry was irrepressible. As health board officer, he objected to the use of "night soils"—human excrement removed from privies around Portland—by the Chinese gardeners who supplied most of the city's vegetables. The gardeners stored the unsanitary fertilizer in stone crocks set along the sides of their gardens, according to ancient custom. When repeated remonstrances failed to halt the practice, Dr. Lane took pot shots at the crocks with a rifle from the hillside above the gardens. He was an excellent marksman, and the gardeners soon found substitute fertilizers.[11] "There is no one else like him on this coast," a medical journal acknowledged, "a good physician and an all around good fellow."[12]

"Good fellow" Lane could not resist the calls of public service. He often sidled in a rear door in Salem to visit the banker Asahel Bush, head of the "Salem clique" that had long controlled the state Democratic party.[13] "Doc" Lane served as a member of the Portland charter commission. And, as a Citizens' party candidate, he ran a close race for state senator against the entrenched Republican machine in Portland in 1902. A campaign by civic reformers in 1905 to end corruption in city hall enticed him permanently from medical practice. Lane announced his candidacy for mayor at a Democratic rally, arriving dramatically late, just returned from the bedside of a patient. Doc Lane declared that he favored reform, but "don't tell 'em I never take a drink."[14]

Mayor Harry Lane, as spectacular a municipal reformer as any of the colorful city officials of the progressive era, fought traction and utilities interests over franchises for street railways, electric power, and water-supply systems. Relishing the opportunity to be obstructive with a civic purpose—as he saw it—he canceled municipal contracts and vetoed agreements. Portland's government probably was more honest under Lane's rule; but the city's efficiency suffered, for the mayor caused considerable turmoil. He wrangled constantly with the Republican-dominated city council. In relatively quiet moments Lane changed the personnel of the Health Department and bypassed civil service procedures to name the police chief and other officers.[15] His administration was, to say the least, highly personal and often arbitrary, and some of his practices resembled the dictatorial methods for which he severely condemned President Wilson a few years later. But Lane described himself as a "benevolent despot."

The city's Republican newspaper, the highly partisan *Oregonian*, inveighed against him constantly, as it had done against his grandfather. Lane, as quick to reply as Old Joe had been, retorted on one occasion with puns: "Nor do I expect fair treatment . . . I know your hands, and for lo, these many years, Have I seen the prints thereof."[16] The Democrats were equally distressed with Mayor Lane, for he retained many Republican officeholders and refused to appoint certain worthies from his own party. Six months after he took office, Lane was unwelcome at the Democratic Andrew Jackson Club.[17] "We want to elect men to office who . . . will conduct a Democratic administration," one party chieftain stormed. "The most we can get out of Mayor Lane, so far, is Biblical quotations such as 'Sufficient unto the day is the evil thereof.'"[18]

Doc Lane enjoyed every skirmish. "Those were joyful times," he recalled later. "Something occurred almost every day."[19] One day the mayor heard that contractors had installed some faulty curbing. Lane inspected personally. He tapped the curb with a hammer. Whenever he heard hollow sounds, he smashed in the paving. Schoolboys gathered round, and the mayor put them to work. The contractor rushed up and threatened to shoot the next boy who tampered with the curb. "That's the way to talk," Lane snapped. "Get a gun, hurry right along and shoot just once. Ten minutes later you will be hanging from the nearest telephone pole."[20] Concerned only with foiling a dishonest businessman, Lane did not seem to recognize the impropriety of what he had done or of his hinting at lynch-law justice.

He was more restrained in the Macleay Park incident, which drew chuckles from many Portlanders. A promoter had applied for permission to build a wooden flume through the park. The city refused to grant the permit, but the promoter went ahead secretly. One quiet Sunday afternoon, reporters saw Mayor Lane enter the police station, send off a force of officers carrying sledgehammers, and depart with the chief. "Nothing doing," His Honor remarked casually to members of the press. The reporters decided to tag along, just in case something should develop. At the park the mayor supervised while the policemen doffed their coats and smashed a section of the flume. Just then the entrepreneur arrived, surveyed the destruction with dismay, and angrily demanded permission to rebuild. Lane swung his arms dramatically and replied, "If you do, I will have you placed under arrest." He and the police chief walked away and amused themselves shooting pistols at a tree.[21] Altogether the occasion was somewhat reminiscent of the behavior of Theodore Roosevelt, who was president at that time.

Those who would banish sin from his city gave Lane more trouble than did corrupt contractors. He ignored the advocates of moral reform as long as he could, for he did not share the view that such action was in the public interest—or popular with many workingmen, who were among his supporters. But the forces of righteousness usually have their day, if they are persistent, and a combination of women's clubs, property owners, merchants, and the Portland ministerial association at last forced Lane to move against the city's gamblers and close the disorderly houses in the North End district.

Once he had made up his mind to act, Lane was relentless and little concerned for legal proprieties and the rights of others. The raids waged by Lane's "flying vice squad" and a series of gross invasions of privacy soon had respectable Portlanders barring their doors. "There may have been some mistakes," the police chief conceded.[22] When the moral reformers demanded that Lane also close a number of saloons, he countered that the churches should provide places where "poor men" might rest. This clever defense of the recreational rights of workingmen aroused more interest among skid row denizens than it did among respectable parishioners.[23]

Reelected in 1907, Lane kept Portland in a mild uproar to the very end of his second term in 1909. "The people had voted me in," he said, "and I meant to give them the worth of their money."[24] Everyone expected him to discharge a number of important city officials, including the fire chief, as a parting gesture. (He didn't.) "Speak softly and carry a big smile, ready to break out tomorrow," the *Oregonian* crowed. "There's only one more day of Mayor Harry Lane."[25]

Soon after he moved out of city hall, Doc Lane acquired a prairie schooner and departed on a six-month tour of the state. Well known to sons of the pioneers, he renewed many old friendships. Even his friends admitted that Harry Lane was a character. Republicans worried that the character was preparing to run for higher office, and they were right. Lane declined to enter the race for governor in 1910 because, he said, he lacked the time and money.[26] In 1912, however, an even better year for Democrats, he filed for United States senator, purchased a cheap automobile, drove it himself, and canvased the state. The divisive struggle between Republican President William Howard Taft and Progressive party candidate Theodore Roosevelt substantially aided Democrat Woodrow Wilson; and it created a three-way split among Lane's senatorial opponents, allowing him to slip into office by the barest of margins.[27] Republicans rightly considered Wilson and Lane accidental victors; but the president and the senator believed that they enjoyed the mandate of the people.

Doc Lane eagerly took up his duties on Capitol Hill. At first he seemed slightly subdued in the Senate, though not from awe at the dignity of that body. "There are a few highly intelligent men," he announced shortly, "but the bulk are just common, ordinary, average mutts."[28] He was annoyed by what he called "the windjamming way they talk and talk, and then talk some more, and you can't shut 'em up."[29] Lane tried ridicule in order to restrict debate. He knew that the bite of the Gila monster paralyzed the vocal cords, so, one hot summer day when the speeches continued endlessly, he circulated a petition on the floor of the Senate. The signers pledged themselves to pay the sums opposite their names for purchase of twelve Gila monsters to be turned loose in the chamber. "A unique character" was the reaction of Vice-President Thomas Marshall.[30]

Temperamentally, Harry Lane was an impetuous man, determined to go his own way. He was equally insistent that the citizens had a right to make their views effective. "I would consolidate power and accountability," he stated repeatedly. Thus, he supported all the devices of popular government—recall, referendum, primary elections, and other political reforms of the populist and progressive movements—that became known as the Oregon System because this state had employed them most extensively. Lane championed the adoption of these measures. "Government by the people has been tried in my state," he bragged. "It has been a success." The senator, an incessant pipe smoker, paused only long enough to reach for a cooler briar before dispensing the remainder of his political philosophy: "I am an incorrigible and inveterate champion of a government by the people directly applied. No agent business for me."[31]

By "the people" he meant the "plain people," and he wanted them to exercise the powers of government directly lest they become the victims of special interests. An antibusiness progressive with strong populistic instincts, he harped constantly on this subject. Early in his political career, he had objected to the railroads' issuing free passes to legislators as an example of dangerous privilege. In his first mayoral campaign he appealed to the man "who does not want anything out of the city for his special benefit."[32] As mayor, Lane appointed some wealthy men to city boards, "thinking they could join a doctor and make it a good business administration. But when I forced them up against a thing that hurt special interests . . . they resigned. I condemned them then."[33] When he ran for the Senate in 1912 he advertised in the *Oregon Labor Press:* "Harry Lane, as Mayor of Portland, Made Good . . . With the Plain People."[34]

Lane considered himself a participant in a struggle between economic classes. "We'll have to go up against moneyed interests," he once warned supporters in a mayoral race.[35] In his campaign for the Senate, Lane reiterated his views: "We find on one side a few men possessed of millions and on the other side the very poor and helpless and between these two a great class of people either striving to get into the first class or struggling to keep from being submerged into the second class until we have growing up in this country a great social unrest."[36]

Lane revealed his pervasive suspicion of "the interests," whose insidious influence he believed was the root of all the nation's ills, even when the issue at hand involved surplus potatoes, unmarketed grapes, and windfall apples. He appealed to President Wilson on behalf of Pacific Coast orchardists in 1913: "At this time, when the country is suffering from the effects of a designed and systematic onslaught on its business affairs by the 'predatory interests,'" a measure of relief might be given to farmers by allowing them to manufacture denatured alcohol from potatoes and fruit that they could not market.[37] Lane typically did not carry through in a systematic way with his idea, and the proposal got nowhere.

The senator, meanwhile, was off to tilt against larger foes. He advocated government ownership of telephone and telegraph facilities. He attacked the House of Morgan for its financial control of the New Haven Railroad. In 1914, he spoke so strongly against the procedures of the Interstate Commerce Commission and the transportation rebate system used by the "steel trust" in the western states that Vice-President Marshall rebuked him for unparliamentary language. Lane grimly withdrew his comments, then stubbornly restated them, saying that if someone would tell him the parliamentary expression he would use it.[38]

Three months later Lane launched a determined but perverse fight to prevent the federal government from accepting money from the Rockefeller Foundation for agricultural demonstration projects and the extermination of boll weevils, which were ravaging the crops of cotton farmers—including impoverished Southern farm tenants and sharecroppers, the plain people whom Lane claimed to champion. Lane did not want to accept the foundation's money because, he insisted, it was "covered with the blood and tears of women and children shot down in the Colorado strike."[39] He referred to the so-called Ludlow Massacre of 1914, a little civil war in Colorado that had resulted from union efforts to organize the Rockefeller-owned Colorado Fuel and Iron Company and which ended tragically when state militiamen attacked a tent colony of strikers.

Lane stood firmly against military force in all its forms. Once again his populistic instincts lay behind his attitude. He told the Portland Labor Council—which, like many union organizations, opposed standing armies because they might be used to break strikes—that the United States should pay its soldiers well but have them building roads throughout the land two-thirds of the time and engaging in military drill only the other one-third.[40]

Following the outbreak of the European war in 1914, Lane quickly involved himself in the first debates over U.S. foreign policy. In late 1915 he coauthored with Socialist representative Meyer London of New York a resolution calling upon the president to convene a Congress of neutral nations to work for peace.[41] As the nation's debate over neutrality policy reached a new degree of intensity in January 1916, Lane informed the Senate, "I am now and at all times have been opposed to the exportation of munitions of war." Instead of selling arms and other matériel to the belligerent powers, he said, the U.S. should send "to those who have suffered from the results of the war in Europe shiploads of baby shoes, of condensed and powdered milk . . . and clothing . . . [and] convoy them with battleships."[42] Lane's idea would not have prevented the belligerents from trying to purchase munitions and other valuable American materials or resolved the problems resulting from the Wilson administration's defense of neutral rights on the high seas, but it revealed his humane instincts—and his characteristic tendency to assume a superior moral position. Unfortunately for Lane, President Wilson assumed the righteousness of his own views and policies.

For a moment in the autumn of 1916, however, Lane returned to his party's fold and campaigned loyally for the president because Wilson had "kept us out of war." Other populistic Democrats who had been critical of the president's foreign policy, such as former Secretary of State William Jennings Bryan, adopted a similar political stand during the election of 1916, so Lane was not alone in his brief reconciliation with Wilson. But the senator's fears surfaced again soon after the election. In his heart he believed that bankers and businessmen really ruled the country. When he observed the yacht of J. Pierpont Morgan lying at anchor in the Potomac, he remarked dryly to a friend, "I see the government has come to town."[43]

The president and Lane did not in fact differ greatly at this time on some issues, such as their views of the belligerents. On January 22, 1917, Wilson asked each of the warring powers to state its terms for peace and called for a "peace without victory." But his address was not well received either at home or abroad, and nine days later Germany listed her impossible conditions—including hegemony over Belgium, part of Serbia, indemnities, and colonies—and simultaneously announced the resumption of unrestricted U-boat warfare. The Berlin government had slight regard for U.S. opinion because the American government then possessed no army of any consequence.

The president responded to the German actions by severing diplomatic relations but did not immediately go further; indeed, he excused German submarine attacks on British ships during February, saying that the British vessels were armed—perhaps offensively—and had virtually invited attack. American interventionists were furious.

Opponents of intervention were equally unhappy with the president because they felt that he had already gone too far and because they feared that he would arm American merchant ships against possible German U-boat attacks. And that is exactly what happened. At the end of February 1917, as the final session of the Sixty-fourth Congress neared an end, Wilson suddenly appeared in person and requested authority to arm American merchant vessels.

Senators of diverse views combined to oppose the president's request. Anti-interventionist members led by Democrat William Joel Stone of Missouri, the chairman of the Foreign Relations Committee, and Republicans Robert M. La Follette of Wisconsin, George Norris of Nebraska, and Asle Gronna of North Dakota joined forces with interventionist Republicans led by Henry Cabot Lodge of Massachusetts, who disliked the president's tactics, to prevent action on the Armed Ships bill. Wilson then revealed the Zimmermann telegram—German Foreign Minister Arthur Zimmermann's order to his minister in Mexico to promote Mexican and Japanese attacks upon the United States—a secret document obtained by British agents and given to the president some days earlier.

The Senate debate began at 4 P.M., on Friday, March 2, and continued without pause until Sunday noon, the close of the Congress. Senators Stone, Norris, Gronna and other opponents of the bill spoke at length; supporters of the president insinuated that a filibuster was under way but themselves took even more of the time that remained. Harry Lane joined in the debate despite the fact that he was seriously ill. Earlier that year the senator had begun to lose weight. He suffered from hemorrhages and even had spells of blindness. As he listened to his colleagues wrangle over the Armed Ships bill, he occasionally wiped blood from his lips. He nevertheless doggedly remained in the chamber hour after hour, and at 7 A.M. on Sunday morning he obtained the floor. For forty-five minutes he denounced those who profited from the war: "I do not care to fight or legislate or appropriate money for a certain gentleman who has made millions and millions . . . out of the misery and the death and destruction of unfortunate people across the seas." He insisted that he favored voting on the bill, however, if modifications were made to protect the ships of other nations, except for vessels carrying munitions.

Later that morning, supporters of the administration asked Lane to find out what the other opponents of the bill wanted. He spoke to Norris, William Kenyon of Iowa, and several other senators who stated that they would agree to the bill if it were modified. But "Battle Bob" La Follette, "just as suspicious of advocates of the bill as they were of him," Lane said, declined to give him any assurances.[44] The Wisconsin senator, an iron-lunged orator who often spoke for hours on end, had a lengthy speech ready to deliver and showed no interest in appearing cooperative. Lane himself refused to sign a round robin—a petition that backers of the bill circulated to show support for the measure—and was one of only five Democrats and eleven senators who thus expressed their opposition to the administration's policy.

As the tension in the chamber mounted, the impulsive Oregon senator grew worried. Earlier in the day, he slipped a rattail file into his pocket. Word had reached him that Democratic Senator Ollie James of Kentucky, an administration stalwart, might attack La Follette physically. Just before noon, when La Follette rushed forward shouting vainly for recognition so that he might have the last word in the debate, Lane saw James move from his seat. He followed quickly. James was carrying a gun, Lane told La Follette later; he claimed that he had seen it when the senator rose from his place. But James never would have drawn his weapon, Lane said, for he knew where to make a single fatal thrust with his file, had it been necessary.[45] Lane was so tired, sick, and emotionally distraught that he might well have imagined that La Follette was threatened when no danger existed, but a physical assault in the Senate was neither unprecedented nor impossible, especially under the circumstances. As it turned out, no incident occurred, but a different kind of attack was to follow.

After the furious struggle over the Armed Ships bill, abuse was heaped on Harry Lane and the other senators who had not signed the round robin. President Wilson himself denounced his opponents as "a little group of willful men." In Oregon, the mayor and city council of Portland signed a statement condemning Lane.[46] The Portland Chamber of Commerce passed two resolutions: one attacked the "willful men" in general as "cowardly, pusillanimous, [and] traitorous"; the other singled out Senator Lane for "complete repudiation."[47]

The Eugene Chamber of Commerce voted to change the name of Lane County, named for General Joseph Lane, setting off an angry local debate in which "the old traitor" had more defenders than did the new one. The city council of Dallas (Oregon), the Democrats of Jackson County, and a joint meeting of Republicans and Democrats in Hood River asked him to resign.[48] There were similar onslaughts from Albany, Medford, Marshfield, Tillamook, and numerous other towns.[49] A group in Corvallis, where Lane had grown up, sent him a German medal. Governor James Withycombe and Chief Justice Thomas McBride headed the lists of hundreds who publicly entered their disapproval. "Considering his brain weight, he is doing the best he can," one prominent Portland clergyman jibed.[50]

"Senator Lane has humiliated Oregon," the Medford *Mail Tribune* complained. "Oregon is disgraced by Senator Lane," resounded from the Grants Pass *Courier*. The Eugene *Daily Guard* labeled Lane "An Unworthy Official," while the Corvallis *Daily Gazette-Times* denounced the "traducer of [Oregon's] honored traditions," and the Salem *Oregon Statesman* protested his "rattling around" in office.[51] Even the Portland *Oregon Journal*, which opposed intervention in the war and had been a friend of Lane for years, criticized him in three consecutive editorials for his failure to back President Wilson.[52]

The strongly interventionist *Oregonian* provided a chorus for the refrain of protests from the press. Beginning on Monday, March 5, with an editorial on "The Shame of Oregon," the newspaper maintained its attack throughout the month. Some issues contained a half dozen pages devoted to articles, quotations from prominent citizens (featuring Democrats), and editorial opinion from other newspapers criticizing the senator. Front-page cartoons ridiculed him; the drawings showed a goose-stepping Lane being awarded the "Order of the Double Cross" or "Jonah" Lane being shoved from the Democratic raft to the whale of public indignation.[53]

Encouraged by the *Oregonian*, a group of citizens began to raise money to recall the senator from office. "Good," Lane responded jovially. "I'll contribute twenty dollars myself, and if they win, I'll give them another twenty dollars."[54] He informed one reporter, "If the people do not want me to work for them, I'm ready to quit." But, he added, "I have no idea of quitting, not yet."[55]

Senator Lane correctly believed that the power of recall did not extend to his office. And he shrugged off the telegrams of criticism sent to him. "Most of the people who approve my action in trying to keep out of war are fellows who do not spend money for telegrams," he explained. "They write letters."[56] Lane argued that the Armed Ships bill would have led to war within thirty days and that the protests from Oregon "emanate from persons who, it seems to me, are endeavoring to push this country into war, which I do not believe the people of this country wish to engage in."[57] His secretary announced that the senator had received thirty-one letters criticizing him and over two hundred letters of commendation.[58] He replied to the writers with a circular in which he repeated that he had favored voting on the Armed Ships bill but wanted changes in it to prevent presidential dictatorship. "I feared," Lane said, "that some day there might come a Díaz," referring to President Porfirio Díaz, who had ruled Mexico with an iron hand for forty years before 1910.[59]

Lane never conceded and probably never recognized the similarities between Wilson's angry treatment of the "willful men" and his own behavior as mayor, when he had been convinced that he stood for justice and the public will and had run roughshod over his opponents. The senator's retort about the danger of a Díaz expressed the fear shared by anti-interventionists in that era and in later times that strong executive leadership in foreign policy will result in war and in despotism at home.

The president's sharp reproof and the bitter public condemnation of the senators who had opposed the Armed Ships bill went beyond the bounds of decent criticism and undoubtedly contributed to Lane's agitation. But the senator's health also affected his state of mind, intensifying his firm conviction that sinister forces were at work. Lane lost fifteen pounds within a short time after the battle over the Armed Ships bill, and he appeared pale and weak. His doctors advised him to leave the Senate for a complete rest, but he would not hear of it.[60] Deeply discouraged by the prospect of war, Lane fixed his attention on international affairs and on friends who stood by him. He wrote to one: "We are in for war. The Morgans are in the saddle and they will ride without mercy. Be careful what you say. You are outspoken and you may get in trouble."[61]

Wilson, following his defeat in the Senate, had gone ahead under his executive powers and ordered the arming of American merchant ships. But armed neutrality proved to be not much different from war, at least in the popular mind, and the policy seemed to divide Americans. By March 20, 1917, Wilson's cabinet was uniformly of the view that there was no alternative to war. The president at last made up his own mind and on April 2 returned to Congress to ask for a declaration of the existence of a state of war with Germany, explaining that German policy made the continuation of armed neutrality an impossibility.

Lane was desperately ill that day, as the new Sixty-fifth Congress organized itself and prepared to hear the president's message. Lane applauded politely when Wilson entered the chamber but sat quietly during the address, never applauding and appearing unmoved when the audience around him cheered enthusiastically. He did not seem to respond even to Senator La Follette, who sat nearby and occasionally whispered to him.[62] Lane's physicians again advised him to avoid taking part in the debate on the war resolution that followed. Once more he was determined to be present during the extended Senate debate and to go on record against the declaration of war. His quiet no was one of six in the Senate and the last vote that Harry Lane cast.

On the following Thursday, he issued a statement to explain his opposition to war. "Commercialism," he maintained, "is undoubtedly behind the war spirit." His conversations with other members convinced him, Lane asserted, that a secret vote would have given the resolution only a narrow margin in the Senate and would have resulted in its defeat by two to one in the House of Representatives. "I obeyed the instructions of an enormous majority of the people who have been writing me from Oregon. Their prayer was for peace. . . . My vote, I may add, represented my honest conviction, and I take the responsibility for it."[63]

Just after noon the next day, which was also Good Friday, President Wilson signed the resolution passed by both houses of Congress, and the United States was officially at war with Imperial Germany. Lane spent the day in his last Senate debate, arguing for greater food production for the war. This stance suggests that he might have modified his opposition during the course of the conflict, but it is highly unlikely that he would have relented in his view of the war.

On Saturday, April 7, Lane, probably a victim of arteriosclerosis and Brights' disease, entered a local hospital. Early in May he recovered enough to return to his office occasionally and to visit the Senate floor. Then he submitted to pleas that he undergo medical treatment. At one o'clock on a morning in mid-May, the Oregon senator said farewell to George Norris, who had joined him in opposing the Armed Ships bill and the war resolution and who waited with him in Washington's Union Station for the train that would carry Lane to the West Coast.[64] On May 23, 1917, Lane died in a hospital in San Francisco.

Agitators in the United States ordinarily have frequented the fringes of the political arena, usually because of their lack of political skills, sometimes because they chose to be aloof critics, occasionally because the major parties absorbed their ideas while repudiating them as extremists. Periodically, however, disturbers of the peace have become active in the parties and even gained political office. This occurred with greater frequency in the progressive era, when a wave of new ideas and reform sentiment rocked both political parties.

Lane was both Democrat and agitator. A partisan by inheritance from his grandfather, who had established the party in Oregon, and a politician by instinct and rearing, Lane was a Democrat almost by proprietary right. Yet, he rarely invoked partisanship for its own sake. From the beginning of his political career to the very end, he ignored the party when he chose. The conditions that he laid down for serving "my party," he insisted in 1907, were that he wanted "my hands left free." A party boss responded bitterly, "Democracy wants a Democrat candidate . . . not an independent."[65] President Wilson and national party leaders felt much the same about him ten years later. But Lane could not be brought into line. He got away with his independent course because he picked his races carefully, shrewdly outmaneuvered the old-line Democratic chieftains, mustered amateurs and independents, drew help from downstate leaders who were jealous of Portland's domination of the party, and won elections that other Democrats would have lost.

Lane's role in the progressive movement, which was peppered with characters, was less distinctive than his privileged position in the Democratic party. The source of his interest in reform remains a matter of speculation. Dr. Lane's social standing in Portland was solid, and his close friend and campaign manager, Charles Erskine Scott Wood, was a wealthy corporation lawyer whom the *Oregonian* described as "the arbiter elegantiarum of our local plutocracy."[66] At the same time, Doc Lane charged so little for his medical services and invested his money in such speculative ventures that he was often compelled to call upon wealthy friends and relatives for financial help.[67] His distress over his financial situation must have festered within him, and his interest in making a quick financial killing and his constant denunciations of those who possessed wealth revealed jealousy and resentment.

His sympathy for the struggling "plain people," however, was genuine if vicarious. But Harry Lane initiated few proposals for legislation, and his campaign pledges were commonplace. Even in 1912, the moment of greatest reform fervor, Lane's senatorial platform would have suited most western Democrats in the heyday of the Gilded Age: honest and efficient government, a lower tariff, rigid exclusion of Chinese laborers, more post roads and expanded postal services, and federal appropriations for river and harbor improvements and reclamation projects in Oregon. Only his planks in support of the Oregon System (already soundly established in the state), stiffer enforcement of the antitrust laws (Wilson's New Freedom, with a punitive fillip), and a banking system that was free from the domination of Wall Street were distinctively progressive.[68]

Lane made a contribution to progressivism, however, both as a mayor and as a member of the Senate. This was in agitation. Full of restless energy and very sure of himself, he was natively gifted for stirring up a fuss and he enjoyed every commotion. He was frankly more interested in dramatizing principles by words or by direct actions than in enacting principles into laws, which he thought tedious and boring work. Lane recognized his special talents. On one occasion, recalling how he became mayor, he observed that what Portland had needed was "a man with an adequate flow of language and sand enough to put his convictions into words or writing."[69] Lane thought that he was just the independent Democrat to fill the bill, and so he went to work smashing hollow curbing, exposing corrupt contractors, and creating a tempest in city hall.

He saw himself in a similar role as a senator. His intent was not to stand by his party and his president but rather to lash out at what he considered greed and selfish interests in the highest places. As he viewed it, only an independent—a Democrat who identified with the plain people rather than the interests—could do what was needed. He would stir things up in the public interest. Convinced that his course was correct, he did not desist even under the greatest possible political pressure and the threat of foreign war.

NOTES

1. Portland *Oregonian*, Aug. 2, 1914.
2. *Ibid.*, May 11, 1861.
3. *Ibid.*, May 18, 1861.
4. *Ibid.*, Aug. 2, 1914.
5. Oswald West, "Reminiscences and Anecdotes: McNarys and Lanes," *OHQ*, Vol. 52 (1951), 148–49.
6. *Oregonian*, Aug. 2, 1914.
7. *Ibid.*, July 28, Aug. 2, 1891.
8. Copy of Report to Trustees, November 30, 1890, Oregon State Library, Salem. Lane observed later: "Some of the wisest men I have ever known were inmates."
9. Harry Lane to Asahel Bush II, April 10, 1892, Bush Papers, Oregon State Library. On John Knox: "What a cantin' old publican he was, I did not dance on his grave but I wanted to."
10. Lane to Bush, Oct. 5, 1892, Bush Papers.
11. Dr. Olaf Larsell, *The Doctor in Oregon: A Medical History* (Portland, 1947), 460–62.

12. *Medical Sentinel*, Vol. 13 (July 1905), 139.

13. Interview with Oswald West, Portland, Sept. 15, 1958.

14. *Oregonian*, May 11, 1905. Asahel Bush sent aid.

15. *Ibid.*, Aug. 8, Dec. 17, 1905.

16. *Ibid.*, Oct. 26, 1905.

17. *Ibid.*, Dec. 27, 1905.

18. *Ibid.*, March 16, 1907.

19. *Ibid.*, Aug. 2, 1914.

20. *Ibid.*

21. *Ibid.*, Feb. 26, 27, 28, 1906.

22. *Ibid.*, Aug. 19, Dec. 2, 1908, March 6, April 4, 1909; *Portland Spectator*, Vol. 1 (March 23, 1907), 2.

23. *Oregonian*, Feb. 13, 14, 1909.

24. *Ibid.*, Aug. 2, 1914.

25. *Ibid.*, June 30, 1909.

26. West, 152.

27. Lane won by fewer than 2,000 votes even with the extraordinary three-way split in Republican ranks.

28. *Oregonian*, Dec. 6, 1914.

29. *Ibid.*

30. Thomas Marshall, *Recollections of Thomas R. Marshall, Vice-President and Hoosier Philosopher* (Indianapolis, 1925), 320–21.

31. *Oregonian*, Aug. 2, 1914.

32. *Ibid.*, May 24, 1905.

33. *Oregon Journal* (Portland), Nov. 3, 1912.

34. *Oregon Labor Press* (Portland), Oct. 24, 1912.

35. *Oregonian*, March 30, 1905.

36. *Oregon Journal*, Nov. 2, 1912. At the banquet given by the Portland Medical Society to celebrate his election to the Senate, Lane spoke on the "whole unholy load" of watered stocks; *Oregonian*, Feb. 7, 1913.

37. Lane to Woodrow Wilson, Aug. 6, 1913, Woodrow Wilson Papers, Library of Congress.

38. *Oregon Journal*, Feb. 1, 1914.

39. *Oregonian*, May 5, 1914.

40. *Oregonian*, Nov. 16, 1915. He proposed such a bill.

41. Lane was not himself a socialist, but some of his ideas resembled those of socialists.

42. *Congressional Record*, 64th Cong., 1st Sess., 1916, p. 1917.

43. Nina Lane McBride Manuscripts, Oregon Collection, University of Oregon, Eugene. Richard Neuberger and Stephen B. Kahn attributed this story to George Norris (*Integrity: The Life of George W. Norris* [New York, 1937], 57.)

44. *Oregon Journal*, March 6, 1917.

45. Interviews with Belle and Fola La Follette, Washington, D.C., Feb. 19, 1959, and with Chester and Suzanne La Follette, New York City, Feb. 16, 1959. Lane gave the file to La Follette for a souvenir.

46. *Oregon Journal*, March 5, 1917.

47. *Ibid.*

48. *Oregonian*, March 6, 1917.

49. *Ibid.*

50. *Oregon Journal*, March 5, 1917. Lane received a number of messages of support from lesser-known persons; only a few had German names, although the German churches on Portland's east side backed him, according to the *Oregon Journal*, March 6–11, 1917.

51. *Ibid.*, March 8, 1917; *Oregonian*, March 6, 1917, quoting other newspapers; Corvallis *Daily Gazette-Times*, March 6, 1917; Salem *Oregon Statesman*, March 6, 1917.

52. *Oregon Journal*, March 5–7, 1917. This was a Democratic newspaper.

53. *Oregonian*, March 6, 7, 1917. The Portland *Evening Telegram* was equally critical. The *Oregon Journal*, March 15, 1917, at last realized that it had contributed to a vendetta

and pointed out the *Oregonian*'s "sweet concord of variations on one theme: 'We want his office, we want his office.'"

54. *Oregonian*, March 7, 1917.

55. *Oregon Journal*, March 6, 1917.

56. *Ibid*.

57. *Oregonian*, March 8, 1917.

58. *Ibid*., March 13, 1917.

59. *Oregon Journal*, March 21, 1917.

60. *Oregonian*, April 8, 1917.

61. Richard Neuberger, "Time Vindicates a Prophet from Oregon," *Oregonian*, Sept. 29, 1935.

62. *Oregonian*, April 3, 1917.

63. *Ibid*., April 5, 1917; *Oregon Journal*, April 5, 1917.

64. *Capital Journal* (Salem), April 22, 1936.

65. *Oregonian*, March 24, 1907.

66. *Ibid*., Nov. 27, 1906.

67. Lane to Asahel Bush III, Feb. 17, Sept. 20, 1913, Bush Papers, Oregon State Archives, Salem.

68. *Oregon Journal*, Nov. 1, 1912.

69. *Oregonian*, Aug. 2, 1914.

IV. The Modern Era

The Great War ended on November 11, 1918, and a dazed and uncomprehending world stumbled through the first months of peace. The "War to End All Wars" and the "War to Make the World Safe for Democracy" had done neither. Each side had sacrificed millions of soldiers, a generation of young men, but the world scarcely seemed better for it. Instead of German imperialism, Americans now feared worldwide communist or Bolshevik revolution. The litany of postwar troubles seemed endless—the cost of living spiraled upward out of control, veterans returned home to find their former jobs belonging to others, and a deadly new killer, the Spanish influenza, claimed thousands of lives. The Pacific Northwest escaped none of these troubles.

So many influenza victims filled Portland hospitals, for example, that the civic auditorium had to be converted into an emergency infirmary. The city allowed football games to be played as usual but barred spectators; people wore masks in public, washed their money, and refused to enter crowded stores, all in a desperate effort to avoid the mysterious killer. In late November 1918 the number of cases started to decline and soon the influenza pandemic was but an ugly memory.

Postwar economic unrest proved a less deadly but more stubborn problem than Spanish influenza. In the major cities of the Pacific Northwest, little groups of jobless and angry veterans organized Workers, Soldiers, and Sailors' councils to voice their grievances. The very name seemed suspiciously like something out of the Russian revolution of 1917 and further fueled the prevailing mood of fear and distrust. The unemployed veterans were only one part of a swelling army of the discontented. Workers in the Seattle shipyards protested against wages that failed to keep pace with the cost of living, which had nearly doubled since 1913. Their plight, attracting the sympathy of other workers, culminated in the Seattle General Strike of February 1919, a short and bloodless demonstration that nonetheless frightened nervous Americans into imagining that revolution had erupted on Puget Sound.

No one did more to foster that impression than Mayor Ole Hanson of Seattle, a one-time progressive reformer who became a national hero overnight by breaking America's first real general strike. He soon resigned his office for the lecture circuit, spinning an incredible tale of revolutionary plots that he published as Bolshevism versus Americanism. *"Laughter and ridicule have never bothered me," Hanson warned his detractors, but his sudden success was scarcely a laughable matter. It was a sobering commentary on the nation's grim and disagreeable mood. In November 1919 that same mood turned a first anniversary celebration of Armistice Day into a violent confrontation between American Legionnaires and Wobblies in Centralia, Washington. A Legion journal described the episode as a nightmare of blood and conflict, "a veritable orgy of passion." In its aftermath, Governor Louis F. Hart called for the organization of Washington residents into state-coordinated Loyal Leagues in an effort to channel vigilantism into more respectable forms of protest.*

During such unsettled times the Ku Klux Klan thrived. The Klan pushed into Oregon and Washington from California in the early 1920s and soon became a potent force in Oregon politics. The targets of its hatred ranged from blacks, Roman Catholics, Jews, and radicals to private and parochial schools. In 1922 the Klan and its allies successfully promoted an initiative outlawing nonpublic elementary and secondary schools, making Oregon the only state in modern American history to create a monolithic educational system. The motivation of the initiative's sponsors was to promote Americanism—that much used and abused keynote of the era—and their rallying cry was "One Flag! One School! One Language!"

The United States Supreme Court overturned the Oregon initiative in 1925, but by that time the Klan was a spent force (see Eckard Toy's essay). The postwar paranoia upon which it thrived disappeared as Americans learned to live with the irrevocable changes brought by war. The 1920s were the years of prohibition and the first decade of nationwide woman suffrage. In 1926 Seattle became the first major city in America to elect a woman mayor (see Doris Pieroth's essay).

People who had earlier cited front-page headlines of the Seattle Union Record, *the city's most prominent labor paper, as evidence of an impending revolution should have turned to the inside pages and followed* Interesting Topics of the Automobile World. *Those columns recorded the real revolution of the era.*

Not until the early 1920s was the automobile's potential to alter lifestyles and challenge the railroad's dominance of land transportation fully established. Before that time, poor roads had discouraged widespread use of the automobile outside urban centers. An important change came in 1919 when Oregon became the first state to enact a gasoline tax to finance improved highways, and the call to "lift Oregon out of the mud" was taken seriously. Before the decade of the 1920s ended, it was possible to speed across the region at the legal maximum of thirty-five or forty miles per hour.

As the public took to the new highways and closed cars that made all-weather automobile travel possible, railroads, particularly the electric interurban lines of the Willamette Valley and the Seattle-Tacoma area, suffered a dramatic loss of passengers. Most of the electric lines went out of business, and the few that survived carried freight only. The major trunk lines, too, discontinued dozens of local passenger trains and boarded up unused waiting rooms. Highways built for automobiles also carried the intercity buses and trucks that first appeared in large numbers in the 1920s.

Overhead, passengers rode in open-cockpit planes from the cities of the Pacific Northwest to California on regular schedules by the mid-1920s. But what the pioneer airline passengers gained in speed they sacrificed in comfort. Goggles protected their eyes, but nothing protected their cheeks, ears, and hands from the biting rush of wind that was sometimes accompanied by rain and hail. Upon arrival, an attendant helped them wipe away the inevitable spatters of oil blown back by the engine. Fortunately for passengers, the heroic phase of air travel lasted only a few years.

Synonymous with major advances in aviation was the Boeing Company of Seattle. William E. Boeing started his "aeroplane" shop on the shores of Lake Union in 1916, and from that modest beginning evolved the flying fortresses, stratoliners, and 747s of subsequent decades. In 1927 Boeing's company pioneered transcontinental air travel with a small fleet of passenger-carrying mail planes, and from that venture ultimately emerged one of the giants of the industry, United Airlines.

Few groups derived a greater benefit from the transportation revolution of the 1920s than the region's farmers. For years they had supported the Good Roads movement as a cure for rural ills. The coming of the automobile freed them from social and cultural isolation, and the truck ended their almost total dependence upon railroads to carry their crops to market. Gasoline-powered tractors and combines decreased their need for seasonal labor, even as many former harvest hands abandoned the life of the hobo, got married, and took their families with them to the job in their own cars. As nothing else, owning a car symbolized admission to the middle class. Wobbly organizers deplored the trend, complaining that it gave workers a false sense of upward mobility.

Significant technological and social changes overtook the mining and forest industries (see Richard White's essay). Electrification made it possible for the metal mines of north Idaho to operate year-round, stabilizing the work force that had once wintered in nearby Spokane. In the woods the federal government's wartime sponsorship of a variety of reforms led to the eight-hour day and better living and working conditions. By the mid-1920s life in the camps had so improved that workers no longer had to pack their bedrolls from job to job. Like the resident farm worker, the resident logger driving to work in his own car or truck replaced the migratory casual laborer.

Although the decade of the 1920s was for many Pacific Northwesterners a time of prosperity, it opened on a sour note of economic trouble and closed the same way. And some farmers suffered economic adversity throughout the decade. Following their dizzying wartime climb, land and crop prices slumped and then collapsed in 1921. Farmers who had enjoyed unprecedented prosperity during the war saw their gains wiped out. In mid-decade prices started inching upward only to drop to new lows during the hard times of the early 1930s. It was then that Washington's desperate apple growers encouraged the unemployed to peddle their crop on the nation's street corners, thereby creating one of the enduring symbols of the Great Depression. Another was the shantytowns—typically named in honor of President Herbert Hoover—that sprang up on tideflats, near garbage dumps, and under bridges in the region's large cities.

During the Great Depression breadlines appeared in Portland, Seattle, Spokane, and other localities. Estimates of unemployment in Seattle ranged from 23 to 60 percent. The jobless there organized self-help projects such as the Unemployed Citizens' League in an attempt to stretch meager welfare payments and assist one another. The first of these grass-roots efforts was organized in July 1931 and attracted national attention (see the essay by William Mullins). The severity of the depression, however, exhausted the scant resources of voluntary aid programs even as the ranks of the destitute swelled with refugees from the Dust Bowl of Oklahoma and Texas. Crossing half a continent in dilapidated and heavy-laden automobiles, they sought jobs in the once fabled promised land. Some found work on federal construction projects like the Grand Coulee Dam, but many were not so fortunate.

Poverty in a region so rich in natural resources was not easy to understand or endure. In the search for solutions, some people embraced radical proposals and endorsed eccentric politicians who promised to enact such measures into law. The consequences were often bizarre and sometimes humorous. Richard Neuberger, Oregon journalist and future United States senator, observed of his neighboring state that "for years in the drama of national affairs, Washington provided the comic relief." After years of Republican rule, Washington voters overwhelmingly favored the Democratic party, which during its years in the political wilderness had become a ragbag of political oddities and a forum for the apostles of radical change.

One state official who dedicated himself to providing comic relief was Washington's lieutenant governor, Victor A. Meyers, a former bandleader in a Seattle nightclub who now presided over the state's senate. "Under Vic," observed Neuberger, "the Washington State senate became the best show on the Pacific Coast outside Hollywood." Despite his occasionally outrageous comments and offbeat style, Meyers proved a canny politician who won reelection to four more terms as lieutenant governor and two terms as secretary of state. Most notably, during the turbulent days of the 1930s he emerged as a valued ally of the Democratic party's radical left. Governor Clarence D. Martin, a member of the party's more moderate wing, scarcely dared to leave the state for fear of what Meyers and his allies might attempt during his absence.

Washington politics had long been marked by a noticeable strain of radicalism. Typically, this took the form of third-party protest movements such as the Populist crusade of the 1890s, but in the 1930s it appeared as the Washington Commonwealth Federation, a pressure group operating within the Democratic party. Its membership comprising reformers as well as communists, the Washington Commonwealth Federation promoted as its main plank "production for use and not for profit." The socialistic-sounding phrase frightened moderates and conservatives. Although its accomplishments were really quite modest, the organization attracted much attention that furthered the *state's reputation as a hotbed of radicalism: "There are forty-seven states in the Union, and the Soviet of Washington," Postmaster General James A. Farley allegedly quipped.*

Depression era politics in Oregon were relatively calm by comparison. Probably the noisiest battles occurred when the state's combative Republican governor Charles A. Martin fought with organized labor. Martin, a former major general from West Point, regularly denounced labor unions and public power.

Pacific Northwest labor was often the center of attention during the turbulent 1930s. A sudden increase in membership nationwide gave the unions new muscles to flex. Strikes were frequent, and several of the largest of them tied up the waterfront in Oregon and Washington. The house of labor itself erupted in a no-holds-barred power struggle between the American Federation of Labor and its aggressive young rival, the Congress of Industrial Organizations, which was the more radical of the two. The chief strategist for the AFL forces was Dave Beck of Seattle, who emerged as one of the most powerful figures in the region and ultimately served as national head of the Teamsters union (1952–58). A shrewd and resourceful man, he won the support of employers by his appreciation of sound business principles and his vigorous opposition to communism and the CIO (see the essay by Jonathan Dembo). In time the rival labor organizations reconciled their differences, but their fights during the 1930s left an unpleasant memory of blackened eyes and broken heads.

Unquestionably the most powerful presence in the Pacific Northwest during the 1930s was that of Uncle Sam. Only once before, during World War I, had the federal government touched the lives of individual citizens in so many different ways, and, in fact, the war experience provided President Franklin D. Roosevelt and his New Deal planners with an appropriate model to follow in their battle with hard times. The scope and variety of federal programs heartened advocates of the welfare state but dismayed its opponents. In any case, Timberline Lodge on the slopes of Mount Hood, Bonneville and Grand Coulee dams on the Columbia River, and numerous other New Deal projects provided people jobs in addition to benefits ranging from cheap electrical power to irrigation water and recreational facilities.

With the surprise Japanese attack on Pearl Harbor in December 1941, the United States plunged into the Second World War, and the unemployment problem vanished almost overnight. The following days and weeks presented complex new challenges to the nation. Instead of too little work, the problem now was to find people to fill the myriad of new jobs created by mobilization. By 1943, Boeing alone employed more than 50,000 workers in various plants in western Washington, some 50 percent of these being women. Washington's 88 shipyards employed more than 150,000 workers, turning out a variety of craft including barges, tugs, destroyers, and aircraft carriers. Even the skilled inmates at the federal prison on McNeil Island built boats for the navy. Shipbuilding boomed in the Portland-Vancouver area, too.

From the giant naval base at Bremerton to the food processing plants of the Willamette and Walla Walla valleys, from Fort Lewis to the backyard "Victory Gardens," the Pacific Northwest was a beehive of war-related activities. One of the most awesome and far-reaching of these was shrouded in secrecy. Along an isolated stretch of the Columbia River near Richland arose an installation to produce the plutonium used in atomic bombs.

Military service and wartime employment opportunities brought thousands of newcomers to the Pacific Northwest. Mainstreets were crowded, as were theaters, restaurants, buses, schools, and nurseries. During the first two years of the war, the shipbuilding center of Vancouver, Washington, for example, grew from 25,000 to 85,000 inhabitants. Eight new schools had to be built there. Seattle gained 150,000 new residents during the same period. Not all population movement was into the region, however. The Japanese were forcibly removed. Encouraged by fear of an imminent invasion of the West Coast after Pearl Harbor, American and Canadian authorities removed the Japanese to remote inland camps. Considering that many of those relocated were American citizens or mere children, the forced move was a dubious step at best, but nonetheless understandable within the context of long-standing racial prejudices on the Pacific Slope (see Howard Droker's essay).

During the war years and after, life in the Pacific Northwest was increasingly shaped by national and international trends. When Pacific Northwesterners contributed to wartime scrap metal drives, shared rides or used their cars less to save gasoline and rubber, and bought victory bonds, they identified their personal interests with those of the nation as a whole. World War II also thrust upon the region important new strategic and economic roles that drew it into close cooperation with the rest of the nation. Moreover, the development of substantial trade with Japan in the postwar era—Seattle being the major American port closest to Asia—and an increased United States military presence in the Pacific meant that the Pacific North-

*west could no longer be regarded merely as a resource-rich but periph-
eral part of the country.*

*Clearly, a major trend in the postwar decades was toward greater
national uniformity at the expense of regional distinctiveness. This
was fostered by network television and franchised, standardized ham-
burgers no less than by jet aircraft that made it possible for Portland
and Seattle residents to fly to New York in less time than it took them
to drive to Spokane. Yet many distinctive regional attributes of the
Pacific Northwest persist, at least for the present.*

*Politics continued to be personality rather than party oriented, one
result being the election of some uncommonly honest and competent
public officials. Since 1945 quite a number of senators and representatives from Oregon and Washington have held influential posts in
Congress. The states' governors, too, were unusually able people.
Daniel J. Evans, three-term governor of Washington and later United
States senator, was selected by a national political analyst as one of the
top ten governors in the country in the twentieth century. The maverick tradition persisted as well and was represented best by Oregon's
Senator Wayne Morse, at various times a Republican, an independent,
and a Democrat.*

*Since the age of discovery the most distinguishing feature of the
Pacific Northwest has been the beauty of its physical setting. Even now
its many natural wonders seem to suggest that the region's environment will always retain a certain pristine quality (see the essay by
Alfred Runte). That, of course, is a deception. Lake Washington and
the Willamette River have been rescued from the ravages of pollution,
but the steady population increase since the 1940s continues to pose a
threat to the region's environment.*

*People have often been attracted to the region by the availability and
variety of outdoor recreation and the belief that the quality of life remains higher in the Pacific Northwest than elsewhere. As a matter of
fact, though Seattle, Portland, and Eugene have consistently ranked
as three of the most livable cities in America, each has occasionally
suffered from air quality problems. And with each new subdivision,
pressure on the environment increases, and in time population growth
may well destroy the desirable qualities that attracted people to the
region in the first place. In the face of mounting population pressures
and the nationalizing influence of space-age transportation and communication, the chief question remains, What distinguishing attributes—other than Mount Saint Helens and an unusual pattern of
rainfall—will the Pacific Northwest retain in the coming decades?*

The Ku Klux Klan in Oregon

ECKARD V. TOY

In less than one-half an hour after signing up [in May 1921], the three of us were obligated into the Klan in a hotel room by a Kleagle, who had just arrived that morning in the state. . . . That afternoon the three of us gathered a group of reliable men and that night obligated twenty-six of these men in the Masonic Hall, Medford, Oregon. Thus the [Ku Klux] Klan started in Oregon.[1]

Mere mention of the Ku Klux Klan today arouses fear and curiosity, usually bringing to mind vivid images of Reconstruction, hooded night riders, and lynching in the rural South. With its birth after the Civil War shrouded in myth and its activities blurred by romanticism, the original Ku Klux Klan stands as a symbol of the South's response to military defeat and Republican rule. Many older histories of the South, Thomas Dixon's novels, and D. W. Griffith's epic movie *The Birth of a Nation* portrayed the original Klan as the protector of white womanhood and Southern rights against rapacious blacks, greedy carpetbaggers, and vengeful Radical Republicans. Periodic revivals of the organization in the twentieth century resurrected the legend but generated less positive stereotypes. Historians now take a negative view of the Klan in all its incarnations, but the Ku Klux Klan remains, in the popular view, a predominantly Southern, rural, and antiblack phenomenon.[2] This brief account of the rise and fall of the Ku Klux Klan in Oregon during the 1920s should alter those popular misconceptions.

When William Joseph Simmons and a small group of followers proclaimed the rebirth of the KKK in Georgia in 1915, few witnesses could have predicted that the revived Klan would become more than a local or regional aberration. Before he transformed the Southern legend into a national symbol of patriotism and racial purity, Simmons was merely an itinerant salesman of fraternal orders and a part-time preacher in the South. His interest in the Klan coincided with the showing of *The Birth of a Nation* in Atlanta and with a massive migration of blacks and whites from the rural South to the industrial North and petroleum-rich Southwest during the First World War. International political unrest and renewed immigration from war-ravaged Europe after 1918 revived nativist fears and contributed to an explosive social atmosphere nourished by the Red Scare, race riots, and labor unrest. Divisive moral and religious issues represented another part of the reaction to social change apparent in the appeal for a return to "normalcy" voiced by the Republican presidential nominee Warren G. Harding in 1920.

On the eve of Harding's presidency, the Ku Klux Klan stood poised as the spearhead of a nationwide resurgence of racial and religious bigotry. With Simmons as Imperial Wizard, its members cloaked in sheets and secrecy and united by fraternal pledges of racial purity, the revived Klan fittingly labeled itself the Invisible Empire. Attracting new members at an astonishing rate by 1921, the Klan grew faster outside the South than within its old heartland. After its introduction on the Pacific Coast, the KKK expanded rapidly in California and Washington but most dramatically in Oregon, where it became a potent political force only a year after its first members were "obligated" in Medford.

There were many reasons for the Klan's success in Oregon. In the years following the First World War, economic problems in shipbuilding, the lumber industry, and agriculture erased many of the gains made in the Pacific Northwest during wartime. The Red Scare of 1919–20 aggravated labor issues and heightened concerns about continuing unlimited immigration. The KKK thrust itself into this volatile atmosphere and challenged the direction of conventional politics. While racial issues were central to Klan dogma, the target was elusive in Oregon. Historically, there had been few black residents in the state and only a small number of blacks had joined the wartime migration of workers to the Pacific Northwest. Thus, much of the attention was focused on lingering fears of Japanese farm laborers, and racial sentiments were generally secondary to political, social, and moral issues for Klansmen in Oregon. Moreover, it was "not the bad people of the State, but the good people—the *very* good people," the journalist Waldo Roberts reported, who were "largely responsible for the transformation of the Oregon commonwealth into an invisible empire."[3]

The social reservoir from which the Klan drew its members represented, in Earl Pomeroy's words, "a collaboration of older and newer strains of population, of advocates and enemies of change."[4] In some communities, where established families dominated politics and the local economy, the Klan served as a countervailing political force that challenged the status quo. In other communities, Klan recruiters (kleagles) appealed to defenders of traditional culture on issues of prohibition, education, and sexual morality. In a decade marked by rapid technological change yet sustaining vestiges of a small-town past and Victorian morality, religious fundamentalism and archaic notions of moral reform blended easily with romantic nationalism and racial bigotry.[5] Klan kleagles found receptive audiences and promoted their version of "One-Hundred Per Cent Americanism" with boosterish enthusiasm. These traveling salesmen of hate, who worked on commission, moved from town to town with lists of potential members in their pockets and samples of Klan paraphernalia in their suitcases.

Following the national pattern, three kleagles appeared in Oregon in the spring of 1921. Major Luther I. Powell, a war veteran and native of Louisiana, arrived in Medford from California, where he had been organizing Klan units. C. N. Jones, who followed Powell north from California, sought recruits in Eugene, and Bragg Calloway, newly arrived from Houston, Texas, worked Portland. After his success in southern Oregon, Powell replaced Calloway in Portland and reaffirmed his worth as an organizer. Imperial Wizard Simmons rewarded him by appointing him King Kleagle of the Pacific Northwest Domain. On August 1, the king kleagle and a new recruit, Fred L. Gifford, robed and masked, held a well-publicized press conference with Portland's Mayor George L. Baker and several city and federal officials. Powell informed reporters that almost one-hundred-fifty policemen were among the thousand members the Portland Klan had enrolled in less than three months. By then, provisional Klans had also been organized in Salem, Eugene, Ashland, Medford, Hood River, and numerous other towns in the state.[6] The Portland Klan continued to grow rapidly, and Powell conducted its first official meeting in October 1921. Gifford, who would soon head the state organization as grand dragon, was elected the first exalted cyclops of Luther I. Powell Klan Number One.

The Invisible Empire had suddenly become highly visible, but few Oregonians believed the KKK posed any threat to the state's political and social stability. In September 1921, Governor Ben Olcott had informed the New York *World* that the Klan had made "practically no impression on our people."[7] The governor's mistaken confidence is not difficult to understand. The sudden and phenomenal growth of the Klan simply could not have been predicted. There was little threat of labor radicalism, despite periodic scares about the revival of the IWW (Industrial Workers of the World). And in a state where native-born citizens were by far in the majority, where Negroes totaled only about two thousand, and where the number of Asians, other than Japanese, decreased with each census, there seemed to be little cause for the formation of a militantly nativist organization.[8] Yet, these very characteristics of social stability and racial and cultural homogeneity assured at least partial success for the Klan's program of patriotic conformity.

If the Ku Klux Klan was new to Oregon, many of its issues were not. Racism, nativism, and anti-Catholicism were deeply rooted in nineteenth-century America. The emergence of nativism in Oregon closely paralleled the great westward migrations, and prejudices against Negroes and Catholics were a part of the cultural heritage of these early pioneers. Oregon was their haven from chattel slavery and from the Church of Rome. The process of self-selection through racial and cultural exclusiveness, seemingly guaranteed by Oregon's constitutional barriers against blacks and Chinese in the nineteenth century, was reinforced in the twentieth century by the belief that the state must be kept free of alien influences, whether papal or Bolshevik. For those individuals who perceived the promised land in these limiting terms, the methods of purification were simple. Reform and nativism each reinforced the conformist pattern of Oregon politics. The Ku Klux Klan would benefit from the historical residue of nativism and also would exploit widespread concerns about maintaining the purity of America's blood and the sanctity of its public and private morals.[9]

For several years after the appearance of the first organizers, the Oregon Klan enjoyed a notoriety greater than that accorded any other fraternal order within the state. The exact size of the Klan in Oregon cannot be determined accurately; the most reliable estimates vary between fifteen thousand and forty thousand members. The active membership fluctuated widely, as political and social issues alternately attracted and repelled supporters. And there was also a tendency for its leaders and some opponents to exaggerate the Klan's size and its influence. At the time of the primary election in May 1922, for example, Fred Gifford claimed nearly fourteen thousand members, nine thousand of them in Portland. One month later, a Klan spokesman in Eugene boasted that membership exceeded thirty-five thousand men in thirty-one klaverns (local chapters). Gifford's figure was probably more accurate for mid-1922; the larger number would be closer to the total in December 1923, when C. C. Chapman, editor of the *Oregon Voter*, reported that there were fifty-eight chartered and seven provisionally chartered Klans in the state.[10]

But the strength and influence of the KKK should not be measured simply by counting members, since the hooded order enrolled many prominent ministers, politicians, and professional men and found thousands of sympathizers outside its ranks.

Leadership was a crucial factor in the success or failure of the Klan, and the schismatic nature of the Oregon Klan was evident from the beginning. Calloway and Powell split over sharing commissions from memberships, and, later, Powell and Gifford fought bitterly for control of the state organization. Formerly a union business agent and a supervisor for the Northwestern Electric Company, Gifford had been active in Masonic circles before joining the Klan. He was ambitious, proved adept at fraternal politics, and his Klan activities apparently had the approval of his utility company employers. Initially, he cooperated with the king kleagle in directing the activities of the Klan in Portland, but they chose opposite sides in the national struggle for Klan power that began in late 1922 between Imperial Wizard Simmons and Hiram Wesley Evans, a credit dentist from Dallas, Texas. Powell naturally supported his benefactor, while Gifford moved adroitly to the side of the successful challenger, who in turn backed Gifford's election as grand dragon (state head) of the Oregon Klan. By 1923, Gifford was the leading Klansman on the Pacific Coast, close to Evans's inner circle and the ruler of a virtually autonomous state Klan.

Gifford established his state headquarters in Portland. Although he had to contend with periodic challenges from rebellious klaverns outside the Portland metropolitan area, he maintained control with the assistance of Lem A. Dever, the colorful editor of the state Klan paper, the *Western American.* As nominal boss of a large voting bloc and with newspapers often neutralized by their ambivalent attitudes toward the Klan, Gifford was in a position to approve or reject politicians seeking Klan support. Chapman of the *Oregon Voter* interviewed the grand dragon in 1922 and conceded that "he radiates a spirit of sincerity, and evidently is very much in earnest, believing he is performing a high patriotic duty . . . in promoting the Ku Klux idea."[11] Other, less charitable, observers described Gifford as opportunistic, unprincipled, and with a streak of authoritarianism in his political practices.

In their search for allies, the aggressive leaders of the Oregon Klan mixed racial and religious prejudice with a dash of political opportunism: the Klan pledged support for an anti-alien land law sponsored by the American Legion, joined with Scottish Rite Masons in opposing parochial schools, and endorsed the Oregon Automobile Association for its advocacy of state motor license law modification. The Klan also bartered for the backing of the Portland Association of

Teachers by promising support for increased salaries and a tenure law.[12]

While the network of Klan political activities reached outward from Gifford's headquarters in Portland to every section of the state, many local Klans exploited issues peculiar to their communities. Pacific Klan Number Two in Astoria capitalized on the local circumstances that made religious and ethnic issues particularly appealing.[13] In Eugene, the KKK made repeated efforts to enroll faculty members and students at the University of Oregon, succeeding despite opposition from the administration. Dean Henry D. Sheldon of the university's School of Education complained to the historian Joseph Schafer: "We are having the hottest campaign you ever heard of here over the Ku Klux Klan. Ben Olcott, the governor, is out against the Klan. One of the other candidates is supposed to be backing it. Several of the members of our august faculty have joined its ranks."[14] The Eugene Klan counted among its recruits several members of Masonic orders, even more members of the Elks Lodge, a half dozen automobile salesmen, at least one local dentist, some city officials, and a county commissioner.

In Corvallis, where kleagles were active on the Oregon Agricultural College campus, the local klavern conducted a public initiation in October 1923 for an estimated five hundred candidates seeking citizenship in the Invisible Empire. Klansmen from Salem, Eugene, Roseburg, Albany, Lebanon, McMinnville, and Portland paraded through Corvallis and joined local Klansmen at a barbecue. One month later, at a rally in Salem, nearly three thousand Klansmen from Portland and nearby Willamette Valley towns marched through the city. Reporters estimated that more than seven hundred Klansmen were initiated in a ceremony at the state fairgrounds before an audience of nearly four thousand persons. Three Klan bands and two airplanes fitted with electric crosses added to the festivities.[15]

This phenomenal growth of the hooded order in Oregon can be traced best in the surviving records of Tillamook Klan Number Eight.[16] By the fall of 1921, Klan organizers had mobilized a solid core of members in this isolated coastal county, which had an economy based on logging and dairying. Most of the Klansmen lived in or near the city of Tillamook, and many were members of local fraternal orders, most notably the Masonic lodges, the Independent Order of Odd Fellows, and the Benevolent and Protective Order of Elks. Religious agitation against the strong Roman Catholic minority there attracted several evangelical Protestant ministers into Klan ranks. In April 1923, Klan officials consolidated the membership in the nearby town of Wheeler with that in Tillamook, raising the total to between 600 and 800. Although only about 200 were ever active at one time, in a city of 1,964 people and a county where the total population was only 8,810 in 1920, Klansmen constituted a significant and powerful group.

The Tillamook klavern experienced its most rapid growth from the spring of 1922 until 1925 and, unlike its counterparts in many other communities, remained relatively large until 1928, a few dozen members continuing to meet weekly at least into 1929. For a decade, the majority of municipal, county, and state officials elected in Tillamook were Klansmen or former Klansmen.[17] Religious issues were only one cause of local conflict, but they effectively bound Klansmen and non-Klan Protestants, thereby reinforcing the KKK's political activities. At first, the membership of the Tillamook Klan represented a cross section of the community, but the records for the years 1924 through 1926 show that the largest percentage of new members came from the county at large rather than from the city of Tillamook. This shift in the source of membership revealed a pattern that other Klans followed as they evolved from an aggressive political force into a social organization on the fringes of respectable fraternalism.

Nationally, the decade of the twenties was an age of joiners, and the Klan exploited this trend. Though membership was restricted to native-born white Protestant males, imaginative Klan leaders in Oregon and elsewhere attempted to organize women, Protestant citizens of foreign birth, and teenage boys. Grand Dragon Gifford established Klan auxiliaries for each of these groups, and Oregon set a standard for entrepreneurship in fraternalism that Klan leaders elsewhere envied and copied. In July 1922, Gifford, Powell, the Reverend Reuben H. Sawyer of Portland's Eastside Christian Church, and fellow Klansman Rush H. Davis established the Ladies of the Invisible Empire, and by 1923 the organization had several hundred members pledged "to unite in one inseparable bond the Protestant women of the world." When the newly established Women of the Ku Klux Klan absorbed the Ladies of the Invisible Empire later that year, Mrs. Fred L. Gifford was named head of the Oregon chapter.[18]

The Oregon Klan also spawned the colorfully garbed Royal Riders of the Red Robe in 1922. Dr. Martin W. Rose, a Portland physician and naturalized citizen from Canada, worked closely with Gifford and Powell in establishing the first chapter of this secret fraternal society for foreign-born citizens in Portland. Within a few years, the Royal Riders claimed nearly three thousand members in Oregon and had a national membership approaching seventy-five thousand. In 1926, the Royal Riders affiliated with the American Krusaders, a similar organization for the foreign-born established by the national Klan.

During a decade when the Boy Scouts of America burgeoned, an appeal to young men was a logical step for the Klan. At a meeting of state grand dragons in 1923, Gifford proposed a Junior Order of Klansmen patterned after the Order of DeMolay. Within a few months, the Salem *Capital Journal* reported that the Oregon Klan had established such a group. The national Klan announced the formation of its Junior Department in the spring of 1924. A prospective member of the Junior Klan had to be "a native, white, Gentile, Protestant American Boy" who was to "love the United States of America better than any other country in the whole world."[19] Although the Junior Klan never achieved the success of the Boy Scouts or similar groups, Junior Klansmen were organized in at least twenty-two states by 1925.

In Oregon as elsewhere, Klansmen exploited religious and racial prejudices, and the highly visible symbols of the robe and the fiery cross made it difficult to ignore the presence of the Klan. In 1922 and 1923, KKK lecturers attracted overflow crowds to the Portland Civic Auditorium, robed Klansmen interrupted church services to present money to friendly ministers, and burning crosses flared in Portland's evening sky from Mount Tabor and Mount Scott. Klansmen conducted similar activities in many towns, and burning crosses were often seen on Skinner's Butte in Eugene and on other hills around the state. In addition, Protestant evangelists, self-proclaimed "escaped nuns," and apostate priests roamed across Oregon stirring anti-Catholic passions. Many of these speakers plumbed the seemingly bottomless depths of hatred and fear. The Reverend Mr. Sawyer, for example, had a standard theme in speeches he delivered to large audiences throughout the Pacific Northwest. This segment of a speech he delivered at the Portland Civic Auditorium provides an example of his inflammatory rhetoric. "Jews," he preached,

are either bolshevists, undermining our government, or are shylocks in finance or commerce who gain control and command of Christians as borrowers or employees. It is repugnant to a true American to be bossed by a sheenie. And in some parts of America the Kikes are so thick that a white man can hardly find room to walk on the sidewalk. And where they are so thick, it is bolshevism they are talking, bolshevism and revolution.[20]

The Reverend J. R. Johnson, the pastor of the Sellwood Christian Church, who had succeeded Gifford as exalted cyclops in Portland, replied to a criticism by a Roman Catholic priest:

I was on the subject of religion; I was on the subject of white supremacy. . . . I believe that a Chinaman could be a Christian; I believe that a Jap could be a Christian; I believe that a nigger could be a Christian; I believe that a dago could be a Christian, that a Greek could be a Christian, but I didn't want the black blood mixed with mine.[21]

Many journalists ridiculed the Klan at first, but by 1922, as the Oregon Klan grew in strength, the majority of newspaper editors took a more ambiguous position. Some publishers feared the economic consequences of boycotts by Klansmen and their sympathizers, and some small-town editors either supported the Klan or maintained a benevolent neutrality. The Oregon Editorial Association revealed the potential for disagreement among its members in a resolution adopted in July 1922:

We deplore the fact that religious issues have been injected into Oregon politics. We, the editors of Oregon, refuse to be dragged into religious entanglements and hereby denounce and condemn any effort of any party, sect, organization or individual to inject religious issues into Oregon politics as un-American and inimical to the welfare of the people of the state of Oregon.[22]

Expressing an ambivalent view of the Klan that resembled the editorial position of two of Portland's major newspapers, the *Oregonian* and the *Oregon Journal*, the *Oregon Voter* stated, "We would not regard membership . . . or activity in the Ku Klux Klan as disqualifying anyone from holding public office, even though we condemn the principles, purpose and activities of the Klan itself."[23] The Portland *Telegram*, on the other hand, conducted a vigorous anti-Klan campaign, and its owners blamed a Klan-backed boycott as the cause of their economic woes. Outside Portland, the Medford *Mail Tribune* and the Salem *Capital Journal* waged the most effective anti-Klan crusades.

Uncertain how to respond to the KKK, many Oregonians simply tried to ignore it, but the organization's rapid growth and insidious influence made that option difficult, if not impossible, to achieve. In fact, the Klan became a divisive political issue within months after it entered the state.

On the eve of the primary election in mid-May 1922, the Republican Governor Ben Olcott, facing a stiff challenge from several opponents, issued an official proclamation condemning the Klan:

Dangerous forces are insidiously gaining a foothold in Oregon. In the guise of a secret society, parading under the name of the Ku Klux Klan, these forces are endeavoring to usurp the reins of government, are stirring up fanaticism, race hatred, religious prejudice, and all of those evil influences which tend toward factional strife and civil terror.[24]

The timing of Olcott's proclamation, coming nearly a month after Klansmen were blamed for a series of night-riding outrages in Medford, drew charges of political opportunism. Klan leaders and rival gubernatorial candidates were immediately drawn into the controversy. The Reverend Mr. Sawyer, speaking for the Klan, charged Olcott with "an unwarranted attack . . . bearing all the earmarks of Roman politics," and Gifford declared: "The only things that the Ku Klux Klan looked at in picking the right man to vote for [were] their loyalty to the free public schools, loyalty to the government of the United States, and the question of the anti-alien land law bills."[25]

The governor's attack on the Klan widened a developing breach in the Republican party. Tax and patronage issues were already divisive factors, but the *Oregon Voter* complained that the Republican primary had suddenly "degenerated into a pow-wow with does-he-belong or does-he-not the principal question."[26] Whether Olcott acted on principle or desperately used the Klan issue to catch his opponents off balance is a question left unanswered. The consequences of his action were evident almost immediately. With the political climate of the state in flux and his party badly split, the governor widened the fissure. The *Oregonian* responded to Olcott's charges by submitting a questionnaire about the Klan to each of the candidates in the primary campaign. While most of the Democrats and Republicans evaded a direct answer, the Republican state senator Charles Hall replied that he saw no sign of the KKK in politics and denied that it was a "menace to political freedom and public safety."[27] A banker and telephone company executive from Coos Bay, Hall represented many Republicans from southwestern Oregon who wanted improved roads for the coast and who resented the traditional dominance of the Portland-Salem wing of their party. But Hall also revealed a willingness to support Klan-related issues. He adopted, as the central plank of his political platform, a measure to abolish private and parochial schools for children in the lower grades, explaining: "The public school is one of the fundamental factors in our system of government. I favor compulsory attendance in the primary grades. Teach pure Americanism to all pupils beginning at an early age. Continue to strengthen and build up this typical American institution."[28] The Oregon Federation of Patriotic Societies (FOPS), which represented a coalition of anti-Catholic fraternal organizations and churches, based its endorsement of Hall on this plank, and the Klan announced its endorsement of Hall for the same reason.

Isaac Patterson of the state senate was considered Olcott's principal Republican challenger early in the primary campaign, but he faded, and Hall came within a few hundred votes of unseating the incumbent governor. Walter Pierce, also a state senator, easily won the nomination of the Democratic party. Although Republicans enjoyed a three-to-one advantage over the Democrats among registered voters, the primary election demonstrated that they were badly divided. Factional politics became the norm. In Multnomah County, the stronghold of FOPS and the KKK, twelve of the thirteen candidates with federation and Klan endorsement were nominated. In other areas of the state, Klan-endorsed candidates achieved only mixed success. But the Klan was just on the verge of its massive growth, and by election time, a slackening economy and tax issues would join with it to defeat Governor Olcott and change the composition of the legislature.

After his narrow victory in the primary election, Olcott renewed his assault on the Klan. In a statement to the New York *Herald Tribune,* he warned: "No greater menace confronts the United States today than this monster of invisible government." The governor ordered the state attorney general to proceed with the prosecution of the Jackson County night riders and removed Dr. R. C. Ellsworth of Pendleton, an acknowledged Klansman, from the state board of chiropractic examiners.[29]

The governor's attack did not prevent the KKK from exploiting the public school issue, which had emerged earlier that year when unofficial representatives of various Masonic groups drafted a "compulsory school bill" initiative. Based on a resolution of the Ancient and Accepted Scottish Rite Masons of the Southern Jurisdiction, which the Oregon lodge had adopted in 1920, the proposed law would require all children between the ages of eight and sixteen to attend public schools, thus virtually abolishing private and parochial schools. P. S. Malcolm of Portland, the inspector general of the Oregon Scottish Rite Masons and the leading figure in drafting the measure, denied that the bill was aimed at Catholics, asserting instead that it would improve patriotism and raise educational standards. On June 15, 1922, barely a month after Olcott's victory in the primary election, Robert F. Smith, president of the Lumbermen's Trust Company Bank of Portland and a prominent Mason, circulated petitions to place the school bill on the November ballot and declared that Oregon would be "an example for the rest of the country." The petition, as expected, gained the immediate endorsement of the Federation of Patriotic Societies and the Klan; indeed, there was ample evidence that Gifford had worked behind the scenes with Malcolm in drafting the measure.[30]

An important symbol of democracy in America, the public school was therefore a potent political weapon. Proponents of the school bill appealed to the patriotic sentiments of the large Protestant majority and attracted educational reformers by emphasizing the "democratic" idea of one school for all. The controversial bill divided Masons and forced politicians to take sides. It became the anvil upon which political careers were forged. Support for the school bill cut across party lines, and like prohibition, the bill became the political manifestation of a moral belief. Governor Olcott attempted to take a neutral stance, but his party, strongly tainted with Klan and FOPS affiliations, endorsed the initiative measure. The Republican Central Committee of Multnomah County made the standard disclaimer about injecting religion into politics, explaining that its endorsement was strictly "from the standpoint of pure Americanism."[31]

Walter Pierce, Olcott's Democratic opponent, emphasized tax issues early in his campaign, apparently considering the school issue a potential political liability. But late in August or early in September 1922, he met with Grand Dragon Gifford and a representative of the Federation of Patriotic Societies; he received the Klan's endorsement in return for supporting the school bill and giving some implied promises of patronage.[32] His statement, which Gifford released to the press, read: "I am in favor of and shall vote for the compulsory school bill sponsored by the Scottish Rite Masonic bodies in Oregon."[33] Even though Pierce continued to treat the school bill as a secondary issue, public attention could not be diverted from it. He handily defeated the incumbent governor in a surprisingly one-sided victory by a vote of 133,392 to 99,164. The school initiative also passed, but by a narrower margin of 115,506 to 103,685. It won in only fifteen of the state's thirty-six counties, gaining much of its majority in Western Oregon and in Portland, which "was the center of strength for both the Klan and the Roman Catholic Church." Scheduled to take effect on September 1, 1926, the new school law did not survive court challenges by its opponents. On January 1, 1925, the United States Supreme Court upheld a federal district court decision and declared it unconstitutional.[34]

Although Pierce won an overwhelming personal victory, his party did not enjoy similar success. The Mississippi-born Democrat Elton Watkins, who also had accepted Klan support, won a narrow victory for Congress over the Republican incumbent C. N. McArthur, but at the state level the Republican party triumphed. K. K. Kubli, a Portland stationer who was coauthor of Oregon's criminal syndicalism law and a Klansman with remarkably apt initials, was elected speaker-designate of the Oregon house, where in 1923 Republicans outnumbered Democrats fifty-one to nine; a similar ratio held in the senate. C. C. Chapman believed that FOPS and the KKK controlled "a majority or nearly a majority of the House and a strong working minority of the Senate." He asserted that there were more inexperienced legislators than ever before in the history of the state. Another significant change was evident. For the first time in over nine years farmers outnumbered lawyers, and their influence on legislation would be evident in a second controversial bill, this one aimed primarily at Japanese Americans.[35]

By 1923, Oregon was the only state on the Pacific Coast without a law restricting the ownership of land by aliens. Oregon lawmakers had briefly considered such a law in 1917 but dropped it at the request of the U.S. Department of State. In 1919, the Hood River post of the American Legion had introduced a resolution at the Legion's national convention proposing restrictions on Japanese ownership of land, a position supported by the Oregon State Grange and other groups of farmers. Even Governor Olcott had supported such a measure. When he addressed the legislature in 1921, he had recommended that

steps . . . be taken by means of proper legislation to curb the growth of the Japanese colonies in Oregon; to preserve our lands and our resources for the people of our own race and nationality. I believe the ultimatum should be issued that it is the sense of the people of Oregon . . . , that this state is a state with a government of Americans, by Americans, and for Americans, and that Americanism is the predominant asset of its citizenry.[36]

The legislature did not approve Governor Olcott's request in 1921, but the election of Walter Pierce and the changed composition of the new legislature assured a more receptive response in 1923. Pierce, who was a rancher and lawyer in eastern Oregon, considered an alien land law desirable and necessary. In his first message to the legislature, Governor Pierce urged passage of "a law prohibiting the selling or leasing of land in Oregon to the Mongolian and Malay," explaining that "European and Asiatic civilizations cannot amalgamate and we cannot and must not submit to the peaceful penetration of the Japanese and other Mongolian races."[37] With the school bill assured, eager house members introduced an anti-alien land bill on the first day of the session, and Governor Pierce signed it into law on February 16, 1923.

The legislature supplemented the land law by requiring county assessors "to list all Chinese and Japanese who own, lease or operate real property in the state of Oregon" and prohibiting aliens from operating specified businesses. The new laws actually offered little hindrance to Japanese-born farmers, who continued to lease land or to purchase it in the names of their American-born children. But the punitive legislation carried the indelible stamp of racism and reinforced fears of economic competition. The 1923 legislature concluded its nativist crusade when it responded to a national campaign by adopting two joint memorials urging Congress to impose additional restrictions on immigration to the United States. The *Oregon Voter* concluded that on the subject of nativist measures "the legislature was simply a goodnatured but determined mob."[38]

Although these nativist measures were only a small part of the legislature's slate, they involved highly emotional issues and stimulated considerable public response. There was a similar reaction to a series of laws affecting education. Legislation adopted in 1923 made it unlawful for teachers in public schools to wear religious garb and required "the teaching of the Constitution of the United States in the public and private schools of the state." On February 12, 1923, Pierce signed into law a bill requiring that "no text-book shall be used in our schools which speaks slightingly of the founders of the republic, or of the men who preserved the union, or which belittles or undervalues their work."[39]

Despite the presence of Klansmen in the Oregon legislature and the prejudices inherent in much of this nativist and patriotic legislation, the extent of Klan influence is difficult to determine. The new laws adopted by the Oregon legislature in 1923 were not simply products of Klan sponsorship or measures of Klan strength; rather, they reflected the opinions of many Americans in the 1920s. The Oregon Klan was neither as strong nor as united as Klan leaders proclaimed. Thus, the laws more likely demonstrated the popular appeal of efforts to legislate conformity in a state with a predominantly white, native-born, and Protestant population. Moreover, the efforts to legislate conformity were not confined to Oregon. Although only Oregon's school bill passed, it was but one of more than a dozen similar measures presented to voters around the country. In the state of Washington, for example, voters in 1924 rejected a compulsory school initiative modeled on the Oregon law.

While the KKK's political and public activities drew the most attention in Oregon, its secret operations and mystique of terror were equally detrimental to community life. The infiltration of its members and philosophy into churches, fraternal organizations, and local politics disrupted social interaction in many small towns. In fact, Klan militancy often stimulated an equal and opposite reaction and contributed to the growth of anti-Klan coalitions. Numerous business and political leaders and prominent Protestant ministers spoke out against the Klan, joining in opposition with religious and racial minorities. Although there were relatively few blacks in Oregon, the Portland branch of the National Association for the Advancement of Colored People worked to influence public opinion and lobbied against politicians identified with the Klan. Roman Catholics, with their principal political strength in Portland, worked with the Catholic Truth Society and the *Catholic Sentinel* to organize anti-Klan programs in parishes throughout the state. And in October of 1923, the state chapter of the American Federation of Labor, meeting in convention in Portland, climaxed a lengthy internal struggle by adopting a resolution condemning the Klan.[40]

The Klan's decline was as rapid as its initial success. Klansmen split with Pierce before the end of 1923, charging that the governor had broken his promise of patronage. The following spring introduced a divisive primary contest for the Republican Charles L. McNary's seat in the U.S. Senate; Kubli, Portland's Mayor Baker, and other candidates scrambled for Klan support, but McNary stood aloof, and he won an easy victory in the primary as Gifford began to lose his tight grip on Klan votes. One history of the Oregon Klan written in the 1920s estimated that Gifford controlled directly only 10 to 20 percent of the Klansmen in the state by the end of 1924.[41]

There were many reasons for Gifford's loss of control over the Klan. External opposition mounted, his running feud with Luther Powell erupted periodically, downstate Klansmen rejected the dominance of the Portland faction, and Lem Dever turned against him. Following his early disputes with Gifford, the king kleagle had moved north of the Columbia River to organize Klans in Washington and Alaska. He returned to Oregon briefly in the fall of 1923, when he once again challenged Gifford. Powell lost, but the renewed dispute widened a breach between Grand Dragon Gifford and Lem Dever, who, in December 1923, resigned his posts as publicity director for the Realm of Oregon and editor of the *Western American*. Dever launched a vigorous attack against Gifford and the Klan in a bombastic exposé, *Confessions of an Imperial Klansman*.[42] Despite this apparent break with the Klan, Dever never strayed very far from the Invisible Empire; he even attempted in 1926 to organize an Independent Order of Klansmen in Oregon. He failed in this effort as he would fail in many others and "remained a political pamphleteer," in the wry words of the historian Malcolm Clark, Jr., "wasting useful talents on small unworthy causes."[43]

Although Klan influence was still evident during the legislative sessions of 1925 and 1927, its strength had ebbed. Wracked by internal dissension, afflicted by apathy, and challenged by its opponents, the Klan would soon wither away. Gifford relinquished control of the Oregon Klan in mid-1925, afterward devoting his time to a partnership in a detective agency and finally working as bailiff for a Portland judge. His successors were unable to stem the Klan's decline. The Atlanta headquarters dispatched M. S. Belser to Oregon in August 1925 with the objective of reviving the organization. Belser repudiated political activities, declaring that the Klan's purpose was "purely and solely educational."[44] Oregon Klansmen elected C. T. Godwin of Baker as the new grand dragon, and his appointments of officers confirmed the shift in strength from Portland to the outlying Klans.[45] He opened a drive for new members and permitted KKK political activities to resume on a limited scale. Political observers even alleged that Governor Patterson, the Republican who had challenged Olcott in 1922 and had defeated Pierce in 1924, appointed more Klansmen to state offices than did his predecessor. Yet, when the presidential contest of 1928 between the Republican Herbert Hoover and the Democrat Alfred E. Smith revived anti-Catholic sentiments nationally, the Oregon Klan remained relatively dormant. Some surviving Klansmen took an advanced fraternal degree, the K-Trio degree of the Knights of the Great Forest, in 1928, and one branch of the Portland Klan and small klaverns in other communities continued to meet into the 1930s.[46]

But the KKK failed to survive the economic trauma of the Great Depression, and other groups took its place. In 1937, after more than a decade outside its ranks, Fred Gifford attempted to revive the Oregon Klan once again. At a press conference on November 24, 1937, he declared that the new organization would "give battle to all fascist and communist groups, no matter under what name they call themselves." He asserted that "advices from Atlanta, Georgia, show a present paid-up membership of slightly more than 16,000 in the state of Oregon" and that "applications are coming in as fast as we can check applicants." But Gifford's estimate of membership was highly exaggerated, and his optimism, unwarranted. There was no rush to join even though he promised that "religion will play no part in the new Klan." Of course, as he explained, "Catholics and Jews will be barred from membership. So will Negroes."[47]

Gifford failed to revive the old Klan spirit but persisted briefly in his effort. In the spring of 1938, the pro-Klan Portland *Times* reported that Klansmen were investigating "vice, dope, and gambling." The newspaper sympathetically stated that "in defense of womanhood, in upholding the lofty standards of the White Race, the Klan today may be sure of the strong support of every decent citizen. Make Portland safe for all women and children!"[48] By then, however, the Oregon Klan resembled other remnants of the formerly massive national membership.

Although it demonstrated greater political strength in Oregon than in neighboring states, the KKK failed to sustain its initial rate of growth and could not replace members who left the organization at an equally rapid rate. The Klan had no constructive values to sustain it; the prejudices it exploited did not lend themselves to positive programs. If the "good people" of Oregon could be blamed for permitting the Klan to succeed, their conservative instincts eventually contributed to its decline. But even though the Ku Klux Klan of the 1920s was discredited and eventually failed, the residue of prejudices it exploited has never been fully cleansed from the state, the region, and the nation.

NOTES

1. *Kourier Magazine* [Atlanta], (July 1931), 32. The author wishes to acknowledge the assistance from a research grant provided by the American Association for State and Local History.

2. Thomas Dixon, *The Clansman: An Historical Romance of the Ku Klux Klan* (New York, 1905), and J. C. Lester and D. L. Wilson, *Ku Klux Klan; Its Origin, Growth and Disbandment* (1884; New York, 1905), give the older view of the Klan. Allen W. Trelease, *White Terror: The Ku Klux Klan Conspiracy and Southern Reconstruction* (New York, 1971); David Chalmers, *Hooded Americanism: The History of the Ku Klux Klan*, 2d ed. (New York, 1981); and Kenneth T. Jackson, *The Ku Klux Klan in the City, 1915–1930* (New York, 1967), are the best general histories of the Klan. For a history of the Klan in Oregon, see Eckard V. Toy, Jr., "The Ku Klux Klan in Oregon: Its Program and Character," M.A. thesis (University of Oregon, 1959).

3. Quoted in Earl Pomeroy, *The Pacific Slope: A History of California, Oregon, Washington, Idaho, Utah, and Nevada* (New York, 1965), 216.

4. *Ibid.*, 226.

5. Stanley Coben, "The Assault on Victorianism in the Twentieth Century" in *Victorian America*, ed. Daniel Walker Howe (Philadelphia, 1976), 160–81.

6. Portland *Oregonian*, July 31, Aug. 2, 1921.

7. Telegram from New York *World* and reply, Sept. 22, 1921, Ben Olcott Papers, Special Collections, University of Oregon, Eugene.

8. *Fourteenth Census of the United States, 1920*, Vol. II, *Population: General Report and Analytical Tables* (Washington, D.C., 1922), 46.

9. Priscilla Knuth, *Nativism in Oregon* [Essay in Armitage Competition in Oregon Pioneer History] (Portland, 1943–44); Malcolm Clark, Jr., "The Bigot Disclosed: 90 Years of Nativism," *OHQ*, Vol. 75 (1974), 108–90; Donald L. Kinzer, *An Episode in Anti-Catholicism: The American Protective Association* (Seattle, 1964).

10. Jackson, 283–84, n8; L. E. Burger in Eugene *Morning Register*, June 30, 1922; and "Purifying the Klan," *Oregon Voter* (Dec. 8, 1923), 16.

11. "Gifford, Head of the K.K.K.," *Oregon Voter* (March 25, 1922), 5–6.

12. *Capital Journal* (Salem), Oct. 23, 1922.

13. *Ibid.*, Nov. 13, 14, 1922.

14. Henry D. Sheldon to Joseph Shafer, May 15, 1922, Henry D. Sheldon Papers, Special Collections, University of Oregon; *Capital Journal*, Oct. 27, 1922.

15. *Oregonian*, Oct. 19, Nov. 11, 1923.

16. See Eckard V. Toy, Jr., "The Ku Klux Klan in Tillamook, Oregon," *PNQ*, Vol. 53 (1962), 60–64; see also, William Toll, "Progress and Piety: the Ku Klux Klan and Social Change in Tillamook, Oregon," *ibid.*, Vol. 69 (1978), 75–85.

17. These findings are based on comparison of membership lists with election results. Records of Tillamook Klan Number Eight, Special Collections, University of Oregon.

18. Quoted in George E. Turnbull, *An Oregon Crusader* (Portland, 1955), 106. See also, *Capital Journal*, July 7, 1922; Portland *Catholic Sentinel*, July 13, 1922; Portland *Western American*, Sept. 14, 1923; and Lawrence J. Saalfeld, "Forces of Prejudice in Oregon, 1920–25," M.A. thesis (Catholic University of America, 1950), 70.

19. Quoted in Bessie Louise Pierce, *Citizens' Organizations and the Civic Training of Youth* (New York, 1933), 124. See Grand Dragon of Oregon, "Responsibility of Klankraft

to the American Boy," *Papers Read at the Meeting of Grand Dragons, Knights of the Ku Klux Klan* (Atlanta, 1923), 84; Saalfeld, 72; and "America's Future," *Kourier Magazine* (February 1925), 23.

20. "Ku Klux and Jews," *Oregon Voter* (April 15, 1922), 16.

21. Stenographic record of speech by the Reverend J. R. Johnson at Oak Grove Community Church, July 12, 1923, in files of Catholic Truth Society of Portland.

22. Quoted in Turnbull, 118.

23. "Ku Klux Is Busy," *Oregon Voter* (Jan. 21, 1922), 14.

24. Proclamation of Governor Olcott, May 13, 1922, Oregon State Archives, Salem.

25. Sawyer quoted in *Oregon Journal* (Portland), May 14, 1922; Gifford quoted in *Oregonian*, May 16, 1922.

26. Clark, 166–67.

27. *Oregonian*, May 16, 1922.

28. Quoted in Turnbull, 68.

29. *Ibid.*, 159 (quotation); Olcott to R. C. Ellsworth, June 17, 1922, Olcott Papers.

30. Smith quoted in *Oregon Journal*, June 16, 1922; Saalfeld, 105; *Western American*, Dec. 7, 1922; Amended Section 5259, *Oregon General Laws* (Salem, 1923), 9 (hereafter cited *Laws* with appropriate year).

31. Turnbull, 134–35.

32. Malcolm Clark believes that Pierce gulled Gifford; Clark, 171. Arthur H. Bone states simply: "There can be little doubt that Pierce played 'footsy' with Klan leaders. Whether he made a bargain with them is a moot point"; see Arthur H. Bone, ed., *Oregon Cattleman/Governor/Congressman: Memoirs and Times of Walter M. Pierce* (Portland, 1981), 168. Also see, Gerald Schwartz, "Walter M. Pierce and the Tradition of Progressive Reform: A Study of Eastern Oregon's Great Democrat," Ph.D. dissertation (Washington State University, 1969).

33. *Capital Journal*, Sept. 13, 1922.

34. "Official Returns," *Oregon Voter* (Dec. 9, 1922), 27; Amended Section 5259, *Laws*, 1923; Pomeroy, 228. See *Society of the Sisters of the Holy Names of Jesus and Mary v. Pierce*, in Clark Spurlock, *Education and the Supreme Court* (Urbana, 1955), 170.

35. Saalfeld, 57; "Next Legislature," *Oregon Voter* (Nov. 11, 1922), 5; "Farmers Exceed Lawyers," *Oregon Voter* (Nov. 18, 1922), 3–11. There were twenty-one farmers, fifteen attorneys, and five bankers in the house and six farmers, nine attorneys, and three bankers in the senate.

36. Quoted in Marjorie R. Stearns, *The History of the Japanese People in Oregon*, University of Oregon Thesis Series, No. 4 (Eugene, 1939), 50.

37. *Ibid.*, 56–57.

38. H.B. 34, 120, and 205, *Laws*, 1923, pp. 145, 77, and 232; "1923 Legislature," *Oregon Voter* (March 3, 1923), 4.

39. S.B. 20 and 57, *Laws*, 1923, pp. 17, 60.

40. *Catholic Sentinel*, Oct. 4, 1923.

41. C. Easton Rothwell, "The Ku Klux Klan in the State of Oregon," B.A. thesis (Reed College, 1924), 139.

42. Lem A. Dever, *Confessions of an Imperial Klansman*, 2d ed. (Portland, 1925).

43. Clark, 182.

44. "Klan Functioning Again," *Oregon Voter* (Feb. 13, 1926), 24–30.

45. *Capital Journal*, Aug. 16, 1927.

46. Membership lists of the Tillamook Klan appear to confirm these reports. A former Klansman told the writer in an interview that many of these men became "life members."

47. *Oregonian*, Nov. 28, 1937.

48. Portland *Times*, May 26, 1938.

Poor Men on Poor Lands:
The Back-to-the-Land Movement
of the Early Twentieth Century

Richard White

Back-to-the-land movements in the United States are usually characterized as occurring only on the fringes of urban and rural society
and as worthy of only passing historical attention. Largely urban in
inspiration, they are perceived as barely affecting the city and as un-
important even in the countryside. Many scholars dismiss them as a
mere romantic or sentimental reaction to industrialization; their literary artifacts reveal intellectual trends, but their concrete social accomplishments are usually assumed to have been negligible. Many
of these movements, however, were more than the stillborn brain-
children of romantic intellectuals, more than mere hankerings after
idealized agrarian pasts. They have often succeeded in placing thousands of families in the countryside and have had important social
and ecological consequences. Furthermore, back-to-the-land movements proceeded from intellectual assumptions more complicated
than mere romanticism, and their remains are more than literary. A
proper understanding must take into consideration the rationale behind the movements, the experience of the people who worked the
land, and the relationship of the settlement to environmental change.
These three interrelated aspects of back-to-the-land settlement are
clearly revealed in the movement to place settlers on the logged-off
lands of western Washington during the first four decades of the
twentieth century.

Early twentieth-century advocates of back-to-the-land settlement
proceeded from the assumption that the cities were overpopulated
and the rural districts were correspondingly underpopulated. From

Originally published in *Pacific Historical Review,* February 1980 (© 1980 by the Pacific
Coast Branch, American Historical Association).

this fundamental imbalance (in their eyes, a development out of step with American history and alien to American institutions) flowed the myriad social problems—unemployment, poverty, disease, moral decline—that they believed would, if unchecked, eventually destroy the nation. In the western United States particularly, the scarcity of small farms and the rapid growth of cities aroused considerable concern. Most back-to-the-land promoters, operating in arid regions, sought to put people ón irrigated lands, but in the Pacific Northwest, as in Wisconsin, Michigan, and Minnesota, the movement attempted to create farms on logged-off timberlands.

The failure of people to settle these cutover lands and create farms without considerable urging is not mysterious. Western Washington consisted of neither fertile virgin land awaiting the plow nor an established rural district. It was a desolate and unproductive waste of huge stumps and shattered trees. An observer sympathetic to the movement to settle the logged-off lands gave a frank description of a typical tract in 1917:

Stumps from two to nine feet in diameter lift their ugly heads above the brush and debris; dead snags reach up here and there to stand twisted, half uprooted and stripped of limbs. Logs, water soaked, interlace the ground, often overlapping three and four deep. A tangle of underbrush covers the ground. The surface is generally broken and is one mass of hummocks and hollows. The ground conceals a network of roots, often massive in size, and running out many yards from the parent tree.

Unlike the stumps of the deciduous forests of the East, or even the pine forests of New England, Minnesota, Wisconsin, and Michigan, these conifer stumps could take a human lifetime to rot. Simply to remove the stumps, which might be up to ten feet in diameter, the new farmer had to work longer and spend more money than his counterpart in any other forested area of the United States. Furthermore, although soil types varied in the cutover region, light podzolic soils composed the bulk of the upland forest area of western Washington. Infertile, leached by heavy winter rains, and easily eroded when vegetation had been removed, these soils were unsuitable for agriculture.

Reforestation did not become the accepted way of dealing with this cutover land until the mid-twentieth century. Between 1900 and 1940 serious institutional and economic problems blocked reforestation: replanting the forests demanded sweeping alterations in existing tax structures, and it promised no economic benefits for at least a generation. Even foresters, such as Burt Kirkland, a University of Washington professor who studied the economics of reforestation, believed that conversion of the logged-off lands into farmlands, not replanting them to Douglas fir, constituted the best hope for reclaiming the cutover districts. The worst lands, a small minority of the total by contemporary standards, might be suited only for reforestation, but settlers could turn most cutover lands into productive farms.

During the first forty years of the twentieth century, settlement rather than reforestation became the accepted way of salvaging logged-off lands. Advocates of settlement were unaware of the infertility of the forest soils that they planned to transform into farms. Since the primitive soil science of the era could not judge fertility with any great accuracy, only experience could disprove their claims that fertile soils awaited the settler. When boosters asserted that "land which grew the sturdy evergreen will grow anything else," few challenged them. As late as 1931 the state director of agriculture for Washington advised prospective settlers to choose land with many big stumps because such land was certain to be the most fertile.

Even if reforestation had been financially feasible, the reasoning of the land boosters would have probably forced them to reject the planting of trees on cutover lands. Reforestation ignored the fundamental social logic of the movement. Planting trees did not correct urban social ills; new forests would not drain large numbers of unemployed workers from the cities. When an advocate of settlement denounced the Forest Service for trying to "grow trees on land that should grow men," he was only underlining the rationale behind the movement.

Despite anti-urban rhetoric, the back-to-the-land movement arose from motives far more complicated than a mere hatred of the city and its ills. The promoters of rural settlement were not themselves farmers. Politicians, lawyers, editors, speculators, businessmen, bankers, foresters, and lumbermen organized and promoted the movement. The Everett Chamber of Commerce called the first Logged-off Land Conference in 1908, and the head of the Seattle Chamber of Commerce was a strong advocate. George S. Long, the manager of the Weyerhaeuser timber interests in the state, helped organize the settlement movement, and lumber trade journals as well as business journals regularly featured articles on the problem of the logged-off lands. In 1912 the movement in the Northwest spawned its own journal, *Little Logged-off Lands*.

Although many of these men, or the corporations they worked for, owned logged-off lands, the movement represented more than a speculation dreamed up by landowners and timber companies. Indeed, boosters condemned timber companies for not selling their land and attacked speculators for selling land at inflated prices. The interest of the supporters of the movement often went beyond immediate profit; they wanted to save the city by redeeming the countryside. Virtually all back-to-the-land movements sprang from this concern for urban problems. For example, George Maxwell, who headed the National Irrigation Congress and made it a pressure group far more formidable than any logged-off land association, saw irrigation not only as a tool for economic development, but also as a safety valve for urban social tensions. Nowhere does the economic and social bias of the movement emerge more clearly than in its autarchic assumptions. The city demanded a productive hinterland; the rapid cutting of the northwest forest, therefore, threatened cities like Seattle and Tacoma with ruin unless the land could be returned to productive uses. Since reforestation seemed slow and unprofitable, agriculture provided the only answer. Proponents of settlement cited figures indicating that Seattle alone consumed $3 million in food monthly, but not over 20 percent of it was produced in the Northwest. According to *Little Logged-off Lands,* residents of Washington sent $26 million out of the state in 1910 for dairy, poultry, and pork products that logged-off land farmers could have produced in Washington. Not only would new settlers help keep needed capital in the state, they would also consume the products of the industries that the capital would create. To fill the lands, boosters sought unemployed urban workers and recent foreign immigrants. In theory, such settlers would perform a double service: by leaving the city they would automatically lessen its social problems, and by settling on the logged-off lands they would feed the urban population and stimulate urban industry.

It is within this economic context that the movement's anti-urban rhetoric should be understood. Propagandists trotted out all the venerable agrarian homilies, but they put them at the service of the city. They argued that the attraction of men to the soil was instinctive, that urban life was unnatural, and that moral and civic virtue sprang directly from the soil. Advocates of stumpland farming even added a corollary: the harder the land is to bring into production the greater is the yield of virtue. As H. W. Sparks, an official of the state college demonstration farm in Pullman, put it in 1913:

I believe it fortunate for this favored country and good people who inhabit it that the land is expensive to prepare for cultivation in that we are practically free from that class of undesirable adventurers who have been for generations moving from one piece of virgin soil to another exhausting the accumulated fertility, giving nothing in return, whose sole motive has been exploitation.

Most prospective settlers were probably more immune to these invocations of agrarian virtue than to the boosters' promises of sure financial success. Organizations from local chambers of commerce to the state government of Washington assured potential settlers that farming logged-off lands would make them comfortable and might very well make them rich.

Between 1900 and 1920 a substantial number of settlers apparently believed such propaganda and began farming the logged-off lands west of the Cascade Mountains. Western Washington gained almost 17,000 farms during this period, and 15,000 contained less than fifty acres. Although no specific enumeration was made, the vast bulk of this settlement was on cutover lands. During the twenties the movement lagged as urban prosperity coupled with rural depression to pull people off the land. With the Great Depression, however, this trend reversed itself, and the movement boomed once more. The number of farms in the logging counties of western Washington increased 51 percent between 1930 and 1940. Between 1930 and 1935 alone, 12,650 families settled on farms in Washington, largely in the west and largely on the worst lands.

The experience of these people on the land has largely been ignored. Who were they and what happened to them? Before 1920 the settlers who took up cutover lands seem to have been in large part the very people urban propagandists were aiming for. A survey by the United States Department of Agriculture (USDA) estimated that the bulk of the settlers on cutover lands in the prewar years were foreign born. Between 1898 and 1903 the foreign born made up 83 percent of all settlers, a percentage that declined to 70 percent between 1910 and 1915. Most of these settlers came from Scandinavia, especially Norway and Sweden. As late as 1921, some 55 percent of cutover farm settlers had been born in Scandinavia, the great majority having acquired their lands before the first world war.

During the 1930s, however, foreign immigration virtually ceased, and two new streams of settlers, unemployed workers from the cities and refugees from the Dust Bowl, dominated the flight to the cutover lands. According to a survey by the Washington agricultural experiment station, slightly over half of the cutover settlers of the 1930s came from within the state of Washington, mostly from urban areas, while the remainder were from outside the state, mostly the drought-stricken states of the northern plains. The urban workers often sought little more than space to grow food while they worked elsewhere. Their farms were only glorified gardens, too small to be counted by census takers. But the people fleeing the northern plains attempted to start more ambitious farms.

The Dust Bowl migrants began arriving in 1932 and peaked between 1934 and 1936. Driven from their homes by crop failures and drought, these uncelebrated companions of John Steinbeck's Okies sometimes moved west only because, as one migrant explained, "We all seem to have our eyes turned that way." Lois Phillips Hudson, whose family finally settled on a cutover farm, wrote years later that "it didn't seem to matter where you were during those depression years. After you'd been in one spot for awhile you decided things couldn't be quite so bad anywhere else and so you moved." But most moves were not so aimless. Migrants sought out relatives and old neighbors, re-creating plains communities in the cutover lands. In some instances entire congregations followed their ministers who had gone ahead to locate land. They settled where the land was cheap and there they largely stayed. Surveys made during the 1930s found that three-quarters of the drought migrants remained in the county where they first settled. Contemporary studies of population found a depressing logic behind these rural migrations: the worse the land, the greater its availability and the greater the influx of immigrants.

The farming experience of the pre-1920 migrants differed from that of the depression migrants: few of the former had ever farmed before. By 1921, according to the USDA, only 27 percent of the farmers (37 percent of the native-born settlers and 23 percent of the immigrants) on the logged-off lands had run a farm prior to settlement. In 1921 some 51 percent of the settlers had held working-class jobs before settlement, but only 5 percent had worked in factories, and indeed the only identifiable urban segment outside of factory workers consisted of small urban businessmen who constituted 11 percent of the settlers. Many settlers, perhaps most, had probably been rural workers—farmhands, loggers, and fishermen.

During the 1930s the situation changed drastically. Since nearly all the Dust Bowl migrants of the depression had been farmers, their participation in the movement boosted the percentage of settlers with prior farm experience to 50 percent. Most of them, however, had farmed in a totally different environment, and their understandable concern with water led them to overrate the cutover lands, where lush growth seemed to promise abundant crops. Before these settlers discovered that bracken did not translate into oats nor fireweed into potatoes, they had often fallen prey to real estate promoters or lumber companies which sold them worthless land on contract.

With or without farm experience and regardless of national origin and time of settlement, these new settlers uniformly arrived with little working capital. In the early years of the century, land was cheap (five to twenty dollars an acre) and available near the cities; but as land values rose, new settlers either had to reduce the size of their farms or move into more isolated areas. Moreover, the cost of bringing cutover lands into production greatly exceeded the original purchase price of the land. Until the 1930s it cost between two hundred and three hundred dollars an acre to clear logged-off land. During the thirties the bulldozer reduced the expense to one hundred dollars an acre. Because of the cost of clearing, the rural migrants became preeminently small farmers. Between 1898 and 1903 the rural migrants bought about 40 acres of land per family, and between 1910 and 1915, 22.4 acres. By 1939 a third of all cutover farms contained less than 20 acres. Such statistics actually overestimate the productive capabilities of these farms. Because of the labor and capital expense involved, farmers cleared very little of their land. In 1915 the average logged-off farm contained only 12.8 acres of improved land. In 1939 some 33 percent of the farms had less than 2 acres cleared, and 43 percent more had from 2 to 10 acres.

This lack of capital and the expense involved in mechanized clearing shaped the settlement experience as much as the infertility of the soil. Recognizing the difficulties, promoters of settlement turned relatively quickly to the state for aid. Asserting that logged-off lands in Washington were more difficult to bring under cultivation than eastern woodlands and that the old individualistic pioneer methods would no longer suffice, they cited federal and state aid to reclamation projects on arid and marsh lands as a precedent. Advocates argued that only government support could assure successful settlement. In 1912, using *Little Logged-off Lands* as their mouthpiece, promoters began a concerted campaign to secure governmental assistance for settlers on the logged-off land. Their lobbying seemed so successful that the journal claimed that only one major newspaper in the state, the Yakima *Republic* (which with remarkable perspicacity protested that logged-off lands were not worth the cost of clearing), opposed state aid.

As a result of this campaign, state legislators in 1913 confronted a formidable array of plans to reclaim the cutover lands. After a joint legislative committee consolidated the proposals, a new law, providing for agricultural development districts that were coextensive with the counties, passed both houses by large majorities. Under the new law each district would have three commissioners who would be selected by the voters. The commissioners could call special elections to vote on the property taxes that would fund reclamation. Once voters approved the necessary taxes, the commissioners could issue bonds, contract for the clearing of logged-off lands, and sell the improved land to new settlers at cost plus 5 percent. Before the law could take effect, however, each county had to vote to organize the development districts.

In county after county voters rejected the formation of the agricultural development districts. The assemblyman Thomas Murphine, who had helped to write the legislation, rather vaguely blamed "interest lackeys" for the defeats. Others explained that voters feared the granting of tax powers to local bodies other than the county government. Corruption and incompetence seemed to be very real dangers if all landowners were taxed to buy and clear land that might prove unproductive and difficult to sell. All subsequent attempts to revise the law to meet these objections failed. Now leery of popular disapproval, the legislature defeated another, far less ambitious, project to build a state powder factory that would provide explosives for stumpage removal to settlers at cost. The state continued to encourage settlement of logged-off lands and eagerly tried to sell the logged-over lands it possessed, but it provided no financial aid to the settlers.

The failure to secure government aid was a crippling blow to logged-off land settlement, but for a period during and after World War I, it appeared that corporate capital might step in. Between 1917 and 1925 the Puget Mill Company, one of the largest lumbering companies in western Washington, seriously considered providing assistance to settlers on its cutover lands. Prior to this date, many (although not all) lumber companies had discouraged settlement on their lands since few regions had yet been totally logged, and the companies feared the effects of settlement of nearby virgin timberlands. Not only would settlers in such regions demand schools and roads, thus raising property taxes that would fall most heavily on valuable virgin timberlands, but in clearing the land settlers also often set fires that spread to adjoining areas and destroyed valuable standing timber.

After World War I new technologies and the rapid pace of cutting dramatically altered this situation. Lumbermen had stripped all marketable timber from huge areas of western Washington, and these deforested lands were valueless to the companies. Indeed, these lands drained corporate resources since, although they produced nothing, taxes still had to be paid on them. Lumbermen continued to reject reforestation of these lands because they considered the price of timber too low to make private reforestation feasible. Instead, they preferred to sell off their cutover tracts for whatever they could obtain and to seek virgin timber on more isolated private holdings and on the public lands.

The failure of standard promotional techniques to dispose of much of this land led the Puget Mill Company to undertake an experiment on seven thousand acres of stumpland it held near Seattle. Since it could not sell unimproved cutover land, Puget Mill decided to establish a farming community on the tract. The company built roads and schools and set up a demonstration poultry farm—the Alderwood Manor Demonstration College and Farm. The company also began a massive campaign, advertising the land in five- and ten-acre tracts, with one acre already cleared, for two hundred dollars per acre and a 10 percent down payment. Puget Mill promised settlers a comfortable living from their small poultry farms, and by 1922 almost fifteen hundred people had settled at Alderwood Manor. Like previous cutover farmers, few of these people had ever farmed before, and, not surprisingly, few made their new farms work. Most ended up as commuters to Seattle, and Alderwood Manor eventually evolved into a suburb of Seattle rather than a colony of independent small farmers. In the end Puget Mill successfully disposed of its land, but the cost of doing so proved so extravagant that the company did not undertake any further settlement projects nor did other companies seek to imitate Alderwood Manor.

The failure of government and corporations to finance settlement meant that farmers had to rely on their own resources. For settlers lacking capital, the chances for success on infertile and unimproved cutover farms were slight. Yet, because they failed to secure government aid or corporate loans, settlers tried for almost forty years to duplicate on the logged-off lands the individual settlements associated with eighteenth- and nineteenth-century pioneers in the eastern United States. Boosters encouraged the settlers to see opportunity instead of disaster. The heavy rains of western Washington (which leached the limited fertility from thin soils) were described by boosters as "just enough to make everything grow to perfection." The logging debris which made clearing so expensive was actually "fuel for all time . . . at the doors of the home." Indeed, promoters claimed that logging debris represented profits of up to $280 an acre through the sale of wood and by-products such as turpentine, charcoal, and tar.

Instead of profits the debris yielded only years of hard work and drudgery. Logging waste had to be cleared before farming could begin. Confidence men promoted miracle chemicals to dissolve stumps, but most farmers followed the carefully researched techniques recommended by the Washington agricultural experiment stations. Before any attempt to remove stumps was made, logging debris had to be gathered into piles and burned. After the whole tract was burned over to destroy the brush, a settler attacked the huge stumps. The methods of removal involved combinations of burning, blasting, and pulling. The cheapest and one of the most common of techniques was the char-pit method, which consisted of making an intense fire in a circle around a stump stripped of its bark and then burying the fire to conserve and focus heat. The char-pit method demanded little equipment and had few material costs, but took days to remove a single stump.

Dynamite removed stumps more quickly, but it cost more and was fast only in comparison with burning. The Department of Agriculture estimated that a farmer working alone required four hundred hours of his own labor, thirty-four hours of horse labor, and forty dollars' worth of dynamite to clear an acre of stumpland. A far faster and more efficient technique involved using a donkey engine to pull the stumps. Almost an acre a day could be cleared by a trained crew, but the estimated cost of clearing with the machines ran as high as three hundred dollars an acre.

Because clearing cutover lands demanded either immense amounts of time and labor or heavy capital expenditures, farmers turned to forms of agriculture that could be undertaken with the stumps still in place. This meant dairying, poultry raising, or berry growing. Before World War I, when many cutover farmers had acquired sizable acreages of cheap land, dairying dominated. As the cities grew, however, lands immediately surrounding them increased in price, and many farmers could not acquire sufficient acreages near cities to pasture a dairy herd. They turned to chicken farming and berry raising on smaller and less expensive farms. But no matter what type of farming was undertaken, farmers in the cutover uplands had to meet the challenge of competition from farmers in the fertile prairies and lowlands. Few of them could. Lack of capital denied cutover farmers access to new technologies and economies of scale, and this along with the high cost of subduing their land and its low productivity made their farms noncompetitive. Nowhere did these disadvantages show up earlier or more clearly than in dairy farming.

The major liability of dairy farmers on the cutover lands was the infertility of their soil. The most productive of the cutover uplands was still less fertile than the least productive of the lowland prairies and diked bottomlands and marshes. Because of the low fertility of upland fields, the grasses adaptable to them had lower nutritive value than those of the lowlands. Cows on logged-off farms thus required more pasture land than cows on lowland soil, and upland herds produced less butterfat per cow than lowland herds. To compensate for insufficient land and the scarcity of nutritious pasture, upland farmers had to expend money for feed, which became the largest single expense on most stumpland dairy farms. Even with purchased feed, however, the cows still produced less butterfat per $100 of feed than cows of the lowland farmers. Under such conditions, upland dairy farmers could not survive the competition of lowland herds. A 1915 survey by the USDA revealed that the average dairy farm, despite advantages in invested capital and in improved and total acreage over other upland farms, earned substantially less annually ($384) than upland poultry and fruit farms ($524).

After World War I, dairying grew less significant on the cutover lands, and chicken raising became the dominant farming activity. During the 1920s, however, many lowland farmers also turned to poultry raising, and once again the superior fertility of their land and greater access to capital gave them significant advantages. Lowland farmers could grow their own feed, invest in modern equipment, and take advantage of economies of scale. By the end of the decade, upland farmers faced a declining competitive position in egg production.

What allowed cutover farming to survive and expand during the 1930s was not an improved competitive position, but rather the near total collapse of farm markets. During the 1930s egg prices in Washington averaged only 72 percent of those of the 1920s, and butterfat prices averaged only 52 percent of the earlier period. New settlement on the cutover land during the thirties was not commercial settlement at all. For the first time since the 1850s, subsistence farming became widespread in western Washington. Between 1930 and 1940 the number of self-sufficing farms west of the Cascades increased from 2,339 to 21,869 and formed the single largest category of farms in the state. Self-sufficing was a census category, however, not an economic reality. In practice, subsistence was synonymous with poverty. Most of these farms neither produced adequate food nor provided adequate shelter for their owners.

This collapse of commercial farming on the uplands was the culmination of a long trend on the cutover lands. Few farms had ever yielded adequate incomes. Earnings were low before World War I; they averaged $386 in 1915, improved during the war, but then declined to $414 in 1921. The average earnings for 1921, however, actually disguised the bleakness of the situation after the war. A comparison of forty-seven farms where the operator had retained ownership between 1915 and 1921 revealed that average net earnings declined from $395 in 1915 to $290 in 1921. In 1921, 20 percent of the one hundred fifty cutover farms surveyed in one sample operated at a loss.

By 1939, according to a study conducted by the agricultural experiment station at Pullman, only the largest (average size of 131 acres) and most atypical cutover farms, with mean earnings of $819, came close to the $901 considered necessary for a comfortable rural standard of living. Other cutover farms, the vast majority, came nowhere near this figure. The abandoned farms resettled during the thirties often remained undeveloped and produced an average cash income of $75 a year. In order to survive, most stump farmers had to work off the farm. The proportion of such farmers in the cutover counties of western Washington varied between 40 and 60 percent. Nonfarm work was not casual labor; it ranged from an average of 129 days a year in isolated San Juan County to a high of 203 in Jefferson County. According to researchers at the agricultural experiment station at Pullman, most cutover farmers in 1938 and 1939 earned more by working off the farm than they did by working on it. During virtually every period of settlement between 1900 and 1940, therefore, the logged-off lands produced relatively little income, and most owners hovered near poverty. To study only income, however, distorts the picture.

The settler's real opportunity for security lay not in what he produced but rather in rising land values. In isolated rural regions, unimproved logged-off land prices remained low (between $5 and $25 an acre) throughout the period, but near the coastal cities they averaged nearly $100 an acre just prior to World War I. Such land, bought for under $20 an acre before 1903 and then improved and cultivated, was worth an average of $227 between 1910 and 1915. If a cutover farmer had been lucky or farsighted enough to acquire land near an urban area while prices remained low, he could reap a profit. Between 1915 and 1921, gains from rising land values represented, on paper, an income far larger than what cutover farmers received for their crops. Economists calculating the return at 7 percent had cutover farmers gaining $809 annually by 1921. Such gains theoretically compensated somewhat for the decline in incomes that increasingly forced settlers to work off the farm, but, unless translated into cash by mortgage or sale, they did little to improve living conditions. Furthermore, these gains largely benefited older settlers who bought land when it was still cheap; the outcome for later settlers who paid higher prices is not so clear. In any case, after 1925 these gains disappeared, for real estate values in the rural cutover regions dropped steadily for fifteen years. In no county west of the Cascades was the average value of an acre of farmland as high in 1940 as it had been in 1925. Despite investments by farmers of time, money, and labor, their lands did not appreciate. As the cutover lands declined in value, the last financial rationale for cutover land settlement disappeared.

The failure of settlers to achieve either an adequate livelihood or financial security is only a partial measure of the social price paid for settling the cutover lands. Boosters of settlement had admitted during their agitation for government aid that cutover farmers sometimes paid a high price for settling logged-off lands. George Long, for example, had conceded that "isolation from markets, lack of roads, lack of neighbors and lack of school facilities" often made farming logged-off lands a life of "dreary existence . . . without any practical rewards." Years of hard and lonely labor without financial gain, families living in isolation and near poverty, and children growing up with an inadequate education represented not only individual failures, but also a larger social failure. Such a failure is, however, statistically unmeasurable. Before 1930 the individual farmers and their families paid the price themselves. Only in the 1930s, with New Deal relief measures, did society compensate, in part, for the failure of the farms and assign a dollar value to suffering.

During the 1930s public relief provided a substantial portion of the income of the people on the logged-off lands. Of the cutover farmers surveyed by the personnel of the agricultural experiment stations in 1938 and 1939, 35 percent had received either direct aid or work relief. A much higher proportion of those families starting their farms during the 1930s (54 percent), however, were on relief at some time during the survey period. A similar survey of drought migrants revealed that approximately 50 percent had received public assistance after arriving in the state. Even with relief, most farm families lacked adequate diets, and they often lived in houses that were little more than shacks. Many families found their farms produced little but tragedy.

The social cost of these farms went well beyond the relief payments and personal suffering. Because of the scattered nature of much cutover land settlement, the price of providing essential public services, such as roads and schools, was often far higher than in more prosperous regions. For example, in one case the cost of educating grade-school children from isolated cutover farms was three times greater than the expense of educating children elsewhere in the county.

The poor did not, however, suffer alone. The land suffered along with these settlers. Ultimately, the social cost of settlement cannot be separated from the environmental cost. Farmers began to damage the land as soon as they started to clear their farms. Fires set to remove debris burned at temperatures as high as 1,814°F and consumed approximately twenty-five tons of organic material an acre, 89 percent of the forest duff layer. These slash fires fed on abundant logging debris and burned much hotter than fires in virgin or second-growth forests where only foliage, dead trees, and broken limbs provided fuel. These were a new and immensely more destructive kind of forest fire.

The burning of slash destroyed soil texture and water retention along with logging debris. It did not, however, eliminate either stumps or native vegetation. Most farming depends on the eradication of native plants from fields and pastures, but cutover farmers found this to be impossible. Because of the stumps and roots remaining even after the logging slash had been burned, settlers could not use the plow effectively to destroy the native plants that quickly returned. This problem was most critical in dairying where the native plants that invaded burned areas could not support cows. Some experts recommended that farmers immediately seed potential pasture land with a timothy clover mixture after the slash had been burned. On sections of the uplands, however, the water retention of the soils was so poor that the domesticated grasses were dead by summer. And elsewhere, even when the plants survived, farmers found that the pastures could not maintain a dairy herd the year around. Most of the grasses recommended for the uplands had relatively short life-spans, and all of them suffered under heavy grazing. Within a very few years unpalatable native plants reinvaded the fields. When this happened, the experts recommended that farmers pull up the stumps, plow the land, and reseed. But for most settlers this course remained financially impossible. Out of necessity they resorted to a type of land clearing similar to the slash-and-burn techniques of the tropics. In the tropics, however, fields were abandoned to the forest after a few years of farming, but in western Washington, farmers continued burning for years at regular intervals to kill the invading vegetation. By burning, farmers only changed the normal ecological succession of the area into a relentless reinvasion of bracken fern. Bracken, with its dense underground network of rhizomes and the death of its top growth in the late summer (before fall burnings), survived the fires and spread as other plants were eliminated. The more often burning occurred, the higher the proportion of bracken in the fields. Since bracken was poor feed after its first growth, this meant fewer and fewer animals could be grazed each successive year. Repeated burning ultimately not only destroyed the ecological basis of the farmer's livelihood, but also blocked natural reforestation after he abandoned his farm. Conifer seedlings could not establish themselves among dense patches of bracken.

If partial clearing, followed by burning, disrupted and degraded the natural succession of plant species, full removal of stumps on the uplands and plowing of pastures brought other dangers. When plowed or overgrazed, steeper uplands tended to erode, and under the winter rains their meager topsoil washed down the slopes toward Puget Sound. A National Resources Board survey in the 1930s found moderate erosion (25 percent to 75 percent of the surface soil removed, infrequent gullies) over much of the cutover region in the western counties. Forest trees returning to the degraded landscape of the cutover land were not commercially valuable fir, the usual natural invader of clear land in the forests of the Pacific Northwest, but rather alder. Alder, the prime deciduous invader of severely disturbed land, found its niche in the gullies and uneven surfaces the farmer left behind. It succeeded where the farmer had failed. With the abandonment of the stump farms, the amount of alder in cutover areas such as Island, Kitsap, and San Juan counties, where logging had largely ceased, increased from 11 million to 408 million board feet. Farming had not only failed, it had helped to ruin the land for commercial logging.

Recognition of this dual social and environmental disaster on the logged-off lands first emerged during the 1930s. The Dust Bowl had done the most to sharpen a national awareness of the relationship between poor land and poor men and between ecological disaster and social disaster, but the insight was eventually applied to the logged-off lands as well. In a series of independent studies, the National Resources Board, the Washington agricultural experiment station, the Resettlement Administration, and the Washington State Planning Commission recommended detailed surveys to locate land suitable for agriculture and proposed reforestation of all remaining lands. They also suggested that the people on the worst lands be resettled and that rural regions be zoned to prevent further settlement and misuse of the cutover areas.

In practice, however, these agencies accomplished little. The Resettlement Administration, along with the Federal Emergency Relief Administration and the Soil Conservation Service, had the authority to purchase marginal lands and to help the farmers on that land relocate. Yet the agency often did little but issue press releases. A Resettlement Administration office bulletin declared that "human tragedy like a wheeling vulture, followed closely the devastation of the forest" and promised to help "stranded" settlers off the land, but the agency did not buy a single acre of marginal land in the Pacific Northwest, and it resettled only 173 farm families in western Washington. Attempts to prevent people from settling marginal cutover lands fared little better. In 1936 the Washington State Planning Council made land classification one of its leading priorities and recommended rural zoning, but the state legislature only created county planning commissions that had little real power.

Those people already on the cutover lands received little assistance. Cutover farms simply were not worth enough to qualify as collateral for loans provided by the Farm Credit Administration. Only a small number of families on the best logged-off lands obtained loans through the Rural Rehabilitation Division of the Farm Security Administration. Not until 1941, when a pilot project was begun in Lewis County, did a concerted and coordinated attempt to deal with the problems of the logged-off lands get under way. This was too late. War industries had begun to draw people into the cities, and the logged-over regions were emptying. The decline in the number of farms began in some western counties after 1935; for other regions the decline set in during the war. By the late 1940s the trend was clear. In 1950 the number of farms was down 16 percent from 1940, and many other farms served only as homes for suburban commuters.

For all its progressive concerns, the back-to-the-land movement was reactionary in its outlook and destructive in its application. It was designed in part to salvage the city for the middle class. Urban discontent might be diffused by removing the poor to the countryside where they would provide food, exports, and markets for the urban economy. Middle-class city dwellers encouraged settlement on the logged-off lands, although they themselves rarely settled on farms. They were hoping to see workers and immigrants transformed into an amalgam of the rural virtue they still believed in and the urban entrepreneurship they fervently practiced. As a result, men and women, usually without any agricultural experience, moved onto stumplands where infertile soils were highly vulnerable to degradation. They came with much encouragement, but without capital and without aid. On the logged-off lands social and environmental disaster mingled and became one. Ultimately, settlers found themselves trapped in a vicious economic and ecological circle that scarred them and their land.

On the logged-off lands a whole series of assumptions was proven wrong. The belief that growth was good for its own sake; that agriculture was the highest use to which land could be put; that merely living on the land, any land, and working it brought prosperity, virtue, and serenity; that, given hard work, almost any land had some kind of agricultural potential—all these cherished beliefs resulted only in personal suffering and environmental damage. There was finally, it seemed, a price to be paid for the human arrogance involved in thinking nature was infinitely malleable. But the cost, in this instance, fell on those who could bear it the least—the poor, the migrants, the immigrants, and the unemployed—and not on those who had urged settlement.

BIBLIOGRPAHICAL NOTE

The basic sources for this paper include *Little Logged-off Lands,* a journal published to encourage settlement on the logged-over lands of Washington and Oregon, and the published *Proceedings of the Washington Logged-off Land Association* (Seattle, 1909). Also useful were articles appearing in the trade journals of the region: *Pacific Northwest Commerce, Pacific Lumber Trade Journal,* the *Timberman,* and the *West Coast Lumberman.* A series of publications by the state of Washington were also important, particularly Secretary of State, *Vacant Logged-off Lands of the State of Washington* (Olympia, 1917), and a series of bulletins published by the Washington Agricultural Experiment Station (numbers 28, 93, 370, 380, 399, 424, and 426). Of the various United States government publications, the U.S. Department of Agriculture, *Department Bulletin 1236* and *Farmer's Bulletin 462* are the most significant.

There are two excellent theses written while settlement was in progress: Campbell Murphy, "Farmers on Cutover Timber Lands in Western Washington State," M.A. thesis (University of Washington, 1943) and Glenn Hoover, "Rural Settlement in Western Washington," M.A. thesis (University of Washington, 1922). For understanding environmental problems on cutover lands, see Leo Isaac et al., "Plant Succession on Cutover, Burned and Grazed Douglas Fir Areas," U.S. Department of Agriculture, *Pacific Northwest Research Note 26* (Portland, Oreg., March 1938) and Douglas Ingram, "Vegetative Changes and Grazing Use on Douglas Fir Cutover Land," *Journal of Agricultural Research*, Vol. 42 (September 1931).

Bertha Knight Landes:
The Woman Who Was Mayor

Doris H. Pieroth

With her election as mayor of Seattle in 1926, during a decade that promised more for women in politics than it delivered, Bertha Knight Landes became the first woman mayor of a major city in the United States. She has been largely ignored by historians or depicted as a prohibitionist killjoy, a figure of ridicule whose term in office can be dismissed simply as "two turbulent years of 'petticoat rule.'" This essay is a look past the caricature to the woman whom Seattle voters trusted enough, and with whom they were sufficiently comfortable, to elect to public office.

She belongs to the progressive tradition, that seeming paradox of altruism and pragmatism that, for all the diversity of its reform efforts, was intent on the moral regeneration of a society becoming increasingly urban, industrial, and multicultural. She was thirty-two years old in 1900—a nineteenth-century woman who, in her twentieth-century career, espoused moral uplift, public decency, and effective civic management in such areas of urban life as health, safety, and wholesome recreation. She championed the city manager form of government and the municipal ownership of utilities. Her public career came during the life of the Eighteenth Amendment, and, for good or ill, her reputation became inextricably tied to enforcement of the prohibition laws. She was dedicated to duty and service, guided by science and reason, a practical, law-abiding, and moralistic woman who operated under an internal restraint that was reinforced by the contemporary culture.

Her political career began in 1922. She and Mrs. Kathryn Miracle

Originally published in *Pacific Northwest Quarterly,* July 1984.

broke the all-male barrier to city government that spring with their election to the Seattle City Council, Mrs. Landes by the unprecedented plurality of 22,000 votes. She came to office as a "nonpolitician," backed primarily by women's organizations and an informal network of establishment groups and individuals. Although she grew as a politician and became more politically astute, she failed to strengthen or broaden her power base and to fashion a strong political organization of her own. She appears to have lacked one thing necessary for her to have made a truly productive and lasting contribution to municipal reform: personal political ambition. Or, if she possessed it, she suppressed it. By the time she glimpsed some vision of her political possibilities, the door had closed on them and she was denied reelection as mayor.

She brought to the role of public servant fifty-three years of previous experience as daughter, sister, student, wife, pioneer, mother, community leader, and clubwoman. She was born Bertha Ethel Knight on October 19, 1868, in Ware, Massachusetts, the daughter of Charles Sanford Knight and Cordelia Cutter Knight. She was the youngest of nine children, the sister of two boys and six girls. On her father's side there was said to be "a dash of French Huguenot," which showed itself "in the olive complexion, dark hair, and big black eyes of his children." In 1926 the New York *Times* described Bertha as "below medium height, with olive skin and drab brown hair," noting that "the keen brightness of her eyes is her most arresting feature."

Although both the Knights and the Cutters could trace forebears to early Massachusetts Bay, there is little to suggest great family wealth. Her father worked as a painter in the village of Ware after his discharge from the Union Army; he moved the family twenty miles east to Worcester and entered the real estate business when Bertha was five years old.

Worcester, an industrial center with a population of 41,000 in 1870, had been, before the war, a center of militant resistance to the Fugitive Slave Law. It was also an important nineteenth-century educational center, the home of Worcester Polytechnic Institute, Holy Cross College, a state normal school, and Clark University.

Bertha Knight grew up in that city, in a family later described as providing "the best of home influences, a father and mother of old American stock, of that sterling uprightness, and devotion to duty, that 'plain living and high thinking' that has produced so many of our best in literature, arts and statesmanship." While the Knight children "were rigidly taught to abide by the law," the family was evidently close, secure, and loving. Bertha thought her mother the most wonderful woman she had ever known; she especially admired her devotion to the nine children and to the care of her husband, whose Civil War wounds had left him an invalid by the time Bertha turned eight.

Indications of a close family with a strong sense of family obligation are apparent in Bertha's years as a young adult. She had graduated from Classical High School in Worcester and was living at home in August 1887, when her sister Jessie married David Starr Jordan, who was then the president of Indiana University. In the fall of 1888, just shy of her twentieth birthday, Bertha went to Bloomington to live with the Jordans and to enroll as a student at the university. She was there that October, undoubtedly providing help and support when Jessie's first child was born into a household that also included Jordan's two children by his first wife.

Following her graduation from Indiana in 1891, Bertha returned to Worcester to live with her mother and to teach until her own marriage three years later. In Bloomington she had met and become engaged to Henry Landes, a geology student from Carroll, Indiana, who had gone on to Harvard for a master's degree.

Bertha seems to have chafed somewhat in the role of single daughter under her mother's roof and she perhaps anticipated difficulty breaking away. In a long and eloquent letter written in the last summer of their long engagement, her fiancé reacted to the latest word from her:

I am so glad that you find your life happier than you had expected. It takes a load off me when I find you cheerful. . . . You must not be blue dearie, it don't pay. Your letter was not blue by any means—but very cheerful. I am very sorry that mother is ill, and that you have to work so hard. Please do not do too much, but keep as strong as you can. . . . I am very much surprise[d] at the turn Charlie [her brother?] and May have taken. I should think that if they came over they would . . . stay there permanently. It certainly would be a nice thing all around. And how easily it will be for you to leave home when you can. It will very [e]ffectively settle your dilemma. Now if other things would only shape themselves in such good fashion we might get married before many months after all. . . . I know but little more than I did a week ago. You must expect developments very slowly.

The "other things" included his finding a job at the end of that summer, which he had spent with a United States Geological Survey team. Despite the precarious state of the nation's economy in 1893, he did secure employment that fall, classifying and arranging the geological collection for the New Jersey State Museum. They were married on January 2, 1894, and made their first home in Trenton.

At Indiana, Bertha Knight and Henry Landes had attended a university that was experiencing an intellectual renaissance and enduring political and economic stress. Its student body of fewer than three hundred included between thirty and forty women. Bloomington, population thirty-five hundred, "was still a backwoods courthouse town," with flickering electric lights and muddy streets; it had no registered saloon, but it boasted twelve churches. Founded in 1820, Indiana University had known only clergymen as presidents prior to the appointment in 1885 of the biologist David Starr Jordan, who helped the school redefine its mission within the context of the humanities and the social and physical sciences. There was extensive curriculum revision, and emphasis on physical science led Henry to a career in geology, while Bertha studied for her degree in the new Department of History and Political Science, whose young chairman, influenced by the Johns Hopkins seminar, stressed American history and politics.

David Starr Jordan touched the lives of thousands of students, and his influence on Bertha and Henry Landes is readily apparent. Although a "Darwinian extrovert among Hoosier fundamentalists" at Indiana, the liberal scientist was still somewhat old-fashioned and strongly opposed to drinking. His sister-in-law was seventeen years his junior, and in her years as a student, living for a time in his home, she had ample opportunity to be exposed to his ideas and style, his commitment to science and reason, and his politics. They corresponded after the Jordans had moved to California, where he served as the first president of Stanford, and she traveled occasionally to the Bay Area during her years in public office. He consoled her following her defeat in 1928, telling her he was not surprised at the election's outcome and asking with Thoreau, "When were the good and true ever in the majority?"

It is quite likely that conversation at the Jordan dinner table in Bloomington included politics, both civic and academic. The university was always faced with appropriations struggles and battles with legislators who at one time wanted "not only to cut the university's . . . funds but even to close the institution." Bertha Landes's experience on a campus pressed politically and financially, and whose administration she had observed from a unique vantage point, came with her to the role of faculty wife the year after her marriage. Henry Landes, on Jordan's recommendation, was appointed professor of geology at the University of Washington, and the Landeses arrived in Seattle in the fall of 1895. Newly occupying its present campus, the school was on the threshold of growth and improvement. Its immediate future was stormy, however; a Populist legislature, elected in the sweep of 1896, cut the university's requested appropriation from $90,000 to $78,000, and faculty salaries were among the nation's lowest. During the Landeses' first seven years, the university saw a succession of four presidents. A fifth, Thomas Kane, served until January 1914, when he was replaced by an acting president—Henry Landes.

The Landeses rightly qualify as Seattle pioneers; the university's new location was on a heavily wooded site well beyond the city, and they were among those university people who chose to live near the new campus and become active participants in the life of the community. They built their home at the pivotal intersection of Brooklyn Avenue and Northeast 45th Street; it was a large, two-story frame house with a hospitable and inviting front porch.

The Congregational Church, long the only church in the district, was a center of community activity; geared intellectually to serve university families, it became a focal point for the Landeses, who had joined the fledgling congregation early on their arrival. By 1899, Henry had become its treasurer and a trustee, and Bertha was to serve two terms as president of its women's league—in 1903 and again in 1918. Dean Frederick Padelford later described their community at the time of his own arrival:

In 1901 the University District was distinctly a town in the making—a few unpaved streets, wooden sidewalks, cottage homes, bits of lawn on which the cows from the Green Lake farms were daily trespassers, a cluster of stores at the corners, and a little community church, bare and graceless as frontier churches are wont to be. But it was a warm-hearted and strictly democratic community, almost entirely made up of people in their twenties and thirties, all of them from somewhere else, and all ambitious and confident of achievement. The atmosphere was electric, charged with youth and energy. The environment, both physical and social, was flexible, and with singular unanimity the members of the community went about the task of molding it into something fine and worthy.

In such an environment and among such people, the Landeses reared their family. Bertha bore three children; the first, a daughter, Katherine, was born when her mother was twenty-eight years old. She was a beautiful and talented child, and her death in 1905 at the age of nine from complications following a tonsillectomy can only have been a crushing blow. There were two sons—Roger, who did not survive infancy, and Kenneth, who followed his father's career choice to become professor of geology at the University of Michigan. Two years after Katherine's death, nine-year-old Viola was adopted into the family, whose circle for many years included a blind and aged uncle of Bertha's. She devoted the period prior to World War I to home and family. Her outside activities were related to the church, to schools and P.T.A., to social services such as the Red Cross, and to women's clubs.

During the year of the acting presidency, the Landeses entertained students and faculty on frequent occasions, giving the first alumni homecoming reception, which was attended by more than four hundred people. Bertha Landes's home was once again that of a university president awash in politics, and in the spring of 1914 there was speculation that Landes would be named to the presidency permanently. The speculation ended with the appointment of Henry Suzzallo.

For any woman carving a career, Henry Landes would have been an exceptional husband; he gave his wife unwavering support. She fully appreciated this and said at one time that he "is as interested in having me live a full, rich life as he is in having one for himself." He understood and acknowledged the contributions of women, and as dean of the College of Science at the university, he provided a source of counsel and support for women on the faculty. Both the nursing and home economics departments considered him one of their best friends. He was described by a long-time friend as "always happy, gallant and gay," and a student who ran afoul of the faculty and was dealt with by Landes said that he was "a man of inflexible honor and exalted ideals. . . . Moreover, he possesses infinite tact, a rare sense of justice, and a rarer sense of humor."

It was widely speculated during Bertha's campaign in 1922 that *he* would be the councilman in truth, and letters to the editor asked such things as, will she "do as Henry tells her—if elected?" There is no evidence that he controlled that council seat, although he obviously was her staunch ally and a chief adviser. She said that he was "a tower of strength in times of stress and made many sacrifices without complaint that I might give my time and strength to my civic service." One such sacrifice by the former Indiana farm boy could have been the postelection move from their home (then at 4511 18th Avenue N.E.) to an apartment in the nearby Wilsonian Hotel, a move that lightened her domestic duties, some of which she continued to carry even while mayor.

Both Landeses saw her career as duty and service rather than opportunity for fulfillment of her own ambition, and they both justified her political activities within the context of woman's proper place. In 1926, Henry Landes found nothing "revolutionary" about his wife's election as mayor, saying, "It's simply the natural enlargement of her sphere. Keeping house and raising a family are woman's logical tasks, and, in principle, there's no difference between running one home and a hundred thousand." The city as simply a larger home was a theme of many of her speeches and public comments; one of the nationwide lecture tours that she made was called "Adventures in Municipal Housekeeping." Throughout her public career she held to the old values, and she sought to reconcile woman's "proper place" with her newly emergent opportunities in a wider sphere.

In 1921 Mrs. Landes was president of the Seattle Federation of Women's Clubs; she was involved in university community affairs, active in campus circles as a faculty wife, and a leader in the University Congregational Church. The quintessential clubwoman, she had honed her skills in public speaking and parliamentary procedure during years of active leadership in such clubs as the Woman's Century Club and the Women's University Club. As federation president, she was a driving force in planning and directing the highly successful week-long Women's Educational Exhibit for Washington Manufacturers. This exhibit of Washington State products was staffed by more than a thousand clubwomen who had become enthusiastic supporters of local industries at a time when the city and the region were in the throes of economic depression and severe unemployment. The business community was impressed with the women's efforts in behalf of the state's economy, and the Seattle Chamber of Commerce president praised Mrs. Landes for her role, telling her that he was "particularly impressed with the character of the interviews you have given out, showing as they do that you have caught the great vision of civic usefulness and responsibility."

That year, Mayor Hugh Caldwell created a five-member commission on unemployment to deal with the city's problem, and he appointed one woman—Bertha Landes. Another member of that commission urged her to run for the city council. She had successfully bridged the gap between woman's traditional world of home, church, and club and the world of business and civic service; she was now a strong, serious, and worthy candidate for public office.

She couched her 1922 council campaign in perfectly acceptable terms for a woman. While asserting that the time had come for women to be represented in governing bodies, she stated clearly that woman's first duty was to home and family. Many of her campaign statements seemed aimed at reconciling those two points, and they frequently smacked of apology for a candidacy justified as duty and service and for a candidate who disavowed any political ambition. As she filed for office she said, "It is not only the right, but the privilege and duty, of women to take part in the administration of public affairs." She stressed time and again the right of 40 percent of the voters to representation on the council and said that if elected she would "support the moral and welfare projects in which women are primarily interested."

During that campaign, noting the large number of women candidates in the country, she said, "This woman's movement is the logical outcome of two things: 1. Suffrage [and] 2. Commercialization of many of the activities which formerly centered in the home, such as the laundry work, baking, sewing and so forth." She also thought, though, that women might not be so anxious to demand the right to representation, which suffrage gave them, if men had "been able to interpret and express women's viewpoint on matters relating to the home, the welfare of women and children and the moral issues." The viewpoints of both men and women, she believed, were "as necessary for a well-balanced theory of city government as for a well-managed house. Home standards should be city standards, and this man has not realized." Since technology had ended much household drudgery, women had more time for outside activities, and "if [a woman] is not to be a parasite, something abhorrent to her nature, she must turn her energies to public service of some kind." While Mrs. Landes emphasized that woman's task is "to make the home and rear the future citizens," she urged civic involvement for the woman "who has reared her family and has . . . a trained intelligence to offer to the service of her country . . . and who can render it without detriment to home or family interest."

That first campaign and its organization were considered "absolutely unique in the political annals of the city." It was run by a group of five women—Mrs. Landes and four staunch backers from among the city's clubwomen, who were described as "typical Seattle housewives." One of them, Mrs. R. F. Weeks, said, "We wanted political experience; we were all amateurs." She stressed that they had run a low-budget operation in order to avoid "slush funds [which] mean either paid campaign workers or promised jobs"; they wanted Bertha Landes to enter office with "clean hands," beholden to no faction.

On May 2, 1922, the day of the general election, the candidate issued one final statement:

Our campaign is over. It has been strictly a women's campaign to elect a woman to the city council without entangling alliances, to represent woman's thought and viewpoint. . . . Our idea was to serve the best interests of the city; not to further the political ambitions of any one woman.

From her seat on the council license committee, Mrs. Landes spearheaded the move for an ordinance that provided for the tighter regulation of cabarets and dance halls. In June 1924, she was elected council president and became acting mayor when Mayor Edwin J. ("Doc") Brown was in New York attending the Democratic National Convention. She caused a furor and received attention in the national press when she fired Brown's police chief, William Severyns, for failing to rid his department of corruption, which he himself had widely publicized, and for his insubordination in an exchange of letters with her. She won reelection to the council in 1925 by a margin well below her phenomenal showing of 1922, but as municipal election time approached the following year, her name cropped up as a potential mayoral candidate.

She was extremely reluctant to run for mayor and saw herself as a candidate only if none other emerged with a chance of defeating Doc Brown. It was not until the last day of filing, during which she changed her mind several times, that she made her final decision. She was heavily influenced by leaders in women's organizations that had been the backbone of her council campaigns and by pressure from supporters of an initiative—also on the ballot—to establish city manager government in Seattle. In favor of the city manager plan and optimistic about its passage, she perhaps felt less diffident about entering the race because of the likelihood of the mayor's office being superseded.

Her mayoral campaign occurred against the backdrop of the celebrated "Rum Trial" of the Seattle policeman-turned-bootlegger Roy Olmstead, a coincidence that kept the spotlight on Mrs. Landes's concern for morality and law enforcement. The trial tended to substantiate links between Brown and bootleg interests and to corroborate assertions she had made during the Severyns firing two years earlier. She was elected on March 9, by a margin of just under six thousand votes in what was then a record voter turnout.

As mayor she sought strict law enforcement, sound management for the municipal electric utility (City Light), a firmer financial base for the troubled street railway department, improved traffic safety, and quality appointments based on merit. She could and did take pride in such accomplishments as enhanced and expanded recreational programs in the park department and the return to profitable operations for the streetcar system. Although she had assured the Municipal League that as mayor she would "attend to other duties than 'greeting actresses at incoming trains,'" Mrs. Landes was gracious in her ceremonial tasks; notable among them was welcoming to Seattle both Charles A. Lindbergh, recently returned from his Atlantic flight, and Queen Marie of Rumania, on her widely heralded tour of the United States.

In 1928, the once reluctant candidate was being touted in some quarters as a potential governor, but she wanted to be reelected mayor. A two-year term was, according to the incumbent, "not long enough to work out and put in effect a constructive program." She told reporters, "Frankly, I like being mayor. I haven't seen any reason, since taking the office, why a woman can't fill it as well as a man." Another thing that appealed to her as a woman was a "hope to show that a woman could not only get an office, but could 'make good' and win indorsement [*sic*] of voters for a second term."

She began her reelection campaign armed with a good record in office and the same type of support she had commanded since 1922. But, "within the space of a short election campaign, the incumbent mayor went from a betting odds' favorite . . . to resounding defeat." She lost to Frank Edwards, a man completely unknown politically and without any record of public service or community involvement. The conventional explanation for her ouster has been that by pressuring the police department into making liquor raids she lost valuable support and that by 1928 "Seattle was tiring of reform and of Mrs. Landes."

Although enforcement of prohibition was without doubt a factor in the election, it was not the whole story. She herself attributed her defeat to a combination of "a nine months' campaign on the part of my opponent, excessive expenditure of funds, and sex prejudice."

Indeed, the Edwards campaign was of unprecedented length and cost; it had started the preceding summer and utilized hundreds of paid precinct workers, citywide billboards, and film footage of the candidate at City Light projects on the Skagit River. Edwards's reported expenditures failed to include much of that, prompting the prosecuting attorney to consider an investigation of his funds. However, such a probe could be initiated only by the defeated candidate, and Bertha Landes never did request an investigation.

Lacking the facts, which might thus have been uncovered, speculation about the source of Edwards's money centers on those favoring a more open city with less stringent law enforcement and on private power interests. Both groups had long-standing cause to oppose Mayor Landes.

A backer of municipal ownership of utilities throughout her career in public office, the mayor sided with J. D. Ross, the popular and increasingly powerful head of City Light, in his plans for developing the power potential of the upper Skagit River. Although overshadowed by her sensational dismissal of the police chief, two other actions Mrs. Landes took as acting mayor in 1924 may have earned her the opposition of private power. One was the signing of a new contract for Ross, which had been held in abeyance by Mayor Brown for six months, and the other was proclaiming June 18 as Power Day, in support of the signature drive to gain ballot qualification for the Bone bill, an initiative that would authorize expanded opportunities for public utilities.

The financial woes of Seattle's street railway system, the city's $15 million white elephant inherited from Mayor Ole Hanson's glory year of 1919, brought Mrs. Landes face to face with the firm that had sold the city the system—Stone and Webster, parent company of Puget Sound Power and Light. The refusal of banks in the Seattle Clearing House Association to honor railway warrants in December of 1927 forced the mayor to go beyond measures that cut operating expenses and to negotiate refinancing of the system. The success of this depended on state enabling legislation, and while making the city's case before the legislature, "she clashed with private power company officials over the bill's contents."

Activities of the Civil Service League also contributed to her ouster from office. That organization of municipal employees actually sought out Edwards and encouraged him to run, and "firemen and policemen openly campaigned for him while on duty." The mayor had alienated many streetcar men by making deep cutbacks in personnel in order to assure the system's solvency.

Sex prejudice, as Mrs. Landes put it, looms as no small factor in her defeat. In her study of the 1928 election, Florence Deacon stresses the pervasiveness of the issue and sees it as both an overt and a subtle factor. She characterized the successful Landes campaign of 1926 as a "non-threatening" one in which the candidate "did not step out of the traditional woman's role: she was simply to be a municipal housekeeper." In contrast, for the reelection race, the mayor "was too busy running the city to present an adequate campaign. She didn't take time to play up the role of 'little woman' and housewifely mother." Deacon concludes that the voters would not accept Mrs. Landes in other than the traditional role. Her opponent stressed his experience as a business*man* and much of his literature promoted "Frank Edwards, the *man* you would be proud to call mayor." The issue of a woman mayor was a constant theme in the press, pro-Landes papers decrying the fact that the only criticism of the incumbent was that she was a woman. It was implied at every turn that a city of Seattle's stature really needed a man for mayor. The Portland *Oregonian* chided the city for defeating a mayor considered the superior of most of her predecessors, saying,

We suspect . . . that Mrs. Landes was defeated solely because Seattle wishes to be known as a he-man's town. . . . [I]t wants a mayor's office where one can put one's feet on the desk. . . . [The commercial club] wants a mayor whose presence does not call also for letting everyone's wife in to the festivities. . . . [I]t is the fashion for cities to personify their dignity and importance through the male sex. Yet out here in the far west where men are reputed to be men a proud and hustling city was mayored by a woman. Many a bearded cheek in Seattle has blushed in the past two years over this imagined shame upon a he-man's town.

If the public woman was beset by the he-man factor, the private woman seemed beset by an inner restraint that kept her from using her political power effectively and to her own advantage. Nonetheless, Bertha Landes held strong convictions about the role of government and the place of women in relation to government, and she was firm in her commitment to progressive measures.

The mayor's progressivism suggests the influence of David Starr Jordan, whose abiding interest in politics comprised a strong opposition to the spoils system and an ongoing concern for civil service reform. Jordan and Theodore Roosevelt, who met when Roosevelt spoke on the Indiana campus in 1888, shared political convictions, and the views of the two men informed those of Bertha Landes. Her appointment policy as mayor was one Jordan could approve, one intended, in Roosevelt's words, "to take politics out of politics." A forgotten element in her clash with Doc Brown in 1924 was his alleged abuse of civil service regulations; after her brief tenure as acting mayor she continued to serve on the council's efficiency committee, which conducted a wide-ranging investigation of the Civil Service Commission.

Mrs. Landes preserved a reprint of the text of a speech Roosevelt gave in 1893, and she quoted from it to advise the 1927 graduating class of Yakima High School to become involved in civic affairs. In choosing to avoid politics, she warned, "You are simply saying that you are unfit to live in a free community." That particular Roosevelt speech could almost have served as her political credo:

The first duty of an American citizen is that he shall work in politics. . . . [He should remain in political life] only as long as he can stay in it on his own terms, without sacrifice of his own principles. . . . [W]hen a public servant has definitely made up his mind that he will pay no heed to his own future, but will do what he honestly deems best for the community, without regard to how his actions may affect his prospects, not only does he become infinitely more useful as a public servant, but he has a far better time. He is freed from the harassing care which is inevitably the portion of him who is trying to shape his sails to catch every gust of the wind of political favor.

She presented her views on municipal government, home, and womanhood in a speech prepared for delivery shortly after her election as mayor. Echoing Frederic C. Howe, she noted that the city "is said to be the hope of Democracy" and deplored people's reluctance to become involved politically: "The majority of our people desire civic decency and public morality but they don't desire them sufficiently to be willing to sacrifice very much of their time, strength or money to procure them." She reminded her listeners that the family is the smallest unit of government, that "government centers around the home," and that "the underlying principle [of government] is the satisfaction of all the needs of the people." For her, the most important function of government "is creating the proper atmosphere, mental, moral and physical, for the rearing of children and the activities of adult life. The city is really only a larger household or family with its problems increased many fold through its diversified interests and the cosmopolitan nature of its members." The city must "supervise and regulate commercial amusements within her borders—keep down vice and immorality with a firm hand and . . . control the moral conditions under which her people live." In a personal message for the women in the audience, she said,

Let me tell you . . . that though I am a public official and a so-called politician, that I am first and always a woman . . . that I am a wife and mother but a mother whose children are grown . . . that I yield to no one in my respect for wifehood and motherhood and regard those professions as the very highest ones which any woman can fill. . . . I now want to urge you to assume your personal responsibility for civic betterment. If woman is indifferent and fails to realize her responsibility . . . then is the outlook gloomy and the future uncertain. . . . [Even the mother of small children] must pay some attention to what is going on outside the walls of her home. . . . The woman of mature years who has raised her family certainly has an added responsibility for civic conditions, for which she has not only leisure but a maturity of judgment which should be used for the public good.

Mrs. Landes remained firm in her belief that a woman should have raised her family before seeking office; she preferred also that a woman not be dependent on the job for a living because financial freedom encouraged objectivity and independence. This sounds naïvely idealistic, but though she did not change her basic belief, she did become more practical. She came to see politics as the art of the possible. While she was mayor, she spoke of the "necessity for compromise in small things in the hope of providing for greater ones," and she acknowledged the difficulty of reconciling one's ideals with reality.

She had assumed that her greatest contribution on the city council would be supporting women's traditional health and welfare measures, representing others rather than initiating and leading. Two things thrust her into a leadership role—the need for a dance hall ordinance and conditions within the police department, including the insubordination of the police chief. In the former instance, she had the active and open backing of leading men in the community; in the latter, she took matters in her own hands, while a few men offered advice in the background. The episode of the police chief weighed heavily on her. She later said that she had been given power; she believed in God; she felt like a martyr; and "Oh, I didn't want to do it!" With something akin to a sense of calling, she did what she had to do, feeling somewhat victimized in the process.

When the call came, or pressure was applied, to be a mayoral candidate, she felt no special urge to be mayor but asked herself, "[Am] I the person to help my city realize its possibilities?" Again, potential power was thrust on her; she had not sought it. Once again she answered the call and did her duty. Toward the end of her term as mayor, as she came to relish the opportunities and the power of her office, she said,

Municipal housekeeping means adventure and romance and accomplishment to me. To be in some degree a guiding force in the destiny of a city, to help lay the foundation stones for making it good and great, to aid in advancing the political position of women, to be the person to whom men and women and children look for protection against lawlessness, to spread the political philosophy that the city is only a larger home—I find it richly worth while!

She had come to public life from among Seattle's middle-class clubwomen, but during her time in office she encountered a much broader spectrum of Seattle's women. She came to appreciate women wage earners and their concerns as well as the business and professional women who made up the Seattle Soroptimist Club, of which she was a charter member. Her expanded contacts seem to have made her more understanding of the economic problems of women and perhaps less prone to sit in judgment. In the dance hall ordinance battle of 1922, she softened her stand to some extent after receiving in her home three women who worked in one of the establishments targeted for closure and who came to plead economic necessity. She was reportedly determined to wipe out vice in the city, having been informed "that the same type of women are here today that were here some years ago, when we had a wide open town, and that gambling and all other vices of those days are again in vogue." Yet her visitors "did not make a bad impression. We had a pleasant talk. I got their viewpoint. It was enlightening, but I have nothing to say about it." Two of the women were working to support their children; they could earn $4.00 or $5.00 a night in the dance halls, in contrast to $13.85 a week in a factory or $2.40 for an eight-hour shift in a restaurant. Whatever her reasons, Mrs. Landes did settle for dance hall regulation and supervision rather than closure in the final version of the ordinance.

She remained sympathetic to women's causes after she left office;

the depression underscored the economic plight of women. In 1931 she was the principal speaker for a successful lobbying of the city council that was organized by the Women's Protective Association in opposition to a proposed charter amendment barring married women from city employment. She headed the women's division of the city's Commission for Improved Employment early in the depression; its main project was the operation of three sewing rooms that provided employment for women and clothing for needy children. Mrs. Landes showed concern for the self-esteem of the women in the sewing rooms: she declared that the city, in helping such women "avoid the dole," must make "every effort to provide work and see that work is paid for so that there is no feeling of accepting charity." During her term as president of the American Federation of Soroptimist Clubs, to which she was elected in June of 1930, one of that organization's major concerns was relief for older women, who as a group suffered disproportionately from unemployment.

That she was a prohibitionist is a fact. But it is open to question that she merits the reputation as a "blue-nose" moralist intent on spoiling all the fun of the roaring twenties. During the mayoral race in 1926, in an effort to divert the issue from being solely "whether you want an open town or a blue law one," the Seattle *Star* said, "Bunk! Mrs. Landes isn't a blue law person. She wants only what the vast majority of our citizens want—a fair degree of decency and some dignity in public office."

She never did promise to "entirely eradicate bootlegging and illegal sale of liquor." She did say, however, "that there would be no longer open and flagrant violation of any law—be it the prohibition law or any other law." She fought repeal and thought that many seeking it were "men and women who can afford financially the 'high cost of drinking' . . .[and who wish to] break down the protective law which the 18th Amendment has built around society. . . . apparently in order that they may go their way unhampered and with a less guilty conscience." She herself personified restraint and self-control, and at the heart of her prohibitionism was her contention that "all prohibitive laws have arisen as a result of a lack of personal restraint on the part of individuals and the placing of an over-emphasis on the right to personal liberty."

Although she cannot be classified as a civil libertarian, neither should she be thought a bigot; in the context of her times, on occasion she appears comparatively enlightened, and her activities and statements indicate an objective and rational approach to race relations. She was a member of the board of directors of the city's Soroptimist Club, which took the lead in eliminating the "white only" restriction for membership; she was president of the national organization when all reference to race as a membership qualification was deleted from its constitution. Her reported opposition in 1921 to interracial marriage was based on the ground that "where the two races are so different, the result could mean nothing more than incompatibility." That is a rational note for an era marked by agitation for immigrant exclusion and by virulent racism—a time in which fifty hooded and robed members of the Ku Klux Klan could be seated in a body for Sunday services at Seattle's First Presbyterian Church and be described by the Reverend Mark Matthews as worshiping "reverentially."

Bertha Landes was blessed with a sense of humor, even in regard to liquor. She saved the printed lyrics of a song parody that had been sung to her while she was mayor. Set to the tune of "Maryland, My Maryland," it went:

> You took our booze and took our gin,
>   Mayor Landes, mayor dear!
> And made it hard for us to sin,
>   Mayor Landes, mayor dear!
>
>   When we had Doc and Roy and Bill
>   We felt quite safe to drink our fill;
>   Now hooch there ain't, though we be ill—
> Mayor Landes, mayor dear!
>
> Now, kindly woman that thou art
>   Mayor Landes, mayor dear!
> Please, prithee, show a woman's heart,
>   Mayor Landes, mayor dear!
>
>   Let down the bars, we'll stand in line;
>   Fill once again ou[r] empty stein;
>   We'll vote for you; we like you fine—
> Mayor Landes, mayor dear!

In her ill-fated campaign for reelection, unable to get her opponent to meet her in debate, she staged mock debates with an empty chair. The New York *Times* reported that "she laughs as she conducts these one-sided debates and appears to get as much 'kick' out of them as her hearers, and the audience is usually in an uproar."

She met defeat in 1928 in much the same manner that she had encountered other developments in her life: realistically and without false modesty; stoically but with some humor. The day after the election she told the Rotarians, gathered for their Citizenship Day luncheon, that they were "imposing a severe test upon her to laud voters for 'intelligent citizenship' in view of their decision of the previous day." She took pleasure in the knowledge that she could leave office with the conviction that she had given Seattle a "constructive administration" and that the city was cleaner than it had been for years.

Later, however, she indicated that she had been abandoned by her supporters. Although she avowed no regrets, there is disappointment in her words:

The people who had put a woman into office to house clean for them "rested upon the comfortable assurance that all was going well and they could rest upon their oars." . . . So . . . they left their woman mayor to the wolves . . . an unguarded sheep. . . . Then the wolves came down *en masse* and, to all practical purposes, devoured her. They sent her back, providentially, to private life. She had worked day and night with very few play days for two years. . . . She was not exactly weary in well doing, for she fought long and hard to win, but at the same time she took her defeat with a certain sense of relief and without bitterness or deep regret.

Reflecting on her performance in office, she once said, "I tried to uphold the ideals of womanhood." For her, that meant exhibiting strength, intelligence, and courage, and taking the slings and arrows stoically. Her formula for political success for women included "courage without tears . . . personal charm . . . poise . . . endless physical energy . . . a sense of humor . . . but most of all—no tears." An oversensitive woman would "be hurt by the many unpleasant things people do and say. And before she knows it she [would] be in tears, which would bring disgrace on womankind!"

She had wanted full equality in name and in truth, once saying she was a council*man*,

not a council woman, please note. And I threaten to shoot on sight, without benefit of clergy, anyone calling me the mayoress instead of the mayor. Joking aside, I am fighting for a principle in taking that stand. Let women who go into politics be the real thing or nothing. Let us, while never forgetting our womanhood, drop all emphasis on sex and put it on being public servants.

In the summer of 1933, she and Dean Landes conducted the first of a series of University of Washington–sponsored study tours to the Far East, and they led a group during each of the next three summers. On the return trip in 1936, Henry Landes became ill, developed bronchitis, and died shortly after arriving back in Seattle. The former mayor agreed to lead the tour alone the following year, but this was among the last of her public activities. Even though by 1939 her own health had become a problem, she continued to live at the Wilsonian, and she maintained her independence. During those later years, she encountered the thinking of the Unity School of Christianity, the Kansas City–based organization that stressed faith healing and a sort of self-help, matter-of-fact approach to the spiritual. That Mrs. Landes would turn to it seems quite in keeping with her character, and it is not surprising that among the Unity School literature that she kept was the motto: "I meet every situation in my life with perfect poise, for I am secure in the realization that God guides, protects, and prospers me." In 1941, in part because of poor health, Bertha Landes moved from Seattle to Pacific Palisades, California. She died on November 29, 1943, at the age of seventy-five, at her son's home in Ann Arbor.

Bertha Landes graduated from college at the dawn of the progressive era of political and social reform, but she was not enfranchised until the age of forty-three. Although a leader in church, club, and community, she remained on the sidelines politically until, as a woman whose personal identity was first and foremost wife, mother, and homemaker, she was called upon at fifty-three to begin a new career in elective office.

Her political career had strong overtones of the progressive tenets of efficiency and regulation in public affairs, but her term as mayor did not mirror institutional reorganization that had taken place under progressives elsewhere, nor did it produce any lasting social change. It seems rather that she fought a rear-guard action in which she tried to reestablish in the city a rational and efficient approach to civic affairs, to strengthen municipal utilities, to improve services and programs for the betterment of the people, and to enforce the laws that she considered essential for the health and welfare of all.

Unlike earlier progressives Mayor Landes built no political machine of her own. The short, two-year mayoral term worked against her enlistment of able, and younger, strategists with long-range goals and ambitions of their own, and her reliance on a core group of women supporters, amateurs all, who lacked political staying power, added neither strength nor breadth to her campaigns.

She failed to effect reforms and she failed of reelection. It can be argued that the causes of the failures were the two things that made her tenure unique—her espousal of progressive measures and her sex. By the mid-twenties, a progressive was already something of a political anachronism, and her 1928 defeat may be seen as further evidence that the progressive movement had died or gone underground to await rebirth in the New Deal. As a woman she confronted the same forces, both subtle and not so subtle, that still account for gender inequality in politics; even within herself she was restrained by having been born and bred to a nineteenth-century woman's "proper place."

322   Doris H. Pieroth

She reconciled the role of woman-in-the-family and that of woman-in-public-office by combining them. She simply proclaimed the city a larger home, a concept acceptable to her and to contemporary culture. But the attempt to achieve political success took her beyond the stereotype of municipal housekeeper to meet politics on its own terms, and she found herself, a woman beyond the home, at odds with her culture if not with herself.

BIBLIOGRAPHICAL NOTE

Primary sources for this essay are the Bertha Knight Landes Papers, University of Washington Libraries; the Seattle Lighting Department Records, University of Washington Libraries; the records of the Seattle Soroptimist Club; the Seattle newspapers, *Star*, *Times*, and *Post-Intelligencer*, for the period 1921–31, and *Argus*, January through June 1928, *Pacific Wave*, April 7, 1905, *University of Washington Daily*, February and November 1914, and *University District Herald*, June 6, 1941; the Portland *Oregonian*, June 29, 1924, and March 15, 1928; and the New York *Times*, March 28, 1926, and March 11, 1928.

Other sources include Florence J. Deacon, "Why Wasn't Bertha Knight Landes Re-elected?" M.A. thesis (University of Washington, 1978); *Notable American Women, 1607–1950*, s.v. "Landes, Bertha Ethel Knight"; David Starr Jordan, *The Days of a Man*, 2 vols. (New York, 1922); *Biographical Cyclopaedia of American Women*, Vol. 2, s.v. "Landes, Bertha E. Knight"; *Encyclopaedia Britannica*, 11th ed., s.v. "Worcester, Massachusetts"; Blanche Brace, "Well . . . Why Not?" *Woman Citizen*, Vol. 11 (September 1926); Julia N. Budlong, "What Happened in Seattle," *Nation*, Vol. 127 (Aug. 29, 1928); G. E. Goodspeed, "Memorial of Henry Landes," *Proceedings of the Geological Society of America, for 1936* (June 1937); Thomas D. Clark, *Indiana University: Midwestern Pioneer*, 4 vols. (Bloomington, 1970–77); Charles M. Gates, *The First Century at the University of Washington* (Seattle, 1961); Frederick M. Padelford, "The Community," *University Congregational Church Fiftieth Anniversary Program*, (1941). Cora Jane Lawrence, "University Education for Nursing in Seattle, 1912–1950," Ph.D. dissertation (University of Washington, 1972); "Interesting Westerners," *Sunset*, Vol. 58 (February 1927); Bertha K. Landes, "Does Politics Make Women Crooked?" *Collier's*, Vol. 83 (March 16, 1929), and "Steering a Big City Straight," *Woman Citizen*, Vol. 12 (December 1927); Norman H. Clark, *The Dry Years: Prohibition and Social Change in Washington* (Seattle, 1965); *Soroptimist Yearbook*, 1925, 1926, and 1932; and Seattle Soroptimist Club, "President's Report," read at Founders' Day Meeting, Seattle, October 8, 1980.

Self-Help in Seattle, 1931–32: Herbert Hoover's Concept of Cooperative Individualism and the Unemployed Citizens' League

WILLIAM H. MULLINS

The past several years the presidency and career of Herbert Hoover have drawn the attention of a number of historians. Their assessments are diverse and have become increasingly complex. Some scholars see the Hoover administration as a contributor, or at least a logical prelude, to the New Deal. Recently Joan Hoff Wilson, Ellis Hawley, and David Burner have tended to reinforce or extend this point of view, put forth earlier by Richard Hofstadter and Carl Degler. Wilson and Hawley point out that, although many of his approaches presaged some of Franklin Roosevelt's actions, Hoover was finally a captive of his ideological framework. Burner identifies a predisposition on Hoover's part to rely on private agencies as the main aspect of this framework.

Other writers have portrayed Hoover's policies as the direct opposite of the New Deal approaches. Interestingly, this camp has room for conservative, liberal, and New Left historians. Conservatives, including Hoover himself, have defended the Hoover administration as the caretaker of the American tradition. Many liberal writers have found the responses of the earlier administration to the depression to be rather timid when compared to far-reaching New Deal policies. William Appleman Williams, critical of a present-day burgeoning government working hand in hand with corporate capitalism, seems willing to praise Hoover and his administration for farseeing and admirable restraint. The business of interpreting Herbert Hoover and his presidency has become rather complicated.

Originally published in *Pacific Northwest Quarterly*, January 1981.

It may be, however, that there is room for even more commentary. Historians have outlined and assessed Hoover's policies and his attitudes toward the political economy, but they have tended to be less thorough in their evaluations of how his views affected the individual American striving to survive in the midst of economic collapse.

Herbert Hoover (and, very likely, the nation that elected him in 1928) placed great store in the values of self-reliance and individualism. An individual was supposed to help himself when problems arose. If necessary, local agencies were to take responsibility for relief. For many Americans, federal direct relief—the dole—was not an acceptable means of alleviating the problems of the depression, and for Hoover, at least, local solutions seemed preferable to any type of federal aid, even federally funded public works. The Reconstruction Finance Corporation, for example, was careful to funnel relief money through the states. The prospect of the national administration stepping into what Hoover considered local matters was, for him, a threat to the "fiber" and "backbone" of the nation.

To Hoover, however, individualism did not mean simply "rugged individualism"—a philosophy which held that a person would succeed or fail entirely on his own. Perhaps a more helpful term to describe his social ideal for Americans is "cooperative individualism." Joan Hoff Wilson, in her biography *Herbert Hoover: Forgotten Progressive,* employs this phrase to explain Hoover's "dream of a humane, voluntarily controlled capitalistic system based on cooperatively sharing the abundance produced by technology." Although Wilson uses the phrase in the context of Hoover's beliefs about the nature of the corporate economy, it effectively describes Hoover's ideal for the individual American citizen, as well as the American corporation.

With the idea of cooperation, Hoover attempted to add another dimension to the concept of individualism. Just as the ruthless individualism of the marketplace had to be tempered, according to Hoover, so too did the rugged individualism of personal relations. In *American Individualism* (1922), Hoover called for "an individualism that carries increasing responsibility and service to our fellows." Neighborliness, service, and cooperative self-help were to be the hallmarks of Hoover's new American individualism.

He continued to voice this belief regularly during his term of office. In his annual message to Congress of December 2, 1930, he said, "Economic wounds must be healed by the action of the cells of the economic body—the producers and consumers themselves. Recovery can be expedited and its effects mitigated by cooperative action." Wilson points out that Hoover finally wearied the public with his unending calls for locally financed self-help programs.

President Hoover's decisions at the national level seem to have borne out his philosophy. Although he created the President's Emergency Committee on Employment in 1930 and the President's Organization on Unemployment Relief in 1931, the role of these groups was restricted by Hoover's assumption that private charity should take primary responsibility for relief. The Wagner-Graham Stabilization Act of 1931 acknowledged the need for federal public works in times of unemployment, and the creation of the Reconstruction Finance Corporation represented an important step toward a federal responsibility for work relief. Nonetheless, the Hoover administration limited the effects of both measures by its concern over excessive federal action. For Hoover, the ability of Americans to function according to his ideal of cooperative individualism was important. It is useful to remember, as David Burner points out, that this philosophy applied not only to those who needed help, but to private individuals who could offer it as well. If individuals, cooperating with one another, could handle their depression-caused problems at the local level (and the president seemed confident they could), then extensive federal intervention ("interference") was not necessary. The national government could refrain from handing out relief; and the economic storms could be weathered without altering the relationship between the American economy and the federal government.

How appropriate was such an ideal for a depression-rocked nation? How successful were the ensuing policies as they were carried out at the local level? These are key questions that must be answered in order to provide a full assessment of the Hoover administration.

Because Hoover, to a great extent, sought to involve individuals and local agencies in relief programs, success at the local level was important to the success of his national policies. To neglect this facet of Hoover's presidency is to overlook a basic and critical aspect of federal policy formation of the period. By evaluating the ideal of cooperative individualism at the local level, we should gain insights that will add to an assessment of the Hoover administration.

The Unemployed Citizens' League (UCL) of Seattle was a group of individuals who dealt with the problems of the depression at the local level. There is no record that Hoover knew of its existence; and no evidence indicates that the league consciously modeled itself on his ideal of cooperative individualism. Yet the UCL seems to have embodied the spirit of voluntary, cooperative self-help, which the president hoped would spontaneously emerge in the nation. By studying this organization we can see how one city coped with the problems of the depression, and we will be able to draw some tentative conclusions about the viability of Hoover's ideal.

By 1931 the Great Depression was a reality in Seattle. Estimates of unemployment ranged from 23 percent to 60 percent; the city's Public

Employment Office reported that almost two and one-half times as many men had registered for work in 1931 than had in 1930; and a Hooverville had sprouted along the tidal flats of Puget Sound. In response to the severe downturn in the economy, the city government had bolstered the public works budget and formed a fact-finding commission. Because Washington's Governor Roland Hartley believed in rugged individualism, the state contributed essentially nothing to aid the unemployed. Even the Community Fund, the traditional source of sustenance for the unemployed and impoverished, barely met its 1931 goal. The stage was set, then, for private citizens to create among themselves an organization to cope with the problems.

On an evening in July 1931, about forty unemployed men met in West Seattle, seeking a way to alleviate their economic situation. By the end of the meeting, they had resolved to work out a plan for unemployment relief for the coming winter, present their needs to city authorities, and make a survey of unemployment in Seattle. To implement this program they formed the Unemployed Citizens' League, which was to have a major impact on Seattle's program of relief for the next sixteen months.

The idea for organizing the unemployed in such a manner originated in informal conversations between Hulet Wells and Carl Brannin. Though the emergent group seemed tailored to Hoover's concept of locally financed self-help, Wells and Brannin were surely not the kind of people Hoover had envisioned as the leaders of a new American individualism. Both were socialists and played major roles in publishing the radical newspaper *Vanguard*, which became the unofficial organ of the UCL. Brannin, whom a contemporary described as "definitely Marxian," was the head of the Seattle Labor College. Wells had had an interesting and long career in Seattle's left-wing community: he had been a Socialist candidate for mayor, the head of the Seattle Central Labor Council, a postal worker, and an attorney. On the eve of World War I, he had issued a circular calling for resistance to conscription. He received a two-year sentence for conspiring against a joint resolution of Congress declaring war. The Industrial Workers of the World (IWW) was later active in seeking his release.

Brannin and Wells quickly recruited Charles W. Gilbreath, who had been in the trucking business and was now a Labor College leader, and John F. Cronin, a 69-year-old unemployed building contractor, former newspaper reporter, and onetime member of the Knights of Labor. These men attracted others to their cause. Despite the strong socialist tinge of this leadership, the UCL itself, in its first year of existence, was not a particularly left-leaning organization—even when judged by the criteria of the time.

The league grew at a phenomenal rate. Soon every neighborhood in the city with a sizable number of men out of work had a local branch of its own. At its peak the UCL could boast of between forty thousand and fifty thousand members. Although the leadership openly advocated a reorganization of the economic structure, the rank and file of the UCL was composed of rather conservative skilled and common laborers. These men joined together simply to help themselves. Wells himself despaired that the UCL was not very encouraging "for those who look to mass intelligence for social betterment."

But the crucial fact was that people were endeavoring, in accord with the president's highest hopes, to overcome their problems without the aid of institutions. According to the constitution ultimately drawn up for the Unemployed Citizens' League, the first objective was employment, primarily through public works, the second was self-help, then came unemployment insurance, and finally, if necessary, direct relief.

Among these goals self-help inspired the most interesting and imaginative responses. Because the organization was one of the first of its kind in the depression era, the Seattle UCL had no pattern to follow. With the spontaneity that characterized its formation, the league threw itself into self-help projects. Beginning with wood cutting on land donated for that purpose, various UCL locals extended their activities to picking unwanted fruit crops in the Yakima Valley and fishing in Puget Sound. The league set up commissaries where the wood and food could be distributed, and a barter economy was created. In return for these goods, able-bodied members chopped the wood, repaired shoes, did tailoring, and performed other services on behalf of their fellow jobless. With a minimum of contributions, UCL members took advantage of available manpower and skills to aid each other during rough times.

Another service that the league sometimes provided was a bulwark against eviction. Usually through negotiation the organization could stave off an ouster. If necessary, however, UCL members would simply move the evicted friends and furniture back in. By the end of 1931 the Unemployed Citizens' League had already become an important force in the city, and city councilmen and mayoral candidates began to meet with and speak to its members.

Just as the UCL was getting under way, the city of Seattle was instituting its own program for dealing with the economic crisis. Somewhat surprisingly, the public response to unemployment did not automatically supersede the private efforts of the UCL. Instead, the Mayor's Commission on Improved Employment, set up in September 1931, joined with the league to deal with the problems. Thus developed a system that almost perfectly represented Hoover's cooperative individualism in action.

I. F. Dix, the man Mayor Robert Harlin chose to head the Commission on Improved Employment, was the kind of person Hoover would have approved. Dix epitomized the "go-getter" businessman of the time. Born in Brooklyn, Dix, fifty years old, was the general manager of Pacific Telephone and Telegraph. Although he had been in Seattle only two years, having worked in Los Angeles the previous twenty, Dix was already serving as the chairman of the Community Fund and was the president of the Seattle Chamber of Commerce. To this full schedule the lean, businesslike man added what was to become his most demanding job. Here, then, was the expert business leader who could guide the local relief effort most efficiently and, according to the Hoover philosophy, most successfully.

The Dix Commission, as it came to be called, was primarily an organizing committee designed to work with and through already established public and private agencies. Although its goals were to stimulate and encourage commerce in the Seattle area, its first order of business was to make a list of the unemployed. By mid-October, five thousand families had registered for aid and employment.

Soon depots opened in five locations in the city to receive donations of food and clothing and distribute them. James F. Pollard, the general manager of Seattle Natural Gas, was in charge of the single men's division; the former mayor Bertha K. Landes headed the women's relief operation. For both men and women the commission sought to provide food and shelter for some minimal amount of work.

Throughout the months of October and November 1931, a multitude of suggestions, estimates, and proposals were bandied about in the city council chambers. The council intended to establish a special emergency fund to finance the mayor's commission, and interested parties called for funds ranging from $140,000 to $1 million to be reapportioned, reserved, or raised through a bond election for a variety of projects. According to the Dix Commission, $35,000 per month would be needed to furnish adequate work relief. The mayor recommended that $4.50 per day be paid to unemployed persons working on city projects, in order to stimulate efficiency and simply to provide workers an adequate living. Naturally, the UCL heartily endorsed this plan. Several councilmen, however, looking toward the taxpayers and a tight budget, proposed a $1.50-to-$3.00 scale (based on how many dependents the worker had to support). Despite the Dix Commission's approval of the sliding scale, the labor wing of the council managed to push through the higher, $4.50 wage. Finally, the city council passed an emergency measure of $1 million.

From this appropriation the Mayor's Commission on Improved Employment created the District Relief Organization (DRO). Dix showed that he was serious in his desire to work through existing agencies by placing the DRO, which was to become the principal relief arm of the municipal government, under the authority of the Community Fund. Thus, city moneys passed through the Community Fund to the DRO, which was administered in conjunction with private charities. Claiming that the citizens' group was better organized and could do more than his agency alone, Dix made the UCL the basis of DRO operations during the early weeks of 1932. Besides the five district depots, the DRO now had three to seven UCL commissaries in each district from which it could dispense relief.

Using the unemployed to administer relief to themselves was a practical, if unusual approach to public relief. It served two purposes. First, many of the jobless were given a stake in society. At a time when their pride was shattered, they could function usefully as administrators, rather than be passive recipients. Second, relief itself became work relief. Many unemployed persons volunteered their services to help in the commissaries. This at least created a feeling that work had been accomplished in return for relief. However, there was also one important disadvantage to this method of administration. The unemployed checked eligibility of relief applicants. Even if those entrusted with this task were scrupulously honest, criticism was inevitable; and, in fact, accusations of fraud were a factor leading to the ultimate failure of the system.

The dual nature of the District Relief Organization engendered a rather chaotic structure. The manager of the operation was Charles F. Ernst. His UCL counterpart was C. W. Gilbreath, who was designated "central contact man." Although Ernst held responsibility for every phase of operation, the success of the DRO depended on the cooperation of Gilbreath, who determined UCL policy and the extent of UCL cooperation in the relief effort. This bifurcated organization pervaded the whole program, and although harmonious relations usually prevailed, it was a definite threat to efficiency.

According to Ernst a "typical" DRO budget for one month called for $155,000. Of this sum, administration and operation costs took a total of $8,000, leaving $147,000 for relief. The DRO furnished both work relief and direct relief in the form of money and food. To be eligible a person had to be unemployed, a resident of the county for at least six months, and receiving relief from no other source. By December of 1931, when the entire project was really getting under way,

$150,000 had been spent. Most of the money had been used to put more than three thousand men to work. Already ten thousand had registered, and Dix expected twelve thousand to be signed up by the end of the month.

The DRO was able to perform a number of services for the unemployed. Its primary function, of course, was to distribute food to the needy. To assure the recipient of a balanced and nutritious diet, the Department of Home Economics at the University of Washington drew up a list of foodstuffs to be included in the distribution. The DRO also furnished free transportation to a mass meeting of the unemployed in early 1932. In addition, the commission intervened on occasion with Seattle City Light, the municipal utility, to maintain electric service to unemployed customers behind in their payments. The DRO did not neglect the UCL tradition of self-help. It encouraged people to continue exchanging the fruits of their skills in sewing, shoe repair, gardening, carpentry, food canning, and wood cutting. From time to time, the city supplied such essentials as seeds, cans, sugar, and transportation to enhance the self-help projects.

As 1931 came to an end, the city of Seattle appeared to be taking meaningful strides toward alleviating the plight of the unemployed. Almost immediately, however, any optimism that its program might solve its problems all but vanished. The unemployment situation in the city steadily worsened. Close to 40 percent of those who had been employed in 1929 in Seattle were without jobs three years later; and almost sixty-five hundred families had registered for aid with the UCL by February 1932. Moreover, the first weeks of 1932 saw the city relinquish a portion of the responsibility for maintaining relief to the administrators of King County. Although it continued to contribute to work relief, the city no longer had sufficient resources to provide full support for the DRO. As early as January, county funds amounting to $125,000 were being funneled through the Community Fund to the DRO. (The organization of the relief program remained essentially the same as the county began to assume increasing authority.)

It was not long before the county found itself in the same straits as the city. In May 1932 the King County commissioners voted $417,000 for relief and announced that the sum represented the last of their funds. The enormity of the problems engendered by the national economic collapse was clearly outweighing the abilities and resources of the local governments. County officials followed what seemed to be their only recourse and approved a bond issue. The commissioners planned to submit the $200,000 relief bond to the voters on a special September ballot; but under law the date had to be set back to the November election. Because of the great need and rapidly emptying coffers, it was impossible to wait until November for approval of funds, so the county government took a test case to the state supreme court to establish whether or not the commissioners could exceed the county's legal debt limit. The court ruled swiftly and humanely. In their June decision the justices declared that it was the government's duty to aid the unemployed, and they authorized King County to appropriate the $200,000 without a special vote of the people.

In May a tired I. F. Dix had stepped down as head of the mayor's commission in order to devote more time to the telephone business and to regain his health. In July the city gave up its remaining power over the local relief program (though it continued to provide some funds); this was a logical step now that the county had court approval to spend money over and beyond its debt limit. With the county heading up the effort to aid the unemployed, the King County Emergency Relief Organization replaced the DRO.

The court decision and the reshuffling of responsibilities, however, could not solve, even temporarily, other serious problems that the relief effort was facing. Most Seattleites, even the conservative elements of the population, accepted the Unemployed Citizens' League as a necessary, even useful, organization spawned by the economic conditions. There had been no notable outcries when the UCL became the foundation for the District Relief Organization. In such a group, however, existed the seeds of social disruption—and this was an important factor that Hoover should have perceived as he encouraged self-help groups among the jobless at the local level. The unemployed—the have-nots—organized themselves into a relatively efficient group. The very nature and function of the group seemed to prepare the way for the UCL to turn itself into a socialistic organization. Moreover, the political stance of the leaders of this group was to the left of center, although Wells, Brannin, Gilbreath, and the rest were probably not sure themselves just where they stood. Their unofficial organ specialized in radical rhetoric. The *Vanguard*, or *Unemployed Citizen* as it was called part of the time, espoused political and industrial action, industrial unionism, and a modified brand of communism. Because of these unmistakably leftward leanings, both city and county officials, along with a number of citizens, kept a close watch on the UCL.

During 1932 two things happened to the league that severely damaged its credibility, destroyed its usefulness in providing relief, and, in turn, deprived the UCL of its power in the community. Externally, as we shall see later, its problem was graft; at least, the accusation was leveled that the UCL was mismanaging relief funds. More critical to its stability and more disastrous to its ongoing role in Seattle were the UCL's internal divisions. Arthur Hillman, a sociology professor at the University of Washington, studied the UCL in 1934. He concluded that certain league members, dissatisfied with the relative mildness of the trade unionists, progressives, and socialists who were the original organizers, began to force out these men and replace them with more radical individuals of their own choosing.

If one reads through the *Vanguard–Unemployed Citizen*, however, it is hard to see how many of the jobless could have found much fault with the radical tone of the views of the original leaders. Although the leaders' actions never matched their words, the divisions within the UCL were probably the result of a struggle for power, not an ideological contest. That is, members of the IWW and the Communist party who were scattered throughout the organization saw in the league a field ripe for harvest and were determined to reap its fruits.

In mid-1932 members of a local branch of the UCL began to acquire control of the league. Composed of Wobblies and supported by Communists, the Capitol Hill Gang was made up predominantly of single men who had been pushing for more militancy among their fellow unemployed. Several times they aggressively forestalled evictions of families. In August 1932 this faction completely took over the UCL. The significance of this change in leadership was demonstrated in a new UCL constitution. Although the first objective of the organization continued to be the unification of the jobless to fight unemployment, the ultimate goal, according to the constitution, was to achieve public ownership of all business and industry to put an end to the intolerable exploitation of the workers. Ultimately, the unemployed were to combine to overthrow the capitalist system.

For the Seattle business community, these political turns meant that the league's brand of cooperative individualism was beginning to take on a sinister appearance. Popular reaction was understandably negative. Many of the unemployed were themselves alienated by the growing radicalism of the league. Businesses withdrew their support from the UCL's self-help program. In November 1932 the former UCL leaders formed a new group, which they called the Economic Security League. It attracted disgruntled UCL members but never achieved the size, power, or significance of the original organization.

The struggle within the UCL continued. After the Wobblies eliminated the socialists and union men, it was the Communists' turn to assert their power. In a Machiavellian ploy the Communists now allied themselves with the more conservative UCL members to oust the IWW men. Ultimately, William Dobbins, a Communist, became chairman of the league. By this time the organization's effectiveness as a mouthpiece for the unemployed was gone. During the IWW days of the summer of 1932, the group staged an essentially fruitless march to see Governor Hartley in Olympia. In February 1933 the UCL held a sit-in at the County-City Building in Seattle without significant results. Members again went to Olympia in March and were ignominiously turned away when "vigilantes" met them at the outskirts of town.

Cooperative individualism in Seattle owed its demise to local relief funding problems, internal strife, and the leftward turn of the UCL; but local politics played an important part as well. In fact, the league's high point in both notoriety and power came on the eve of its decline. In March 1932, before radical elements began to seize control of the UCL, the league had made its first and last significant foray into Seattle politics. The most important contest in that election was the mayoral race. The three major candidates were the incumbent Harlin, the former mayor Frank Edwards, who had been ousted in an earlier recall election, and John Dore, a criminal attorney. Edwards hoped for support from conservatives and some factions of labor, while Harlin advertised himself simply as "A Safe Pilot in a Troubled Sea." Dore, a Democrat, was the most interesting candidate in the field. A flamboyant speaker, called by some a demagogue, he campaigned for greater economy and lower property taxes, thus endearing himself to beleaguered taxpayers. He was also able to cast himself as the friend of Seattle's liberal community. Most significant, Dore won UCL endorsement with promises of jobs.

In addition to Dore, the UCL supported Frank Fitts and Roy Misener for city council spots. The conservative Seattle *Times* labeled these three men radicals. If they accepted such an evaluation, *Times* readers woke up on March 9, 1932, to find themselves under a radical government. Seattle gave Dore the largest margin of victory ever accorded a mayor up to that time; the UCL-endorsed councilmen did almost as well.

The Unemployed Citizens' League quickly claimed a share of the credit for the victories, and Dore, Fitts, and Misener all acknowledged the importance of UCL support. The two councilmen estimated that the league's approval could have made a difference of twenty thousand votes; and Fitts generously gave the league credit for sixty thousand votes in the general election. Even many community leaders were willing to acknowledge the organization of the unemployed as a significant political force, although I. F. Dix did not agree. The important thing, no matter how much political clout the UCL actually did have, was that the group had entered politics. Up to this time it had concerned itself with feeding and aiding the unemployed on its own or in tandem with local government. Now the

UCL was taking its new role in politics seriously—and so were many other Seattleites. Yet this March election was to be the highwater mark of organized activity among the unemployed. Never again could they successfully exert their influence in such a way.

Although the UCL and liberal Seattleites had endorsed Dore, the new mayor began to dismay these supporters as he put his platform into operation. In the campaign he had promised to cut the wages of only the highest-paid members of the municipal bureaucracy. In June, however, he quickly antagonized six councilmen and his supporters by calling for across-the-board pay slashes. The editor of the Seattle *Star*, once an adamant Dore supporter, now assailed the mayor for attempting to destroy the city's wage scale. When the councilmen opposed Dore's demands, he called them "public enemies" and the "six sillies." For two months the city council and the mayor wrangled bitterly over salary cuts for city employees. While the council sought a reduced work week, Dore continued to call for a 10 percent slash in wages.

To the chagrin of Dore's campaign supporters, the bankers soon came in on the mayor's side. The city had been giving its employees pay warrants, which had to be cashed at banks. From time to time, especially when they thought the municipal government was practicing unsound finance, the banks would stop cashing the warrants. With such powerful backing, the mayor got his economy message across, at least to the employees. Despite city council resistance, Dore circulated a petition among city employees. By signing, the workers agreed to accept voluntarily a wage reduction. Their alternative, they were told, was dismissal as an "economy measure." Caught between the banks, which would not honor their pay warrants, and the mayor, few employees hesitated to sign. Later in the year the mayor and the banks coaxed and coerced the council into another boon for the taxpayer—a lower budget. The split between the mayor and his supporters continued to widen. Although he had promised the unemployed jobs, a councilman observed, by October he was calling them radicals and communists.

Thus, John Dore, friend of liberals and labor alike during his campaign, turned out to have much in common with conservatives and bankers once he assumed office. Because the Unemployed Citizens' League had become a success in relief administration and politics, and because it seemed to be moving steadily leftward in 1932, neither the now conservative mayor nor the county commissioners, who were in charge of administering relief, could sanction the major role the league was playing. Soon Dore, along with several others, was voicing the opinion that paid checkers should be placed at the commissaries to watch over the administration of relief. After charges of extravagance and mismanagement had been bandied about, the UCL itself called for a county inspection to stop the rumors. In June an unpaid observer selected by the county was placed at each commissary to watch for fraud. With this step the crisis seemed to pass; Commissioner Donald Evans said that there was no reason to change the operation as long as it was well run.

But the calm was short-lived. Anxious county commissioners, monitoring the leftward leanings of the UCL throughout the summer of 1932, readied for action. In September, league members at the Ballard District commissary complained that the meat from Frye's Packing Company, which was distributed at the commissaries, was inferior and—possibly more significant—that the nonunion company was unfair to labor. Although the controversy was settled, it led to the county's reappraisal of relief administration. At the end of the month, the commissioners decided that a more permanent system should be created, and they began to replace the UCL workers with paid managers. League members, of course, objected strongly and refused to cooperate. In numerous cases the new managers were unable to obtain the lists of relief recipients from their UCL predecessors. The county was obliged to set up several new depots when relief workers would not countenance the new managers of the old ones. Justifying the takeover, Commissioner John Earley claimed that the UCL had padded the lists of relief recipients and had been lax in its record keeping.

The Unemployed Citizens' League by the end of 1932, then, had declined in status drastically. It had lost its position in the relief operation, and its political clout had dwindled. In November 1932 the league made one last attempt to recoup its power by supporting John C. Stevenson and Louis Nash for county commissioners, assuming that the two would reinstate the UCL in the relief program. Although they were elected and did remove the paid managers from the food depots, the two new commissioners replaced them with jobless people, regardless of whether they belonged to the UCL. This arrangement did not significantly change the operation of the relief system, but it sealed the fate of the moribund league.

Several of the important ingredients for the Hoover ideal of cooperative individualism were present in Seattle in the early 1930s. Citizens independently formed a self-help organization in order to avoid public relief. Local authorities, not the state or federal government, provided the financial undergirding for the grass-roots effort. Although the beneficences that Hoover hoped would come forth from wealthy private sources were notably absent, a business expert—I. F.

Dix, the qualified technician—set up and initially ran the operation. The UCL appears to have been the kind of group Hoover sought, and its relationship with local government seems to represent cooperative individualism. But the effort failed. What happened? Where did Hoover's ideal fall short?

More than anything the severity of the economic situation defeated Seattle's attempt at self-help. The relatively meager resources of the UCL could not hold out long in the face of overwhelming problems; the funds of the city, then the county, were quickly exhausted; and it seems reasonable to believe that the same thing would have happened to state support, had it been forthcoming.

Moreover, the cooperative ideal itself—at least as it was manifested in Seattle—appears to have been afflicted with problems Hoover did not anticipate. Arthur Hillman identified several factors that might have doomed the Seattle effort even under less trying conditions. First, the internal organization of the UCL changed in ways unacceptable to city and county leaders. Most were reluctant to support or defend a relief program manned by members of a radical organization. Second, graft and waste charges leveled at the UCL had a ring of truth and were never satisfactorily answered. Third, politicians had reason to fear the growing power of the UCL machine. After the league demonstrated its influence in the mayoral election, no candidate could afford to ignore it. The county commissioners, therefore, decided to remove the UCL from the relief program, reducing its visibility and its power base. Finally, once it became clear that the economic crisis and its problems would not soon pass, the commissioners sought to establish a relief organization more permanent than the UCL and more directly under their control.

Hillman's conclusions seem sound, and it would be difficult to judge the relative importance of one factor over another. Apparently each played its part in the league's downfall. Frank Foisie, a member of a committee that studied unemployment relief for the Washington State Legislature in 1932, wrote that the UCL was replaced because of a substantial increase of fraud and the county's fear—shared by some citizens—of the league's growing political power. Unless lists containing fraudulent entries were totally fabricated, it would appear that the UCL-administered program was not an entirely honest operation. Moreover, since both the mayor and the county administrators had reason to fear the UCL's political power (especially after radicals took control of the organization), they must have been eager to limit league influence. Furthermore, the commissioners, uneasy at the unemployed administering relief to themselves, would logically have seized any opportunity to put the program under their supervision.

Hoover, perhaps more idealist than politician in many ways, was reluctant to admit that local solutions, even augmented with federal aid, were not proving effective; nor did he seem to perceive that his ideal of cooperative individualism was fraught with so many political pitfalls. A self-help organization composed of unemployed people would seem a likely, even easy, target for those who would guide such an organization in a far different direction than that which Hoover would approve. The league's entry into politics is not surprising, for a well-organized power bloc might reasonably seek political influence as a means of attaining its goals. Nor is it surprising that those already in power would combat the UCL as a threat to their positions—and portray it as a threat to the stability of the city. Hoover's ideal, it appears, was a somewhat simplistic one. As it worked itself out rather spontaneously in Seattle, cooperative individualism began to encounter a variety of very real problems. Neither local government nor the UCL would overcome these problems or the larger one of the failure of the national economy.

If the Seattle experience is any indication, cooperative individualism could not have succeeded in many, if any, other American cities. It had too many weaknesses. There was too much to be done. There were too many opportunities for it to go awry. Although it was a basically conservative ideal, its cooperative aspect invited a socialistic interpretation that was unacceptable to most Americans of the time. Those who seek to revise interpretations of the Hoover administration must keep the failure of this ideal in mind, for belief in local solutions was the foundation for the president's other policies and actions. It is true that a federal government far more complicated and overladen with bureaucracy has developed since the Hoover era. Yet even if we find the present system inefficient, insensitive, if not uncontrolled and dangerous, we must seriously question the wisdom of upholding as an alternative the Hoover policy of cooperative individualism.

BIBLIOGRAPHICAL NOTE

For assessments of Hoover see: Robert H. Zieger, "Herbert Hoover: A Reinterpretation," *AHR*, Vol. 81 (1976), 800–10; Albert U. Romasco, "Herbert Hoover's Policies for Dealing with the Great Depression," and Ellis Hawley, "Herbert Hoover and American Corporatism," both in Martin L. Fausold and George T. Mazuzan, eds., *The Hoover Presidency: A Reappraisal* (Albany, N.Y., 1974); Joan Hoff Wilson, *Herbert Hoover: Forgotten Progressive* (Boston, 1975); David Burner, *Herbert Hoover: A Public Life* (New York, 1979); Richard Hofstadter, *The American Political Tradition* (New York, 1948); and Carl

Degler, "The Ordeal of Herbert Hoover," *Yale Review,* Vol. 52 (1963), 563–83. Hoover states his philosophy in *American Individualism* (Garden City, N.Y., 1922).

Bernard Sternsher, ed., *Hitting Home: The Great Depression in Town and Country* (Chicago, 1970), seems to be the major effort to document the depression at the local level.

Sources that reveal the situation in Seattle include the Charles F. Ernst Papers and Hulet Wells Papers at the University of Washington Libraries (the Wells Papers include an autobiography); "Constitution of the Unemployed Citizens' League," Seattle Public Library; Mayor's Commission for Improved Employment, "Questions and Answers," Northwest Room, Seattle Public Library; the Seattle *Post-Intelligencer,* Seattle *Star,* and *Vanguard–Unemployed Citizen;* Journal of the Proceedings of the City Council of Seattle; Arthur Hillman, *The Unemployed Citizens' League of Seattle* (Seattle, 1934); John Arthur Hogan, "The Decline of Self-help and Growth of Radicalism among Seattle's Organized Unemployed," M.A. thesis (University of Washington, 1934); Ronald M. Leistra, "Seattle's Radical Press, 1930–1934," M.A. thesis (University of Washington, 1964); Tom Jones Parry, "The Republic of the Penniless," *Atlantic Monthly,* Vol. 150 (1932); and Hulet Wells, "They Organize in Seattle," *Survey,* Vol. 67 (1932).

Dave Beck
and the Transportation Revolution
in the Pacific Northwest, 1917–41

JONATHAN DEMBO

Between the beginning of World War I and the beginning of World War II, a series of vast and fundamental upheavals transformed virtually every aspect of life—economic, social, and political—in the Pacific Northwest. Technological change, the basic source of these upheavals, became ever more dramatic. New industries arose; old ones declined. The automobile and truck replaced the horse and cart. People became more mobile, and whole populations fled their rural isolation and poverty for the prospect of urban prosperity. The factory displaced the farm as the dominant American institution. Although change uprooted many people, it provided opportunity for even more. Those who had the insight to see where the future lay, who had the courage to seize their chance, and who had the energy and strength to overcome adversity won rich rewards. The story of Dave Beck and the transportation revolution in the Pacific Northwest is the story of just such a man and of his struggle to win for the Teamsters union its rightful place in the regional economy.

The transportation revolution—some would even call it a counter-revolution because it helped re-create patterns of settlement that had been upset by the railroads—is easily documented. In 1910, as in the 1890s, the primary means of land transportation in the Pacific Northwest was the transcontinental railroad.[1] Their routes and depots determined the location and pace of economic development and subsequent population growth. Railroads thus ended the nation's dependence on wagon roads and water routes. After the arrival of the Chicago, Milwaukee, Saint Paul and Puget Sound Railway in Seattle in 1909, however, the great era of railroad construction slowed. Between 1880 and 1910, total railroad mileage in Idaho, Oregon, and

Washington had increased from 1,003 to 9,339 miles. Regional mileage peaked at 11,963 in 1930 and then began to decline.[2]

Simultaneous with the greatest surge of transcontinental building was the rise in steam- and then electric-powered commuter railways, which quickly claimed the urban and interurban passenger markets in the Northwest. The transcontinental lines retained the freight business and the long-distance passenger service, but downgraded local service as unprofitable.[3]

The first appearance of gasoline-powered vehicles after 1900 did not threaten either the local or transcontinental rail markets. Due to the lack of good roads, automobiles and trucks were limited to urban areas. Soon, however, as roads improved, and as vehicles themselves became safer, more durable, and more comfortable, they began to have a noticeable impact. Beginning in 1915, gasoline-powered taxis known as jitneys began to compete with electric- and horse-powered urban transit systems for local passengers.[4] Then, when freight traffic burgeoned in response to the defense buildup during World War I, the combustion engine found another application. Trucks began to compete with the railroads for the long-distance freight business as well. By 1920, the trucking industry was well established in the Pacific Northwest.[5]

Initially, trucking companies served local urban markets. This was a logical outgrowth of the days when horse-drawn wagons did most of the wholesale and retail delivery work in urban areas. In the 1920s and 1930s, however, the trucking industry expanded rapidly into a wide range of markets, including the vital long-distance, intercity market. One of the keys to this expansion was supportive state legislation. In 1919, Oregon passed the nation's first tax on gasoline and devoted the revenues to highway construction, improvements, and maintenance. Washington and Idaho followed suit in 1921 and 1923. Beginning in 1932, the federal government also levied a tax of 1 cent per gallon on gas and contributed part of the revenues to the states for their highway programs. By 1940, Washington and Oregon had raised the gas tax to 5 cents per gallon, and Idaho to 5.1. As a result, state highway expenditures increased rapidly and remained high until the outbreak of World War II.[6]

During the period between the wars, Pacific Northwest state and local highway systems grew at a rate that has never been equaled. By 1940, highway mileage in the three states exceeded railroad mileage. Even more important, however, were the improvements the states made to the roads themselves. In the 1920s and 1930s, the Pacific Northwest states spent the vast majority of their highway dollars to improve and modernize existing highways. They upgraded their roads from unsurfaced to gravel, stone, and stabilized soil surfaces, to a variety of bituminous surfaces, to Portland cement, and to brick and block-type surfaces. Prior to 1923, the highways in the Northwest were little more than rutted tracks, often impassable in bad weather. In less than two decades, the mileage of hard-surfaced roads in Idaho and Washington nearly tripled, and in Oregon it increased by 250 percent. By 1941, virtually all of the public roads and streets in the three states were usable in all weather. Equally dramatic technological improvements in automobile, truck, and tire manufacture, coupled with easy credit and reductions in the cost of fuel and equipment, gave a powerful boost to the trucking industry in the region.[7]

The rapid expansion and improvement of the region's road network had other profound consequences. Hitherto, product markets—the area within which companies do business—tended to be small. Consumers were limited to neighborhood stores. Corner grocers and other small shopkeepers were limited by the number of potential customers within walking distance. Service firms like plumbing, trucking, or construction companies were also restricted to a small geographical area by the difficulty of transporting men, supplies, and equipment by horse-drawn vehicles. Likewise, trade unions in these industries were circumscribed by the geographical limits of the firms that employed them. The automobile, truck, and highway changed all this. Product markets expanded in size. Consumers now had a citywide choice of stores. With greater numbers of potential customers, shopkeepers expanded the range and quality of their merchandise. With easier, faster transportation, contractors bid for jobs over a much wider area. This produced tremendous benefits for society as a whole: increased competition produced lower prices and better goods and services. Those individuals, companies, and industries favored by the new trends, those with the knowledge, capital, and vision to take advantage of their opportunities, prospered as never before. Unfortunately, however, many thousands did not. Businessmen who expanded their operations attracted trade away from their competitors and drove them out of business. In the same way, these developments forced unions to organize on a far wider scale if they hoped to survive.

A beneficiary of the dramatic growth in highway transportation in the Pacific Northwest was the International Brotherhood of Teamsters (IBT), once one of the weaker unions affiliated with the American Federation of Labor (AFL). Its original jurisdiction—men working on or near horse-drawn vehicles—had expanded naturally with the development of the gasoline-powered truck. The first Teamsters unions in the Pacific Northwest were established in Seattle before 1900. At that time the trucking industry—also known as the cartage or dray-age industry—consisted of numerous small, highly competitive firms that did business entirely within their own product markets, mainly hauling goods to and from railway stations and docks, or between retail and wholesale outlets. A few companies, such as milk, bread, and laundry retailers and beer distributors, also used trucks to deliver goods directly to retail customers. The largest firms employed no more than a few dozen men. Teamsters local unions were correspondingly small, weak, and transient.

The largest and most powerful Teamsters local in the Pacific Northwest was General Teamsters Local 174. In 1910, when it affiliated with the King County Central Labor Council,[8] however, it paid dues on only 190 members. Its survival was by no means certain. It had neither contracts with its employers nor immediate prospects of winning any. Yet, despite great hardships, Local 174 did prosper. In 1913, it first won recognition from its employers after a hard-fought, year-long strike prolonged by the intervention of outside interests. By 1916, when it won an industry-wide contract with the Truck Owners Association of Seattle, Local 174 had 500 members and was serving as the defender of a growing number of smaller Teamsters locals in the Seattle area. To coordinate the activities of these locals, and to insure communication with the leadership, the International Brotherhood of Teamsters chartered the Seattle Joint Council of Teamsters, which would also endorse political candidates, assist in the prosecution of strikes, and provide expert advice to the locals.[9]

As General Teamsters Local 174 grew larger and more diverse, the international union mined its membership to create a number of new, specialized locals. In 1917, for example, the IBT chartered locals of Auto Drivers (taxis), of Garbage Wagon Drivers, and of Laundry and Dye Wagon Drivers. Together, they had a membership of 1,211, or 7.8 percent of the Seattle Central Labor Council's entire membership. Between 1918 and 1925, while membership in the CLC as a whole declined, membership in the Teamsters locals increased to 1,853, or 13.4 percent of CLC membership. By then, the council contained eight Teamsters locals, and the Teamsters was the single most influential union in Seattle.[10]

Meanwhile, the international union also began to charter a number of Teamsters locals outside of the Seattle area. Of these, the most important was Tacoma General Teamsters Local 313. Significantly, these locals affiliated with Seattle's joint council, being too small and too weak to establish their own. As yet, the Teamsters had no locals in either Idaho or Oregon. In California, the only region of Teamsters strength was the Bay Area, where Michael ("Bloody Mike") Casey had led the union since the turn of the century.[11]

It is perhaps ironic that, despite its relatively small size and weakness, it was Seattle Laundry and Dye Wagon Drivers Local 566 that produced Dave Beck, the most powerful and dynamic leader in Teamsters history. Beck was born on June 16, 1894, in Stockton, California, into an impoverished Irish-German family. In 1899, Beck's father moved his family to Seattle in a vain search for financial security. During his early years Beck's family lived close to destitution, and he had to sell newspapers and catch fish to supplement its meager income. After dropping out in his third year of high school, Beck held a variety of temporary jobs to help support the family. He delivered typewriters. He worked in an electrical company warehouse. Eventually, he won a position as an inside worker in a laundry, which also employed his mother. At length, he became a commission driver-salesman there and joined the Laundry Workers Union. When, on April 3, 1917, the Teamsters chartered Seattle Laundry and Dye Wagon Drivers Local 566, Beck became one of its first members. That year, before he enlisted in the Naval Air Service, Beck participated in the bitter but victorious strike that resulted in the local's first union contract.[12]

After overseas service, Beck returned to Seattle, married, and went to work for a different laundry, one that offered higher commissions than he had received before. Soon, because of his business sense and his relentless energy, he won a promotion to route supervisor. Meanwhile, he also achieved recognition for his union activities. In 1923 he was elected president of Local 566 and became the Laundry and Dye Wagon Drivers local's delegate to the Joint Council of Teamsters. In 1924 he was elected secretary-treasurer of the local and became a rising figure on the joint council. There, he discovered that he had a talent for leadership and public speaking. He was so effective, in fact, that in 1924 he won election to the executive board of the joint council. As a member of the board, Beck used his influence to criticize radicalism and sympathy strikes. But this was a troubled period in his life, and he was soon in conflict with his employers. After one argument, Beck resigned and returned to his old job at the laundry where his mother worked. There, he found a new arrangement that had much to do with his future course as a union leader. Formerly, laundry truck drivers had been company employees; they received a basic minimum wage plus a commission on the business they brought to the laundry. After the war, however, expanding businesses and increased competition caused companies to seek ways of reducing expenses. In firms that employed truck drivers—laundries, bakeries, milk and beer distributors, construction firms, and drayage or highway trucking companies—the biggest expense was labor. In order to meet the competition, employers reduced maintenance on

their trucks, they went without insurance, they neglected safety practices, and they and their employees worked dangerously long hours.
But these steps were insufficient. To survive, small businessmen
needed even stronger controls on their labor costs. The owner-
operator system, by which the employers eliminated wages altogether, forced drivers to become virtual subcontractors. As owner-
operators, they worked on a straight commission basis and had to
buy their own trucks. This arrangement placed most of the risks and
costs of doing business on the backs of the drivers and allowed the
companies to skim off more of the profits; it also engendered intense
competition among the drivers. Many laundries, including the one
that employed Beck, adopted this system, reducing the minimum
wage and forcing their driver-salesmen to become owner-operators.
Because of his energy and ambition, Beck was one of the few drivers
to profit under this system. Soon, he was earning between $100 and
$110 per week and was one of the best-paid Teamsters in Seattle.
Nevertheless, he was very much aware of the inequity of the
system.[13]

Meanwhile, Beck also came into conflict with the leadership of his
local. The disputes began in 1923, the year he was elected president
of the Seattle Joint Council of Teamsters, an unpaid position. In office,
Beck criticized the Laundry and Dye Wagon Drivers leaders for their
lack of progress since the war and their failure to relieve the competitive pressures on the members. His views led him to enter the local's
elections in December 1924. The decision to seek office in the local
was not an easy one. It meant abandoning his career as a driver, with
a loss of $45 per week, or very nearly half his income. He was gam-
bling that he could make the union grow dramatically. He was also
making a personal point: that he was willing to make personal sacrifices in the interests of the union. This was a highly significant gesture at a time when the distinction between organized labor and organized crime was not very clear and many Teamsters locals were run
by criminal elements.[14]

As the new secretary-treasurer of Seattle Laundry and Dye Wagon
Drivers Local 566 and as president of the city's Joint Council of Teamsters, Beck was a typical "business unionist" of the 1920s. He did not
believe that organized labor should try to reform society. According
to Beck, the only commodity that working people had to sell was
their labor. The role of the union was to get for them the best possible
price for the least amount of work. He was militant only in the sense
that he would go to virtually any lengths to secure this end. He also
believed in the right and the necessity of employers to earn a profit.
He made speeches and wrote articles extolling the virtues of free enterprise, profits, and private property. His position helped assuage

employers' fears of unions, and it helped build up support for organized labor among the middle class. By the same token, Beck's pro-business propaganda helped establish a close alliance between himself and President William Short of the Washington State Federation of Labor (WSFL).[15] Impressed, Short adopted Beck as a sort of protégé. Through Short, Beck established close ties to the conservative Samuel Gompers wing of the AFL.[16] With increasing frequency, chambers of commerce, medical societies, the American Legion, the Elks clubs, and other fraternal organizations invited him to address their gatherings.

Immediately upon taking office as his local's secretary-treasurer, Beck launched a vigorous organizing drive and began negotiating directly with the employers. First, he studied the laundry industry carefully. Having attended law and business classes at the University of Washington's night school, Beck often knew as much about the operations and economic problems of the laundries as the employers did. Moreover, he was prepared to see both sides of any problem. As a result of his investigations, Beck concluded that labor and management should cooperate in the regulation of the laundry industry and should transfer any new costs to the customers. The first step was to "stabilize," that is to equalize, labor costs within the industry by forcing the laundries to pay their drivers a standard, guaranteed minimum wage. Beck reasoned that if he could reduce differences in labor costs among various firms, he could reduce the competition on labor costs. That is, if employers knew that all their competitors faced the same labor costs, regulated by Beck and the Teamsters, they would compete with one another in other areas, such as improved services, better advertising, or greater efficiency. At the same time, if they could equalize labor costs by establishing minimum wages, Beck and the Teamsters could place a floor under the truck drivers' incomes and remove one of the greatest uncertainties in their lives.[17]

To achieve his goal of minimizing the competitive pressures that forced employers to cut labor costs, Beck developed organizational devices and tactics that went far beyond labor's traditional practices. By themselves, they were not great innovations, but Beck practiced them with such energy that they virtually transformed labor negotiations. One of the most effective of these tactics was to encourage employers to form regional trade associations and to empower the associations to engage in collective bargaining. This had two great benefits for the Teamsters. By negotiating a single area-wide contract for all the firms in a particular product market, the Teamsters eliminated in a single stroke all the differences in wages and conditions among different firms. No less important, this tactic greatly reduced the cost and time involved in contract negotiations. Instead of having to negotiate hundreds or even thousands of separate contracts for each firm in a product market, the union only had to worry about a single bargaining session. Paid Teamsters officials could spend their time recruiting and providing more extensive services to members instead of constantly renegotiating individual contracts. Collective bargaining soon became such a valuable tool for the Teamsters that when employers complained they could not afford the expense of establishing a trade association, Beck offered to subsidize them, giving them office space in the Teamsters headquarters building and even paying their officials' salaries. But he ruthlessly suppressed those who refused to agree to area-wide bargaining through trade associations. Recalcitrant employers found that no truck driver would handle their products. Most soon saw the wisdom of compliance.[18]

Of course, Beck and the Teamsters wanted more than to stabilize wages and conditions. They wanted to improve them. If members of an employers association claimed inability to raise wages, Beck was prepared to be understanding. He would analyze the employers' situation and try to find ways to enable them to raise their prices or improve their efficiency, thus increasing their profits and allowing them to raise wages. If he found that a particular industry had too much competition to pay higher wages, he was even prepared to use Teamsters power to shut down a few of the weaker firms and so provide larger markets for the survivors.[19]

Beck's most innovative and important organizational tactic, however, was to employ one jurisdiction to increase the union's economic leverage within its other jurisdictions and as a device for projecting that power to organize new jurisdictions far from the union's base of support. Specifically, Beck used the long-distance highway truckers—a group created by the transportation revolution—to extend and strengthen Teamsters power throughout the 11 western states.[20]

In putting this vast organizational campaign into effect, Beck's most pressing need was for allies. He knew that he could expect no help from the International Brotherhood of Teamsters. Its unalterable policy was to oppose the growth of local dynasties within the union by prohibiting the use of IBT funds to help local organizing campaigns. Beck's own local, the Seattle Laundry and Dye Wagon Drivers, was too small and weak to be of use. For assistance, therefore, he turned to Seattle General Teamsters Local 174. During World War I, Local 174 had been the first local in the nation to organize the rapidly growing long-distance highway trucking jurisdiction. It had also signed the first union contract in this jurisdiction. In California and on the East Coast, organization of over-the-road jurisdictions proved difficult and unprofitable. In such populous areas, highway trucking locals frequently overlapped the jurisdictions of other locals. They also undermined long-established local drayage operations by taking business away from the railroads, a main source of Teamsters employment in those areas. Because it was relatively isolated and because there were few other Teamsters locals in the Pacific Northwest, Local 174 had few impediments to its work with the highway truckers. By 1925, it had organized a majority of the approximately two hundred carriers operating between Seattle and Portland. But Harry Dail and Frank Brewster, president and secretary-treasurer of Local 174 and the dominant figures in the Seattle Joint Council of Teamsters, were highly dubious of Beck's plans. Like their California counterparts, they were not empire builders. They lacked the vision to see the potential of using the highway truckers to organize in distant localities. Therefore, Beck began a diplomatic campaign to change their minds and win them to his purposes.

Gradually, over a period of several years, he demonstrated how he could use the highway truckers and Local 174's treasury to organize the weaker outlying locals of the state. Although they continued to entertain serious doubts, Dail and Brewster eventually agreed to help finance Beck's organizing strategy. Using Local 174's strategic economic position and financial resources, Beck, ultimately, fully organized and even expanded beyond the IBT jurisdiction into many nontraditional areas such as warehouses, canneries, breweries, and dairies.

Dave Beck's rise to power was meteoric, and it quickly brought him to the attention of the IBT officers. In the spring of 1925, Beck proved instrumental in preventing a strike between the General Teamsters and the Truck Owners Association of Seattle. During the summer and fall, he played a critical role in negotiating an agreement between the Laundry and Dye Wagon Drivers local and the Laundry Owners Association of Seattle. These activities, not unusual in themselves, gave Beck special prominence because they occurred while Teamsters delegates from all over the U.S. and Canada were arriving in Seattle for the 1925 convention. Among those who sat in on the bargaining sessions were Dan Tobin, president of the international union, and Mike Casey of the San Francisco Teamsters. Beck's adroit performance impressed them both.[21]

During the convention, Beck won more laurels. He served, with distinction, as chairman of the arrangements committee (responsible for entertaining the visiting delegates and their wives) and as a member of several other committees. At a critical moment he also helped President Tobin avert an embarrassing constitutional fight between American and Canadian members of the union by making a timely motion from the floor. In gratitude, Tobin and Casey began to take close personal interest in his career. Their support served Beck well as long as they remained active in the Teamsters union.[22]

Beck's alliance with Tobin and Casey first bore fruit in 1927. In that year, Louis Schwellenbach and Robert MacFarlane offered Beck a much higher salary to manage the new chain of laundries they were in the process of establishing. When they heard of it, Tobin and Casey arranged to subsidize Beck's salary from IBT resources in order to keep him in the labor movement. And, later that same year, Tobin appointed Beck to be a full-time organizer for the international union in the Pacific Northwest, with an appropriate salary increase.[23]

Meanwhile, Beck continued his local organizing activities. In 1927, he negotiated a new contract with the Laundry Owners Association of Seattle, one that included a minimum salary for union members. From that date on, regardless of commissions, no matter how few customers he had or how little he worked, a driver had to be paid a basic salary. In future contracts, Beck won regular increases in the basic salary level and thus discouraged the use of owner-operators.[24]

By the time the Great Depression struck, in 1929, Beck was a well-established union leader. It was during this devastating period that he proved his worth. While other union leaders became cautious and defensive, Beck became even more aggressive and expansive. Without consulting the IBT leadership, he began to broaden the functions and scope of the Seattle Joint Council of Teamsters to include organizing over the entire state of Washington. He even used the Seattle council and the highway truckers to organize a joint council in Portland. The more Beck organized, the greater his strength became. Through his control of the long-haul trucking jurisdiction, he could shut down deliveries to virtually any firm in the region that refused to recognize the Teamsters. Other unions undertook numerous long and expensive strikes during this period, but most Teamsters strikes were short and relatively inexpensive.

The expansion of Teamsters jurisdiction brought about by Beck's organizing required an elaboration of the union's structure and a professionalization of its leadership. In the 1920s, Beck had pioneered in the field of area-wide multi-employer bargaining, by which employers negotiated with the Teamsters through trade associations. In the 1930s, Beck established trade councils, within the Seattle joint council, so that the stronger locals within each of the Teamsters market areas could be used to support the newer, weaker locals with money and expert advice. Later, he also established a union school to train professional union officials for the Teamsters. In 1936, he combined these innovations when he established the California Highway Drivers Council, whose purpose was to coordinate a campaign to organize the entire state of California. Again, he moved independently of the international union's leadership. The following year, when Tobin appointed him West Coast organizer, Beck used the highway drivers council to break the power of the open shop forces in Los Angeles. By simply shutting down all truck movements into and out of southern California, he forced employers throughout the region to recognize the union. The struggle was over in a matter of days. Beck, however, did not stop with this success. In 1938, he established and brought under his control the 11-state Western Conference of Teamsters to coordinate local activities and provide advice and financial assistance to local unions on a regional basis. By the end of the decade, Beck was, by far, the most powerful regional leader in the Teamsters union.

During the 1930s, however, Beck's relations with other unions deteriorated. Many weaker unions sought to enlist Teamsters support in their battles with employers. Beck declined to assist a good many of them; sympathy strikes could require the Teamsters to violate valid contracts, and more important, they would embroil the Teamsters in endless controversy. Yet, Beck and the Teamsters did assist some unions. In 1934 and again in 1936, they helped the International Longshoremen's Association win recognition from the waterfront employers on the Pacific Coast. Similarly, in 1936, Beck's support proved the margin of victory in the American Newspaper Guild's strike against the Seattle *Post-Intelligencer*.[25] Teamsters did business with virtually every firm in the nation. The union simply could not afford to strike every time another union needed its assistance.

Another cause of irritation between the Teamsters and other unions was Beck's vigorous defense of Teamsters jurisdiction—its right to organize certain categories of workers—against the inroads of other unions and his equally strong defense of the AFL in its wars with the rival CIO. For example, in 1933 and 1934 following the repeal of Prohibition, the United Brewery Workers Union demanded that the newly legalized beer producers employ only its members, even those workers who drove beer trucks. When the IBT leadership turned away from this challenge, Beck took up the fight on his own— and won. Today, Teamsters produce all the beer made in the U.S. except for Coors. Also, in 1937 and 1938, when Harry Bridges and his International Longshoremen's and Warehousemen's Union tried to "march inland" from the waterfronts of the Pacific Coast to organize warehousemen for the CIO, Beck again accepted the challenge and led the tumultuous fight against them on behalf of the AFL. He proved victorious almost everywhere on the Coast.[26]

By the late 1930s, Beck had amassed a great store of economic and, hence, political power. He had organized a huge and disparate collection of workers into the Teamsters union: condensery workers in dairies, cannery workers, aircraft company warehousemen, automobile salesmen, office employees, retail clerks, optical technicians, rag pickers, and many others in addition to truck drivers. His organizing efforts knew few bounds. He was hated, feared, and envied. Employers and rival union leaders accused him of using strong-arm tactics and of employing goon squads of former prizefighters and criminals to intimidate his opposition. Beck admitted that many of the charges were true but denied that he had ordered violence. It was, he said, simply impossible to control the violent tendencies of his membership. Teamsters refused to run away from a fight. On the other hand, he claimed they never started trouble. Teamsters practice under Beck was to win by superior force, tactics, endurance, or whatever else victory required. As a result, Beck was respected but his popularity suffered.[27]

In an effort to counteract his bad public image, to win friends for the Teamsters, and to gain greater acceptance from businessmen, Beck became increasingly active in politics in the late 1930s. In doing so, he followed a characteristically pragmatic policy. He wanted to support winners who could be relied upon as friends of the union. In close election contests, therefore, he occasionally supported both sides in order to assure the election of a sympathetic candidate. Beck, however, never relied upon politics to maintain Teamsters power: he believed that political successes were transient; only economic power could last.[28]

To further build up their public support, Beck and the Teamsters contributed thousands of dollars to charities and civic programs, but these activities had only a marginal impact. Real improvement in the Teamsters public image occurred only after the CIO emerged, in 1937 and 1938, with its militant organizing campaigns and left-wing political agenda. Suddenly, businessmen, conservative politicians, and community leaders began to see the Teamsters as a bulwark against radicalism, and Beck's political influence grew.[29] In 1940, he was elected vice-president of the international union and took a seat on its executive board. By then, he was widely recognized as President Tobin's heir apparent. In fact, he could probably have defeated Tobin had he chosen to challenge him. However, Beck chose instead to amass power and leave the symbols of it to Tobin.[30]

World War II brought an end to the great highway construction and improvement projects of the 1920s and 1930s. Production of automobiles, trucks, and tires for civilian use practically ceased. Gasoline rationing limited motor travel. Nevertheless, Beck and the Teamsters became ever more powerful. The nation's highway system was basically complete. The railroads were even less able to meet the nation's transportation needs than they had been in World War I. With military service putting truck drivers in short supply, employers, operating under lucrative cost-plus contracts, readily consented to Teamsters demands. Take-home income for Teamsters rose dramatically as wages, benefits, and overtime hours increased. Beck was a vital cog in the transportation network; national and international political and business leaders, including Britain's Prime Minister Winston Churchill, consulted him. Both Presidents Roosevelt and Truman asked Beck to serve as secretary of labor. (He declined both offers because he disliked politics.) Meanwhile, attacks on Beck and the Teamsters from within the labor movement also declined. Many of the left-wing labor leaders in the CIO moderated their views in the interests of wartime labor unity.

By the end of the war the Teamsters were firmly entrenched as the most powerful union in the Pacific Northwest, and the transportation system of the region had assumed the basic shape it retains to this day.

NOTES

1. Sol H. Lewis, "A History of the Railroads in Washington," *WHQ*, Vol. 3 (1912), 168–97; Randall V. Mills, "Recent History of Transportation in the Pacific Northwest," *OHQ*, Vol. 47 (1946), 281–312.

2. Otis W. Freeman et al., eds., *The Pacific Northwest: A Regional, Human, and Economic Survey of Resources and Development* (New York, 1942), 392, 434–35; see also 2d ed. (1951), 389–435.

3. Mills, 295–305; Leslie F. Blanchard, *The Street Railway Era in Seattle* (Forty Fort, Pa., 1968); Dorothy O. Johansen and Charles M. Gates, *Empire of the Columbia: A History of the Pacific Northwest* (2d ed. New York, 1967), 313–15.

4. On jitneys, see Seattle *Star*, Oct. 18, 19, Nov. 10, 1915; also see Seattle *Town Crier*, June 10, 1916, 1–2; Mills, 303.

5. Jonathan Dembo, *Unions and Politics in Washington State, 1885–1935* (New York, 1983), 136–37; U.S. Dept. of Transportation, Federal Highway Admin., Bur. of Public Roads, *Highway Statistics, Summary to 1965* (Washington, D.C., 1967), 25–36.

6. *Highway Statistics*, 17–18, 90–91, 100–106.

7. *Ibid.*, 111, 124, 129; Freeman (1st ed.), 430.

8. The King County Central Labor Council is a policy-making body open to all local unions, and joint councils of local unions in Seattle and King County. It makes political endorsements, sanctions strikes, and adjudicates disagreements between locals.

9. "Membership and per Capita Tax Records, 1907–1957," Box 11, King County Central Labor Council Records, University of Washington Libraries. My statistics are conservative; for a comparison, see Carl G. Westine, "The Seattle Teamsters," M.A. thesis (University of Washington, 1937), 24. Donald Garnel, "Teamsters and Highway Truckers in the West," 2 vols., Ph.D. dissertation (University of California, Berkeley, 1967), I, 116–19; *idem, The Rise of Teamster Power in the West* (Berkeley, 1972), 52–53.

10. "Membership and per Capita Tax Records, 1907–1957"; Garnel, "Teamsters," I, 118–19; Western Conference of Teamsters, *Report of the Proceedings of the First Meeting* (1937?), 2.

11. *Ibid.*

12. Garnel, "Teamsters," I, 143–44; *idem, The Rise,* 53; Dembo, 400–401.

13. Garnel, "Teamsters," I, 147–48, 155–56; *idem, The Rise,* 68; Dembo, 401.

14. Garnel, "Teamsters," I, 148–49; Dembo, 402.

15. The Washington State Federation of Labor was a statewide organization open to all AFL affiliates. Its main purposes were to lobby the state legislature and to coordinate organizational activities.

16. Gompers (1850–1924) was president of the AFL 1886–94, 1896–1924. He opposed radical political philosophies and plans to reorganize the AFL.

17. Garnel, "Teamsters," I, 119–59, 198–99; *idem, The Rise,* 68–72.

18. Richard Neuberger, *Our Promised Land* (New York, 1938), 184; Dembo, 402–403.

19. Dembo, 404; Daniel Bell, "Labor's New Men of Power," *Fortune,* Vol. 47 (June 1953), 156; "Life on the American Newsfront: Labor Leader Dave Beck Is the Boss of Seattle," *Life* (Oct. 25, 1937), 56–60.

20. The following discussion of Beck's use of the highway truckers to consolidate Teamsters power comes from: Garnel, "Teamsters," I, 182–201; *idem, The Rise,* 56–60.

21. Garnel, "Teamsters," I, 91, 149; Washington State Federation of Labor, *Proceedings of the Annual Convention* (1925), 10–11; Dembo, 405–406; Seattle *Union Record,* Sept. 9–14, 1925.

22. International Brotherhood of Teamsters, *Proceedings of the Ninth Convention* (Seattle, 1925), Officers Reports, pp. 92, 112; Fifth Day, A.M., pp. 3–6, P.M., pp. 13–14; author's interview with Dave Beck, Feb. 25, 1975; Dembo, 406–12.

23. Garnel, "Teamsters," I, 152–53.

24. For Beck's increasing success, see *ibid.,* 153–60, 183–200, 220–39, 251–52, 269–92; II, 363–73; Walter Galenson, *The CIO Challenge to the AFL: A History of the American Labor Movement, 1935–1941* (Cambridge, Mass., 1960), 471–78.

25. Seattle *Times,* May 8, 1934; William E. Ames and Roger A. Simpson, *Unionism or Hearst: The Seattle Post-Intelligencer Strike of 1936* (Seattle, 1978).

26. Galenson, 488–94; Herbert C. Prouty, "Seattle's A.F. of L.–C.I.O. War of the Warehousemen," M.A. thesis (University of Washington, 1938); Beck interview; J. B. Gillingham, *The Teamsters Union on the West Coast* (n.p., 1956), 54–63.

27. Beck interview.

28. Robert D. Leiter, *The Teamsters Union,* (n.p., 1957), 49–50; Garnel, "Teamsters," I, 167, 176–81.

29. *Ibid.;* Alva Johnston, "Seattle's One-Man Revolution," *Saturday Evening Post,* Vol. 76 (1937), 27–37; Beck interview.

30. Garnel, "Teamsters," I, 179–81, 285–92; II, 420–21.

Seattle Race Relations
during the Second World War

HOWARD A. DROKER

Bernard E. Squires, the new executive secretary of the Seattle Urban League, and his wife, Melvina, were surprised to find Asian redcaps looking after their bags when they arrived by rail in Seattle in 1939. At their hotel, Japanese bellhops served them. They soon discovered that Asians performed many jobs traditionally done by blacks in other parts of the country. Seattle's black population, a smaller minority than the Japanese, numbered only 3,789 in 1940—less than half the total Asian population. Mr. and Mrs. Squires also found that more than a quarter of the black community was native to Washington State; but the movement of blacks to the area had been impeded by the lack of economic opportunity following the boom years of the First World War. Cautious and conservative on the eve of World War II, the black community occupied a tenuous position on the margins of Seattle's economic and social life.

The outbreak of war in Europe suddenly ended the depression in the United States as the nation geared up to become the "arsenal of democracy." But the new prosperity did not extend equally to black workers and whites, and A. Philip Randolph, head of the Brotherhood of Sleeping Car Porters, organized the March on Washington movement to protest. The threatened march of one hundred thousand blacks in the summer of 1941 produced President Roosevelt's Executive Order 8802, creating the Fair Employment Practices Committee (FEPC).

Seattle's black community did not become strongly involved in the national protest movement. As early as May 1940, however, the com-

Originally published in *Pacific Northwest Quarterly,* October 1976.

munity produced a multiorganizational group to deal with discriminatory employment policies in local war production contracts. The
Committee for Defense of Negro Labor's Right to Work at Boeing Airplane Company, made up of black church groups, clubs, unions, fraternal organizations, and political groups, focused on the principal
war contractor in Seattle and on Local 751 of the Aero-Mechanics
Union.

Awarded major defense contracts in late 1939, Boeing had refused
to admit blacks to its newly established training schools. Initially,
Boeing attributed this discrimination to company policy, but soon
shifted the blame to the Aero-Mechanics Union of the International
Association of Machinists (IAM), labor's sole bargaining agent with
the company. On March 8, 1940, the headlines of the *Northwest Enterprise*, the local black newspaper, charged, "Conspiracy Bars Negro
Labor at Boeing." And the June 7 headlines angrily accused: "Jim
Crow Labor Unions Hitlerize U.S.A."

In response to a speech given by Bernard Squires in July, Local 751
voted to accept blacks and to propose to the annual convention of
machinists that the union's discriminatory initiation oath be
dropped. But the admission of blacks became a side issue in a juris-
dictional dispute when Local 751 split in October 1940. The local officers, who had Congress of Industrial Organizations (CIO) leanings,
were charged with communistic activities and ousted by the IAM.
The new executive board of the Aero-Mechanics Union, appointed
by Harvey Brown, IAM president, met and rescinded the decision to
admit blacks. This action was taken without consulting the membership, on the grounds that the July meeting had been controlled by
communists. The ousted faction attempted to organize a local affiliated with the United Auto Workers and the CIO, both of which prohibited racial discrimination, but it was unsuccessful.

As the defense industry expanded, employment rather than segregation of the armed services or the anti-lynching bill became the
central issue for the nation's black press. The *Northwest Enterprise*
hammered at the subject of job discrimination and took every opportunity to expose the hypocrisy of opposing Hitler's blatantly racist
regime with Jim Crow industry. When Roosevelt established the
FEPC in June 1941, the paper reported: "The president's memorandum issued to quiet the rising tide of Negroes' protest against the
hypocritical stand of industry and labor denying the Negroes' right
to work in plants holding contracts for national defense falls on deaf
ears in the far northwest."

In September 1941, following a complaint lodged by the National
Association for the Advancement of Colored People (NAACP), William Green, president of the American Federation of Labor, contacted

the Aero-Mechanics Union on behalf of the FEPC. After further informal action, in April 1942 the FEPC, backed by Roosevelt, persuaded the union to issue work permits to blacks. Local 751 gave little, and that grudgingly. "We have officially gone on record as agreeing to live up to the letter and spirit of the executive order whole-heartedly and without reservation," said one official of the IAM. "At the same time we rather resent that the war situation has been used to alter an old-established custom, and do not feel it will be helpful to war production." Furthermore, the permits that cost blacks $3.50 monthly did not afford them the status or job security of union membership.

Despite the union's hostility, there were sixteen hundred black workers at Boeing—2.9 percent of the total work force—when employment peaked in the summer of 1944. That percentage might have been higher if the company's labor recruiters, competing with other industry, had been able to promise southern blacks adequate housing in Seattle. Another two thousand blacks worked in Seattle area shipyards.

After the Japanese population was evacuated in the spring of 1942, other jobs were opened to blacks. These were the kinds of jobs that blacks traditionally held in other parts of the country, positions as bellhops, dishwashers, redcaps. Although the *Northwest Enterprise* denounced discriminatory action against the Japanese and later protested more strongly than any other Seattle paper against the evacuation, it was quick to urge that blacks take advantage of the new opportunities. Black business improved considerably; on May 22, 1942, the *Northwest Enterprise* noted that the holdings of one businessman had increased 25 percent due to the Japanese evacuation.

Yet discriminatory practices continued to keep blacks out of some jobs. For example, in an advertisement for Christmas help placed by Frederick and Nelson in the *Post-Intelligencer* of November 12, 1941, the store requested "white applicants only." By mid-1942, however, and until the end of the war, employment had ceased to be a problem for blacks. It is true that lack of job security continued to cause concern among blacks who looked beyond the wartime manpower crisis. But although the *Northwest Enterprise* persisted in its attack on work permits at Boeing, it turned its attention to other matters.

Expanded employment opportunities led directly to the rapid growth of Seattle's black population. In early 1944 it was estimated that the black community had at least doubled since 1940 (from under four thousand to over eight thousand) and possibly tripled. In the context of latent racist feeling, this radical change in the population posed new difficulties. Seattle experienced the same kinds of problems (though on a lesser scale) that occurred in every major northern and western city where the black population increased during the world wars. As black people became more visible and harder to ignore, racial tensions began to mount. Problems arose mainly in housing and in the use of such public facilities as parks, restaurants, and transportation. Jim Crow policies multiplied along with the black population.

Migrants of all races found housing a particularly acute problem in Seattle. Construction of private residences could not keep up with the demand. Once the defense industries were operating at maximum capacity, public housing might have been able to provide for the migrants' needs; but the local public housing authorities could not convince officials at Boeing and Todd Shipyards that their projections were correct. In addition, industry representatives to the mayor's housing committee, perhaps under pressure from real estate interests, blocked action on requests made by the Seattle Housing Authority (SHA) for more public housing.

According to Jesse Epstein, the director of the SHA from its inception in 1939, "Public housing was still considered too much government, a lot of New Deal." He summed up industry's sentiments: "Let's go slow on it now, there's a war on and we may need some but let's not go overboard and let's certainly not build so many permanent ones because that means they'll be used for low rent afterwards." Soon, however, Seattle industry was experiencing difficulty recruiting in the South because people had heard that housing was not available.

For blacks the problem was especially difficult because they were excluded from all new private housing as well as any already existing outside black neighborhoods. Restrictive covenants still had the force of law. Blacks were barred from all-white neighborhoods by various methods, which may have included violence: in March 1941 the *Northwest Enterprise* reported that the home of a black teacher was bombed, but there is no corroborating evidence of this.

Even before the war, housing for blacks was unsatisfactory. The incidence of substandard housing in the Central Area was twice that of the city as a whole, and overcrowding was a major problem. In April 1944 Epstein reported that at least seven thousand blacks were "living in the same areas, and for the most part in the same buildings, housing 3,789 Negroes in 1940." The Seattle *Times* of August 15, 1943, reported a "share-the-housing" drive that encouraged Seattle residents to take war workers into their homes. The federal War Housing Center dealt with the problems of overcrowding and deficient facilities by promoting remodeling to accommodate more people in existing space; its Homes Lease Program assumed all such construction costs and also paid for leasing houses while the war lasted.

As a result of the shortage of private housing, a high percentage of black migrants turned to the SHA. Seattle was one of the few cities in the country to have integrated public housing, an accomplishment of Jesse Epstein, who recalled:

I made the decision administratively, early, that there would be no discrimination, no segregation, and, to me, that particular approach . . . was so obvious that I did not ask the [SHA] Board to declare a policy in writing. . . . I was also a little concerned that if I raised the question there might be some consideration given to such matters as quotas, maybe even segregation.

The federal government never tried to influence this decision or to change it. The Roosevelt administration, while maintaining a low profile on racial matters, was willing to let local administrators use their discretion.

Integration went smoothly at the SHA's only prewar project, Yesler Terrace, in the cosmopolitan area known as the International District. But when the SHA built in the all-white areas of West Seattle, Holly Park, Rainier Vista, and Sand Point, local businesses and residents brought pressure on Epstein to segregate the projects. Although constructed to house defense workers, they were also designed as permanent public housing. The SHA administered all defense housing for the federal government, permanent and temporary. Tenant clashes occurred but Epstein did not consider them racial in nature. "I had most of the trouble before anyone moved in," he remembered.

The last element of the population to be tapped for the war effort, blacks (especially those from the South) constituted the majority of the labor force that sought employment on the West Coast. Toward the end of the war, they made up an ever-increasing percentage of the people residing in temporary public housing. In Seattle this meant that the projects were developing with an unbalanced racial mix that Epstein never wanted, but there was no alternative. The number of black residents at Duwamish Bend rose to 40 percent before war production tapered off and migration ceased. But on the West Coast as a whole, temporary war housing became permanent ghettos for those blacks who remained. San Francisco's Hunter's Point was (and is) an example of that fact.

The increase of the black population in Seattle magnified other problems. Congestion in the Central Area produced conditions similar to those of other cities with racial ghettos. Overcrowding led to deterioration of health, growth of crime, and deflation of the human spirit. Jim Crow institutions became more prevalent as a result of the black migration and more prominent as a result of the black community's growing commitment to do away with them. Blacks were discriminated against at public swimming pools, Longacres Race Track, and roller rinks, on city buses, in hotels, restaurants, and movie houses. Local branches of the NAACP and the Urban League reacted strongly to such policies with suits and protests and in some cases succeeded in alleviating the practice of discrimination. Black university students challenged the city's segregation policy at Colman Pool in 1941, but it was not until 1944 that the policy was changed.

In Washington State, black soldiers were often discriminated against, especially in smaller cities with military installations, such as Walla Walla, Yakima, and Bremerton, which experienced a large influx of blacks where there had been few or none before. The *Northwest Enterprise* reported that almost 95 percent of the restaurants in Walla Walla refused to serve blacks; 80 percent of Bremerton's restaurants, soda fountains, and beer parlors followed the same policy. At the Bremerton Navy Yard the racial situation had become so tense by mid-1943 that the commander requested that the Civil Service Office route all blacks to San Francisco Bay installations.

Black soldiers stationed at Fort Lawton or visiting Seattle from Fort Lewis were more fortunate than those in the small cities. For one thing, they could find a welcome in the established and growing black community. Initially, sections of that community strongly opposed the establishment of all-black United Services Organization clubs in the city, and the NAACP denounced the black members of the city's War Defense Council who had recommended them. But segregated armed forces could hardly justify integrated USOs, and by October of 1943 the black community proudly announced plans to open its second all-black USO. Growing racial tensions in the city, however, made the presence of black soldiers a matter of concern to black residents, who were well aware that frustration and anger were increasing among black servicemen as the war continued to be fought by a Jim Crow army.

The reaction of the older, prewar black families to the migrants provides an interesting barometer by which the change in Seattle's racial climate may be measured. At first the newcomers were resented, both because they were largely an unskilled rural working class and because their behavior and numbers made all blacks conspicuous and increased discrimination by whites.

In early 1943, with the black migration in full swing, the *Northwest Enterprise* became concerned with increasing crime committed by blacks. The editor, Edward I. Robinson, praised the police and the daily papers for not making a racial issue out of recent incidents. "Let us do a little missionary work among our new comers," Robinson continued in his editorial. "Pipe down these loud mouth bus riders . . . and maintain a wholesome respect for the rights of others." Race relations were damaged, the paper paraphrased a black leader as saying, by the "public discourtesy, boorishness, uncleanliness, obscene language, garish display, and drunkenness of a small minority of Negroes."

Horace Cayton, nationally known sociologist and Seattle native, scolded local blacks for their lack of hospitality when he visited the city in August 1943. He urged black leaders to stop complaining about the behavior of the migrants.

Both Negroes and whites will have to realize that the migrants are a city-wide responsibility and are there to stay. The old Negro settlers will have to realize that they must "carry the cross" for the behavior of the newcomers, whether they approve of them or not. If they do, and work toward a program to integrate them in the social fabric of the city, they will reap rewards in the form of new business opportunities and a greater political strength.

The black community tried to meet the challenge by publicizing the work of the American Association for Tolerance, and in September 1943 launched its own program, including a "Good Conduct Drive." In late 1944 some black churches formed fellowship committees "for the purpose of orienting the new residents into our way of life." The East Madison YWCA held classes to teach migrants how to use electrical appliances.

It took time for the migrants to accustom themselves to their new way of life in Seattle, and it took the old black families even longer to get used to their new black neighbors and the heightened visibility of blacks in the city. Cayton had been right about the increased business and political opportunities that would come as a result of the black influx to Seattle. He had also been right about the newcomers being there to stay, though most people at the time apparently hoped that the migrants would go back where they came from when the war was over. The war years also made white Seattleites more conscious of the black community and its place in the city. Black Seattleites could no longer be ignored.

White Americans, unsettled by growing black assertiveness, were defensive when confronted by demands for racial equality that were tied to the war's democratic rhetoric. Many considered the campaign of the black press for domestic justice both opportunistic and bordering on treason. Led by Roosevelt, whites believed that the winning of the war took precedence over all social problems and that the agitation over such issues interfered with the conduct of the war.

Not surprisingly, the conflict of viewpoint between whites and blacks led to tensions that were compounded by competition for housing and recreation in the overcrowded centers of war industry.

In the South, violence against black soldiers in uniform is largely attributed to the whites' fear that blacks were becoming too aggressive. But racial violence was not confined to the South. The black press, by giving extensive coverage to individual violent acts and to race riots (largely ignored by the white press), helped create a determined attitude among blacks to stand up to attacks and to fight back. Despite the increasing occurrences of racial violence, little was done to prevent more outbreaks until three major riots shook local governments out of their lethargy. The Harlem riot, the Los Angeles "Zoot Suit" riot involving the Spanish-speaking minority, and especially the Detroit race riot—all of which occurred in the summer of 1943—were so destructive of life and property, and so imperiled the war effort, that many cities could no longer ignore the problem of racial tensions.

In the eighteen months following the Detroit riot, more than one hundred state and local committees were set up across the nation to deal with conflict between the races. On the surface at least, this "civic unity movement" was a spontaneous phenomenon, a chain reaction; but there is reason to suspect that an initiating force operated from the White House or the military. Some attempts at federation were made, including efforts by the newly formed American Council on Race Relations and by such established groups as the Southern Regional Council, the NAACP, the National Urban League, and the president's FEPC. Local and state committees remained autonomous, however, and displayed diverse methods, purposes, and authority.

Lester B. Granger, executive secretary of the Urban League, conducted a survey of fifty-seven such committees in 1944. He found that interracial membership was universal and that "prestigious" or influential people, representative of the establishment, were recruited to serve. Professional people were heavily overrepresented. "Generally speaking," Granger wrote, "committee membership is eminently respectable, but not remarkable for qualities of dynamic leadership." Few of the state committees had any legislative sanction, few of the municipal committees had the endorsement of their city councils, and most committees had to rely on volunteers because of inadequate budgets. Granger singled out only two, in Massachusetts and West Virginia, as potentially effective. Many committees received some aid from such federal agencies as the Office of Community War Services, the War Manpower Commission, and the National Housing Agency.

In February 1944 Seattle's Mayor William F. Devin created his Mayor's Civic Unity Committee in response to the black community's concern, his own new awareness (which grew out of the Detroit riot), and the suggestion from Ann Madsen of the Civilian War Commission (who became the first secretary of the CUC). Black leaders, most sensitive to the changes occurring in Seattle's race relations, were the first to become apprehensive about the possibility of racial violence in their city. One black citizen recalled that the black leadership worked very hard to avoid violence. "The organizations [NAACP, Urban League, churches] really got together and said to industry and the power structure, 'If you don't change some of these things [job and housing discrimination, Jim Crowism, racial insults], the lid is going to blow off.'"

Mayor Devin told the first meeting of the CUC that the members had been brought together "to give study to growing tensions and to attempt to make recommendations to avoid any outbreaks of violence that might occur because of such tensions." A study committee suggested the name, outlined the purpose, and proposed a means of financing the new committee. Although many people denied that racial tensions existed and, therefore, denied the need for such an organization, Devin disagreed.

The problem of racial tensions is one which is fraught with a great deal of dynamite because it deals with long established fears that have brought about prejudices. It is going to affect us as a city not only during the war, but also after the war. Now, it is our duty as citizens to face the problem together; if we do not, we shall not exist as a civilized city or nation very long.

Devin's sincerity has not been questioned even by those far to the left of his mildly conservative, business-oriented politics. The appointment of the CUC may also have been politically motivated; it was announced a few days before the mayoral election of 1944 (which Devin went on to win) and was publicized only in the black press. That the *Times* and *Post-Intelligencer* were silent is not surprising when the CUC's low-keyed, quiet approach is considered. In the committee's view, widespread knowledge of its existence was undesirable.

The purpose of the CUC, Devin recalled, was "to create in our city a committee of respected, reliable individuals to whom the whole community looked and admired and respected because of their positions and their reputations, and then to have them explain to the people why they should not discriminate." The original committee included "two members of the Negro race, one a minister and one a dentist, one Jewish member, one Chinese, two labor representatives (one CIO and [one] AFL), two women who have [been] interested in community work for years, one educator, one industrialist, one protestant clergyman, one lawyer and one banker." "Left-wingers" were excluded and politically conservative people predominated. Most were professional people who represented the upper economic and social levels. Ideally, the CUC was to be "non-political" and "balanced as to conservative-progressive viewpoints." Its "majority viewpoint" was intended to "coincide as nearly as possible with that of the community," which, given the prevalent conscious and unconscious racism of white Seattle, is somewhat ironic.

The Seattle Civic Unity Committee had the same general characteristics that were found in most of the committees studied by Granger. The members were chosen as much for their standing in the city as for their knowledge and experience in intergroup relations. There were, however, some notable exceptions. The first chairman was George Greenwood, a bank president who took what was for his day a courageous position on the race issue, especially for a prominent businessman. According to Irene B. Miller, race relations officer for the Northwest Public Housing Authority and CUC secretary from 1946 to 1952, Greenwood was one of the few prominent civic leaders on the West Coast "with the guts to take a strong stand against the removal of the Japanese." The two black members, the Reverend F. Benjamin Davis and Dr. Felix B. Cooper, had both been active in civil rights work. Arthur G. Barnett was active in the unpopular cause of defending Japanese-American rights and was attorney for Gordon Hirabayashi, whose case against the relocation of the Japanese went to the U.S. Supreme Court.

Like most municipal committees on race relations, Seattle's CUC lacked endorsement by the city council and, without adequate financing, relied heavily on voluntary work from its members. The CUC was under the jurisdiction of the Civilian War Commission, and its only salaried employee, part-time secretary Ann Madsen, was paid by the King County Community War Chest. It was directly responsible to the mayor and during the war years was known as the Mayor's Committee. Without any authority or powers, the CUC relied wholly on persuasion to accomplish its aim of decreasing racial tensions.

The Seattle CUC was part of an informal national network of race relations agencies that shared information and experiences. These groups shaped the incipient civil rights movement in the years before protests against racial discrimination gained widespread national attention. From its very beginning, the CUC relied to a significant degree on correspondence with other local committees and national coordinating agencies for its organizational rules, ideas of appropriate targets and tactics, and information on the successes and failures of various programs. The Chicago committee was a popular model, and the Seattle group combined many of its features with scattered ideas from other committees. By pooling its own experiences with those of other committees, the CUC was able to overcome some of the inherent limitations on its effectiveness.

The tactics of many civil rights advocates were rejected by the CUC because, whether successful or not, they tended to increase racial tensions. Although the threat of litigation under the state's civil rights statutes and of adverse publicity had been effective in breaking down discrimination, these devices antagonized discriminators. Furthermore, the public in general distrusted both white and black civil rights groups. They viewed the former as typically left of center and the latter as narrowly focused and self-interested.

CUC members made a sincere effort to understand the position of the discriminator and avoided intimidating tactics at all costs. Their principle duty was to defuse discriminatory incidents and troubleshoot tense situations through private meetings with those concerned and with the media. Their main method of persuasion was to invoke the concept of democracy and the logic of self-interest. In its public relations, the CUC highlighted progress rather than the problem of remaining discrimination. It was also prepared to initiate a "constructive program and activities through community organizations and other appropriate channels," to educate the public on race relations, and to utilize factual information compiled by existing agencies and by individuals.

According to the committee, its approach was a pleasant surprise to businessmen who had been criticized by "left-wing" groups. Arthur Barnett recalled: "When a couple of nice people from the Mayor's Office would go out and talk to somebody, what were these people going to do? It wasn't the sort of thing that would create a problem, it was a healing approach." Correctly assuming that prejudice was common and not easily changed, the committee went about its work accordingly. "It had to gain the confidence of the community by the fairness of its attitude, its willingness to understand the contrasting interests and philosophies."

So great was the commitment of the CUC to a quiet, behind-the-scenes approach that most Seattleites were unaware of the committee's existence. During the war, publicity was avoided, and except for its campaign to ease the return of the Japanese, the committee attracted little attention. Although it was commended by the *Northwest Enterprise* for its role in bringing the War Department film *The Negro Soldier* to Seattle, the CUC limited itself primarily to private dealings with individuals in order to accomplish its aims; only after the war did the committee subsidize local studies that compiled and disseminated facts to the public.

At a CUC meeting in March 1944, employment, transportation, housing, and recreation were identified as the areas requiring immediate attention. Anticipating a major industrial cutback, the committee expressed concern for the postwar employment situation and advocated that dismissals be made by racial quota to avoid trouble. Although a member proposed that the matter be taken up with the chamber of commerce, there is no record of any follow-up action, and the CUC never produced a plan to mitigate the effects of defense layoffs on blacks. Subsequently, the black work force suffered much more drastic cuts than did the white. The CUC did become active, however, in the state's postwar fair employment campaign.

During the war, the CUC's major case of discriminatory hiring practices concerned the refusal of the Seattle Transit Company to hire black drivers despite a severe manpower shortage. After gathering information on the successful integration of San Francisco transit drivers, the committee presented its findings to Lloyd Graber, the company's general manager, in March 1944. In August of that year, Graber maintained that the occurrence of racial clashes on the buses "was making it increasingly difficult to discuss the subject of hiring Negro drivers." By then the situation had become more acute. In Philadelphia, white transit employees had gone on strike over the issue of hiring black drivers and consequently had disrupted war production and antagonized blacks. Del Castle, a radical spokesman, called for CUC hearings in the Washington Commonwealth Federation newspaper, *New World*.

Undertaking to work privately with the transit company, bus drivers' union, and the Urban League, the CUC urged the latter to encourage blacks to apply for driving jobs. In February 1945, when ten blacks had submitted applications, the committee met with the company and the union. By midmonth blacks were enrolled in the training program at Seattle Transit. During the course of the program, however, all the black trainees were disqualified or left voluntarily, save one—and he failed to receive a passing score in the obligatory final driving test conducted by a white driver. Although the company came under fire from the *Northwest Enterprise* and the Urban League, its good faith was upheld by the committee chairman, George Greenwood. The CUC met with league members and representatives of the newspaper in an effort to tone down their attacks on the company. When the first black was finally hired in late April 1945, the CUC sent letters of commendation to the company, the union, and the new driver.

The public transit system was a source of concern for the CUC not only in terms of discriminatory hiring practices but also because the buses provided a potential site for violence. The *Northwest Enterprise* and the transit company shared the committee's fear of clashes resulting from the unavoidable racial mixing at close quarters. In March 1944, a black woman was evicted from a bus by the driver and arrested by four policemen who manhandled and cursed her. The general manager, Graber, invited to speak to the committee, attributed increased racial tensions to the attitude of recent white migrants from the South and to overcrowding on the buses. One witness to the incident described the police action as "Gestapo tactics," and the *Northwest Enterprise* speculated that the presence of black soldiers at the scene could have fomented a riot. The paper reported that one soldier had said, "And this is what I am wearing this uniform for." Although other incidents occurred, the press, at the request of the CUC, either minimized or refrained from reporting them.

In the areas of employment and transportation, the CUC enjoyed a limited success, but the housing issue proved too large and complex for it during the war. Jesse Epstein's report on overcrowding in the black neighborhoods was submitted to the committee, but it lacked power to improve these conditions. In the area of recreation, the CUC made some progress; although it failed to alleviate discrimination at roller rinks, it succeeded in integrating the city's Colman Pool.

When the Japanese began to return in January 1945, Seattle confronted its gravest racial problem. Although the blind racism and fear that were largely responsible for the evacuation of the Japanese had abated to some degree, self-styled "patriotic" anti-Japanese groups had formed. These, together with certain economic groups, were opposed to the move back to the West Coast. But a public sense of guilt, the efforts of civic groups, and the favorable publicity given to Japanese-American soldiers by the federal government helped to lessen racial tensions and ease the return.

In a letter to Lieutenant General Delos Emmons, Western Defense Command chief, in early 1944, Mayor Devin joined the chief executives of several large Pacific Coast cities in protesting against any return of Japanese Americans to the coast. Once the government decided to allow the Japanese to move back, however, Devin turned the matter over to the CUC. The committee adopted a resolution that agreed with the government's reasons for rescinding the evacuation order, cited the heroism and sacrifice of Nisei soldiers, and concluded with the expression of hope "that Seattle will respond as a truly American city and grant the returning American-Japanese citizens all the rights to which they are legally entitled."

Greenwood met with representatives from the daily papers, who assured him that "the situation would be played down" in the press. The *Times* editorial of December 20, 1944, entitled "Loyal Citizens Should Be Received on Their Merits," questioned the justice of the indiscriminate evacuation, praised the loyal Japanese for tolerating temporary injustice, and counseled Seattle citizens to welcome their return. Similarly, the *Post-Intelligencer* published an article that emphasized the heroism of the Japanese-American soldiers who were fighting in Europe and the Pacific. The papers also countered statements by hate groups such as the Japanese Exclusion League and the Remember Pearl Harbor League. The third daily paper, the pro-labor Seattle *Star*, minimized the issue but avoided the sympathetic stance of the other dailies.

Late in 1944, an army general visited the city on the assignment of clearing the way for the return of the Japanese. The CUC coordinated his meeting with representatives of potentially troublesome groups, including the Veterans of Foreign Wars, the American Legion, the Teamsters union, and the Central Labor Council. To encourage free expression, no minutes were kept. Arthur Barnett, a representative of the CUC at the meeting, recalled what took place.

We were assured by the general . . . that we would have no problem with patriotic groups because they seldom ever took a position opposite to that taken by the Army. And this was true. The American Legion said, "Oh, we go along with the Army". . . . So we just had Charlie Doyle (representing the Central Labor Council), he was a wild one. He said, "You bring them back, we won't be responsible for how many are hanging from the lamp posts."

Dillon S. Meyer, national director of the War Relocation Authority, which administered the Japanese evacuation and the relocation camps, claimed that the return of the Japanese was opposed almost entirely by "professional race mongers" and special economic interests. Washington's Governor Mon Wallgren's disapproval of the return as late as January 1945 indicates that the opposition was somewhat more widespread than Meyer claimed. Elements of organized labor, fearing renewed competition, were hostile. The *Washington Teamster*, looking ahead to the postwar contraction of employment, blamed industry for trying to use the Japanese as cheap labor to drive down wages. Dave Beck, head of the Teamsters union, was a prominent spokesman for the opponents of Japanese return. The *Washington State Labor News*, which was published by the Seattle Central Labor Council, echoed Charles Doyle's opposition to the return, but there is no way of knowing how the rank and file responded to Doyle's exhortations. The *Washington State CIO News* ignored the issue.

Produce dealers formed another group that opposed return. Seeking to protect their economic interests, they couched their arguments in patriotic jargon. In a letter to ten produce dealers who had displayed "no Jap" signs, the CUC appealed to "your spirit of fair play, . . . your basic American neighborliness and your desire to see that the principles of Democracy for which our men are giving their lives may not be stamped out and forgotten here at home." But the signs remained, and the CUC, unwilling to resort to pressure tactics, lacked the power to force their removal. Most of the other opposition around the Seattle area was located in the Kent Valley, where farmers feared Japanese competition.

The successful, nonviolent return of the Japanese to Seattle was possible because of a combination of factors in which the CUC was an important element. Since the committee represented the responsible policy of the city government, it was able to gain the cooperation of the press and thus moderate public opinion. Another major factor was the federal government's commitment to the return and its propaganda on behalf of Japanese-American soldiers. Finally, the most important element in the preservation of civic peace was the demeanor of the Japanese themselves: their acceptance of evacuation, their suppression of bitterness, and their quiet determination to rebuild their lives.

In its involvement with the return of the Japanese, to which it devoted considerable effort, the CUC achieved its greatest wartime success. The threat of violence had been most real in this instance, and perhaps the urgency occasioned by this threat made the committee more forceful than usual in countering the arguments of the opposition. In addition, the issue was somewhat less complicated than that of minority employment or housing, and it was more susceptible to the kind of actions the CUC was best suited to carry out. One member of the committee, Arthur Barnett, housed one of the first returning Japanese families, and the CUC helped place many more in homes and jobs.

The impact of the Second World War on Seattle was enormous; it changed forever the city's economy, its population, and the outlook of its citizens. The war transformed the city into a major industrial center and added to the population a large number of migrants who brought their own habits, customs, tastes, manners, and ideas to the Northwest. From April 1940 to November 1943, thirty-five states had a net civilian population loss, and the largest gainers were California, Washington, and Oregon, in that order. By 1960, less than half of Seattle's 557,000 residents were native to Washington State.

Earl Pomeroy's contention that the West, as a separate and unique entity in the nation, was disappearing during the middle decades of the twentieth century is applicable to the Pacific Northwest's largest city. Regional differences diminished once the unique racial makeup of the West Coast and Seattle had been modified, with the subsequent altering of race relations. When blacks became the largest minority group, and race relations became a vital though too often avoided concern of business and political leaders, Seattle began to resemble other urban centers.

In general, the civic unity movement represented a recognition by powerful and responsible people of the dangers of racial injustice. Carey McWilliams may have overstated the case when he called civic unity "the first seriously undertaken attempt 'to do something about' the racial problem" on the part of the white power structure. But inasmuch as it brought the prestige of respectable and influential people to the case of racial justice, the movement was a new departure in social action by civic groups.

In Seattle the new commitment to racial justice, as evidenced by the creation of the Civic Unity Committee, was genuine; it constituted a forward step in the white community's involvement in social problems. The outlook of the community, as well as the experiences and knowledge of CUC members themselves, dictated the committee's practical and low-keyed methods. In the context of the times, a more flamboyant style was unthinkable for such a group and, in the reactionary postwar decade, was increasingly untenable for *any* group. During the early years, the CUC's approach was viable and its contributions to Seattle's race relations valuable. Operating until 1964, Seattle's CUC was one of the longest lived of the wartime race relations committees, and one of the most effective.

BIBLIOGRAPHICAL NOTE

Primary sources of information for this essay include Calvin F. Schmid, Charles E. Nobbe, and Arlene E. Mitchell, *Nonwhite Races: State of Washington* (Olympia, 1968); Robert Bedford Pitts, "Organized Labor and the Negro in Seattle," M.A. thesis (University of Washington, 1941); Robert W. O'Brien and Lee M. Brooks, "Race Relations in the Pacific Northwest," *Phylon*, Vol. 7 (1946); and the 1940s issues of *Northwest Enterprise* (Seattle). During the early 1970s, the author interviewed Melvina Squires, Jesse Epstein, William F. Devin, Arthur G. Barnett, and Robert W. O'Brien.

See also Richard M. Dalfiume, *Desegregation of the U.S. Armed Forces* (Columbia, Mo., 1969); Herbert Garfinkel, *When Negroes March* (Glencoe, Ill., 1959); Robert C. Weaver, *Negro Labor* (New York, 1946); Richard Polenberg, *War and Society: The United States, 1941–1945* (Philadelphia, 1972); and Richard Lingeman, *Don't You Know There's A War On?* (New York, 1970).

Burlington Northern
and the Legacy of Mount Saint Helens

ALFRED RUNTE

The American people, for all their love of spectacular scenery, have largely forgotten their debt to the railroads of the West for first suggesting and promoting many of our great national parks. Washington State's Mount Saint Helens, whose eruption on May 18, 1980, electrified the public as a geological spectacle, also represents that unique period of history when the railroads helped saved our scenic heritage. The key link historically lies in the square mile of property on the crest of the mountain then owned by Burlington Northern Inc. With the donation of this property to the federal government in 1982, it is now appropriate to consider the gift in its historical context.

The presentation of this land is symbolic of that long and remarkable commitment among the western railroads to the establishment, protection, and development of national parks and related reserves. Granted, few executives were motivated by pure altruism or environmental concern; their primary objective was to promote their railroads in general and tourism in particular, thereby adding to corporate profits. The mere suggestion, as a result, that the national park idea—hailed worldwide as America's purest expression of landscape protection—received a crucial boost from a major corporate group may seem almost sacrilegious. Yet often preservationists themselves have been the first to admit, however begrudgingly, the validity of that interpretation. To be sure, the dedication of the summit of Mount Saint Helens is no exception but, more appropriately, a reaffirmation of one of the most positive and colorful traditions of corporate history.

Originally published as a commemorative brochure for Burlington Northern Inc. and in *Pacific Northwest Quarterly*, July 1983.

Prior to 1980 Mount Saint Helens slumbered in relative obscurity. Nationally, if not regionally, her fame and beauty were largely over-shadowed by the popularity of her renowned sisters to the north and south, Mount Rainier and Mount Hood.

Meanwhile, by the 1960s, the automobile and the airplane had out-stripped railroad transportation in the United States; gradually, as use of passenger trains declined, the railroads' role in opening the Pacific Northwest became only a dim recollection in the public mind. Until the eruption of Mount Saint Helens, for example, few people realized that the peak fell within the boundaries of the federal land grant awarded to the Northern Pacific Railroad (NP) in 1864 to help offset the cost of its construction. Similarly, hardly anyone in 1970 noticed when the remainder of this grant, with the merger of the NP into the Burlington Northern, became the property of the new cor-poration.

Then suddenly, early on Sunday morning, May 18, 1980, Mount Saint Helens shook the Pacific Northwest with a thundering assertion of her own special place in the history of the region. The north face of the mountain literally blew apart, spewing smoke and ash tens of thousands of feet into the atmosphere. Simultaneously, millions of tons of mud, shattered tree trunks, and other debris swept down the northern slope, choking Spirit Lake and flooding the Toutle River.

All told, the area devastated by the blast encompassed two hun-dred miles; approximately sixty lives were also lost. Obviously, no amount of training could have prepared the government agencies as-signed to the disaster to cope with such a powerful and relentless force. Only weeks later, when no other major eruptions seemed im-minent, could everyone concerned begin to appreciate the unique opportunity that presented itself to chronicle the rebirth of the sum-mit and its environs.

Burlington Northern, as co-owner of Mount Saint Helens with the federal government, was especially concerned about the future of the peak, now hollowed out into a gaping crater 1,313 feet lower in ele-vation than the original summit. Extending from the lip of the crater down the slopes opposite the blast area, arcing 90 degrees from due south to due west, lay the remainder of the square mile that originally had formed part of the NP's land grant. Clearly, this portion of the mountain had no commercial use but great value as the nucleus of the national park or monument already proposed by environmental groups. In recognition of the popularity of these proposals, Burling-ton Northern in 1982 restored the area to the federal government. With the donation, the corporation added another chapter to a legacy of involvement in scenic preservation dating as far back as 1871.

For several years reports had filtered back east about a breathtaking wonderland newly discovered in the northwestern corner of Wyoming Territory. Here, awed explorers found, were geysers of great power and fountains of bubbling mud, interspersed with deep canyonlands and a waterfall twice the height of Niagara. Apparently, some of the adventurers first suggested that they and their companions should confiscate their discoveries for private gain. Fortunately, they agreed instead to publicize the wonders and to lobby for their protection in a reserve that all Americans could enjoy.

At least, this is the popular version of the origins of Yellowstone National Park. Recently, however, historians have determined that the actual park campaign got under way in Congress only after Jay Cooke, the noted financier, began to press for the park with an eye to boosting the Northern Pacific's transcontinental aspirations. In fact, Cooke had already retained Nathaniel P. Langford, a leading member of the Yellowstone expedition of 1870, to lecture throughout the East about the region's potential as America's grandest and most fashionable tourist resort.

Also keeping in mind the need to confirm the Yellowstone wonders visually, Cooke's agent, A. B. Nettleton, urged that the landscape painter Thomas Moran be allowed to accompany government surveyors into the area in 1871. Cooke further loaned the artist five hundred dollars to make the trip and thereby indirectly patronized Moran's most famous oil painting, "The Grand Canyon of the Yellowstone," now housed in the National Museum of American Art in Washington, D.C.

With such effective publicity and political support, the Yellowstone Park legislation was swiftly approved on March 1, 1872. Unfortunately for Cooke, his hopes of turning the reserve into a profitable attraction for tourist traffic were dashed by the depression of the following year. Not until 1883 was the transcontinental line completed, and the spur track to Yellowstone—heading due south from Livingston, Montana—also in place. Nevertheless, the efforts of Jay Cooke and his colleagues to win approval for the park eleven years earlier had been instrumental in its creation.

Now that the task of promoting Yellowstone also could go forward, the NP spared little expense. As early as 1886, for example, it underwrote the construction of a series of hotels located near the primary attractions. Similarly, to publicize both the railroad and the accommodations, Charles S. Fee, chief passenger agent in Saint Paul, Minnesota, commissioned a colorfully written and illustrated series of guidebooks, beginning with his personal compilation, *Northern Pacific Railroad: The Wonderland Route to the Pacific Coast, 1885.*

Through the quotations of articulate travelers and renowned personalities, these guidebooks introduced Americans not only to Yellowstone, but to Mount Rainier, the Columbia River Gorge, the Cascade Mountains, and similar landmarks accessible via the Northern Pacific. Even Mount Saint Helens, visible from the trains approaching Portland, Oregon, was featured at this early date for its appeal to observers as "the great Sugar Loaf" of the Pacific Northwest.

Obviously, what modern Americans would recognize as ecological awareness was rarely evident in such guidebook testimonials. The primary objective of the descriptions, after all, was to publicize the West's tourist attractions; more visitors, in turn, promised the NP greater revenues from its hotels, transcontinental trains, and other passenger-related operations.

This commercial motive, however, made the long-range impact of the publicity on the preservation movement in the U.S. no less positive or significant. The railroad's own dependence on unspoiled scenery to attract tourists tempered its purely extractive aims, such as the promotion of logging, mining, and settlement. Its passenger department, at the very least, put the NP on record as one of the first and most outspoken defenders of Yellowstone National Park. Barely had the railroad come to the gates of Wonderland, as promoters billed it, when Fee declared on behalf of his employers:

We do not want to see the Falls of the Yellowstone driving the looms of a cotton factory, or the great geysers boiling pork for some gigantic packing-house, but in all the native majesty and grandeur in which they appear to-day, without, as yet, a single trace of that adornment which is desecration, that improvement which is equivalent to ruin, or that utilization which means utter destruction.

As if to underscore the pledge, the Northern Pacific in 1893 adopted a new logo, patterned after the Chinese symbol of the universe, and suspended it above the caption "Yellowstone Park Line."

By the turn of the century, as wildlife conservation also grew in importance, the NP's passenger department again spoke out strongly in defense of Yellowstone. More Americans now recognized that the protection of wild animals required greater amounts of land than the safeguarding of scenic areas. Migratory wildlife populations paid no heed to park boundaries laid out to preserve scenery, but instead followed their traditional routes back and forth between the park and their wintering grounds. For the first time Yellowstone's ecological shortcomings were dramatically apparent. Despite its great size, the park still lacked enough territory to protect its larger mammals, particularly elk, deer, and antelope. Every fall, as these species deserted the park for their winter range at lower elevations, they were forced to run a gauntlet of poachers and sportsmen with no respect for bag limits. For Yellowstone to support its native wildlife effectively, either the park itself would have to be greatly enlarged, or the animals themselves better protected while outside its borders.

The Northern Pacific, through another of its spokesmen, Olin D. Wheeler, supported both options with equal enthusiasm. "In order . . . to properly preserve these fast disappearing relics of wild animal life to future generations," he wrote in the Wonderland guidebook for 1902, "additional territory should be added, either to the park proper or to the forest reserve about it, so that absolute protection can be maintained." Poachers and "game hogs" cared "only for their own selfish pleasure in killing as many deer or elks as they can," he bitterly continued. Perhaps the solution therefore lay in "the boys and girls" of America, those with the greatest stake in the destiny of Yellowstone. From their "irresistible" efforts, their "vim and enthusiasm," he concluded, might spring the "national movement" that finally would compel Congress to "arrange for game protection in the Yellowstone Park region for all future time."

Actually, another half century would pass before the protection of Jackson Hole, lying just to the south, complemented Yellowstone as a wildlife preserve. But again, the delay does not compromise the significance of that first crucial step of stating unequivocally the need for park expansion. The NP, through Wheeler, fully shared in the credit for that endorsement.

Meanwhile, the railroad, obviously successful in its Yellowstone promotion and revenues, supported the establishment of Mount Rainier National Park in Washington State. Approved by Congress in 1899, the park was carved in large part from square-mile sections of the peak, sections the railroad had acquired in its original land grant. In agreement that these properties were best suited for scenic enjoyment, the NP exchanged them with the federal government for public lands elsewhere in the Pacific Northwest.

The merits of the exchange were somewhat controversial. Historians, for example, have noted that the railroad seemed eager to forfeit its holdings on Mount Rainier, especially since the lands it received in lieu of the commercially worthless peak were richly forested. It is probable, however, that without the exchange there would not have been a park of any kind, at least not as early as 1899. Instead, much like Mount Saint Helens, Mount Rainier would have entered the twentieth century as a checkerboard of properties alternately owned by the railroad and the federal government. Because of the exchange, Mount Rainier was spared any possible conflicts over jurisdiction and became a national park decades sooner than it might have.

Besides, the NP had no intentions of ignoring Mount Rainier, at least insofar as tourist promotion was concerned. Throughout the

1890s the company lavishly introduced the mountain to prospective travelers and, after the park itself was created, published literature that federal officials—held back by fiscal conservatism and bureaucratic restraint—could not always afford to produce. Although Uncle Sam protected the parks, without the cooperation of the railroads of the West, the government seemed little interested in promoting or improving the parks unilaterally.

The Northern Pacific, as the first company to become involved with the national parks, set an example that others followed. Across the West, railroads had come to appreciate the goodwill that could be won by sponsoring scenic preservation in the areas they served. The Southern Pacific Railroad in California, for example, lobbied in 1890 for the establishment of Yosemite, Sequoia, and General Grant national parks, all in the High Sierra. Eight years later the company also founded *Sunset* magazine to bring these parks and other attractions in California to the attention of tourists and prospective settlers. Similarly, in 1901 the Atchison, Topeka and Santa Fe Railway pushed a spur track up to the south rim of the Grand Canyon in Arizona and in 1905 opened the luxurious El Tovar Hotel, also on the canyon brink. In this instance, too, the publicity of the railroad immeasurably contributed to the protection of a scenic area; in 1908 the Grand Canyon was set aside as a national monument by order of President Theodore Roosevelt.

The Santa Fe expected national monument status to focus greater public attention on the Grand Canyon and—like the designation of Yellowstone as a national park—to arouse the curiosity of literally millions of Americans. Obviously, if the other western railroads were to approach either the success or prestige of the NP, Yellowstone was the model they must strive to re-create.

Another railroad in the lineage of the Burlington Northern today, the Great Northern Railway (GN), added to this Yellowstone legacy of promoting national parks. The GN, completed in 1893 by James J. Hill, paralleled the NP from Minnesota to Washington, except that Hill chose a right-of-way much closer to the Canadian border. As a result, the Great Northern bypassed the Yellowstone country by more than two hundred miles and instead pierced the jagged ranges of the Rocky Mountains in the northwestern corner of Montana.

As early as 1901 the noted explorer and sportsman, George Bird Grinnell, endorsed government protection of this region as a forest preserve, describing it for *Century Magazine* as "the Crown of the Continent." Indeed, he observed: "Here are cañons deeper and narrower than those of the Yellowstone, mountains higher than those of the Yosemite." In other words, properly protected and developed, the territory was eminently worthy of national park status. Hill, noted for his skepticism about rail passenger service, seemed little interested in park promotion. Then, in 1907, his son, Louis W., was appointed president of the GN. The younger man recognized this magnificent opportunity—after all, immediately south of the region Grinnell had described ran the railroad's main line.

The following year, 1908, Congress did in fact begin debating the merits of a national park bill. As prospects for its passage improved, Louis Hill's initial interest swelled into unbridled enthusiasm. For years the Montana Rockies had been out of reach to all but a few hardy sportsmen. Now that a national park might actually hug the tracks of the GN, this trickle of visitors conceivably could be turned into a flood. Perhaps even Yellowstone, Hill mused, might be forced to sacrifice some of its patronage to this newest competitor. Hill would get his opportunity to find out, for in May of 1910 Congress approved and the president signed the act establishing Glacier National Park.

With the park a reality, Hill's next course of action seemed clear: he must do everything possible to see to the accommodation of visitors. Personally, he disliked committing the GN to the construction and operation of a hotel chain. The park season, only three months long, offered little hope of ever breaking even on such a substantial investment. Still, he had no choice. Luxury accommodations were the prerequisite for attracting visitors to Glacier in the days when only the wealthy could afford to take a vacation in the national parks. Besides, every extra passenger filling an otherwise empty seat aboard one of the railroad's existing transcontinental trains would constitute a net profit, inasmuch as the costs of operating a full train were unchanged.

These, of course, were the practical considerations that inevitably crossed Hill's mind. But on the emotional side loomed a thought that proved to be no less compelling. Simply, Hill took deep personal pride in opening Glacier National Park as his gift to the nation. Visitors to the park were quick to note his dedication to the project. Mary Roberts Rinehart, for example, a popular writer for *Collier's* and the *Ladies' Home Journal*, informed her readers in 1916: "Were it not for the Great Northern Railway, travel through Glacier Park would be practically impossible." Of course the railroad was "not entirely altruistic," she confessed, "and yet I believe that Mr. Louis Warren Hill, known always as 'Louie' Hill, has had an ideal and followed it—followed it with an enthusiasm that is contagious."

Proof for these claims could be found throughout the backcountry, where Hill had scattered a striking assortment of Swiss-style alpine chalets, conveniently located a one-day hike apart. But nowhere was his commitment more grandly displayed than at East Glacier Park station and Many Glacier, on the banks of Swiftcurrent Lake. At these locations, dipping lavishly into native stores of timber and stone, Hill had personally supervised the construction of two sprawling rustic hotels, each capitalized at $500,000. The "Glacier Park Hotel . . . is almost as large as the National Capitol at Washington," Rinehart observed, exhibiting perhaps a slight tendency to exaggerate. Still, the structure was impressive, and in combination with its counterpart at Many Glacier, it moved her to reemphasize that the GN "has done more than anything else to make the park possible for tourists."

Although as much credit could be given to the other western railroads that had developed national parks, Hill's degree of personal involvement was unique. Nationwide, his spirit fired the preservation movement at this very critical time in its history. His efforts to improve Glacier coincided with a twofold campaign to protect the national parks from damaging encroachments and, equally important, to establish a national park service. In California, preservationists had just lost a bitter fight to save the Hetch Hetchy valley— within Yosemite National Park—from being turned over to the city of San Francisco for its municipal water supply. The loss of Hetch Hetchy's inviting meadows and woodlands to a dam and reservoir stunned the Sierra Club and its supporters. Never before, they concluded, had the need for a park service to defend the parks been more critical.

Under the existing arrangement, the Department of the Interior, War Department, and U.S. Forest Service all shared responsibility for managing the reserves. In other words, no single centralized federal agency had the power to protect the national parks as a system. But how, preservationists asked themselves, could such an agency be established, especially over the objections of the existing federal departments, each one jealous of its own authority?

Preservationists needed allies. It was clear that they must strengthen their ties with the railroads, whose own desire to boost travel to the national parks in no way jeopardized the scenic integrity of the areas. Richard B. Watrous, secretary of the American Civic Association, and Allen Chamberlain, a leading activist of the Appalachian Mountain Club, were among the first to publicize the advantages of such an alliance. According to Chamberlain, the Hetch Hetchy debate was the most compelling example of the need to work even harder "to stimulate public interest in the national parks by talking more about their possibilities as vacation resorts." For only if more Americans "could be induced to visit these scenic treasurehouses," he concluded, would the public "come to appreciate their value and stand firmly in their defense."

Watrous, searching for his own analogy, decided that tourism might therefore be defined as the "dignified exploitation of our national parks." Accordingly, in 1911, he also urged preservation groups nationwide to publicize "the direct material returns that will accrue to the railroads, to the concessionaires, and to the various sections of the country that will benefit by increased travel." The support of the railroads especially, he emphasized, was "essential" as "one of those practical phases of making the aesthetic possible."

As if to underscore his remarks, the National Park Service bill, introduced to Congress in 1911, ran into stiff opposition from powerful opponents in the federal bureaucracy. Consequently, five years later, hearings on the legislation were still being held. Only the support of the western railroads seemed unshaken. Like the preservation interests, the railroads looked forward to working with a single government agency, one committed to promoting the parks full time rather than as a sideline to a more compelling—and often conflicting—philosophy of government.

Meanwhile, with passage of the bill still in doubt, preservationists welcomed another major railroad (and another in the lineage of Burlington Northern) to their fold of active allies—the Chicago, Burlington, and Quincy. The approval in 1915 of Rocky Mountain National Park, sixty miles northwest of Burlington's terminus in Denver, Colorado, had provided special incentive for the company to endorse the creation of a national park service. Similarly, Burlington had access to Yellowstone National Park via Cody, Wyoming, a two hour drive due east of the park boundary, and so had begun to promote the Cody Road as a new and more scenic gateway into the area. A recent agreement with the GN also enabled Burlington to sell through tickets to landmarks farther west, including Glacier and Mount Rainier national parks.

Similar arrangements among Burlington's competitors were offered as a sign of good faith, as another expression of the railroads' sincere hope that a national park service would soon be established. In this new spirit of cooperation, P. S. Eustis, general passenger agent of the Chicago, Burlington, and Quincy, concluded four years of hearings on the National Park Service bill before the House Committee on the Public Lands. "We offer every diversity of route possible," he testified, "all on one ticket."

Three separate national parks conferences, called in 1911, 1912, and 1915 by the Department of the Interior, likewise reaffirmed that support for a park service among the western railroads was unanimous. The opposition, once confident of success, no longer could withstand such a powerful tide of enthusiasm from such a prestigious quarter. On August 25, 1916, preservationists cleared their potential hurdle when President Woodrow Wilson signed the National Park Service Act into law.

The alliance forged by the western railroads, preservation groups, and—now—the National Park Service survived intact for the next half century. As late as 1960 the pages of *Holiday, National Geographic,* and similar magazines sparkled with advertisements depicting the joys of rediscovering the American West by rail, especially by visiting the national parks. Having promised to make the journey worthwhile, the railroads had constructed many of the hotels, spent heavily on publicity, and, in some instances, actually developed the first roadways and trails.

"Our relations with the parks are naturally very close, and I believe they should be closer," Louis Hill said in defense of GN's $1.5 million investment in Glacier. In fact, his hotels and chalets, assigned to the railroad's subsidiary, Glacier Park, Inc., were not sold until 1961. Today managed by the Greyhound Corporation, the buildings are still there, rising against their mountain backgrounds, blending the manmade with the natural in a fitting memorial to Hill's idealism and philanthropy.

For this architectural heritage to have survived under railroad management, passenger trains in the West would have had to post dramatic increases in ridership. Instead, the passenger business barely held even during the 1960s. Though the federal government invested billions of dollars in transportation, the money went to highways and airports, not railroad facilities. In addition, many of the railroads in the East were dismantling their passenger operations, depriving trains in the West of vital connections with major population centers. Consequently, the promotion of the national parks among the western railroads no longer seemed justified, and public awareness of the unique relationship between the parks and the railroads finally dimmed. By the time the NP, GN, and Burlington themselves merged in 1970 into Burlington Northern Inc., the new corporation's inheritance of involvement in scenic preservation through the activism of its original companies—dating all the way back to the American invention of national parks at Yellowstone—had also been largely forgotten.

With the eruption of Mount Saint Helens, fate intervened on behalf of Burlington's Yellowstone legacy. A century ago, when the NP planned its right-of-way across Washington State, no one could have foreseen how the route finally chosen would help in 1982 to bring the history of promoting Yellowstone, Glacier, and Mount Rainier national parks full circle.

Of course, the precise boundaries of the park or geological area around Mount Saint Helens may never be fully resolved to the satisfaction of everyone concerned. But this much already is certain: not since the discovery of the wonders that inspired the creation of the first national parks in the West has any landmark so captivated the American mind, so reaffirmed the nation's pride in its breathtaking natural heritage.

BIBLIOGRAPHICAL NOTE

Until recently, information about the development of the national parks by western railroads was widely scattered. This history, from Yellowstone to Mount Saint Helens, is now available in Alfred Runte, *Trains of Discovery: Western Railroads and the National Parks* (Flagstaff, Ariz., 1984). Edward W. Nolan, *Northern Pacific Views: The Railroad Photography of F. Jay Haynes, 1876–1905* (Helena, Mont., 1983), further develops the career of Charles S. Fee, general passenger agent of the Northern Pacific, specifically with regard to his publication of the *Wonderland* series of guidebooks promoting Yellowstone, Mount Rainier, and other landmarks of the Pacific Northwest.

The *Wonderland* guides, now collectors' items, graphically portray railroad interest in national park promotion. Another important primary source is U.S. Department of the Interior, *Proceedings of the National Park Conference Held at the Yellowstone National Park September 11 and 12, 1911* (Washington, D.C., 1912). The conference itself began with lengthy reports from major railroad officials, including Louis W. Hill, regarding their work in behalf of national park publicity and development. Rufus Steele, "The Son Who Showed His Father: The Story of How Jim Hill's Boy Louis Put a Ladder to the Roof of His Country," *Sunset*, Vol. 34 (1915), 473–85, and Mary Roberts Rinehart, "Through Glacier National Park with Howard Eaton," part 2, *Collier's*, Vol. 57 (April 29, 1916), 20–28, are two other contemporary accounts of great value.

Further Reading

Abbreviations

Agr. Hist.: Agricultural History
AH: American Heritage
Am. Q.: American Quarterly
Ariz. West: Arizona and the West
AW: American West
Cath. Hist. R.: Catholic Historical
   Review
Church Hist.: Church History
For. Hist.: Forest History
IY: Idaho Yesterdays
JFH: Journal of Forest History
J. Lib. Hist.: Journal of Library History
J. Negro Hist.: Journal of Negro History
J. Soc. Arch Hist.: Journal of the Society
   of Architectural Historians

J. Urban Hist.: Journal of Urban
   History
Journalism Q.: Journalism Quarterly
JW: Journal of the West
Labor Hist.: Labor History
M: Montana, the Magazine of Western
   History
Mo. Hist. R.: Missouri Historical
   Review
OHQ: Oregon Historical Quarterly
Pac. Historian: Pacific Historian
PHR: Pacific Historical Review
PNQ: Pacific Northwest Quarterly
WHQ: Western Historical Quarterly
WPQ: Western Political Quarterly

Introduction

Books

America's Spectacular Northwest. Washington, D.C.: National Geographic Society, 1982.
Bancroft, Hubert Howe. History of Oregon. 2 vols. San Francisco: History Company, 1886.
——. History of Washington, Idaho, and Montana. San Francisco: History Company, 1890.
Bingham, Edwin R., and Glen A. Love, eds. Northwest Perspectives: Essays on the Culture of the Pacific Northwest. Seattle: University of Washington Press, 1979.

Clark, Norman H. *Washington: A Bicentennial History.* New York: W. W. Norton, 1976.
Dicken, Samuel N., and Emily F. Dicken. *The Making of Oregon: A Study in Historical Geography.* Portland: Oregon Historical Society, 1979.
Dodds, Gordon B. *Oregon: A Bicentennial History.* New York: W. W. Norton, 1977.
———. *The American Northwest: A History of Oregon and Washington.* Arlington Heights: Forum Press, 1986.
Johansen, Dorothy O., and Charles M. Gates. *Empire of the Columbia: A History of the Pacific Northwest.* 2d ed. New York: Harper & Row, 1967.
Lavender, David. *Land of Giants: The Drive to the Pacific Northwest, 1750–1950.* Garden City, N.Y.: Doubleday, 1958.
Meinig, D. W. *The Great Columbia Plain: A Historical Geography, 1805–1910.* Seattle: University of Washington Press, 1968.
Pomeroy, Earl. *The Pacific Slope: A History of California, Oregon, Washington, Idaho, Utah, and Nevada.* New York: Alfred A. Knopf, 1965.
Robbins, William G., Robert J. Frank, and Richard E. Ross, eds. *Regionalism and the Pacific Northwest.* Corvallis: Oregon State University Press, 1983.
Vaughan, Thomas, ed. *The Western Shore: Oregon Country Essays Honoring the American Revolution.* Portland: American Revolution Bicentennial Commission of Oregon and Oregon Historical Society, n.d.

Articles

Deutsch, Herman J. "Pacific Northwest History in Some World Perspectives." *PNQ* 64 (1973): 1–7.
Frykman, George A. "Thoughts toward a Philosophy of Northwest History." *IY* 8 (1964): 26–32.
Gastil, Raymond D. "The Pacific Northwest as a Cultural Region." *PNQ* 64 (1973): 147–62.
Griffith, Thomas. "The Pacific Northwest." *Atlantic Monthly* 237 (April 1976): 46–93.
Stratton, David H. "Hell's Canyon: The Missing Link in Pacific Northwest Regionalism." *IY* 28 (1984): 3–9.

I: Discovery, Exploration, and Settlement

Books

Anderson, Bern. *Surveyor of the Sea: The Life and Voyages of Captain George Vancouver.* Seattle: University of Washington Press, 1960.
Bakeless, John. *Lewis and Clark: Partners in Discovery.* New York: William Morrow, 1947.
Beckham, Stephen Dow. *Requiem for a People: The Rogue Indians and the Frontiersmen.* Norman: University of Oklahoma Press, 1971.
Bowen, William A. *The Willamette Valley: Migration and Settlement on the Oregon Frontier.* Seattle: University of Washington Press, 1978.

Burns, Robert Ignatius, S.J. *The Jesuits and the Indian Wars of the Northwest.* New Haven: Yale University Press, 1966.

Cole, Douglas. *Captured Heritage: The Scramble for Northwest Coast Artifacts.* Seattle: University of Washington Press, 1985.

Cook, Warren L. *Flood Tide of Empire: Spain and the Pacific Northwest, 1543–1819.* New Haven: Yale University Press, 1973.

Drury, Clifford M. *Marcus and Narcissa Whitman and the Opening of Old Oregon.* 2 vols. Glendale, Calif.: Arthur H. Clark, 1973.

Faragher, John Mack. *Women and Men on the Overland Trail.* New Haven: Yale University Press, 1979.

Graebner, Norman A. *Empire on the Pacific: A Study in American Continental Expansion.* New York: Ronald Press, 1955.

Hendrickson, James E. *Joe Lane of Oregon: Machine Politics and the Sectional Crisis, 1849–1861.* New Haven: Yale University Press, 1967.

Jeffrey, Julie Roy. *Frontier Women: The Trans-Mississippi West, 1840–1880.* New York: Hill and Wang, 1979.

Johannsen, Robert W. *Frontier Politics on the Eve of the Civil War.* Seattle: University of Washington Press, 1955.

Josephy, Alvin M., Jr., *The Nez Perce Indians and the Opening of the Northwest.* New Haven: Yale University Press, 1971.

Merk, Frederick. *Manifest Destiny and Mission in American History. A Reinterpretation.* New York: Alfred A. Knopf, 1963.

Morgan, Murray. *Puget's Sound: A Narrative of Early Tacoma and the Southern Sound.* Seattle: University of Washington Press, 1979.

Murray, Keith A. *The Modocs and Their War.* Norman: University of Oklahoma Press, 1959.

Newsom, David. *David Newsom: The Western Observer.* Portland: Oregon Historical Society, 1972.

Ramsey, Jarold, ed. *Coyote Was Going There: Indian Literature of the Oregon Country.* Seattle: University of Washington Press, 1977.

Richards, Kent D. *Isaac I. Stevens: Young Man in a Hurry.* Provo, Utah: Brigham Young University Press, 1979.

Ronda, James P. *Lewis and Clark among the Indians.* Lincoln: University of Nebraska Press, 1984.

Stern, Theodore. *The Klamath Tribe: A People and Their Reservation.* Seattle: University of Washington Press, 1966.

Thompson, Erwin N. *Shallow Grave at Waiilatpu: The Sagers' West.* Portland: Oregon Historical Society, 1973.

White, Richard. *Land Use, Environment, and Social Change: The Shaping of Island County, Washington.* Seattle: University of Washington Press, 1980.

Zucker, Jeff, Kay Hummel, and Bob Hogfoss. *Oregon Indians: Culture, History and Current Affairs.* Portland: Press of the Oregon Historical Society, 1983.

Articles

Ashworth, William. "Hell's Canyon: Man, Land, and History in the Deepest Gorge on Earth." *AH* 28 (1977): 12–22.

Baker, Abner S., III. "Experience, Personality and Memory: Jesse Applegate and John Minto Recall Pioneer Days." *OHQ* 81 (1980): 229–59.

Boyd, Robert T. "Another Look at the 'Fever and Ague' of Western Oregon." *Ethnohistory* 22 (1975): 135–54.

Castile, George P. "Edwin Eells, U.S. Indian Agent, 1871–1895." *PNQ* 72 (1981): 61–68.

Clark, Malcolm, Jr. "The Bigot Disclosed: 90 Years of Nativism." *OHQ* 75 (1974): 109–90.

Cloud, Barbara. "Oregon in the 1820s: The Congressional Perspective." *WHQ* 12 (1981): 145–64.

Cramer, Richard S. "British Magazines and the Oregon Question." *PHR* 32 (1963): 369–82.

DeLorme, Roland L. "Westward the Bureaucrats: Government Officials on the Washington and Oregon Frontiers." *AW* 22 (1980): 223–36.

Deutsch, Herman J. "The Evolution of the International Boundary in the Inland Empire of the Pacific Northwest." *PNQ* 51 (1960): 63–79.

———. "The Evolution of Territorial and State Boundaries in the Inland Empire of the Pacific Northwest." *PNQ* 51 (1960): 115–31.

Doig, Ivan. "Puget Sound's War within a War." *AW* 8 (May 1971): 22–27.

Drury, Clifford M. "The Spokane Indian Mission at Tshimakain, 1838–1848." *PNQ* 67 (1976): 1–9.

Edwards, G. Thomas. "Benjamin Stark, the U.S. Senate, and 1862 Membership Issues." *OHQ* 72 (1971): 315–38, and 73 (1972): 31–59.

———. "Holding the Far West for the Union: The Army in 1861." *Civil War History* 14 (1968): 307–24.

Fendall, Lon W. "Medorem Crawford and the Protective Corps." *OHQ* 72 (1971): 55–77.

Fisher, Robin. "Indian Warfare and Two Frontiers: A Comparison of British Columbia and Washington Territory during the Early Years of Settlement." *PHR* 50 (1981): 31–51.

Gough, Barry M. "British Policy in the San Juan Boundary Dispute, 1854–72." *PNQ* 62 (1971): 59–68.

———. "The North West Company's 'Adventure to China.'" *OHQ* 76 (1975): 309–31.

Hanft, Marshall. "The Cape Forts: Guardians of the Columbia." *OHQ* 65 (1964): 325–61.

Hansen, William A. "Thomas Hart Benton and the Oregon Question." *Mo. Hist. R.* 63 (1969): 489–97.

Hunt, Jack. "Land Tenure and Economic Development on the Warm Springs Indian Reservation." *JW* 9 (1970): 93–109.

Husband, Michael B. "Senator Lewis F. Linn and the Oregon Question." *Mo. Hist. R.* 66 (1971): 1–19.

Jackson, Donald. "Ledyard and Lapérouse: A Contrast in Northwestern Exploration." *WHQ* 9 (1978): 495–508.

———. "The Public Image of Lewis and Clark." *PNQ* 57 (1966): 1–7.

Josephy, Alvin M., Jr. "A Most Satisfactory Council." *AH* 16 (1965): 26–31, 70–76.

———. "The Last Stand of Chief Joseph." *AH* 9 (1958): 36–43, 78–81.

Knuth, Priscilla. "'Picturesque' Frontier: The Army's Fort Dalles." *OHQ* 67 (1966): 292–346, and 68 (1967), 4–52.

Kushner, Howard I. "Visions of the Northwest Coast: Gwin and Seward in the 1850s." *WHQ* 4 (1973): 295–306.

Lavender, David. "The Hudson's Bay Company." *AH* 21 (1970): 4–27.

Loewenberg, R. J. "Elijah White vs. Jason Lee: A Tale of Hard Times." *JW* 11 (1972): 636–62.

———. "New Evidence, Old Categories: Jason Lee as Zealot." *PHR* 47 (1978): 343–68.

Menefee, Leah Collins, and Lowell Tiller. "Cutoff Fever." *OHQ* 77 (1976): 309–40, and 78 (1977), 41–72, 121–57, 207–50, 293–331.

Norwood, Frederick A. "Two Contrasting Views of the Indians: Methodist Involvement in the Indian Troubles in Oregon and Washington." *Church Hist.* 49 (1980): 178–87.

Paul, Rodman W. "After the Gold Rush: San Francisco and Portland." *PHR* 51 (1982): 1–21.

Peters, Robert N. "Preachers in Politics: A Conflict Touching the Methodist Church in Oregon." *PNQ* 63 (1972): 142–49.

Reid, John Phillip. "Replenishing the Elephant: Property and Survival on the Overland Trail." *OHQ* 79 (1978): 65–90.

Richard, K. Keith. "Unwelcome Settlers: Black and Mulatto Oregon Pioneers." *OHQ* 84 (1983): 29–55, 173–205.

Richards, Kent D. "The Methodists and the Formation of the Oregon Provisional Government." *PNQ* 61 (1970): 87–93.

Sackett, Lee. "The Siletz Indian Shaker Church." *PNQ* 64 (1973): 120–26.

Schroeder, John H. "Rep. John Floyd, 1817–1829: Harbinger of Oregon Territory." *OHQ* 70 (1969): 333–46.

Smith, Eugene O. "Solomon Smith, Pioneer: Indian-White Relations in Early Oregon." *JW* 13 (1974): 44–58.

Stern, Theodore, Martin Schmitt, and Alphonse F. Halfmoon. "A Cayuse-Nez Percé Sketchbook." *OHQ* 81 (1980): 340–76.

Taylor, Quintard. "Slaves and Free Men: Blacks in the Oregon Country, 1840–1860." *OHQ* 83 (1982), 153–70.

Teiser, Sidney. "Reuben P. Boise, Last Associate Justice of the Oregon Territory Supreme Court." *OHQ* 66 (1965): 5–24.

Thompson, Erwin N. "Narcissa Whitman." *M* 13 (1963): 15–27.

White, Richard. "Indian Land Use and Environmental Change: Island County, Washington: A Case Study." *Ariz. West* 17 (1975): 327–30.

Whitner, Robert L. "Grant's Indian Peace Policy on the Yakima Reservation, 1870–82." *PNQ* 50 (1959): 135–42.

———. "Makah Commercial Sealing, 1860–1897: A Study in Acculturation and Conflict." In *Rendezvous: Selected Papers of the Fourth North American Fur Trade Conference, 1981,* edited by Thomas C. Buckley. St. Paul: North American Fur Trade Conference, 1984

II. From Frontier to Urban-Industrial Society

Books

Abbott, Carl. *The Great Extravaganza: Portland and the Lewis and Clark Exposition.* Portland: Oregon Historical Society, 1981.

Athearn, Robert G. *Union Pacific Country.* Chicago: Rand McNally, 1971.

Clark, Malcolm, Jr., ed. *Pharisee among Philistines.* 2 vols. Portland: Oregon Historical Society, 1975.

Cox, Thomas R. *Mills and Markets: A History of the Pacific Coast Lumber Industry to 1900.* Seattle: University of Washington Press, 1974.

Hedges, James B. *Henry Villard and the Railways of the Northwest.* New Haven: Yale University Press, 1930.

Hidy, Ralph W., Frank Ernest Hill, and Allan Nevins. *Timber and Men: The Weyerhaeuser Story.* New York: Macmillan, 1963.

MacColl, E. Kimbark. *The Shaping of a City: Business and Politics in Portland, Oregon, 1885–1915.* Portland: Georgian Press, 1976.

McGregor, Alexander Campbell. *Counting Sheep: From Open Range to Agribusiness on the Columbia Plateau.* Seattle: University of Washington Press, 1982.

Mills, Randall V. *Railroads down the Valleys: Some Short Lines of the Oregon Country.* Palo Alto, Calif.: Pacific Books, 1950.

———. *Stern-Wheelers Up Columbia: A Century of Steamboating in the Oregon Country.* Palo Alto, Calif.: Pacific Books, 1947.

Morgan, Murray. *Skid Road: An Informal Portrait of Seattle.* 1951. Rev ed., Seattle: University of Washington Press, 1982.

Nesbit, Robert C. *"He Built Seattle": A Biography of Judge Thomas Burke.* Seattle: University of Washington Press, 1961.

Oliphant, J. Orin. *On the Cattle Ranges of the Oregon Country.* Seattle: University of Washington Press, 1968.

Paul, Rodman Wilson. *Mining Frontiers of the Far West, 1848–1880.* 1963. Reprint, Albuquerque: University of New Mexico Press, 1974.

Sale, Roger. *Seattle, Past to Present.* Seattle: University of Washington Press, 1976.

Throckmorton, Arthur L. *Oregon Argonauts: Merchant Adventurers on the Western Frontier.* Portland: Oregon Historical Society, 1961.

Trimble, William J. *The Mining Advances into the Inland Empire.* Madison: University of Wisconsin, 1914.

Turnbull, George S. *History of Oregon Newspapers.* Portland: Binfords & Mort, 1939.

Weinstein, Robert A. *Grays Harbor, 1885–1913.* New York: Viking, 1978.

Articles

Beckham, Stephen Dow. "Asa Mead Simpson, Lumberman and Shipbuilder." *OHQ* 68 (1967): 259–73.

Berner, Richard C. "The Port Blakely Mill Company, 1876–89." *PNQ* 57 (1966): 158–71.

Blackford, Mansel G. "Civic Groups, Political Action, and City Planning in Seattle, 1892–1915." *PHR* 49 (1980): 557–80.

———. The Lost Dream: Businessmen and City Planning in Portland, Oregon, 1903–1914." *WHQ* 15 (1984): 39–56.

Brackett, Barbara Young, and Evelyn Hyman King. "King of All the Mountains: Scaling the Heights of Mighty Rainier in 1883." *AW* 11 (May 1974): 4–13.

Bright, Verne. "Blue Mountain Eldorados: Auburn, 1861." *OHQ* 62 (1961): 213–36.

Carstensen, Vernon. "The Fisherman's Frontier on the Pacific Coast: The Rise of the Salmon-Canning Industry." In *The Frontier Challenge: Responses to the Trans-Mississippi West,* edited by John G. Clark. Lawrence: University Press of Kansas, 1971.

———. "The West Mark Twain Did Not See." *PNQ* 55 (1964): 170–76.

Cochran, John S. "Economic Importance of Early Transcontinental Railroads: Pacific Northwest." *OHQ* 71 (1970): 26–98.

Conlin, Joseph R. "'Old Boy, Did You Get Enough of Pie?' A Social History of Food in Logging Camps." *JFH* 23 (1979): 164–85.

Corbett, P. Scott, and Nancy Parker Corbett. "The Chinese in Oregon, c. 1870–1880." *OHQ* 78 (1977): 73–85.

Coulter, C. Brewster. "The New Settlers on the Yakima Project, 1880–1910." *PNQ* 61 (1970): 10–21.

Cox, Thomas R. "Single Decks and Flat Bottoms: Building the West Coast's Lumber Fleet, 1850–1929." *JW* 20 (1981): 65–74.

———. "William Kyler and the Pacific Lumber Trade: A Study in Marginality." *JFH* 19 (1975): 4–14.

DeLorme, Roland L. "The United States Bureau of Customs and Smuggling on Puget Sound, 1851 to 1913." *Prologue* 5 (1973): 77–88.

Dodds, Gordon B. "Artificial Propagation of Salmon in Oregon, 1875–1910: A Chapter in American Conservation." *PNQ* 50 (1959): 125–33.

Edwards, G. Thomas, "'The Early Morning of Yakima's Day of Greatness': The Yakima County Agricultural Boom of 1905–1911." *PNQ* 73 (1982): 78–89.

Epstein, Donald B. "Gladstone Chautauqua: Education and Entertainment, 1893–1928." *OHQ* 80 (1979): 391–403.

Etulain, Richard W. "Basque Beginnings in the Pacific Northwest." *IY* 18 (Spring 1974): 26–32.

Fahey, John. "When the Dutch Owned Spokane." *PNQ* 72 (1981): 2–10.

Finger, John R. "The Seattle Spirit, 1851–1893." *JW* 13 (1974): 28–45.

———. "Seattle's First Sawmill, 1853–1869: A Study of Frontier Enterprise." *For. Hist.* 15 (1972): 24–31.

Frykman, George A. "The Alaska-Yukon-Pacific Exposition, 1909." *PNQ* 53 (1962): 89–99.

Henderson, Robert A. "Culture in Spokane: 1883–1900." *IY* 11 (1967): 14–19, 32.

Husband, Michael B. "Morton M. McCarver: An Iowa Entrepreneur in the Far West." *Annals of Iowa* 40 (1970): 241–54.

Johnston, Norman J. "The Frederick Law Olmsted Plan for Tacoma." *PNQ* 66 (1975): 97–104.

Katz, William A. "*The Columbian:* Washington Territory's First Newspaper." *OHQ* 64 (1963): 33–40.

Kenny, Judith Keyes. "Early Sheep Ranching in Eastern Oregon." *OHQ* 64 (1963): 101–22.

Kensel, W. Hudson. "Inland Empire Mining and the Growth of Spokane, 1883–1905." *PNQ* 60 (1969): 84–97.

———. "Spokane: The First Decade." *IY* 15 (Spring 1971): 18–23.

McClintock, Thomas C. "Henderson Luelling, Seth Lewelling and the Birth of the Pacific Coast Fruit Industry." *OHQ* 68 (1967): 153–74.

MacDonald, Norbert. "Population Growth and Change in Seattle and Vancouver, 1880–1960." *PHR* 39 (1970): 297–321.

McGregor, Alexander C. "The Economic Impact of the Mullan Road on Walla Walla, 1860–1883." *PNQ* 65 (1974): 118–29.

Mahar, Franklyn D. "The Millionaire and the Village: Jesse Winburn Comes to Ashland." *OHQ* 64 (1963): 323–41.

Martin, Albro. "James J. Hill: Entrepreneur in the Classic Mold." *JW* 17 (1978: 62–74.

Merriam, Paul G. "The 'Other Portland': A Statistical Note on Foreign-Born, 1860–1910." *OHQ* 80 (1979), 258–68.

———. "Urban Elite in the Far West: Portland, Oregon, 1870–1890." *Ariz. West* 18 (1976): 41–52.

Mills, Hazel Emery. "The Emergence of Frances Fuller Victor—Historian." *OHQ* 62 (1961): 309–36.

Miyamoto, S. Frank. "The Japanese Minority in the Pacific Northwest." *PNQ* 54 (1963): 143–49.

Nash, Lee M. "Scott of the *Oregonian:* The Editor as Historian." *OHQ* 70 (1969): 197–232.

———. "Scott of the *Oregonian:* Literary Frontiersman." *PHR* 45 (1976): 357–78.

Northam, Janet A., and Jack W. Berryman. "Sport and Urban Boosterism in the Pacific Northwest: Seattle's Alaska-Yukon-Pacific Exposition, 1909." *JW* 17 (1978): 53–60.

O'Bannon, Patrick W. "Technological Change in the Pacific Coast Canned Salmon Industry, 1900–1925: A Case Study." *Agr. Hist.* 56 (1982): 151–66.

Pursinger, Marvin Gavin. "The Japanese Settle in Oregon: 1880–1920." *JW* 5 (1966): 251–62.

Robbins, William. "Community Conflict in Roseburg, Oregon, 1870–1885." *JW* 12 (1973): 618–32.

———. "Opportunity and Persistence in the Pacific Northwest: A Quantitative Study of Early Roseburg, Oregon." *PHR* 39 (1970): 279–96.

———. "Social and Economic Change in Roseburg, Oregon, 1850–1885: A Quantitative View." *PNQ* 64 (1973): 80–87.

Rothstein, Morton. "West Coast Farmers and the Tyranny of Distance: Agriculture on the Fringes of the World Market." *Agr. Hist.* 49 (1975): 272–80.

Rydell, Robert. "Visions of Empire: International Expositions in Portland and Seattle, 1905–1909." *PHR* 52 (1983): 37–65.

Saum, Lewis O. "William Lightfoot Visscher and the 'Eden of the West.'" *PNQ* 71 (1980): 2–14.

Shaffer, Ralph E. "The Race of the *Oregon.*" *OHQ* 76 (1975): 269–98.

Sullivan, Margaret L. "Conflict on the Frontier: The Case of Harney County, Oregon, 1870–1900." *PNQ* 66 (1975): 174–81.

Taylor, Quintard. "The Emergence of Black Communities in the Pacific Northwest: 1865–1910." *J. Negro Hist.* 64 (1979): 342–54.

Toll, William. "Fraternalism and Community Structure on the Urban Frontier: The Jews of Portland, Oregon—A Case Study." *PHR* 47 (1978): 369–403.

Tracy, Charles Abbott, III. "Police Function in Portland, 1851–1874." *OHQ* 80 (1979); 5–29, 134–69, 287–322.

Tyack, David. "Bureaucracy and the Common School: The Example of Portland, Oregon, 1851–1913." *Am. Q.* 19 (1967): 475–98.

Walton, Elisabeth, "A Note on William W. Piper and Academy Architecture in Oregon in the Nineteenth Century." *J. Soc. Arch. Hist.* 32 (1973): 231–38.

Waters, W. Kenneth, Jr. "The Baker Stock Company and the Community." *OHQ* 82 (1981): 229–70.

Weinstein, Robert A. "Lumber Ships at Puget Sound." *AW* 2 (Fall 1965): 50–63.

Yonce, Frederick J. "Lumbering and the Public Timberlands in Washington: The Era of Disposal." *JFH* 22 (1978): 4–17.

III. Reform and Repression

Books

Allen, Howard W. *Poindexter of Washington: A Study in Progressive Politics.* Carbondale: Southern Illinois University Press, 1981.

Clark, Norman H. *The Dry Years: Prohibition and Social Change in Washington.* Seattle: University of Washington Press, 1965.

———. *Mill Town.* Seattle: University of Washington Press, 1970.

Dembo, Jonathan. *Unions and Politics in Washington State, 1885–1935.* New York: Garland, 1983.

Hyman, Harold M. *Soldiers and Spruce: Origins of the Loyal Legion of Loggers and Lumbermen.* Los Angeles: University of California Press, 1963.

LeWarne, Charles Pierce. *Utopias on Puget Sound, 1885–1915.* Seattle: University of Washington Press, 1975.

Moynihan, Ruth Barnes. *Rebel for Rights: Abigail Scott Duniway.* New Haven: Yale University Press, 1983.

Schwantes, Carlos A. *Radical Heritage: Labor, Socialism, and Reform in Washington and British Columbia, 1885–1917.* Seattle: University of Washington Press, 1979.

———. *Coxey's Army: An American Odyssey.* Lincoln: University of Nebraska Press, 1985.

Tyler, Robert L. *Rebels of the Woods: The I.W.W. in the Pacific Northwest.* Eugene: University of Oregon Books, 1967.

Articles

Beeton, Beverly, and G. Thomas Edwards. "Susan B. Anthony's Woman Suffrage Crusade in the American West." *JW* 21 (1982): 5–15.

Bennion, Sherilyn Cox. "The New Northwest and Woman's Exponent: Early Voices for Suffrage." *Journalism Q.* 54 (1977): 286–92.

Borgman, H. J. "The Reluctant Dissenter: Governor Hay of Washington and the Conservation Problem." *PNQ* 42 (1971): 27–33.

Blackford, Mansel G. "Reform Politics in Seattle during the Progressive Era, 1902–1916." *PNQ* 59 (1968): 177–85.

Boylan, Bernard L. "Camp Lewis: Promotion and Construction." *PNQ* 58 (1967): 188–95.

Broyles, Glen J. "The Spokane Free Speech Fight, 1909–1910: A Study in IWW Tactics." *Labor Hist.* 19 (1978): 238–52.

Byler, Charles. "Austin E. Griffiths: Seattle Progressive Reformer." *PNQ* 76 (1985): 22–32.

Edwards, G. Thomas. "Chamberlain Hoel, Zealous Reformer." *PNQ* 66 (1975): 49–60.

Ficken, Robert E. "Gifford Pinchot Men: Pacific Northwest Lumbermen and the Conservation Movement, 1902–1910." *WHQ* 13 (1982): 165–78.

Hallberg, Gerald N. "Bellingham, Washington's Anti-Hindu Riot." *JW* 12 (1973): 163–75.

Holl, Jack M., and Roger A. Pederson. "The Washington State Reformatory at Monroe: A Progressive Ornament." *PNQ* 67 (1976): 21–28.

Hynding, Alan A. "The Coal Miners of Washington Territory: Labor Troubles, 1888–89." *Ariz. West* 12 (1970): 221–36.

Johnson, Warren B. "Muckraking in the Northwest: Joe Smith and Seattle Reform." *PHR* 40 (1971): 478–500.

Kerr, William T., Jr. "The Progressives of Washington, 1910–1912." *PNQ* 55 (1964): 16–27.

Kessler, Lauren. "A Siege of the Citadels: Search for a Public Forum for the Ideas of Oregon Woman Suffrage." *OHQ* 84 (1983): 116–49.

———. "The Ideas of Woman Suffrage and the Mainstream Press." *OHQ* 84 (1983): 257–75.

Kingsbury, Mary E. "'To Shine in Use': The Library and War Service of Oregon's Pioneer Librarian, Mary Frances Isom." *J. Lib. Hist.* 10 (1975): 22–34.

Kizer, Benjamin H. "May Arkwright Hutton." *PNQ* 57 (1966): 49–56.

Larson, T. A. "The Woman Suffrage Movement in Washington. " *PNQ* 67 (1976): 49–62.

LeWarne, Charles Pierce. "The Aberdeen, Washington, Free Speech Fight of 1911–1912." *PNQ* 66 (1975): 1–12.

———. "The Anarchist Colony at Home, Washington, 1901–1902." *AW* 14 (1972): 155–68.

———. "Equality Colony: The Plan to Socialize Washington." *PNQ* 59 (1968): 137–46.

Loy, Edward H. "Editorial Opinion and American Imperialism: Two Northwest Newspapers." *OHQ* 72 (1971): 209–24.

McClintock, Thomas C. "Seth Lewelling, William S. U'Ren and the Birth of the Oregon Progressive Movement." *OHQ* 68 (1967): 197–220.

Messing, John. "Public Lands, Politics, and Progressives: The Oregon Land Fraud Trials, 1903–1910." *PHR* 35 (1966): 35–66.

Pendergrass, Lee F. "The Formation of a Municipal Reform Movement: The Municipal League of Seattle." *PNQ* 66 (1975): 13–25.

Rakestraw, Lawrence. "Before McNary: The Northwestern Conservationist, 1889–1913." *PNQ* 51 (1960): 49–56.

Rice, Harry E. "Columbia River Kid." *OHQ* 74 (1973): 293–332.

Riddle, Thomas W. "Populism in the Palouse: Old Ideals and New Realities." *PNQ* 65 (1974): 97–109.

Schwantes, Carlos A. "Farmer-Labor Insurgency in Washington State: William Bouck, the Grange, and the Western Progressive Farmers." *PNQ* 76 (1985): 2–11.

———. "Free Love and Free Speech on the Pacific Northwest Frontier," *OHQ* 82 (1981): 271–93.

———. "Leftward Tilt on the Pacific Slope: Indigenous Unionism and the Struggle against AFL Hegemony in the State of Washington." *PNQ* 70 (1979): 24–34.

———. "Making the World Unsafe for Democracy: Vigilantes, Grangers and the Walla Walla 'Outrage' of June 1918." *M* 31 (Winter 1981): 18–29.

Soden, Dale. "Mark Allison Matthews: Seattle's Minister Rediscovered." *PNQ* 74 (1983): 50–58.

Tripp, Joseph F. "An Instance of Labor and Business Cooperation: Workmen's Compensation in Washington State (1911)." *Labor Hist.* 17 (1976): 530–50.

Trow, Clifford W. "'Something Desperate in His Face': Woodrow Wilson in Portland." *OHQ* 82 (1981): 41–64.

Voeltz, Herman C. "Coxey's Army in Oregon, 1894." *OHQ* 65 (1964): 263–95.

Weisberger, Bernard A. "Here Come the Wobblies!" *AH* 18 (1967): 30–35, 87–93.

Woodward, Robert C. "W. S. U'Ren and the Single Tax in Oregon." *OHQ* 61 (1960): 46–63.

Wunder, John R. "The Chinese and the Courts in the Pacific Northwest: Justice Denied?" *PHR* 52 (1983): 191–211.

IV. THE MODERN ERA

Books

Bone, Arthur H. *Oregon Cattleman/Governor/Congressman: Memoirs and Times of Walter M. Pierce.* Portland: Oregon Historical Society, 1981.

Brown, Bruce. *Mountain in the Clouds: A Search for the Wild Salmon.* New York: Simon & Schuster, 1982.

Burton, Robert E. *Democrats of Oregon: The Pattern of Minority Politics, 1900–1956.* Eugene: University of Oregon Books, 1970.

Chasan, Daniel Jack. *The Water Link: A History of Puget Sound as a Resource.* Seattle: University of Washington Press, 1981.

Ficken, Robert E. *Lumber and Politics: The Career of Mark E. Reed.* Seattle: University of Washington Press, 1979.

Friedheim, Robert L. *The Seattle General Strike.* Seattle: University of Washington Press, 1964.

Lowitt, Richard. *The New Deal and the West.* Bloomington: Indiana University Press, 1984.

McCall, Tom, with Steve Neal. *Tom McCall: Maverick, an Autobiography.* Portland: Binfords and Mort, 1977.

MacColl, E. Kimbark. *The Growth of a City: Power and Politics in Portland, Oregon, 1915 to 1950.* Portland: Georgian Press, 1979.

McKinley, Charles. *Uncle Sam in the Pacific Northwest: Federal Management of Natural Resources in the Columbia River Valley.* Berkeley: University of California Press, 1952.

Metzler, Ken. *Confrontation: The Destruction of a College President.* Los Angeles: Nash Publishing, 1973.

Nash, Gerald D. *The American West Transformed: The Impact of the Second World War.* Bloomington: Indiana University Press, 1985.

Neuberger, Richard. *Our Promised Land.* New York: Macmillan, 1938.

Peirce, Neal R. *The Pacific States of America: People, Politics, and Power in the Five Pacific Basin States.* New York: Norton, 1972.

Sanders, Jane. *Cold War on the Campus: Academic Freedom at the University of Washington, 1946–64.* Seattle: University of Washington Press, 1979.

Seufert, Francis. *Wheels of Fortune.* Portland: Oregon Historical Society, 1980.

Smith, A. Robert. *The Tiger in the Senate: The Biography of Wayne Morse.* Garden City, N.Y.: Doubleday, 1962.

Sundborg, George. *Hail Columbia: The Thirty-Year Struggle for Grand Coulee Dam.* New York: Macmillan, 1954.

Articles

Abbott, Carl. "Greater Portland: Experiments with Professional Planning, 1905–1925." *PNQ* 76 (1985): 12–21.

————. "Portland in the Pacific War: Planning from 1940–1945." *Urbanism Past and Present* 6 (1980–1981): 12–24.

Allman, Joseph M. "The 1968 Election in Oregon." *WPQ* 22 (1969): 517–25.

Balmer, Donald G. "The 1964 Election in Oregon." *WPQ* 18 (1965): 502–508.

————. "The Role of Political Leadership in the Passage of Oregon's Migratory Labor Legislation." *WPQ* 15 (1962): 146–56.

Bartholomae, Annette M. "A Conscientious Objector: Oregon, 1918." *OHQ* 71 (1970): 212–45.

Beckett, Paul, and Celeste Sunderland. "Washington State's Lawmakers: Some Personnel Factors in the Washington Legislature." *WPQ* 10 (1957): 180–207.

Bone, Hugh A. "The 1960 Election in Washington." *WPQ* 14 (1961): 373–82.

————. "The 1964 Election in Washington." *WPQ* 18 (1965): 514–22.

Bone, Hugh A., and Robert C. Benedict. "Perspectives on Direct Legislation: Washington State's Experience, 1914–1973." *WPQ* 28 (1975): 330–51.

Cameron, David A. "The Silverton Nursery: An Early Experiment in Pacific Northwestern Reforestation." *JFH* 23 (1979): 122–29.

Clark, Norman H. "Roy Olmstead, A Rumrunning King on Puget Sound." *PNQ* 54 (1963): 89–103.

Cotroneo, Ross R. "Timber Marketing by the Northern Pacific Railway, 1920–1952." *JFH* 20 (1976): 120–131.

Cox, Thomas R. "Conservation by Subterfuge: Robert W. Sawyer and the Birth of the Oregon State Parks." *PNQ* 64 (1973): 21–29.

————. "The Crusade to Save Oregon's Scenery." *PHR* 37 (1968): 179–99.

Daniel, Cletus E. "Wobblies on the Farm: The IWW in the Yakima Valley." *PNQ* 65 (1974): 166–75.

Dembo, Jonathan, "John Danz and the Seattle Amusement Trades Strike, 1921–1935." *PNQ* 71 (1980): 172–82.

Dodds, Gordon B. "Hiram Martin Chittenden, Historian." *PHR* 30 (1961): 257–69.

Fahl, Ronald J. "S. C. Lancaster and the Columbia River Highway: Engineer as Conservationist." *OHQ* 74 (1973): 100–44.

Ficken, Robert E. "Mark E. Reed: Portrait of a Businessman in Politics." *JFH* 20 (1976): 4–19.

Fine, Sidney. "Mr. Justice Murphy and the Hirabayashi Case." *PHR* 33 (1964): 195–209.

Friedheim, Robert L. "Prologue to a General Strike: The Seattle Shipyard Strike of 1919." *Labor Hist.* 6 (1965): 121–42.

Friedheim, Robert L., and Robin Friedheim. "The Seattle Labor Movement, 1919–1920." *PNQ* 55 (1964): 146–56.

Frykman, George A. "Edmond S. Meany, Historian." *PNQ* 51 (1960): 159–70.

Herrera, Philip. "Megalopolis Comes to the Northwest." *Fortune* 76 (1967): 118–123, 194.

Hitchman, James H. "The Bellingham Port Commission, 1920–1970." *JW* 20 (1981): 57–64.

————. "Northwest Leadership in Education: Henry Davidson Sheldon at Oregon, 1900–1946." *IY* 24 (Spring 1980): 2–11.

Hoffman, George. "Political Arithmetic: Charles L. McNary and the 1914 Primary Election." *OHQ* 66 (1965): 363–78.

Hogg, Thomas C. "Black Man in White Town." *PNQ* 63 (1972): 14–21.

Holsinger, M. Paul. "The Oregon School Bill Controversy, 1922–1925." *PHR* 36 (1968): 327–41.

Hood, Susan. "Termination of the Klamath Indian Tribe of Oregon." *Ethnohistory* 19 (1972): 379–92.

Hoover, Roy O. "Public Law 273 Comes to Shelton: Implementation of the Sustained-Yield Forest Management Act of 1944." *JFH* 22 (1978): 86–101.

Johnson, Ralph W. "Regulation of Commercial Salmon Fishermen: A Case of Confused Objectives." *PNQ* 55 (1964): 141–45.

Johnson, Roger T. "Part-Time Leader: Senator Charles L. McNary and the McNary-Haugen Bill." *Agr. Hist.:* 54 (1980): 527–41.

Jones, David C. "The Strategy of Railway Abandonment: The Great Northern in Washington and British Columbia, 1917–1935." *WHQ* 11 (1980): 141–58.

Jorgenson, Lloyd P. "The Oregon School Law of 1922: Passage and Sequel." *Cath. Hist. R.* 54 (1968): 455–66.

LeWarne, Charles P. "The Bolsheviks Land in Seattle: The *Shilka* Incident of 1917." *AW* 20 (1978): 107–22.

Lovin, Hugh T. "The CIO and the 'Damnable Bickering' in the Pacific Northwest, 1937–1941." *Pac. Historian* 23 (1979): 66–79.

McClelland, John M., Jr. "Terror on Tower Avenue." *PNQ* 57 (1966): 65–72.

McGregor, Alexander C. "Industry on the Farm: McGregor Land and Livestock and the Transformation of the Columbia Plateau Wheat Belt since 1930." *PNQ* 73 (1982): 31–38.

Melanson, Richard A. "The Social and Political Thought of William Appleman Williams." *WPQ* 31 (1978): 392–409.

Morgan, George T. "The Fight against Fire: Development of Cooperative Forestry in the Pacific Northwest." *IY* 6 (Winter 1962): 20–30.

Newbill, James G. "Farmers and Wobblies in the Yakima Valley, 1933." *PNQ* 68 (1977): 80–87.

Oliver, Egbert S. "Sawmilling on Grays Harbor in the Twenties: A Personal Reminiscence." *PNQ* 69 (1978): 1–18.

Pieroth, Doris "With All Deliberate Caution: School Integration in Seattle, 1954–1968." *PNQ* 73 (1982): 50–61.

Richardson, Elmo. "The Interior Secretary as Conservation Villain: The Notorious Case of Douglas 'Giveaway' McKay." *PHR* 41 (1972): 333–45.

———. "Olympic National Park: Twenty Years of Controversy." *For. Hist.* 12 (1968): 6–15.

Robbins, William G. "The Social Context of Forestry: The Pacific Northwest in the Twentieth Century." *WHQ* 16 (1985): 413–27.

———. "The Willamette Valley Project of Oregon: A Study in the Political Economy of Water Resource Development." *PHR* 47 (1978): 585–605.

Saloutos, Theodore. "Alexander Pantages, Theater Magnate of the West." *PNQ* 57 (1966): 137–47.

Sanders, Jane A. "The University of Washington and the Controversy over J. Robert Oppenheimer." *PNQ* 70 (1979): 8–19.

Seligman, Lester G. "Political Change: Legislative Elites and Parties in Oregon." *WPQ* 17 (1964): 177–87.

Shepherd, James F. "The Development of New Wheat Varieties in the Pacific Northwest." *Agr. Hist.* 54 (1980): 52–63.

———. "The Development of Wheat Production in the Pacific Northwest." *Agr. Hist* 49 (1975): 258–71.

Swarthout, John M. "The 1960 Election in Oregon." *WPQ* 14 (1961): 355–64.

Tanaka, Stefan. "The Toledo Incident: The Deportation of the Nikkei from an Oregon Mill Town." *PNQ* 69 (1978): 116–26.

Taylor, Quintard. "The Great Migration: The Afro-American Communities of

Seattle and Portland during the 1940s." *Ariz. West* 23 (1981): 109–26.

Toll, William. "Voluntarism and Modernization in Portland Jewry: The B'nai B'rith in the 1920s." *WHQ* 10 (1979): 21–38.

Toy, Eckard V., Jr. "The Oxford Group and the Strike of the Seattle Longshoremen in 1934." *PNQ* 69 (1978): 174–84.

———. "Spiritual Mobilization: The Failure of an Ultraconservative Ideal in the 1950s" *PNQ* 61 (1970): 77–86.

Tripp, Joseph F. "Toward an Efficient and Moral Society: Washington State Minimum-Wage Law, 1913–1925." *PNQ* 67 (1976): 97–112.

Utley, Jonathan G. "Japanese Exclusion from American Fisheries, 1936–1939: The Department of State and the Public Interest." *PNQ* 65 (1974): 8–16.

Warren, Robert, and James J. Best. "The 1968 Election in Washington." *WPQ* 22 (1969): 536–45.

Woolley, Ivan M. "The 1918 'Spanish Influenza' Pandemic in Oregon." *OHQ* 64 (1963): 246–58.

Contributors

Edwin R. Bingham received a Ph.D. from the University of California, Los Angeles. He recently coedited *Northwest Perspectives: Essays on the Culture of the Pacific Northwest* with Glen Love. He has taught history for many years at the University of Oregon.

Karen J. Blair teaches women's studies and women's history at the University of Washington. She is the author of *The Clubwoman as Feminist: True Womanhood Redefined, 1868–1914*. She holds a Ph.D. from the State University of New York at Buffalo.

Richard Maxwell Brown is Beekman Professor of Pacific and Northwest History at the University of Oregon. He holds a Ph.D. from Harvard and is the author of several publications, including *Strain of Violence: Historical Studies of American Violence and Vigilantism*.

Robert E. Burke has taught history at the University of Washington since 1957 and is the managing editor of *Pacific Northwest Quarterly*. A native Californian and recipient of a Ph.D. from the University of California, Berkeley, he has recently edited the seven-volume *Senate Diary of Hiram Johnson*.

Norman Clark is the author of several books including *Mill Town*, a social history of early-day Everett, Washington. He holds a Ph.D. in history from the University of Washington and is a member of the faculty at Everett Community College.

Jorgen Dahlie holds a Ph.D. from Washington State University and has written *A Social History of Scandinavian Immigration, Washington State, 1895–1910*. He is chairman of the Department of Social and Educational Studies, University of British Columbia.

395

JONATHAN DEMBO, who received a Ph.D. in history from the University of Washington, is the supervisor of manuscripts and archives at the Cincinnati Historical Society. He is the author of several studies on Pacific Northwest labor history.

HOWARD A. DROKER holds a Ph.D. in history from the University of Washington. He is the author of *Seattle's Unsinkable Houseboats*, and is currently attending law school.

G. THOMAS EDWARDS is a native of Oregon. The recipient of a Ph.D. from the University of Oregon and author of several monographs, he teaches history at Whitman College.

ROBERT E. FICKEN has a Ph.D. from the University of Washington, where he has also taught courses in Pacific Northwest history. He is the author of *Lumber and Politics: The Career of Mark E. Reed*.

PAUL HOLBO is vice-provost of the University of Oregon. He is a native of the Upper Midwest and holds a Ph.D. in history from the University of Chicago. His most recent book is *Tarnished Expansion: The Alaska Scandal, the Press, and Congress, 1867–1871*.

DOROTHY O. JOHANSEN is a native of Oregon and coauthor of the well-known text *Empire of the Columbia*. She holds a Ph.D. from the University of Washington and taught history at Reed College from 1935 to 1969.

ALEXANDER C. McGREGOR received a Ph.D. in history from the University of Washington and is the author of *Counting Sheep: From Open Range to Agribusiness on the Columbia Plateau*.

WILLIAM H. MULLINS earned his Ph.D. in history at the University of Washington, and teaches history at Oklahoma Baptist University.

KEITH A. MURRAY is a native of the Pacific Northwest. He received a Ph.D. from the University of Washington, is the author of several local histories, and taught for many years at Western Washington University.

LEE NASH holds a Ph.D. in history from the University of Oregon and since 1975 has been at George Fox College, Newberg, Oregon, as administrator and faculty member.

DORIS H. PIEROTH, a Seattle historian, is currently editing a collection of letters dating from World War I and the Allied intervention in Siberia.

KENT D. RICHARDS has a Ph.D. from the University of Wisconsin, Madison. The author of *Isaac I. Stevens: Young Man in a Hurry*, he is an administrator and faculty member at Central Washington University.

WILLIAM G. ROBBINS received a Ph.D. from the University of Oregon and teaches history at Oregon State University. He is the author of several studies including *Lumberjacks and Legislators: Political Economy of the U.S. Lumber Industry, 1890–1941*.

ALFRED RUNTE teaches history at the University of Washington. He holds a Ph.D. from the University of California, Santa Barbara, and is the author of *National Parks: The American Experience*.

CARLOS A. SCHWANTES is associate professor of history at the University of Idaho. He received a Ph.D. from the University of Michigan and is the author of *Radical Heritage: Labor, Socialism, and Reform in Washington and British Columbia, 1885–1917*.

ECKARD V. TOY is a native of Oregon. He holds a Ph.D. from the University of Oregon, has authored several monographs, and has taught history in several universities in Oregon and Washington.

RICHARD WHITE teaches at the University of Utah. He received a Ph.D. in history from the University of Washington and is the author of *Land Use, Environment, and Social Change: The Shaping of Island County, Washington*.

ROBERT C. WOODWARD holds a Ph.D. from the University of Oregon and currently is chairman of the Department of History at Northwest Nazarene College.